Bakke, DeFunis, and Minority Admissions

Bakke, DeFunis, and Minority Admissions

The Quest for Equal Opportunity

Allan P. Sindler
University of California, Berkeley

LONGMAN
New York and London

BAKKE, DeFUNIS, AND MINORITY ADMISSIONS
The Quest for Equal Opportunity

Longman Inc., New York
Associated companies, branches, and
representatives throughout the world.

Developmental Editor: Edward Artinian
Editorial and Design Supervisor: Linda Salmonson
Interior Design: Pencils Portfolio, Inc.
Exterior Design: Albert M. Cetta
Manufacturing and Production Supervisor: Louis Gaber
Composition: American Book–Stratford Press
Printing and Binding: The Book Press

Library of Congress Cataloging in Publication Data
Sindler, Allan P
  Bakke, DeFunis, and minority admissions.
  Includes index.
  1. Discrimination in education—Law and legisla-
tion—United States. 2. Medical colleges—United
States—Admission. 3. Law schools—United States—
Admission. 4. Bakke, Allan Paul. 5. DeFunis, Marco.
I. Title
KF4155.S53   344'.73'0798   78–63057
ISBN 0–582–28054–0
ISBN 0–582–28053–2 pbk.

Manufactured in the United States of America

To Lenore

PREFACE

This book deals with one of the most difficult and divisive social problems of our time: how to promote equal opportunity for disadvantaged minorities through affirmative action without engaging in reverse discrimination. To give focus and shape to this large subject, I have grounded it on the problem of minority admissions to law and medical schools, where there are many more applicants than available places, and on two nationally controversial Supreme Court cases. Both cases—*DeFunis* (1974) and *Bakke* (1978)—involve a rejected white applicant who claimed he was a victim of reverse discrimination because the school accepted minority applicants with poorer records than his through special admissions arrangements based on race.

When writing an account of the *DeFunis* problem for a volume of original studies I edited, *America in the Seventies* (Boston: Little, Brown, 1977), I became aware that a California trial court had upheld Allan Bakke's claim against the University of California medical school at Davis. After the California high court in fall 1976 also decided for Bakke and the U.S. Supreme Court in early 1977 agreed to review the case, I began writing the present book. With the exception of the closing sections, which cover the Court's decision on *Bakke,* this study was completed before that decision was handed down in late June 1978.

It is a pleasure to express my gratitude to Elizabeth Keyser, whose skilled and rapid transformation of my undecipherable scrawl into typescript never ceased to amaze. My appreciation also to Edward Artinian of Longman Inc. for his unfailing cooperation and for the prompt publication of this study.

CONTENTS

A Ripe and Pressing Controversy

Bakke confirmed a prediction made by U.S. Supreme Court Justice William Brennan. In April 1974 the Court was faced with the *DeFunis* case, which raised policy and legal questions comparable to those that *Bakke* would bring. A bare majority of the Court chose to escape having to deal with the substance of *DeFunis* by holding the case moot on technical grounds. Sharply dissenting, Justice Brennan urged that *DeFunis* was ripe for the Court's resolution and pointedly predicted that its momentous issues would soon reconfront the Court:

> The constitutional issues which are avoided today concern vast numbers of people, organizations and colleges and universities, as evidenced by the filing of twenty-six amici curiae [friends-of-the-court] briefs. Few constitutional questions in recent history have stirred as much debate, and they will not disappear. They must inevitably return to the federal courts and ultimately again to this Court.

As things turned out, the Court's mooting of *DeFunis* set events in motion that quickly led to the fulfillment of Justice Brennan's prediction. Among those closely watching *DeFunis* was Allan Bakke, who was weighing whether to file suit to gain entry to the University of California medical school at Davis, on grounds similar to those put forward by Marco DeFunis. Shortly after *DeFunis* aborted, Bakke sued in the California courts, which supported his position. When the U.S. Supreme Court agreed to hear the case, *Bakke* became the successor case to *DeFunis* that Justice Brennan had anticipated, the one that spotlighted anew those "constitutional issues" that "must inevitably return . . . to this Court."

What *Bakke* and *DeFunis* presented was—and remains—a controversial, vexing, and painful policy problem. This study explores that problem by focusing on the two cases, though with heavier emphasis on *Bakke,* and the issues they raise.

A Watershed Case?

Because the Court had been expected to decide *DeFunis* on its merits, the case attracted extraordinary public attention and visibility. It was widely acknowledged, closely followed, and much argued about as a "big" case, one of that rare kind whose judicial resolution might have major and lasting effects. When the Court, ducking the issues, provided only anticlimax, the large set of attentive and affected interests associated with *DeFunis* transferred its hopes and fears—and invested them with even greater intensity— to the emerging *Bakke* dispute. As a result, *Bakke* soon ballooned into a bigger, more prominent, and more controversial case than *DeFunis.* "No lawsuit," observed a law professor about *Bakke,* "has ever been more widely watched or more thoroughly debated in the national or international press before the [U.S. Supreme] Court's decision."[1] The range and quality of the *Bakke* debate profited, of course, from its dress rehearsal in *DeFunis.*

What was at issue in *Bakke* and *DeFunis?* In each case a private suit was brought by an applicant against a public professional school that had twice rejected him. Allan Bakke and Marco De- Funis, Jr., both claimed that they had been denied the constitutional guarantee of equal protection of the laws (Fourteenth Amendment) because a school, in accord with a policy it had voluntarily adopted, had used racial categories to admit less qualified minority students on a preferential basis. DeFunis's claim against the University of Washington law school was turned down by the highest state court in Washington; but the California Supreme Court upheld Bakke, in sweeping terms, in his suit against the Davis medical school. By pressing adjudication of this constitutional claim, first DeFunis and then Bakke transmuted a personal quest for school admission into *the* case on which the highest court in the land was expected to make a precedent-setting decision on the legality of "reverse racial discrimination." Further, the reach of such a ruling might extend beyond the question of selective admissions to public professional schools to affect or embrace the whole gamut of Affirmative Action government programs.

Once *Bakke* had succeeded *DeFunis* on center stage, therefore, many observers considered it as potentially the most important decision for policy and law in race relations and education since the watershed judgments of the Court on education desegregation in 1954–55. A sense of the high stakes and severe issue conflicts associated with *Bakke* can be had by the following sampling of a few of the friend-of-the-court briefs submitted to the U.S. Supreme Court in the case:

> If this Court errs, and [broadly] affirms the *Bakke* decision [of the California Supreme Court] . . . it risks bringing to a halt all programs and policies which have been regarded as permissible since the beginning of reconstruction after the Civil War. That consequence would be more costly to the nation and to the education of all citizens than any error since 120 years ago when this Court decided *Dred Scott* v. *Sanford*.[2]

> . . . there can be no other name for a program so designed to benefit a given race or group of races than discrimination on the basis of race—pure, simple and unadulterated. The best of motives cannot disguise this worst of practices, which carries with it the seeds of self-destruction for the very system which spawns it, by submerging the rights of the human individual which are sacred to our social system in favor of the interests of the amorphous group.[3]

> . . . we face a cruel irony if we adopt a construction of the Equal Protection Clause that requires absolute governmental neutrality in all circumstances towards the races in their presently unequal positions. Such a move will . . . guarantee the perpetuation of preferential access of whites to the benefits and rewards of our society. . . . And the promise of true civil equality between the races would remain forever a mirage.[4]

> Does equal protection by the State, commanded by the Fourteenth Amendment, mean one thing as applied to whites and another when applied to nonwhites? Since whites and nonwhites, by definition, exhaust the universe, to what are the rights of nonwhites to be equal, if not the rights of whites? . . . Equality denotes a relationship between or among those who are to be treated equally by the government. And the Equal Protection Clause means that the constitutional rights of a person cannot depend on his race, or it means nothing.[5]

Those who attributed great importance to the *Bakke* case could only speculate on the extent to which the Court would attempt this time, in contrast to *DeFunis*, to deal with the key issues. Predicting how the Court may decide a specific case is always chancy, and with *Bakke* the risk was even greater because new judicial doctrine was called for; a divided Court might reasonably be anticipated. Still, there was no dearth of educated guesstimates of how far the Court might choose to take *Bakke*.

At one extreme was the possibility of an abortive outcome similar to that of *DeFunis*. Most observers discounted this, on the practical assumption that the Court would not likely disappoint again by coming up with another false alarm. At the other extreme was the possibility of the Court's broadly and definitively disposing of all the central legal issues through this one decision. Although some *Bakke*-watchers hoped (or worried) that this might occur, the more realistic anticipation was that the Court's beginning move into the highly charged terrain of reverse discrimination would be undertaken cautiously and somewhat narrowly, in keeping with its standard strategy for grappling with large, contentious constitutional questions. When considered as a specific case for judicial decision, rather than as the centerpiece of a wide-ranging debate, *Bakke* was bounded by the particulars of its fact situation. It dealt with but one form of minority preference in admissions to but one category of professional schools and involved nothing directly about employment or other areas in which the use of minority-preference devices was also in dispute. Thus the Court could elect to confine the legal issues to this narrower focus and await a flow of post-*Bakke* cases over the year; in this manner it could slowly work out its full position on whether and how government might permissibly engage in various kinds of race-conscious activities intended to benefit minorities.

Yet even if the Court's holding turned out substantively to be much less than a blockbuster, it was almost certainly not going to be a dud either. However circumspect or circumscribed the decision, it would likely signal at least the direction of the Court's views on the broader range of reverse discrimination policies and practices. Moreover, the buildup of public expectations about the import of the *Bakke* case constituted something of a self-fulfilling prophecy. It ensured that many key antibias participants in the public and private sector would tend to interpret (or overinterpret) the decision in the largest possible terms.

In sum, as long as the Court avoided another *DeFunis*-like non-decision and came down either for Allan Bakke or for the Davis medical school, that action alone (especially if it was buttressed by a well-formed rationale endorsed by a majority of the justices), had to have major symbolic and practical consequences. As one of the briefs observed:

> . . . the decision in the instant case—whichever way it goes—will have great effects on the behavior of Americans in everyday transactions and decisions, not because of the narrow holding therein, but because, in the popular mind, the instant case is viewed as dealing with the legality of preferential treatment in *any* selective process, wherein only some persons can be chosen and others must be rejected. . . . [F]or a large number of Americans indeed, the decision herein will be *the* decision on the legality of such preferential policies and practices.[6] (Emphasis in original)

A Policy Dilemma

In another and no less important sense, *Bakke* and *DeFunis* qualified for a place in the history books almost without regard to how the Supreme Court would decide. Taken together, the two cases served to focus public attention on a complex and contentious problem in public policy and law that had taken on increasing urgency and was now ripe for resolution. Acting as a catalyst, the cases provoked a wide-ranging and intense review of the problem, one that quickly took on the character of a fundamental clash of needs, interests, and values. "Not since the assassination of Martin Luther King [1968]," commented *Change,* a respected journal covering higher education, "has this country engaged in as much soul searching about its race relations as has been triggered by *Bakke.*"[7]

"Soul searching" was an apt term for the morally wrenching dilemma created by a reliance on reverse discrimination to aid historically disadvantaged minorities. As with any genuine dilemma, there were no easy answers; for many who were in conflict on the question, there were no satisfying answers either. Not surprisingly, then, public-spirited persons and organizations found themselves disagreeing profoundly, often passionately, on what balance should be struck between divergent compelling objectives. One side emphasized historic justice for minorities, the social imperative of the need for minority-group advancement, and the obvious effectiveness of applying color-conscious discrimination to promote that objective. The other side's overriding concerns were current justice for all, irrespective of race, and the social imperative of holding fast to the values of color-blind policy and individual advancement through personal qualifications and merit. Typically, both sides invoked the same goals—greater fairness, equality, and justice and an ultimate vision of race-neutral law and policy—but they differed greatly on how best to achieve them. Was there some sound way to reconcile these disagreements, and did racial preference in admissions constitute such a way?

Both the dilemma's complexity and the intensity of dispute it stimulated reflected the impossibility, for this problem, of promoting minority inclusion without producing an equivalent nonminority exclusion. In any highly selective admissions process involving many more applicants than available places, there was no feasible way to increase minority enrollments as a simple "add-on" that would leave undisturbed the admission chances of nonminority applicants. Consider, by contrast, the absence of the exclusion factor in the following policy change on financial-aid awards to minorities by the University of California. In 1969, the university regents voted to discontinue accepting gifts or bequests that required or requested the selection of student beneficiaries on the "basis of race, color, descent, creed or national origin." (Ironically, 1969 was also the year that the university's Davis medical school adopted its preferential minority admissions policy.) In March 1977, well after the California Supreme Court had decided against them in *Bakke*, the regents lifted their ban on such gifts, citing the increased interest of foundations and individual benefactors in providing special funds to help minority and women students. University counsel took pains to emphasize, however, that nonminority or male students in need of aid would not be adversely affected because they would continue to get their regular share from other funds. In counsel's view, the legality of the new policy was assured as long as an equal amount of nonrestricted university funds was available to "offset" the restricted bequests.[8]

But restricted school places could not be offset in the manner of restricted gift dollars. To let in X number of minority applicants on a preferential basis meant, by the inexorable laws of arithmetic, that X number of nonminority applicants could not be let in. Justice Thurgood Marshall, the present Court's only minority member, made the point bluntly in an observation to Bakke's lawyer during the oral argument held in October 1977:

You are arguing about keeping somebody out [Allan Bakke and some other nonminority persons] and the other side is arguing about getting somebody in [some minority persons]. . . . So it depends on which way you look at it, doesn't it?[9]

Much the same point was made at the oral argument on *Bakke* before the California Supreme Court in March 1976, in an exchange between Chief Justice Donald R. Wright and Donald Reidhaar, general counsel of the regents of the University of California:

Chief Justice Wright: We have [before us today] whether it is constitutional to use race as a classification for excluding students— that's what we really have, isn't it?
Mr. Reidhaar: That certainly is a basic issue, Your Honor.
Chief Justice Wright: It is the basic issue.[10]

At the core of the dilemma, then, was the use of race to determine inclusion or exclusion in a situation where "getting somebody in" required "keeping somebody out." And what was at stake was not simply admission to a school but entry to a profession; law and medical schools serve as "gatekeepers" to their respective professions. Most everyone accepted the importance and desirability of enrolling more minority persons in professional schools and the professions, but the means—preferential admissions—was deeply disquieting to many. If, as some insisted, only this particular means could effectively achieve the agreed-on end, how should the quandary be resolved? If the offensiveness of this means was acknowledged, then what of the offensiveness of the social reality of minority disadvantage it sought to alter? Did the employment of race-conscious means, when motivated to bring minorities into the American mainstream rather than exclude them, promote or deny equality of opportunity and equal protection of the law? Was it, in terms of political realities and public attitudes, a self-defeating means, or was it the most feasible way to accomplish what just about everyone said needed to be accomplished?

"Something More" for the Unshackled Runner
Most Americans recognize the extensive past deprivation of minority groups and subscribe to the broad objective of moving minorities into, as the overworked phrase puts it, "the mainstream of

American life." Nevertheless, this substantial consensus favoring minority progress toward full equality does not carry over to how to achieve that objective. Indeed, *Bakke* and *DeFunis* may be said to rest, fundamentally, on the question of what means should be used to promote a broadly endorsed end, and that issue has dramatically split opinion in the nation.

So severe a disagreement over how to facilitate minority gains was not always the case. During the civil rights movement of the early and middle 1960s—at least when seen in retrospect from today's vantage point—the evils addressed had an enviable simplicity, directness, and clarity. Who could really argue, on the merits, against ending southern state laws or state-enforced customs that had long denied voting rights to blacks? Or that had assigned blacks to a public education composed of separate and inferior schools? Or that had required blacks to eat in segregated areas of restaurants and sit at the back of the public buses? Or that had prevented blacks from access to many places of public accommodation?

The statutory and policy remedies for these intolerable conditions were, for the most part, as straightforward and obvious as the evils themselves; hence, they enjoyed unified support. True, an occasional voice not associated with southern defense of its racial caste system expressed worry about the maintenance of federalism in the face of accelerated interventions by the national government, but such anxieties were generally treated as marginal to the problem. The overriding commitment was, in the words of Hubert H. Humphrey (then mayor of Minneapolis) to the cheering delegates at the 1948 Democratic National Convention:

> To those who say that this civil rights program is an infringement on States' Rights, I say this, that the time has arrived in America . . . to get out of the shadows of States' Rights and to walk forthrightly into the bright sunshine of human rights.

The enactment of civil rights measures in this earlier period signaled a determination to put an end to deliberate negative racial discrimination and establish the norm of nondiscrimination in its place. Underlying these dramatic changes in law and policy was the belief—honest but naive, as it turned out—that eliminating the barriers of racial discrimination would be sufficient by itself to bring about equality of opportunity. Reflecting that belief, efforts to enforce nondiscrimination were stepped up from the late 1960s, in the wake of the assassination of the Reverend Martin Luther King, Jr., and of riots in the inner-city ghettos, to the present. But that something more than nondiscrimination was needed is a lesson that many of us have come to learn and accept—"something more" to counter or offset the long-term effects of extensive previous discrimination. What that "something more" should be, however, has become precisely the major bone of contention.

A good way to appreciate the "something more" quandary is to consider the metaphor of the shackled runner, an analogy frequently advanced by spokesmen for minorities:

> Imagine two runners at the starting line, readying for the 100-yard dash. One has his legs shackled, the other not. The gun goes off and the race begins. Not surprisingly, the unfettered runner immediately takes the lead and then rapidly increases the distance between himself and his shackled competitor. Before the finish line is crossed, however, the judging official blows his whistle, calls off the contest on the grounds that the unequal conditions between the runners made it an unfair competition, and orders removal of the shackles.

Surely few would deny that pitting a shackled runner against an unshackled one is inequitable and does not provide equality of opportunity. Hence, canceling the race and freeing the disadvantaged runner of his shackles seem altogether appropriate. Once beyond this point, however, agreement fades rapidly.

The key question becomes: what should be done so that the two runners can resume the contest on a basis of fair competition? Is it enough, after removing the shackles, to place both runners back at the starting line? Or is "something more" needed, and if so, what? Should the rules of the running be altered, and if so, how? Should the previously shackled runner be given a compensatory edge, or should the other runner be handicapped in some way? How much edge or handicap? How do we determine when the point has been reached that ensures "fairness" for the newly unshackled runner? And is "fairness" for one runner likely to result in "unfairness" for the other?

Today's racial issues, in sum, lack the enormous advantages of those in the mid-1960s, when the compelling, dramatic, and simple goal was to remove the many shackles from the long-time shackled runner. We now must deal with what additionally should be done to help the recently unshackled runner. So profound a shift in the focus and complexity of the problem has led, not surprisingly, to a breakdown of the moral, political, and legal consensus that spawned the minority gains of the earlier period. The divisiveness and un-certainty that have taken its place reflect the sobering fact that the "something more" problem, when compared to the displacement of southern racial discrimination by national nondiscrimination, is in-herently much more difficult to resolve and is thoroughly national in scope. As one civil rights veteran has ruefully noted, "It's not that the moral problem [of racial advance] has gone away, but the morality of any given solution is no longer self-evident to many people."[11] It is one thing to provide blacks access to southern voting booths and lunch counters, but quite another to assist blacks over the nation to secure their "share of higher education admissions" or their "share of jobs." Indeed, many of the most pressing current needs of minorities relate to national concerns, such as housing, health, employment, and social services, which are not seen by the public as primarily civil rights or minority issues at all.

2 Divergent Notions of Equal Opportunity

The popular consensus supporting minority gains is most strongly a consensus on direction, endorsing minority progress. It then divides, though still exhibiting a majority view, on how to promote that progress and on the meaning of the larger objective as well. The central concept and catchword is "equality" (or, in this context, "equal opportunity"), a term subject to greatly different interpretations and understandings. When considered as a concept, we tend to endorse equal opportunity for all, including minorities, as a desirable value and objective. Our differences emerge as we move on to explore the meaning of the concept and ways to promote it. Few of us see equal opportunity as an absolute value to be pursued doggedly no matter how adverse the consequences for other values and interests. Rather, most of us are also committed to other intersecting or competing values against which the quest for equal opportunity must be judged. We find, then, that our disagreements turn on the different balances we draw.

The American version of equal opportunity, to the despair of generations of reformers and critics, has always involved acceptance of a large inequality of results among individuals (in income, status, and the like). The dispute over ways to promote equal opportunity for minorities has not, by and large, basically challenged that prevailing outlook. Minorities see themselves, and are seen by others, as seeking their share of what the system offers, not as rejecting or overhauling the system. This widespread acceptance of unequal results is linked, in turn, to popular beliefs in social mobility, in the chance of individuals to progress in line with their ability and effort.

In an earlier period this view took the form of a ruthless social

Darwinism that sanctified the wealthy and society's other status winners and morally condemned the poor and society's other losers. Today's majority view is less harsh and somewhat more humane. Among other modifications of the earlier outlook, it has accepted in principle and practice the obligation to cushion the inequality of results by providing a minimum base of support for those at the bottom, which includes a disproportionate share of the nation's minority population.

The Traditional View

The traditional concept of equal opportunity, when applied, say, to jobs, emphasized a fair process of evaluation among the applicants competing to be hired. This involved assessment of applicants on an individual basis by use of nongroup criteria relevant to satisfactory handling of the job in question. The result of such a meritocratic process was the selection of the persons best qualified to do the job, judged in terms of the current performance abilities of the competitors. By definition, a genuinely meritocratic process was fair and, therefore, both guaranteed and defined a fair outcome and equality of opportunity. The elimination of racial discrimination in hiring thus represented a belated purification of the traditional concept, not a challenge to it. Hence both nondiscrimination and government enforcement of nondiscrimination have become comfortably incorporated within the prevailing notion of equal opportunity.

The antidiscrimination principle initially attracted broad public backing because its meaning was clear, limited, and closely tied to traditional attitudes on equal opportunity. When the Civil Rights Act of 1964 established a national policy of nondiscrimination, it was broadly understood to involve the eradication of intentional and overt discriminatory practices against minorities and the adoption of color-blind procedures in their place. Rapid and sizable minority strides toward equality would follow, it was assumed, once these discriminatory barriers were leveled. Putting the policy into practice was a relatively straightforward matter, at least conceptually, and it led to an emphasis on ways to eliminate considerations of race from selection and evaluation processes.

Within but a short time, this initial view of what nondiscrimination meant and entailed was considered to be too confining to achieve the results desired and, therefore, to be in need of supplementation. Additional and special efforts were required, it was felt, to promote equal opportunity more effectively for members of minority groups extensively discriminated against in the past. In their justification and explanation of these special programs and procedures, government officials customarily represented them as constituting a complementary expansion of the earlier concept of nondiscrimination, one that was faithful to its spirit and to traditional equal-opportunity values. In light of the escalating public controversy provoked by the numerous and varied "something more" procedures that government antibias policy mandated, however, there obviously was considerable dissent from that judgment.

Some types of special actions on behalf of minorities were linkable without strain to traditional antidiscrimination attitudes. They could be interpreted entirely as "competition perfecting" activities intended to confirm the integrity of the accepted equal-opportunity concept by genuinely improving its operation in the real world. For example, the evidence indicated that minorities had less knowledge of job opportunities and, because of previous negative experiences, were less motivated to apply for those job openings of which they were aware. To reduce this inequality, it was reasonable for employers to provide wide notice of jobs and also take other "affirmative actions" to attract minority persons to apply. In principle, such special efforts squared thoroughly with the traditional notion of equal opportunity because they removed inappropriate competitive disadvantages and enlarged the competition, while leaving all else intact.

Other types of affirmative actions were more mixed in character. Many of these sought to help minority persons who were less able, because of past discrimination, to compete effectively now for available opportunities (e.g., special minority training and educational programs, special financial aid to minority students to relieve them of the need to take on a job while at school). Such programs could appropriately be construed as perfecting competition because they aimed to increase the number of qualified minority persons who could hold their own in an open competition. Depending upon circumstances, however, these special benefits could also be seen as having competition-reducing effects. With limited funds, for example, assigning extra financial aid to minority students would result in a cutback of funds available to nonminority students with equivalent needs. Further, the restriction of special programs solely to minorities invariably raised some concern about official use of explicit race categories and about the treatment of persons as members of a group rather than as individuals. Because of these complications, programs in this category of special actions had a more divided reaction from those holding the traditional view of equal opportunity. Still, substantial support for varied kinds of special minority arrangements could usually be counted on, especially when they did not obviously handicap nonminorities.

Broadly speaking, for most Americans the boundaries for doing "something more" to assist minorities were set by a nonrigid reading of the terms of the traditional view of equal opportunity: vigorously enforced nondiscrimination, special programs to bring more disadvantaged minority persons into the pool of qualified candidates, and provision of minimum support for those unable to compete effectively. By strengthening the openness and fairness of individual competition—the core of the traditional view—these actions were seen to promote opportunities for minorities in ways that were consistent with other key values.

An Alternate View
From another perspective, the chief virtues of the means endorsed by the traditional view appeared as its principal liabilities. Means that fully respected the individualistic "competition perfecting" standard could not ensure predictable group outcomes. The traditional concept's stress on developing a larger supply of qualified minority applicants was doubly chancy in this regard: first, as to how rapid and sizable that development would be and, second, as to what proportion of the qualified minorities placed on the starting line actually would win in their competition against nonminorities. The most direct way to eliminate this uncertainty and unreliability was to predetermine what proportion of wins should go to minorities and then to achieve that proportion by some form of preferential selection of minority candidates.

Many of the justifications for preferential treatment of minorities were, paradoxically, backhanded affirmations of the traditional equal-opportunity concept. One much-used argument, for example, stressed that minority-preference policy should be understood as a temporary deviation from equal-opportunity means. A return to traditional values would follow once minorities no longer needed or deserved special preference to promote their equality. Today's departure from equal opportunity, in other words, was necessary to assure tomorrow's renewed commitment to it.

At least one justification embodied an alternative view of equality. In contrast to the traditional concept, it stressed groups and outcomes, not individuals and process. If all other things were truly equal, asserted this view, a genuinely fair and meritocratic process would result in roughly the same proportion of nonminorities and minorities gaining the school admissions, the jobs, or whatever the competition. Where disparate group proportions were the outcome, that indicated the existence of unfairness and unequal opportunity for the underrepresented groups, for which the selection process had acted simply as a "pass-through" rather than a corrective. The proper measure of fair process and equal opportunity was, then, proportional group results.

Applied to the issue of professional school admissions, this view argued that the disproportionate exclusion of minorities by traditional equal-opportunity standards produced unequal opportunity because it rewarded and extended differential group achievement rooted in past unfair group inequalities. The only quick and certain way to break this circle was to make sure that minorities actually got into the school or the profession, as distinct from competing for admission relatively ineffectively as a result of inequalities unfairly imposed on them by society. The surest way to make sure was to apply some method of preference for minorities.

Table 1, which presents the results of a *New York Times*/CBS national survey conducted in October 1977, highlights the cutting points of public sentiment on the intersection of the "something more" problem with these divergent notions of equal opportunity.[1] A clear majority of whites opposed the assigning of a minimum number of jobs or admissions places to minorities, but supported the more moderate means of special job training or the rather ambiguously worded "special consideration to the best minority applicants" to college or graduate school. Among blacks, more approved than disapproved of each item and by margins markedly greater than those of whites. Still, the direction of change in black sentiment on each question paralleled that among whites, which suggested the common tug of shared values. Particularly noteworthy was the last question, dealing with a *Bakke*-like situation, on which blacks were almost evenly split and whites expressed disapproval by an almost two-to-one ratio.

TABLE I. Aiding Minority Advance: Equal-Opportunity Special Assistance, Not Absolute Preference

QUESTION	Whites		Blacks	
	Approve	Disapprove	Approve	Disapprove
"How about requiring large companies to set up special training programs for members of minority groups?"	63%	32%	88%	9%
". . . would you approve or disapprove of requiring business to hire a certain number of minority workers?"	35%	60%	64%	26%
"What about a college or graduate school giving special consideration to the best minority applicants, to help more of them get admitted than otherwise. Would you approve or disapprove of that?"	59%	36%	83%	16%
"What if a school reserved a certain number of places for qualified minority applicants. Would you approve or disapprove of that even if it meant that some qualified white applicants wouldn't be admitted?"	32%	60%	46%	42%

Within the context, then, of high support for the promotion of minority equality, public sentiment appeared to favor a "flexible" application of traditional equal-opportunity values. This flexibility seems to offer legitimacy to a wide range of "something more" policies and programs that stay well short of pronounced preferential treatment. Adherence to the traditional concept of equal opportunity leads to an emphasis on stepping up the skills and qualifications of minorities to hasten the entry of many more of them on the supply side of the equation. Provision of special resources and assistance to promote that development appears to pass public muster also, as long as it operates to strengthen an open and fair competition and not to penalize nonminorities. Even "special consideration" for minorities, an unclear term that perhaps suggests slight modification but not elimination of competition, may fall within the allowable bounds of flexibility, depending on the particulars of the situation. It remains to be seen whether this broadly supportive public posture provides an adequate base for reconciling the disagreements encapsulated in *Bakke* on how best to bring about a fuller measure of equality for minorities.

Goals or Quotas?

As antibias programs expanded in number, coverage, complexity, and regulative detail, public controversy inevitably intensified. The quarrel centered, broadly, on whether the pervasive Affirmative Action and nondiscrimination programs—as they actually operated, not in terms of their stated or claimed intent—were promoting equal opportunity for minorities in ways that discriminated against nonminorities.

Marked disagreement of judgment on how particular programs really worked in practice was readily understandable. For one thing, the administration of antibias programs was so fragmented, inconsistent, and confusing that all sides were united in condemnation of its deficiencies. For another, program operation necessarily involved thousands of key participants in the nongovernmental sector around the nation; the actions of all these people could scarcely be monitored, let alone standardized. Perhaps most basically, even with a more favorable program administration setting it still would have been no simple task to agree on how to distinguish conceptually between what was minority assisting, minority favoring, or minority preferring. The difficulties were multiplied when attempting to apply these often elusive distinctions in evaluation of the complicated procedures characteristic of antibias programs.

As a consequence, plausible judgments on the appropriateness of specific antibias programs could go either way. Which was exactly what happened, with some asserting the propriety, and others the impropriety, of one or another minority-sensitive program, based on different readings of its actual workings. A good example of this process of disagreement is provided by an examination of what was perhaps the most heated and persistent clash in the controversy over Affirmative Action, namely, whether "goals" were or were not "quotas." Before reviewing that quarrel, a brief description of Affirmative Action would be appropriate.

Affirmative Action derived from a series of executive orders, especially those issued by President Lyndon Johnson in 1965 and 1967, based on the national government's procurement authority to set conditions for all who contracted to supply it with goods and services. (The government's interest in promoting greater economic efficiency among federal contractors provided the legal rationale for imposing the condition of nondiscriminatory employment.) It was conceived in the belief that positive ("affirmative") actions were needed, in addition to nondiscrimination, in order to prevent indefinite perpetuation of inequalities caused by past discrimination. Central to its implementation as a program was the requirement that highly detailed written plans be developed by each contractor and approved by the appropriate government agency. In the words of the Department of Labor's Revised Order Number 4, which governed employment practices in industry and higher education:

> An affirmative-action program is a set of specific and result-oriented procedures to which a contractor commits himself to apply every good faith effort. The objective of these procedures plus such efforts is equal employment opportunity. Procedures without effort to make them work are meaningless; and effort, undirected by specific and meaningful procedures, is inadequate.

In working up a written plan, the employer first had to survey his current work force to determine whether there was "underutilization," in any of the firm's job classifications, of blacks, persons with Spanish surnames, persons of Oriental ancestry, American Indians, or women. Underutilization was held to exist whenever the proportion of any of these specified groups within a job classification was significantly smaller than would be expected if the employer had

hired persons from the available work force in a random, nondiscriminatory way. Discrimination, therefore, was defined in terms of
effects, independent of whether the employer had or still was engaged in overt discriminatory practices, and underutilization was
its statistical measure. Where underutilization was found, the contractor had to establish goals for each underutilized group, specify-
ing the number of persons in each group that should be employed
in each job classification and establishing a timetable for reaching
that numerical goal through good-faith efforts.

In the light of these key concepts and procedures, Affirmative
Action could be likened to the "proportional group results" view of
equal opportunity discussed earlier in this chapter. And that view
was associated with advocacy of minority preferences. But the matter was hardly that simple because, to repeat what Revised Order
Number 4 stated, ". . . effort, undirected by specific and meaningful procedures, is inadequate." It could be argued, and antibias
officials did so argue, that the setting of group underutilization was
a proper and valuable procedure. It established a reasonable and
explicit target for achievement and permitted the employer and the
government alike to measure the rate of progress in reaching the
goal. Furthermore, goal setting was logically distinguishable from
quota setting, and government officials emphasized the distinction
and insisted that no quota setting was intended or expected. Thus,
to take but one difference, quotas had to be filled but goals did not
have to be met. Although an unmet Affirmative Action goal might
trigger a fuller inquiry, the employer was then entitled to provide
evidence and to explain why his good-faith efforts had not been fully
successful. If the employer's position was supported by the agency's
review, no penalties could be levied for failure to meet the goal.

Nevertheless, such justifications of group employment goals left
the central question at issue wide open. That question was not
whether goals and quotas were theoretically the same thing; clearly
they were different. Nor was it whether Affirmative Action mandated
quotas, because plainly the procedures called for setting goals. The
core of the dispute was, rather, whether the procedures in their
actual operation often resulted in the conversion of goals into quotas because they encouraged or tolerated the employer's use of
minority-preference devices to achieve his hiring goals.

In probing that central question, a full canvass of experiences
could not be realistically undertaken because literally thousands of

Affirmative Action plans were continuously in operation. Moreover, antibias agencies differed in the criteria they applied to these plans and in their monitoring and enforcement of them. In such circumstances, the critics of Affirmative Action could provide only scattered evidence documenting instances of the translation of goals into quotas, and this evidence was discounted by Affirmative Action supporters and treated by them as inconclusive. For example, the "goals or quotas" quarrel was especially fierce in the world of higher education, with reference to the hiring of faculty members. The evidence introduced on quota behavior in that area often took the form of a department chairman's letter informing an unsuccessful white male applicant that the faculty opening had to be filled by a minority person or woman. In explanation of such incidents, it could be argued that they were random mistakes, reflecting misunderstanding of what goal setting entailed, which were only to be expected in any new, large-scale program involving highly decentralized implementation. Such letters could also be characterized as an effort by some academic employers to use Affirmative Action as a scapegoat, either to provide the unaccepted applicant with an impersonal reason for his turndown or, on occasion, to discredit the program.

Since neither systematic nor mutually acceptable hard evidence was available to the disputants, the argument came to focus on an analysis of the structure and dynamics of the Affirmative Action process. Did the diverse incentives and pressures generated by that process work, on balance, to encourage employers to maintain or to blur the critical goal-quota distinction? On this fundamental question those who argued that goals often became quotas presented a view that illuminated the tensions, contradictions, and confusions latent in Affirmative Action.

Affirmative Action, they noted, called for the maintenance of an extraordinarily delicate balance: a co-joining of minority-sensitive and nondiscriminatory activities that would accomplish a rather specific predetermined numerical result. This balance meant that race-conscious activities had to be constrained by respect for the nondiscrimination principle and that as much attention had to be paid to the integrity of the process as to the satisfactoriness of the results. As these critics saw it, antibias programs had upset the delicate balance by overemphasizing a concern for results, which then skewed the operation of the program toward goal achievement at the expense of fidelity to nondiscrimination. This bias of the antibias agencies, most of these critics felt, was not an accidental development that could be easily remedied through corrective action, but was something built into the fiber of the policy and the dynamics of its implementation by government.

An Affirmative Action program, they pointed out, officially defined itself as "a set of specific and result-oriented procedures." Since it was obviously far easier to monitor results than process, it was incumbent on antibias agencies to take special care to encourage employers to hire through genuinely nondiscriminatory processes. Instead, the agencies all too frequently sent signals that went in the opposite direction: the employer who failed to realize his group hiring goal, and not the one who achieved his goal by use of quota-like means, was the one who might have to face vigorous investigation, bad publicity, and the threat of contract cancellation. The political environment of antibias policy and of the enforcement agencies—especially the political constituencies whose interests were most directly served and the ideological and program commitments of the government officials most directly involved— helped explain this greater concern for deficiencies of outcomes than of methods.

The critics' suspicion that a "quota mentality" often lay behind agency thinking about Affirmative Action goals was reinforced by occasional, but highly publicized, incidents in which high officials departed from the standard government position that goals and quotas were entirely different things. In March 1977, for example, in an interview with the *New York Times,* Joseph A. Califano, Jr., secretary of the Department of Health, Education, and Welfare, observed that it was possible and necessary to endorse preferential hiring for jobs and admissions policies in higher education:

How am I, as Secretary of HEW, ever going to find first-class black doctors, first-class black lawyers, first-class black scientists, first-class women scientists, if these people don't have a chance to get into the best places [schools] in the country?

. . . For a long time, I didn't think quotas would work [but he subsequently changed his mind because of his work with women at *Newsweek* and with employees of the El Paso Natural Gas Company, which he represented in private law practice]. I noticed in recruiting that if you press people hard enough to cast the net wide enough, you find [minority and female] people.[2]

Later that month, on NBC's "Meet the Press" television show, Califano enlarged on his view:

> . . . as a society, we have a constitutional and . . . moral obligation to encourage and give . . . some preferential treatment to minorities. . . . I don't think this involves reverse discrimination against the white male. I think he will have his full opportunity.[3]

What followed these assertions by the HEW secretary was thoroughly predictable. Several groups called on Califano to resign and on President Carter to repudiate Califano's position. An HEW spokesman stated that the secretary was "expressing a personal opinion" and that he felt quotas should "apply to jobs, in employment, but that he didn't mean it to apply to schools, though he wants strong affirmative-action programs there."[4] Califano himself recanted in the face of the ministorm of criticism. Noting, in understatement, that "quotas" was "obviously a nerve-jangling word," he now aligned himself with affirmative action "to rectify past or on-going discrimination," and not with quotas that would require the admission of a certain percentage of blacks or women.[5]

From the viewpoint of Califano's critics, the episode was an egregious example of the general absence of sensitive program implementation committed to preserving the fine balance between race-conscious activities and nondiscrimination. Without that agency commitment, employers were given cues that encouraged them to treat goals as quotas. Since it was improbable that this administrative sensitivity would be developed voluntarily, two implications followed for those who shared this critique. One was a growing disenchantment generally with Affirmative Action on the grounds of its practical inability to promote minority equality without engaging in reverse discrimination. The other was to look more to the courts, especially the U.S. Supreme Court, in the hope that judges might prove less tolerant than administrators of reverse discrimination. The *Bakke* case, because it involved a major test of the legality of explicit racial preferences (albeit in professional school admissions, not jobs), naturally became a focal point for these hopes.

One did not have to subscribe fully to this critique to agree with the more moderate propositions that the goal-quota distinction was much harder to sustain in practice than in theory and that Affirmative Action, by appearing to encourage both nondiscrimination and minority preference, greatly aggravated the goal-quota confusion. As a consequence of this confusion, employers were placed in the unenviable position of running serious risks no matter what they did. "We have no desire to break anybody's law, if we can figure out what the law is," plaintively observed a perplexed dean faced with a federal government requirement that his university consider the sex of applicants when hiring faculty and with a federal judge's ruling prohibiting the university from doing so.[6] And the U.S. Chamber of Commerce, in a lengthy friend-of-the-court brief filed on *Bakke,* complained of "the present uncertainty created by conflicting principles simultaneously pursued by the state and federal governments"[7] and asked the U.S. Supreme Court to end that uncertainty by its decision in *Bakke.* The dilemma for employers, as the Chamber saw it, was as follows:

> On the one hand, employers are confronted with a complex array of federal and state antidiscrimination laws making illegal any racial discrimination or racial preference in employment. On the other hand, many employers have been required as a condition of doing business with federal, state and local agencies to commit themselves to affirmative action programs to increase the employment and promotion of minorities and women according to prescribed statistical representation formulae. The consequences to an employer of a failure to reach such imposed affirmative action "goals" are so severe, that employers inevitably treat the goal as a quota and give preferences to applicants and employees on the basis of their race or sex. Such action may, of course, violate the antidiscrimination statutes. Employers thus are on the horns of a dilemma: they may refuse to use quotas and goals and forego valuable government contracts or they may come into compliance and face the risks of back pay liability [in suits brought by employees on grounds they were illegally discriminated against by the preferences accorded members of other groups] for violations of Title VII [of the Civil Rights Act of 1964, banning employer discrimination] and similar legislation.[8]

The response of the Equal Employment Opportunity Commission (EEOC) to the dilemma posed in the Chamber's brief was instructive. (In its proposed reorganization of federal antibias programs submitted to Congress in early 1978, the Carter administration assigned considerable centralized control to EEOC.) This leading antibias agency proposed new rules in late 1977 that would give employers protection from reverse discrimination charges filed with

EEOC, if they had Affirmative Action plans that passed the agency's criteria for reasonability. Those who thought the plans were not affirmative enough could still challenge them through EEOC, but claims of reverse discrimination would have to be litigated in the courts. If these proposed rules provided a fair indication of how antibias officials defined their own role and position in "settling" the goal-quota confusion, little wonder that persons holding a different viewpoint sought to impose contraints on those administrators by turning to the courts.

Discriminating to End Discrimination?

Broadly speaking, the government's promotion of "something more" activities on behalf of minority advance, both as a concept and as a set of operating programs, was no less novel in law than in policy. Lacking any solid or reliable body of precedent for its justification, Affirmative Action was, as one observer aptly put it, "a fragile commodity" that had "a sort of tenuous existence between the lines of the Constitution."[9] Its programs had expanded so rapidly within a decade that authoritative judicial resolution of the severe disputes it provoked inevitably had lagged well behind. Few definitive lines had been established between what was constitutionally permissible in the generic name of affirmative action and what was impermissible. As a consequence, *Bakke* acted as a magnet for all disputants in the larger controversy, who took the opportunity to press on the Court widely divergent views of where those lines should be drawn.

What faced the Court—and the nation—was a ripe and pressing controversy over what means could be used to hasten the equalization of opportunities for minorities. Some maintained that the touchstone of legal and desirable policy was race-free treatment of individuals by the same or comparable standards. Others urged that positive race-conscious policy based on minority-group membership offered the most effective means. But in any situation of competition for scarce goods, such as selective school admissions or jobs, to prefer members of some groups was to disfavor members of other groups. Hence the policy issue was whether the government could "discriminate to end discrimination" by applying racial-preference policies, and the concomitant legal issue was the consistency of such "benevolent" discrimination with the right of all

Americans to equal protection of the laws, as guaranteed by the Fourteenth Amendment.

Bakke, which involved the reservation of a number of competitive admissions places to members of certain minority groups, presented a clear instance of an award of minority preference at the expense of nonminority aspirants. Each side framed the problem, as would be expected, by emphasizing the half of it that supported their position and slighting the other half. Thus, for example, the University of California offered the following formulation of the central question in its brief:

> When only a small fraction of thousands of applicants can be admitted, does the Equal Protection Clause forbid a state university professional school from voluntarily seeking to counteract effects of generations of pervasive discrimination against . . . [specific] minorities by establishing a limited special admissions program that increases opportunities for well-qualified members of such racial and ethnic minorities?[10]

In contrast, several friend-of-the-court briefs submitted on behalf of Allan Bakke put the central question as follows:

> Does the Equal Protection Clause, held to protect blacks from discrimination in state university admissions, also protect whites?[11]

> May a State, consistently with the commands of the Fourteenth Amendment, exclude an applicant from one of its medical schools solely on the ground of the applicant's race?[12]

What made *Bakke* a genuine dilemma and potentially a landmark case was, of course, having to come to grips with both of these partial perspectives and, ultimately, to favor one more than the other.

The community of liberals, fresh from their enthusiasm and unity of the 1960s, found itself rent asunder by the "something more" quandary. Organized labor, which had supplied the civil rights movement with much of its money and political skills in the past, now opposed any alteration of job-seniority rights to facilitate redress to minorities for past discrimination. Many liberal Democrats in Congress had become lukewarm in support of, or openly hostile to, school busing once that issue left the confines of the South and became national in scope. Now *Bakke* added to the rift because it was seen as an attempt to justify giving minorities preferential school admissions or, even larger, to discredit meritocracy and replace it by a "proportional equality of results" standard.

Liberals remained ostensibly as one in their vision of a "color-blind" society that "neither knows nor tolerates classes among citizens,"[13] but their identity of objective seemed only to exacerbate their differences on how to get from here to there. Even as they made appeal in the name of the same values, their divergent reading of how to realize those values led to mutually exclusive routes. Thus, while both sides sought justification in the common language of equal opportunity, the minority preferences that one side supported as necessary to promote equality were rejected by the other side as antithetical to equality:

> It is by now well understood . . . that our society cannot be completely colorblind in the short term if we are to have a colorblind society in the long term. After centuries of viewing through colored lenses, eyes do not quickly adjust when the lenses are removed. Discrimination has a way of perpetuating itself, albeit unintentionally, because the resulting inequalities make new opportunities less accessible. Preferential treatment is one partial prescription to remedy our society's most intransigent and deeply rooted inequalities.[14]

> If the Constitution prohibits exclusion of blacks and other minorities on racial grounds, it cannot permit exclusion of whites on racial grounds. . . . For at least a generation the lesson of the great decisions of this [U.S. Supreme] Court and the lesson of contemporary history have been the same: discrimination on the basis of race is illegal, immoral, unconstitutional, inherently wrong and destructive of democratic society. Now this is to be unlearned and we are told that this is not a matter of fundamental principle but only a matter of whose ox is gored. Those for whom racial equality was demanded are now to be more equal than others. Having found support in the Constitution for equality, they now claim support for inequality under the same Constitution.[15]

For large numbers of persons, the split within the liberal camp had its counterpart in an almost schizoid conflict within themselves. Many on the anti-Bakke side also had an ingrained distaste for officially sanctioned racial discrimination, whether positive or negative in intent. Many on the pro-Bakke side were also deeply concerned about satisfying the need for social justice through policies that would hasten achievement of minority equality. President

Richard W. Lyman of Stanford University expressively conveyed the anguish of such persons, when confronting *Bakke* in their minds, in these comments about himself:

> I never felt in a greater agony of tension between two passionate commitments, both of which I entertain and which are in conflict with each other. . . . I don't know what I would do if I were a [U.S.] Supreme Court justice. . . . I would hope for some Solomon's judgment that will help us to have our cake and eat it.[16]

The hope for "some Solomon's judgment," though understandable psychologically as a wish to escape from having to make uncomfortable choices, also suggests a popular misreading of the judicial role. The exquisitely complicated problems presented by *Bakke* (and *DeFunis*) can never be "settled" through case law, no matter how reasoned the Court's decision in *Bakke* or subsequent cases. Rather, they are enduring problems not amenable to full resolution at any one time but in process of partial and changing resolution at all times. The Court's role can be enormously influential, of course, in setting the boundaries for policy in the *Bakke* area and shaping the continuing dispute. At bottom, however, it rests on the political process, not on the courts, to work out a shifting reconciliation of conflicting claims, interests, and values that will be popularly accepted as sensible and legitimate. *Bakke* and *DeFunis* pose, in short, a dilemma for the nation and for each of us as citizens, not simply for the nine justices of the U.S. Supreme Court.

Law School Admissions and Marco DeFunis, Jr.

"There was a time," Justice William O. Douglas reminded, "when law schools could follow the advice of Wigmore, who believed that 'the way to find out whether a boy has the makings of a competent lawyer is to see what he can do in the first year of law studies.' In those days [Wigmore's comment was made in 1929] there were enough spaces to admit every applicant who met minimal credentials, and they all could be given the opportunity to prove themselves at law school."[1] Although Wigmore's recommended procedure has long since ceased to be the rule, competition to enter law school was generally slack up through the early 1960s. With but a college degree and a high-C grade average, an applicant was virtually assured of entry into some American Bar Association-approved law school. In 1960 at Boalt (the University of California's law school at Berkeley), for example, a college average of *B* earned automatic admission, and those with a lower average often were admitted if they could persuasively explain why their academic record understated their actual abilities. Only applicants with less than a *B* average were required to take the Law School Aptitude Test (LSAT), and a middling score in the 500s sufficed for admission. On the basis of these criteria, Boalt admitted 73 percent of those who applied.[2]

It was 1970, though, not 1960, when Marco DeFunis, Jr., first applied to law school; by then, the admissions picture had changed fundamentally. It had become the fierce competition that it has remained to date, one in which schools and applicants alike were only too aware that "letting somebody in" meant "keeping somebody out."

Increasing Numbers of Applicants and Rising Standards of Admission

In the period from the 1964–65 academic year through that of 1975–76, applications to law school increased at a much higher rate than the increase in available spaces. The number of persons who took the LSAT, which provided a rough measure of demand, jumped three and one-half times in those dozen years, up to about 134,000 in 1975. The supply side of the equation also expanded: the number of enrolled first-year students nearly doubled to 39,000, the amount of J.D. or LL.B. degrees awarded tripled to 30,000, and new admissions to the bar tripled to 35,000. This increase in student places was accomplished more through an enlargement of existing law schools (by an average of two-thirds) than by the creation of new ones, although the number of ABA-approved schools did move up modestly from 134 in 1963 to 157 in 1975. That the increased supply lagged behind the heightened demand was evident: in 1964 the number of first-year seats represented 61 percent of the number of LSATs taken, but by 1975 that had declined to 29 percent.[3]

Applicants typically apply to more than one law school, of course, and hence the applicant rejection rate of law schools shot up even more dramatically, more than eightfold during the 1964–75 period. From the perspective of the applicant, the gross data suggested the chances of admission to *some* law school were about 50–50. In 1970, for example, which was the year in which Marco DeFunis was initially turned down by the University of Washington law school (UWLS), the number of available spaces in all law schools allowed enrollment of only about 35,000 of the 70,000 students who sought admission. For an applicant to UWLS, however, the statistics were far grimmer: in 1971, when he was rejected for the second time, DeFunis was one of 1601 applicants competing for about 300 acceptances. The 5:1 ratio of applications to acceptances at UWLS, which was not in the top tier of law schools, was about the same as that in the mid-1970s for such prestigious undergraduate colleges as Harvard-Radcliffe, Dartmouth, Williams, Amherst, and Princeton. In further contrast, it might be noted that more than half of all colleges currently accept at least 80 percent of their applicants and another 10 percent accept virtually every applicant.

This scale of demand/supply imbalance, broadly characteristic of professional schools since the late 1960s, was new to law schools. It reflected heightened student interest in the utility of law school training and the law degree, whether for engaging in a legal career, public service, or other lines of endeavor. For some, a desire to improve society was the impetus; students wished to enter law school because of the prominent place of law, lawyers, and judges in public leadership and policy making. For others, practical considerations were dominant, such as a declining job market for advanced-degree holders in the social sciences or humanities. Although the United States already had more lawyers per capita than any other country except Israel, the market appeared far from sated; the projection for the mid-1980s was for at least a one-third increase over the present number of lawyers. Then too, career choice was subject to transient swings of favor and disfavor, and in recent years many college students felt that law was where the action was.

As a consequence of the oversize number of applicants relative to places, admissions standards escalated rapidly, and law schools became increasingly selective in admitting students. In view of the important role assigned to the LSAT in this development, a brief comment on its origin and operation would be appropriate. In the pre–World War II period, most law schools drew their students from their own particular set of "feeder" colleges with whose quality they had become thoroughly familiar. By the immediate postwar years, however, the applicant pool had increased in size, and many students came from undergraduate institutions not well known to the law schools. In order to provide law schools with a single measure to assess the credentials of applicants from widely diverse colleges, several law schools met in 1947 and promoted the development of the Law School Aptitude Test (LSAT). After that device had demonstrated its utility for predicting the academic performance of applicants, more and more law schools adopted it, and by 1967 about nine of every ten first-year law students in the nation were enrolled in schools that required the LSAT. Today, the American Bar Association requires the applicant's inclusion of his or her LSAT scores as one of its standards for accreditation of law schools.[4]

The LSAT thus originated as a democratizing reform, as a strengthening of the meritocratic concept of rewarding academic ability wherever it was found. If a law school wished, it could rely more on the LSAT scores to discriminate among candidates than, for example, on the relative prestige of the undergraduate college of the applicant. Most law schools responded to the crush of applicants by doing just that: by 1975 every law school was more selective with respect to basing admission on high LSAT scores than at least 80 percent of law schools had been in 1961.[5] At Boalt, to make continued use of an earlier example, the median LSAT score of those admitted under the regular admissions program (excluding minorities preferentially admitted) went from 622 in 1966 to 712 in 1976; the latter score represented the top 3 percent of all those taking the LSAT.[6] Similarly, the undergraduate grade-point average (GPA) of admitted candidates rose from an average for all law schools of about 2.8 ($B-$ to B) in the mid-1960s to about 3.4 ($B+$) a decade later; this increase was much greater than could be accounted for by the "grade inflation" that has occurred in many colleges over the last ten years.[7] One effect of the latter phenomenon was to lead law schools to rely even more heavily on the LSAT, which was considered to be the more credible and discriminating of the two academic measures.

With the average applicant applying to more law schools and with each law school having more applicants from which to choose, many law schools shifted from local to regional and national in their standing and student mix. In the prewar period, most applicants and admittees to most law schools were from in-state, but by the mid-1970s every ABA-approved law school received more applications from out-of-staters than from in-staters. Almost two-thirds of all applicants tried to gain entrance to at least one out-of-state law school,[8] just as DeFunis sought to do in 1970. The desire of public law school faculties for their institution to develop a more national and less local image was partially checked, in many states, by legislative pressure to limit the proportion of student enrollees from outside the state. In this connection, it warrants mention that one of DeFunis's claims in his suit was that UWLS should give precedence to Washington residents (of which he was one) over out-of-staters; neither the trial court nor the state supreme court found any merit in that position.

Minorities

As of 1965, blacks comprised about 11 percent of the country's population but less than 2 percent of the legal profession and only

1.3 percent of law school enrollees, nearly half of whom were in black law schools.* The ABA-approved predominantly white law schools had a total of 434 black students, or an average of 3 black students apiece. By 1970, there were about 4000 black lawyers in the nation, representing slightly more than 1 percent of the profession.

The enrollment of blacks and other minorities in law schools began to increase significantly from the late '60s and on, with the advent of "special admissions" efforts by the schools. Undertaken voluntarily, not by administrative or judicial order, these efforts reflected a mix of motives, including a genuine and well-intentioned desire to promote minority advance, a psychological need of faculty and university officials to assuage their guilt feelings about past American treatment of minorities, and a practical concern to respond to the moral and other more direct pressures (including student militancy) exerted on the schools by minority organizations and their white allies to open up their admissions to minorities. The context, it should be recalled, was that of the latter phase of the civil rights movement and the early flush of commitment via Affirmative Action to do "something more" to accelerate minority progress.

These special efforts were directed in part, of course, at stimulating a larger number of minorities to apply. Thus, for example, more active recruitment was undertaken through visits to black colleges and financial disincentives to apply were reduced, such as the elimination of LSAT and application fees for blacks. In addition, programs of summer training for disadvantaged minority prelaw students were begun, and better provision was made for the financial support of minority students once enrolled in law school. But during this same period the imbalance between numbers of applicants and numbers of seats grew rapidly, and higher and higher competitive admissions standards were set. As the law schools saw the situation, then, use of their regular admissions criteria (which heavily stressed past and current academic abilities) for all candi-

---

* Because data on blacks constitute often the best or only available data on minorities, they are typically used in the literature as a surrogate for all minorities. Broadly speaking, the lot of the other minorities standardly recognized in Affirmative Action was comparable to, or worse than, that of blacks, with the exception of Americans of Chinese or Japanese extraction.

dates would result in knocking out of the competition nearly all minority persons, including those they had encouraged to apply. This would leave the racial composition of admittees and enrollees not much different from what it had been.

To avoid this outcome, which they felt to be unacceptable, most law schools chose some form of preferential minority admissions, which became, subsequently, the central legal issue in *DeFunis* (and, with reference to equivalent medical school actions, in *Bakke* as well). This involved keeping their regular admissions standards for nonminority applicants and deviating markedly from them for evaluating and admitting minority applicants. Fearing legal challenge or political conflict or both, most schools operated their "special admissions programs" covertly, either without any public disclosure or in the guise of a program for the disadvantaged, without mention of race preference; in only a few law schools was an explicit minority admissions program openly set up.

As a result of these special admissions programs, minorities comprised 4.3 percent of total enrollment in ABA-approved law schools in 1969–70 and 8.2 percent in 1976–77; in absolute rounded numbers, respectively, 2900 of 68,400 and 9500 of 115,500. Whereas total enrollment during this time span increased by 85 percent, minority enrollment increased by 225 percent. Within minorities, blacks comprised 73 percent in 1969 and 58 percent in 1976; there were more black students in law schools in 1972–73 than there were black lawyers in the profession in 1970. As of 1976, persons with Spanish surnames (two-thirds of whom were Chicanos) made up 25 percent of total minority enrollment, and Asian-Americans 14 percent. Comparing 1976 to 1969, law schools added 10,090 new places and took in 2301 more minority students; in other words, minorities were awarded 23 percent of these new seats.[9] Much the same proportions, it might be noted, characterized the results of comparable special admissions programs of medical schools.

Because law school applicants had to have a college degree, provision of some data on college enrollment trends would help to put the preceding law school data on minority admissions in better perspective. From 1966 to 1976, black enrollments at colleges and universities more than tripled (from 282,000 to 1,062,000) while white enrollments increased by slightly better than one-half. In 1965, 9 percent of black and 20 percent of white 20-to-24-year-olds were enrolled in institutions of higher education, but by 1974 the contrast had sharply narrowed to 17 percent and 22 percent. Of more than 11 million full-time undergraduate, graduate, and professional school students enrolled in 1976, blacks constituted 9.3 percent, Spanish-surnamed 4.3 percent, and Asian-Americans 1.8 percent. Currently, blacks (though not the Spanish-surnamed minority) constitute about the same proportion of undergraduate enrollees as of the general population. These trends dovetailed with the special admissions efforts of law schools by producing greater numbers of minorities within the supply pool. The increase in supply was not as large as the numbers suggested, however, because blacks and other minorities were disproportionately concentrated in low-status urban commuter campuses, two-year colleges, and black colleges, and because their attrition rate was higher than that of nonminorities. As a result, the college supply of minorities did not translate into an applicant pool for post–B.A. education at anywhere near the same rate, let alone the same level of academic achievement, as that for nonminorities.

Ironically, the women's movement virtually coincided with that of the minorities, and the gains registered by women's enrollment at law schools were the more spectacular of the two. Women comprised about one-fourteenth of total law school enrollment in 1969 and about one-fourth in 1975. In contrast to minorities, women applicants had about the same distribution of LSAT scores (and a somewhat higher GPA) as men, and within each range of LSAT scores and GPA records their acceptance rate was comparable to that of men.[10] Thus the heightened mutual interest of women and law schools was easily accommodated without recourse to significant deviation from regular standards for admission.

Admission to the University of Washington Law School

The University of Washington law school (UWLS) shared in the overall law school trends reported earlier in this chapter. In 1967, for example, it had 618 applicants, but this rose to 1601 for fall 1971 admissions; in both years, about 150 places were available. To get its 150, UWLS planned to admit about 310, anticipating that about half would enroll there and the other half would elect to go elsewhere.

In 1970, blacks represented 2 percent of the law school body, a proportion identical to their percentage of the total state population. Furthermore, there was neither allegation nor evidence of past racial discrimination at UWLS. Still, of the school's 3812 graduates from 1902 until 1969, only 12 were blacks and only 15 black lawyers were practicing in the state, which represented a ratio for the black population that was one-eighth the ratio of white lawyers relative to the white population. In addition, UWLS saw itself as a regional or national school; almost half of those it admitted and about one-quarter of those who enrolled came from outside the state. Accordingly, UWLS felt on obligation to increase the number of its minority students to well above the 2 percent level that then obtained for blacks.

In applying to UWLS, an applicant made available the transcript of his or her college study, the LSAT score, letters of recommendation, and a written personal statement. No personal interviews were held. In addition, the application materials permitted a candidate to identify himself or herself as a member of one of the four minority groups then so designated by the federal government: black, Spanish-surnamed, Asian-American, or American Indian.

The school's admissions criteria, as set forth in its *Guide* for applicants, emphasized the applicant's "potential for outstanding performance in law school." What this meant was a heavy reliance on past academic performance as the predictor of future academic performance in law school, for example, LSAT score, GPA (grade-point average), quality of the college attended, and grades earned in difficult courses. More than academic indices were considered, however, as the UWLS brief in *DeFunis* made clear:

> An applicant's ability to make significant contributions to law school classes and the community at large was assessed from such factors as his extracurricular and community activities, employment, and general background.
>
> An applicant's social or ethnic background was considered as one factor in our general attempt to convert formal credentials into realistic predictions.

In its actual operation, the essentials of the UWLS admissions process went as follows. An index based entirely on academic factors was established for each applicant. Called a Predicted First Year Average (PFYA), it was a composite mostly of the applicant's

LSAT score and junior-senior years' GPA. The PFYA measure was then applied to evaluate the pool of aspirants in the following manner, using fall 1971 admissions as the data base.

1. Those with a PFYA of 77 or higher were accepted virtually automatically: all 56 applicants with a PFYA of 78 or better were accepted, as were 93 of 105 (89 percent) who had between 77 and 78. Neither race nor ethnicity was considered for persons in this top PFYA tier.

2. Those with a PFYA of 74.5 or less were rejected, typically without further consideration. (The admissions committee chairman quickly reviewed them—about 1000 in number—to spot any whose potential seemed much greater than indicated by the PFYA. These exceptions, which were very few, were then referred to the full committee.)

3. Two groups were handled in special ways:
   a) Returning military veterans who had been admitted to UWLS in earlier years were routinely readmitted; they numbered 23.
   b) Members of three of the four designated minorities were separated from the regular admissions process and evaluated differently; they numbered 63. Asian-Americans were not handled this way because UWLS found that "enough" of them—7 students—had a PFYA above the cutoff level and hence were accepted through the regular admissions process.

As a result of this screening process, two-thirds of the nonminority candidates—about 1000 of 1530—were summarily rejected because they scored below the PFYA cutoff point. (This early turndown procedure reflected the administrative needs of UWLS, especially the need to reduce to a manageable size the number of applicants who would be fully reviewed; it carried no judgment that rejectees were inadequately qualified to complete the law school curriculum satisfactorily. Most law schools operated their applicant review process similarly, and for the very same reason.) Having been exempted from this cutoff procedure, however, no minority applicant was rejected for having a PFYA less than 74.5.

The competition for about 310 acceptances, after this large-scale first cut, thus took on the following configuration. About 179 acceptances were committed: 149 to those with a PFYA of 77 or better, 23 to returning veterans previously admitted, and 7 to Asian-Americans.[11] About 131 acceptances remained to be decided, and competing for those places were about 360 nonminority applicants, nearly all of whom had a PFYA between 76.9 and 74.6, and 63 minority candidates.

Applications from nonminorities were randomly distributed for review to faculty and student members of the admissions committee. Each member read an average of 70 or so and made a recommendation on each to the full committee, which then made the final determination. Applications from blacks, however, were reviewed by a black faculty member and a black student; those from Chicanos and American Indians (and from a few Filipinos) were reviewed by the associate dean. Every minority candidate who was favorably recommended by this separate review process was subsequently accepted by the admissions committee and was admitted.

The outcome of this stage of the review process was a markedly different acceptance rate for the minority and nonminority applicants: 30 of 63 (48 percent) and 101 of 360 (28 percent). Stated another way, of the 423 competitors for the 131 acceptances, minority persons constituted 15 percent but gained 23 percent of the acceptances. Overall, combining both stages of the selection procedure and excluding Asian-Americans from the computation, minorities made up 4 percent of the applicants (63 of 1594) and 10 percent of those admitted (30 of 305). Thus the chance of admission for a minority applicant was about 50–50, while that for a nonminority candidate was only about 1 out of 5 (280 acceptances for 1530 applicants).

Of the 37 minority acceptances, the PFYA of all but the 7 Asian-Americans was below the cutoff point of 74.5, and hence lower than that of DeFunis; about one-third were below 71. (A PFYA of about 71 represented, for example, the following combinations of LSAT score and GPA: 603/2.11, 529/2.29, 481/2.63, 427/3.22.) About half of these 30 minority admittees had a GPA under 2.75 (B−); only 5 of 280 nonminority acceptances had that low a GPA (and possibly most or all of these were returning veterans). In short, *had these 30 minority admittees been white, they would have been turned down summarily.* Both those in support of DeFunis's position and those opposed to it gave emphasis to that point but, as might be supposed, to support very different arguments.

Marco DeFunis, Jr., Gets Turned Down

A resident since birth of the state of Washington, Marco DeFunis, Jr., was a white Jewish male of Spanish-Portuguese origin whose family went back several generations in America. In terms of the government's definition of disadvantaged minorities, DeFunis was considered simply as a white male, in the residual category of "other" on the race-ethnic identification forms used in Affirmative Action employment programs in the early 1970s. Earning his B.A. degree in 1970 from the University of Washington as a concentrator in political science, he graduated magna cum laude and Phi Beta Kappa; his GPA was 3.6 (*A*−) for his four years and 3.7 (*A*−) for his junior-senior years.

UWLS, at Seattle, was the only public law school in the state, and DeFunis strongly preferred to go there. As insurance, he applied to two private law schools and three other public law schools —Idaho, Boalt (California at Berkeley), and Oregon—with the last-named as his fallback choice. The results: rejection by UWLS and Boalt, acceptance by the other four schools. Respecting the advice that if he got a higher LSAT score he would have a better chance to get into UWLS, DeFunis decided to wait it out a year. He attended graduate school for that year, taking more political science; he earned 6 *A*s, a *B*, and an Incomplete as course grades, and during the same period worked over 30 hours a week for the Seattle Park Department. He also retook the LSAT and scored 668, which placed him within the top 7 percent nationally. His earlier LSAT scores, however, had been 512 (about average) and 566 (above average but well below the top tier), and UWLS computed his score at the average of the three scores (582).

When UWLS turned down DeFunis again in 1971, he was in a predicament. True, if he went to the University of Oregon law school at Eugene, his tuition costs would be no greater than at UWLS because, by interstate compact, Idaho, Oregon, and Washington each permitted the other's residents to attend its public university for the same tuition fees the student would have to pay to attend his own state university. In moving to Oregon, however, DeFunis would have to give up his part-time Seattle job, worth

$1500 a year, and his working wife, a dental technician, had no assurance of gaining reemployment in that occupation in Eugene. These money considerations loomed large because DeFunis's family was not in a position to offer much financial help. UWLS remained a live possibility in DeFunis's mind because he felt the school had treated his candidacy unfairly and, therefore, he was unwilling to accept his turndown as final. His PFYA was 76.23; he believed he had been denied the admission he had earned by his record because UWLS had assigned a number of places on racial grounds and had awarded them to minority applicants whose performance had been inferior to his own.

DeFunis told his plight and his views to a young friend, a lawyer, who passed the story on to Josef Diamond, the senior partner of his law firm. Diamond, it turned out, was highly interested in the principle at issue with respect to UWLS and minority admissions. With DeFunis's active cooperation, the senior lawyer arranged for meetings with the UWLS dean, the admissions committee, and the regents, all in an effort to have DeFunis's application reconsidered favorably. When these discussions proved unsuccessful, DeFunis decided to file suit in summer 1971, with Diamond as his lawyer. The litigation was a civil suit, entered in the state court system, and it claimed that DeFunis had been deprived of equal protection of the laws, under the Fourteenth Amendment, because UWLS had racially classified applicants and had preferentially admitted members of favored racial groups who had poorer records than his. The suit sought, as DeFunis's personal objective, his court-ordered admission to UWLS.

Had DeFunis applied to UWLS several years earlier, his record (and his PFYA of 76.23) almost certainly would have gained him admission. By the outset of the '70s, however, the increased demand for entry, the greater severity of the competition, and the heightened school standards made his chances of admission far more uncertain. Had he, then, actually been a victim of reverse discrimination, as he had come to conclude?

That conclusion could not really be subjected to firm proof or disproof, then or now. UWLS's reliance on academic ranking in determining admission or rejection for nonminority candidates was heavy but not exclusive, so the statistical relationship, while strong, was imperfect. For example, when DeFunis was compared to all nonminority applicants who were not returning veterans, 29 rejectees had higher PFYAs and 16 admittees had lower PFYAs. Of all applicants with a PFYA between 76.0 and 76.99, about one-third were accepted and two-thirds were not. Would Marco De-Funis, Jr., have been admitted, then, if some or all of the 30-plus seats awarded to minorities had been reallocated to accept that additional number of nonminority applicants? Because the particularized evidence needed to settle that question was not available, no confident answer could ever be forthcoming.

Yet, however frustrating and untidy it was to have to leave that question unresolved, it had no real effect on the importance or character of the broad policy problem raised by DeFunis's challenge. The uncertainty related only to the specific fate of DeFunis himself. There was no doubt whatsoever that a goodly number of nonminority rejectees—perhaps including DeFunis, perhaps not—would have been accepted by UWLS in the absence of the special admissions program for minorities. And that was precisely the conflict that lay at the heart of the dilemma.

Race Preference Is Something Special

Any selective admissions process, by definition, must prefer; admitting by academic merit, for example, expressed one kind of preference policy. What was at issue, then, was not preference as such, but racial or minority-group preference. But what was so distinctive or special about a minority-group preference as compared to the variety of other preferences engaged in by higher education?

The traditional admissions practices of many colleges and universities often involved deviations from strict adherence to academic merit criteria. The objects of favor varied from place to place and from one time to another but frequently included children of alumni, residents of geographically distant places, those skilled in some sports activity, military veterans, children of the institution's own faculty members, or persons of unusual accomplishments or talents (drama, music, photography, etc.). These preferences reflected the varied concerns of any higher education institution as they bore on the composition of its student body, such as nurturing the loyalty and generosity of its alumni, providing a valued fringe benefit to its faculty, acknowledging society's debt to its military veterans, increasing its own prestige, enabling it to undertake diverse internal campus activities, and enriching its educational setting through a nonhomogeneous student mix. Should a preference policy intended to secure minority representation or a racially diverse student body be viewed as anything different from these other sorts of preferences? When, for example, it was said of an Ivy League university that "its academic standards [were] bent to admit students from desirable groups—chiefly minority students, football players, and the very rich"—should these exceptions be considered as being all on the same plane?

These preferences usually were given freer play in admissions to undergraduate institutions than to professional schools (e.g., the recruitment of athletes, the receptivity to the oboe player). Still, law and medical schools were by no means entirely devoid of the practice. For example, the UWLS procedures described earlier included a preference for returning veterans who had earlier been admitted or enrolled, and many public law schools sought a geographically diverse student body within the limits set by a ceiling on out-of-state enrollment. In *Bakke*, the Davis medical school had an admissions preference for applicants who intended to reside in rural, underserved northern California or who were spouses of previously admitted applicants. State medical schools generally favored in-state over out-of-state applicants. Further, all sides to both the *DeFunis* and *Bakke* controversies, together with the California Supreme Court in its *Bakke* decision, were agreed that a race-free special admissions program for disadvantaged persons would be an unquestionably legal and entirely appropriate undertaking for a professional school. Plainly, though, the effect of these preferences—like that accorded to minorities—was to lessen the chances of admission for all those not qualifying for the preference. Once again, then, why should minority preferences be singled out for special concern?

A relevant though not necessarily controlling response was that the exercise of these preferences usually required minimal or no adjustment of the regular admissions criteria related to academic abilities. For example, however much UWLS may have desired a geographically varied student class, it confined its pursuit of that objective to choosing among applicants within a relatively similar range of academic credentials, from those having a PFYA between 74.5 and 76.9. Suppose, however, that UWLS had faced a situation in which each year its out-of-state applicants had PFYAs below the cutoff point applied to in-state applicants. In such circumstances UWLS would not likely have persisted in admitting out-of-staters for a significant fraction of its places. The willingness of professional schools to adopt and apply such preferences, in other words, seemed to be implicitly contingent on the expectation that applicants in the preferred categories would have academic records roughly comparable to the rest of the admittees. Minority applicants as a class, however, have not satisfied that expectation, as shown in the 1974 admissions data for UWLS reported earlier.

There were more fundamental reasons why minority preferences should not be considered merely as but one of many different kinds of preferences routinely practiced in higher education. Minority status was simply not just "another factor." Skill at football, for instance, was an acquired personal trait; but race was an unchosen and unchangeable group characteristic bestowed at birth, not open to personal acquisition or divestment. Race was an indelible and unalterable "unearned" characteristic; it said nothing about individual merit. Moreover, the special history of race in America had inescapably made race and race-related policy something special. The law recognized this distinctive character of race: race-based policy, at least when aimed negatively against minorities, was viewed as an arbitrary or constitutionally suspect category. Whether race-conscious policies intended to aid minorities should be treated differently in law was, of course, one of the central questions raised by *DeFunis* and *Bakke*. If significantly different legal treatment were given to "benevolent discrimination," the potential effects would extend well beyond the immediate issue of minority gains to involve such core concerns as whether membership in one's racial/ethnic group would become a basis, or perhaps even *the* basis, for individual identity, rights, claims, and benefits.

In sum, to reduce minority preferences to the level of just another item in a range of allowable preferences open to adoption by higher education units would be to deny altogether that *DeFunis* and *Bakke* raised a genuine problem, much less a dilemma. HEW Secretary Califano, in a speech at City College of New York in 1977 urging greater minority enrollment in colleges, inadvertently highlighted the essential point:

For years, our colleges have with special energy sought out students who enrich the diversity of their campuses: athletes, musicians, students from distant regions or from the families of alumni. No national controversy has raged over the special attention and access given these students.

The contrast in treatment, however deplored by the HEW secretary, simply testified to the broad public persuasion that race was, indeed, something special.

Medical School Admissions

Not very long ago, only two educational institutions, both expressly created for blacks and financed with federal funds, were the primary suppliers of medical training for blacks in America. As recently as 1961–62, of 771 black medical students in the country, only 171 of them (22 percent) were enrolled in predominantly white medical schools; the remaining 78 percent were at Howard University in Washington, D.C., or Meharry Medical College in Nashville, Tennessee. And it was not until 1968 that the American Medical Association banned racial bars to membership in its state and local affiliates. By 1975–76, the two black medical schools (themselves less black in enrollment by then) accounted for only 19 percent of all first-year black medical students in the nation. This shift reflected the adoption by over 90 percent of medical schools of special recruiting and admissions programs aimed at stepping up enrollment of blacks and other minorities.

The medical schools' efforts to do "something more" for disadvantaged minorities were open to the same legal challenge that Marco DeFunis had mounted against comparable law school activities in his suit against the University of Washington law school. It fell to Allan Bakke, a research engineer in his early thirties who had a burning ambition to become a doctor, to press that challenge in his attempt to gain entry to the University of California medical school at Davis.

Greater Demand, Rising Standards
In medicine in recent years, as in law, applicant demand for school entry shot up faster than the increase in available seats. In the middle '50s, some medical schools had a shortage of applicants,

but that situation changed rapidly and was not likely to recur soon. In the ten-year period from 1966–67 through 1975–76, medical school applicants more than doubled in number (from 18,250 to 42,303) while the number of first-year openings went up only by two-thirds (from 9123 to 15,365). Thus, an average of one of every three applicants has been admitted in recent years, compared with one of every two a decade ago.[1] The increase in available places was brought about in good part by federal funds for expansion of existing schools and creation of new ones; the number of medical schools grew from 88 to 114 from 1960 through 1976.

The attractiveness of a medical career, which was already very great, took on added luster in the past dozen years. For one thing, the fear of curtailed professional autonomy implicit in the introduction of new major health policy by the federal government proved to be unwarranted. Medicare and Medicaid not only made no serious inroads in that regard but they in effect strengthened the economic position of doctors by affirming their traditional fee-for-service practices. Since the 1950s, the cost of doctors' services rose almost twice as much as the increase in prices generally, and the average income of doctors grew rapidly to over $60,000 a year by 1976, more than twice that of lawyers, which visibly made medicine the best-paid profession in the country. For another thing, medical schools during this period became increasingly committed to the values and practice of scientific research and to an emphasis on science in the academic preparation of applicants to medical school. (The initial impetus came from governmental and public reaction to Russia's launching of *Sputnik I* in 1957.) As a result, many able undergraduate students in the sciences considered medical school a genuine alternative to graduate school, an option that took on further appeal as the economic insecurity facing prospective Ph.D.s in science fields became more evident. In addition, some medical schools sought to broaden the variety of undergraduate majoring fields represented in their student bodies; they attracted applications from students who had completed the core of required science courses but who were concentrators in fields other than the usual premedical ones of biology, chemistry, physics, or zoology.

Faced with an enlarging oversupply of applicants, medical schools responded by raising admissions standards, just as law schools had done. For example, the mean score on the science part of the Medical Colleges Admissions Test (MCAT) for candidates accepted by medical schools rose from 516 in 1957 to 615 in 1975, and on the quantitative part from 517 to 620.[2] Because entrance standards were lifted much above the minimum level necessary to ensure student completion of the course of study leading to the M.D. degree, the large majority of applicants who had to be denied admission were qualified for admission. Some of these rejected students, it might be noted, enrolled in medical schools in foreign nations, such as Mexico, the countries of Western Europe, and even Rumania. (In 1977–78, nearly half of the 5500 medical school students at the Autonomous University of Guadalajara were Americans; more United States citizens were enrolled there than at any medical school in any of the 50 states.) A disproportionate number of them, it was estimated, were residents of New York, New Jersey, and California. Each year perhaps several hundred of them were successful in seeking admission to the third year of an American medical school to take their clinical training; the large majority completed their school training out of the country with the intention of subsequently returning to the United States to practice.[3]

To compensate for their statistically declining chances of admission, candidates increased the number of schools to which they applied. The average number of applications submitted by each candidate rose from 4.8 in 1966–67 to 8.6 in 1975–76; in the latter year the 114 medical schools were confronted with over 366,000 applications, or an average of 3711 applicants for 135 places (a 28-to-1 ratio) for each school. To cope with this flood of candidates, medical schools generally relied heavily on academic criteria to establish minimum cutoff levels and determine actual acceptances. Compared to law schools, however, medical schools gave greater weight to noncognitive factors, including relevant personal characteristics of the candidates. And in contrast to most law schools, medical schools typically interviewed those in the applicant pool deemed worthy of the fullest review; nearly all admitted students, therefore, had been personally interviewed by school personnel.

California's medical schools provided an aggravated instance of the imbalance between applicant demand and available spaces. To a greater degree than public law schools, state medical schools restricted their enrollments almost entirely to residents of their own states. Private medical schools that accepted state aid also often agreed in return to admit a certain number of state residents. Two implications followed. First, an applicant's chances for admission generally were stronger at schools within his or her state of residence than at out-of-state schools. And second, a candidate's in-state chances varied by which state he or she resided in, because the number of medical school places relative to population varied from state to state.

Applicants from sparsely populated Wyoming and the two Dakotas, for example, had the best prospects for admission because a higher proportion of the relatively few applicants they produced could be accommodated by their state's medical schools. In 1975–76, over one-half the applicants who were residents of those three states were accepted into medical school, as against a national average of about one-third. For Californians, however, the odds were loaded in the opposite direction. In 1974–75, for example, California residents constituted about 9 percent of all applicants in the country, but the number of first-year places in all California medical schools (public and private) comprised only about 6 percent of the national total. (In spite of its rather niggardly provision of in-state medical education, California had no overall shortage of doctors; over half the doctors in the state had received their medical schooling outside the state and then had either relocated or returned to California.)

Consequently, California residents fared quite poorly on entry to medical school. For the 1974–75 year discussed above, only 29 percent of California-based candidates were accepted, well below the average of 36 percent for residents of the other 49 states. California ranked third from the bottom among the states in the percentage of applicants admitted to medical school, notwithstanding the fact that California applicants had average MCAT scores higher than the national average. Summed up a University of California at Berkeley student advising official, "The accident of being a California resident is a severe disadvantage. You really have to be good. Applicants from [the University of California at] Berkeley who are residents of other states have a better chance [than those who are California residents]."[4]

The other side of this coin was that California's medical schools were customarily deluged by an unusually heavy number of applicants (e.g., ratios of applicants to seats ranged from 30 to 1 to over 50 to 1). At the Davis medical school, for example, California residents constituted the overwhelming majority of applicants (84 percent in 1973 and in 1974) and an even larger share of enrollees (all but 5 of the 200 places in those two years).

Minorities

In 1970, as in 1950, slightly over 2 percent of the country's physicians were black, and the ratio of black doctors to the black population was about one-seventh that of white doctors to the white population. From 1947 to 1969, blacks constituted about 2.5 percent of medical school enrollment. In 1969, the year that the Davis medical school adopted its special admissions program, 1042 black medical students were in the nation's schools, about half of whom were enrolled in Howard or Meharry. By 1975–76, black enrollment more than tripled (to 3456) while total enrollment increased by only 56 percent (to 55,818), and blacks constituted 6.2 percent of all medical students.[5] Because other minority groups started from a lower base, their rise in the same period was even steeper. For example, Chicanos (Mexican-Americans) increased from 0.2 to 1.3 percent of total enrollments (from 92 to 699 students).[6]

Comparing 1975 and 1969, medical schools added 4873 new places and enrolled 890 more first-year minority students; expanded minority enrollment accounted, therefore, for 18 percent of the new seats established since 1969.[7] The comparable figure for law schools, it may be recalled, was 23 percent and, in general, the data on minorities were similar for the two sets of professional schools.[8] Thus, for example, for both law and medical schools the gains for minorities, especially for blacks, were much greater in the first half of the 1969–76 period than in the latter half (e.g., first-year enrollments of blacks plateaued in 1973 at medical schools and in 1972 at law schools). As a consequence, the goal for minority enrollment in 1975 set by a task force of the Association of American Medical Colleges in 1970 still has not been met: 12 percent of first-year enrollment (about 1800 students) for four minority groups (blacks, Mexican-Americans, mainland Puerto Ricans, and American Indians; Asian-Americans were not included). The actual proportion varied narrowly between 8.5 and 10.1 percent from 1971–72 through 1975–76.

Women, on the other hand, progressed as rapidly in admissions to medical schools as to law schools. From 1969–70 to 1975–76, the first-year enrollment of women jumped almost four times; the latter year's entering group of 3647 women constituted almost one-fourth of all beginning medical students, just a shade under the counterpart figure for law schools.[9] At the Davis medical school, for example, for the 1971–74 period women comprised 19 percent of the applicants and were awarded 26 percent of the places. In schools of veterinary medicine, it might be noted, women constituted 28 percent of first-year enrollment in 1975, and 12 percent in dentistry schools.[10]

Admissions Procedures at the University of California Medical School at Davis

Davis is one of eight general campuses of the University of California (UC), which enjoys the reputation of being the leading public university system in the country. Located near Sacramento, the state capital, UC Davis sits in the Sacramento Valley midway between the High Sierras and San Francisco. It originated as an agricultural institution offering instruction in the management of crops, soil, and water resources and became a general campus in the late 1950s. With a present enrollment of about 17,000 students, UC Davis, together with UC Santa Barbara, constitutes the medium-size tier of campus units; Berkeley and Los Angeles are larger, and Irvine, Riverside, San Diego, and Santa Cruz are smaller. Noted for an on-campus transportation system in which bicycles displaced cars (the latter are confined to peripheral parking lots), UC Davis's academic prominence rested mostly on its agricultural research and its school of veterinary medicine.

There were five state medical schools, all of which were part of the UC system. Four of them were on general campuses—Davis, Irvine, Los Angeles, and San Diego—and the fifth was at a separate UC medical complex in San Francisco. The Davis medical school (UCDMS) first opened its doors in 1968 with 48 entering places, which was increased to 100 seats in fall 1971. As a new and expensive school in a state not overly generous in its support of medical education, UCDMS has had to concern itself with developing reliable backing from the state legislature for its maintenance and expansion. That effort continues, and its outcome is not yet certain.

Admissions policies for UC institutions, though subject to some systemwide standards and controls, were matters left largely to each campus. Within the campus, in turn, admissions policy was set by the faculty members of each component unit; this decentralized pattern was especially pronounced for professional schools, including the Davis medical school. On special admissions programs for minorities, each professional school made its own decision whether to have such a program and how to run it.

UC central administrators and the UC regents (the governing board) were aware, of course, of the existence of these programs on the campuses. For example, Donald C. Swain, UC vice president for academic affairs, reported that "under race conscious admissions procedures instituted [by the various schools on all the campuses] the enrollment of minorities in the University's professional and graduate programs has increased from 6 percent in 1968 to 20.8 percent in 1975." UC officials took care, however, neither to undertake any systemwide review of such programs nor to endorse them openly; this pattern of behavior suggested either implicit approval or a divided regental board. In fact, regents and top administrators were recipients of opposing messages from vocal partisans on both sides of the issue, the one complaining that "too little was being done to gain access for minorities" and the other that "too much reverse discrimination was taking place." Given that charged political context, the regents' strategy seemed to be to avoid having to take a position, in the hope that the *DeFunis* case, which was working its way through the courts in 1971–74, might settle the matter for everyone. History had a different scenario in store for the regents.

Applicants to the Davis medical school had to submit their scores on the Medical College Admissions Test (MCAT), which examined competence separately in science, quantitative, verbal, and general information areas; transcripts from schools previously attended; a description of extracurricular and community activities and of work experiences; a personal statement; and two letters of recommendation, at least one of which was from a science instructor. There were 2464 applicants for 1973–74 admission and 3737 for 1974–75, the two classes for which UCDMS rejected Allan Bakke, and the school expected to admit about 160 to fill its 100 places.

The admissions process consisted in effect of two processes. One was for regular admissions, and it was applied to nonminority and nondisadvantaged minority applicants. Of the 100 seats, 84 were available for these applicants; in 1974, of the 3737 candidates, 3109 (83 percent) were considered under regular admissions. The other process, which will be discussed shortly, dealt with special admissions for disadvantaged minority persons, for which the balance of 16 seats was available. For regular admissions, the relevant applicant pool was initially reduced by summary rejection of all candidates whose college grade-point average (GPA) was less than 2.5 (C+ to B−).

The membership of the regular admissions committee was selected by the dean and consisted of a dozen-plus faculty and a lesser number of medical students. Several faculty members screened the applications of the "above 2.5 GPA" candidates to determine who would be invited for an interview. No one was accepted without an interview; in 1973, 38 percent of these applicants were interviewed, of whom 20 percent were offered admission, and in 1974, the figures were 15 percent and 28 percent, respectively. According to the trial record, there were no written standards for deciding which applicants were to be interviewed.

In 1973 and 1974, interviews were conducted by one faculty member of the admissions committee; in the latter year, a student member of the committee interviewed in addition. The interviewer prepared a summary of the meeting, with emphasis on the applicant's potential contribution to the medical profession, reviewed the total file on the applicant, and graded him or her on a scale of 0 to 100. The candidate's file, including the summary of the interview but without the numerical score assigned by the interviewer, was then reviewed by four other committee members chosen at random. By secret ballot, these four independently rated the applicant on the same scale. The scores on each applicant were then totaled; the maximum score possible was 500 in 1973 (1 faculty interviewer, 2 faculty and 2 student committee members) and 600 in 1974 (1 faculty and 1 student interviewer, 2 faculty and 2 student committee members). Although the trial record left unclear whether written guidelines were available for evaluating candidates, all committee members attended an orientation session for discussion of the importance of the various factors entering into the admissions judgment.

This composite numerical score, it should be emphasized, represented assessment of *all* the information in a candidate's file, including the interview report covering noncognitive factors, such as the applicant's personality, motivation, and the like. (The breadth of these factors reflected UCDMS's interest in having effective physicians as well as bright medical students.) Called the "benchmark" score, this rating was ordinarily used to determine admissions decisions, subject to some variation in practice. Receipt of new information after the rating was made, for example, might result in an upgrading of an applicant's relative position. Further, applications were handled in monthly batches from December through May, and a "rolling admissions" procedure was used in which admission was offered to some applicants in each batch. It was possible, therefore, for some earlier admittees to have lower benchmark scores than some later rejectees; this happened to Bakke in his 1973 candidacy. Finally, an "alternate list" made up of those whose benchmarks were "very close to admission" was set up to facilitate filling seats for those places that initial admittees declined. The applicants on the alternate list were not ranked, and the dean of admissions had discretion to select for admission those he felt would bring "special skills or balance" to the class.

UCDMS began its operations in 1968 and 1969 with only the regular admissions process and found that its first two entering classes consisted of 83 whites, 14 Asian-Americans, 2 blacks, and 1 Chicano. Minorities made up about 3 percent of all applicants; Asian-Americans constituted three-quarters of these minority applicants and four-fifths of minority enrollees. Reflecting on that experience and on the activities of other medical schools to enroll more minorities, the school faculty decided in 1969, effective for the 1970 selection process, to institute a special "program to increase opportunities in medical education for disadvantaged citizens." When the school had 50 entering places, 8 seats were available to the program; this was increased to 16 from 1971 on, when the first-year class doubled in size to 100.

Candidates were asked to indicate on their application whether they wished to be considered under the special admissions program. The 1973 form, prepared by the school, called for such an applicant to identify himself or herself as an "economically and/or educationally disadvantaged person." For 1974, however, UCDMS used a form prepared by a nationwide application processing service that over half the nation's medical schools also used. It asked, "Do you wish to be considered as a minority group applicant?" Elsewhere on the form, it asked, "How do you describe yourself?" Regarding this question, the form offered the following nine boxes for the applicant's choice: "Black/Afro-American, American Indian, White/

Caucasian, Mexican-American or Chicano, Oriental/Asian-American, Puerto Rican (Mainland), Puerto Rican (Commonwealth), Cuban, Other."*

The applications of those who requested consideration under the special program were referred to a special subcommittee of the regular admissions committee. The subcommittee was composed of nonminority and minority faculty members and minority medical students. In 1973, for example, there were 5 white and 2 Asian-American faculty members on the subcommittee, plus 11 students (6 Chicanos, 3 blacks, and 2 Asian-Americans), all but one of whom was first-year or second-year. The faculty members formally were members of the regular committee, but they served primarily on the special subcommittee. The faculty chairman of the subcommittee screened the applications to determine who was in fact disadvantaged and hence eligible for the program. Although no written definition of "economically and/or educationally disadvantaged" existed, the evidence looked for in the application, in addition to minority status, included whether the applicant was granted a waiver of application fee, worked during undergraduate years or interrupted his or her education to support family or himself or herself, or participated in an educational opportunity program in college; the occupational and educational levels of the applicant's parents were also considered. Applicants who were judged not to be disadvantaged were referred to the regular admissions process. This procedure covered minority applicants as well, as Dr. George Lowrey, a pediatrics professor, associate dean of student affairs, and chairman of the admissions committee, made clear in trial court:

> If we had a black student whose father was a physician and who had gone through four years of pre-med school with little difficulty, and by this I mean consecutive years, he would not be considered a minority student as designated on the question here [1974 application form]. He would not be considered a [special admissions program] applicant.[11]

* UCDMS's adoption of this national application form probably explained the startling jump in its number of applicants from 2464 in 1973 to 3737 in 1974. Under the procedures available through this national service, a student was able to fill out just one application and, for a fee, instruct that it be sent to any or all of the medical schools that subscribed to the service.

Once the applicant pool was pruned to retain only those deemed disadvantaged, the subcommittee reviewed applications in the same manner as the regular admissions committee. Minority applicants reviewed under special admissions constituted less than 9 percent of all applicants in 1973 and less than 12 percent in 1974. Unlike the regular procedure, however, applicants with a GPA lower than 2.5 were not automatically eliminated; no minimum GPA cutoff point was established. The subcommittee chairman determined who would be invited for an interview; the trial record did not indicate what criteria were used. About one-quarter of the applicants were selected for interviews in 1973 and one-seventh in 1974. Subcommittee members were given no formal instructions on selection of students, but were familiarized with the purposes of the program. Parallel to the procedures for regular admissions, benchmark ratings were developed for each candidate. At intervals the subcommittee chairman referred its recommendations for admission to the regular admissions committee, which had the formal authority to accept or reject them. In practice, the recommendations were followed, and that process continued until 16 applicants were admitted under the special program.

Minority Groups and Special Admissions
UCDMS's special admissions program billed itself as open to all disadvantaged persons without reference to race. Yet, as it actually operated, only those disadvantaged persons who were members of four specific minority groups appeared eligible for its benefits. Numerous whites—73 in 1973 and 172 in 1974—applied to special admissions, and though the trial record was silent on whether any were interviewed, not one was admitted through the program.

The university's counsel initially argued that, despite the program's results, its intention was not necessarily to admit only minorities. Rather, went the explanation, the program was genuinely accessible to everyone, but in assessing relative personal disadvantage minorities were given first priority because they were the most "disadvantaged of the disadvantaged." Whites were eligible and in fact would be admitted if qualified minority applicants did not fill the 16 seats assigned to the program. That no whites had been accepted was due, then, only to the large numbers of minority applicants at the head of the line and not to the categoric exclusion of whites from the program.

However one chose to characterize that explanation, it failed to persuade. The trial court concluded, reasonably enough, that "[i]n practice this . . . program is open only to members of minority races and members of the white race are barred from participation therein." Throughout the remainder of the litigation, the university accepted the description of the program as one that involved a reservation of 16 places for personally disadvantaged qualified minority persons, and not open to whites. The covert operation of race preference in the guise of a race-free program was, as noted earlier, rather common among professional schools in their efforts to increase minority enrollments.

Under UCDMS's procedures, nondisadvantaged and disadvantaged persons of the preferred minority groups were assigned, respectively, to the regular and special admissions programs. Taking both programs together for the four-year period from 1971 to 1974 (in which 100 seats were available annually), minorities comprised about 11 percent of the applicants but were awarded 27 percent of the seats.[12] They accomplished this by securing, in addition to 100 percent of the 64 seats set aside for special admissions, 13 percent of the remaining 336 seats available for regular admissions. Compared to nonminority applicants, minority candidates had twice as good a chance for admittance under special admissions and even better odds under regular admissions.

Of the 108 minority first-year enrollees in the 1971–74 period, 63 entered through the special program and 45 through the regular procedure. Had these two groups been comparable in their racial composition, it would have been difficult to defend the existence of the special program in light of the demonstrated success of minorities in gaining regular entry. When these gross data were examined in detail, however, it turned out that the special program was the route of entry for blacks and Chicanos; Asian-Americans enrolled mostly through regular admissions. Of the 45 minority regular admittees, 37 were Asian-Americans; while of the 63 special admittees, 51 were black or Chicano. Stated another way, 21 of 22 black enrollees and 30 of 36 Chicano enrollees came through special admissions, while only 12 of 49 Asian-Americans did so.

According to the 1970 census, 14.7 percent of California's population was Spanish speaking or had Spanish surnames (such persons could be of any race but presumably were mostly Chicanos), 7.0 percent was black, 2.65 percent Asian-American (Japanese,

Chinese, or Filipino descent), and 0.45 percent American Indian; the four groups totaled slightly under 25 percent of the state population. UCDMS's minority enrollment, however, was skewed toward Asian-Americans: of all entering students in the 1971–74 period, Asian-Americans constituted 12 percent, Chicanos 9 percent, and blacks 6 percent.* Asian-Americans made up almost half of all minority enrollees, Chicanos about one-third, and blacks the remaining one-fifth. Each of the three minority groups had roughly the same number of applicants, so enrollment proportions derived from different acceptance rates: 15 percent of Asian-American candidates became enrollees, 12 percent of Chicano applicants, and 7 percent of blacks.

The most obvious question suggested by these comparative data on the three minority groups was whether UCDMS was justified in including Asian-Americans within the list of preferred groups under special admissions. (As will be discussed later in this study, the Department of Justice made exactly that point in the friend-of-the-court brief it filed with the U.S. Supreme Court.) These data also suggested more basic questions that were not raised in the *Bakke* controversy. *Bakke* focused on the issue of minority preference versus reverse discrimination against nonminorities, but what of the issue of discrimination among different minority groups? On what basis did UCDMS distribute its set-aside seats among the component minority groups? Were some stronger minority applicants rejected in favor of weaker ones because of the allotment of group shares in the 16 places? Such queries could not be answered because the required information was not supplied in the record developed in trial court.

Comparable questions, also necessarily speculative in the absence of the data required to answer them, could be raised about the Davis medical school's handling of Asian-American applicants. For regular admissions, Asian-Americans comprised about 3 percent of the applicants but 11 percent of the enrollees. Was this simply a reflection of the superior records of members of that group? Asian-Americans constituted 35 percent of all minorities who applied to the school, but only 19 percent of those enrolled under special admissions. Did this reflect nothing more that a lower proportion of disadvantaged persons among Asian-Americans

---

* The one American Indian who was enrolled during this four-year period came through the regular admissions process.

than among Chicanos and blacks? Or were the two patterns related? For example, were some economically disadvantaged Asian-American applicants who had strong academic records referred to the regular admissions process for consideration, so as not to use up special admissions seats "needlessly"? If an academically competitive Asian-American candidate was turned down under regular admissions, was his or her application then shifted to special admissions for review? Was the low acceptance rate of Asian-American applicants to special admissions a function of their high admission rate under regular admissions? In sum, was the regular admissions program, and not just the special program, also used to increase minority enrollment?*

Personally Disadvantaged Minority Member versus Minority Member
The speculative possibilities about the data on three minority groups could be entertained because of the unusualness of UCDMS's procedures in preferring personally disadvantaged minorities. Relatively few professional schools gave emphasis to the factor of personal disadvantage in addition to that of minority status, and most of them did so quietly and not as an announced policy. The distinctiveness of the Davis medical school's admissions practices in this respect was little commented on in the *Bakke* discussion because the primary issue was the use of preferential minority admissions, not which classes within the preferred minority groups were favored.

Why UCDMS shaped its minority enrollment program as it did could only be conjectured because no explanation was entered in the trial record. Two possibilities have already been touched on: (1) an estimate that a stress on personal disadvantage rather than on minority status per se might be less subject to legal challenge, and (2) a desire to increase the number of minority enrollees beyond 16 through the flexibility afforded by admitting minorities under either of two programs. A concern for political palatability might also have played a role; the Davis program, unlike most others, did not call for giving preference to solidly middle-class

---

* An opposite set of speculations could be raised about why so few blacks and Chicanos were entered through regular admissions. For example, were members of those two minority groups who were qualified to compete for regular admissions nonetheless assigned to special admissions?

minority applicants over lower-class whites. Yet another possibility was that the Davis faculty believed its real contribution to facilitating minority equality lay in favoring minority applicants from poor rather than good educational and economic backgrounds. Since the former's academic credentials generally were weaker than the latter's, they could not otherwise compete effectively for the limited number of minority seats available. It could be argued on behalf of personally disadvantaged minority members in contrast to middle-class minority persons that they were the most deserving of compensatory preference, that their earlier academic performance did not reveal their true abilities, that they were more likely to use their training to serve a minority clientele, and that they provided a greater diversity to the school.

Whatever Davis's rationale for its variant of minority preference, the large majority of medical and other professional schools did not share its views. What was unsatisfactory to most about the Davis scheme was that its losses were certain but its gains more chancy. Under procedures like those of UCDMS, a school would find itself in the odd position of turning down many of the academically most promising minority candidates because they were ineligible for special admissions and yet not strong enough to win out in the regular admissions competition. In their place academically less qualified minorities would be enrolled under special admissions, in the uncertain hope that their academic potential was much higher than indicated by their record and that after completion of school they would apply their skills for the direct benefit of minority communities. From any number of perspectives—the efficient allocation of manpower and school resources, minority needs for competent health care, less adjustment of admissions standards, the reduction of negative racial stereotypes—most schools decided oppositely from UCDMS and emphasized the admission of the most academically qualified minority applicants.

"Fully Qualified"?
For admission to UCDMS in 1973 and 1974, the years in which the school rejected Allan Bakke's candidacy, the difference in academic credentials between regular and special admittees was marked. The Medical College Admissions Test (MCAT) was divided into science, verbal, quantitative, and general information sections; the first two were considered more significant for predicting student perform-

ance in the first half (science courses; nonclinical) of medical school education. For 1973, the data on the average score of regular admittees compared to that of special admittees was as follows: science, 83rd percentile nationally to 35th percentile; verbal, 81st/46th; quantitative, 76th/24th; and general information, 69th/33rd. The counterpart data for 1974 repeated the contrast: science, 82nd/37th; verbal, 69th/34th; quantitative, 67th/30th; and general information, 72nd/18th.

On another academic measure, the undergraduate grade-point average (GPA) in science courses, those entering under regular admissions averaged $B+$ to $A-$ in 1973 and 1974 (3.5 and 3.4) compared with $C+$ to $B-$ (2.6 and 2.4) for those admitted under the special program. Other than these types of statistics, which covered only the averaged MCAT and GPA scores for the two streams of admittees, the trial record contained little further information on this subject. The range of GPA scores for 1973 and 1974 was also provided, and these data revealed that in each year at least one special admittee had an overall GPA of C to $C-$ and another of $A-$. The cutoff point for regular admissions, it will be recalled, was $C+$ to $B-$; the average for regular admittees in those two years was $B+$ to $A-$.

In his sworn declaration submitted to the California trial court, Dr. Lowrey, the admissions committee chairman, stated:

> Every admittee to the Davis Medical School, whether admitted under the regular admissions program or the special admissions program, is fully qualified for admission and will, in the opinion of the Admissions Committee, contribute to the School and the profession.[13]

But, Dr. Lowrey also indicated, in response to a question from Reynold Colvin, Bakke's lawyer, the following about the role of the MCAT score in the evaluation process:

> I think most of us who are doing the screening have been on admissions committees long enough. We do put some value on a percentile of where this score of that particular individual lies, and I suspect most of us would look very hard at other things that would be very positive for that individual if he scored lower than 50 [50th percentile] in science and verbal ability.[14]

For each of the four entering classes from 1971 to 1974, the average score of special admittees on the science and verbal sections of the MCAT was below the 50th percentile; the four-year averaged score was 37th percentile on science and 39th on verbal. What were those "other things" that Dr. Lowrey said the admissions committee would review as a possible offset to such low MCAT scores? "I think," stated Dr. Lowrey, "we would want to look at the individual's motivation, we would want to look at his background and this may explain, perhaps, why his score is not as strong as another individual's."[15]

Did the fact that the special subcommittee's recommendations for admission had to be acted on by the admissions committee ensure that all such admittees were, as Dr. Lowrey stated, "fully qualified for admission?" Justice Mathew Tobriner, the lone dissenter in the California Supreme Court's decision for Allan Bakke, sought to establish that position in his friendly questioning of UC counsel at the oral argument:

> *Justice Tobriner:* . . . the [admissions] committee has to pass upon the recommendations made by the special committee . . . in order to make sure that nobody who is not qualified will be admitted—is that correct?
> *Mr. Reidhaar:* That's exactly correct, . . . and it does seem to me that this element of the process provides reasonable assurance against arbitrary action in admissions decisions.[16]

In his written opinion, Justice Tobriner concluded that

> . . . the special admission program did not contemplate, nor sanction, the admission of *unqualified* applicants simply because they were minorities. . . . [N]o minority applicant was admitted into the medical school without being found fully qualified for medical school study by the *same* admissions committee that passed on all other applicants. (Emphasis in original)

Dr. Lowrey's statements in the trial record, however, lent no support for interpreting the admissions committee's role as that of an active reviewer of the admission recommendations sent to it by the subcommittee. Although Dr. Lowrey said that the admissions committee had not accepted all the subcommittee's recommendations for fall 1973 admissions, he could not recall how many were rejected.[17] When Bakke's attorney asked him about 1974 admissions (this courtroom examination took place on July 23, 1974), Dr. Lowrey cited two instances when the admissions committee had returned the subcommittee's recommendations; in one case because the applicant "had not actually taken all the required courses for admission" and in the other because the candidate "had received a less than satisfactory grade in a course which was required for admission."[18] In Dr. Lowrey's characterization, the admissions committee did not function as a quality-control mechanism in any significant sense; it simply checked that the subcommittee's recommendees had met the formal undergraduate course prerequisites for admission. Moreover, the two instances cited by Dr. Lowrey, which revealed that in the fifth year of the special program's operation some who were recommended for admission had not satisfied the minimum college course requirements for admission, plainly did not add to the persuasiveness of his judgment that all special admittees were "fully qualified."

Colvin (Bakke's counsel) sparred with, but never fully engaged, the issue of whether all of UCDMS's special admittees were qualified for admission. His interest was not in that question directly, but rather in using the factor of qualifications to buttress his core argument that the reservation of 16 places constituted an illegal racial quota. In oral argument before the U.S. Supreme Court, for example, he described the medical school's special admissions program as "a quota where the number is first chosen [16] and then the number is filled regardless of the standard."[19] Acknowledging that "we are not making the argument that they [special admittees] were disqualified," Colvin insisted that "we do not agree that there is a showing that they were qualified."[20] Similarly, Colvin had argued before the California Supreme Court, "There is nothing in the record one way or another on that point except a conclusionary statement of Dr. Lowrey that they were all qualified."[21]

But the school did not have to prove its point; it was up to Colvin to *dis*prove UCDMS's judgment that all its special admittees were "fully qualified." This would have been difficult to do even had full data been available because of the ambiguity surrounding the meaning of "qualified" as the medical school used the term. Nevertheless, whether by design or oversight, Colvin never pressed UCDMS to supply a detailed accounting of the academic and other credentials of the special admittees, and the school presumably had no incentive to provide it voluntarily. By the rules of litigation, therefore, in the absence of effective challenge at the trial court stage the "basic finding that everybody admitted under the special program was qualified"[22] was established as the fact situation binding on the appellate courts, state and federal.

As noted earlier, though, the question whether every special admittee was qualified for admission was not central to Bakke's claim. What was central was the argument that regardless of how well or poorly qualified the special admittees were, he had been denied an opportunity to compete for any and all of those 16 seats in 1973 and 1974, because as a white person he was excluded from the special admissions program.

Allan Bakke Gets Turned Down

It was a UCDMS internal memo, dated 4/22/74, from "Nancy" to someone in the admissions office, and it was headed "BAKKE, Allan." The typed portion read:

> Initiating legal action for admittance into medical school. Similar to DeLunis [*sic*] case sueing [*sic*] the University of Washington Law School.
>
> Info needed:
>   statistics on his application as compared to average accepted applicants for last three years (info needed for white and black students).

Below, there was written in hand, "Average age and age range over last 3 years." And below that, in another hand, "Dr. Levitt [associate dean, academic affairs] asked that we [have?] the info ready when counsel asks for it."[1]

Bakke's Background

Allan Paul Bakke was born in February 1940 in Minneapolis, Minnesota. Of Norwegian ancestry, his father was a mailman, his mother a teacher. His family later moved to Florida, and he was graduated from Coral Gables High School in 1958. Returning to his former home community to do his college work, Bakke earned a B.S. in mechanical engineering in 1962 at the University of Minnesota and took further nondegree graduate work in that subject during 1962–63. His college GPA, both overall and in science courses, was $B+$ to $A-$ (3.5) and, upon graduation, he was elected to Pi Tau Sigma, the national mechanical engineering honor society.

To help pay his way through college, Bakke served in the Naval Reserve Officers Training Corps; the government paid for his tuition and living expenses in exchange for his acceptance of the obligation of four years' military service. He discharged that obligation by serving as an officer in the U.S. Marine Corps from September 1963 to September 1967. Commissioned a second lieutenant, he rose to the rank of captain after seven months in Vietnam, where he was commander of a combat antiaircraft missile unit. Because of his stint in the Marine Corps, he was eligible for veterans' educational benefits through fall 1976.

Immediately after his military discharge, Bakke took a position as a research engineer for the National Aeronautics and Space Administration's Ames Research Center in Moffett Field, California, and participated in that unit's efforts in the race to the moon. (He has remained with that space-agency lab to the present day.) Beginning in the spring quarter 1968, Bakke took a number of engineering courses at Stanford to complete the work he had earlier begun at Minnesota, and Stanford awarded him an M.S. degree in mechanical engineering in June 1970.

During his military service in Vietnam, Bakke got interested in the possibility of going to medical school and becoming a doctor. That interest deepened into a focused ambition after he met and talked with physicians at the NASA lab who were studying the effects of outer space and radiation on the human body. From 1971 on, while holding down his full-time job, Bakke took courses at Stanford and at San Jose State University to complete all undergraduate biology and chemistry prerequisites for entry to medical school. To make up the hours lost in class and commuting, he worked early mornings and also evenings at his NASA job. Bakke also undertook volunteer emergency-room work in El Camino Hospital in Mountain View, a position ordinarily filled by "pink ladies," and often worked late at night with victims of car accidents or fights. As these activities suggested, Bakke's desire to be a doctor had become close to an obsession by this time; it was motivated at least as much by deep religious conviction as by ambition in the usual sense. Observed an admissions official of UCDMS:

> Bakke was a man who felt as strongly as anyone I've ever known about his potential as a healer of the sick and as a benefactor of the community. . . . He struck me as a character out of a [Ingmar]

Bergman film—somewhat humorless, perfectly straightforward, zealous in his approach; . . . he was an extremely impressive man. . . .[2]

Bakke himself explained his passion for doctoring at the close of his personal statement in his second application to UCDMS:

I have an excellent job in engineering and am well-paid. I don't wish to change careers for financial gain, but because I truly believe my contribution to society can be much greater as a physician-engineer than in my present field. I'm not afraid of hard work, I enjoy and have been successful at working with others, and know my motivation is as strong and honest toward a career of service in medicine as that of any applicant. More than anything else in the world, *I want to study medicine.*[3] (Emphasis in original)

What worried Bakke most about his chances of admission to medical school was his age.* In mid-September 1971, he bluntly inquired of a number of schools, including UCDMS, about their policy on the matter:

I am 31 years old, and my purpose in writing this letter is to determine whether my application would receive your consideration. I wish to avoid the wasted effort of applying to medical schools whose policy is automatic rejection of applicants my age.[4]

In his 1973 application to UCDMS, Bakke began his personal statement page by directly addressing the question of his age:

Although I am 32 years old, the usual factors which detract from an older applicant do not apply in my case. First, my only dependent is my wife, who is well qualified to assist in earnings if needed. Second, since receiving a B.S. degree, I have been in graduate school or taking medical prerequisites continuously (although part time) with the exception of my period of military service. This removes the question of current academic inclinations and aptitudes. Third, and perhaps most important, I am in excellent health. Actuarially it may be predicted that I might not serve as a physician as long as a younger applicant. But I believe my high general level of health, good health maintenance habits, and balanced outlook offset these cold statistics.[5]

---

* It was not until the Age Discrimination Act of 1975 that discrimination on the basis of age was prohibited in any program that received federal financial assistance, including medical schools. Enforcement of that statute, after HEW prepared the necessary regulations detailing its meaning, was scheduled to go into effect on January 1, 1979.

And in a mid-1973 letter to Dr. Lowrey, after his first turndown by UCDMS, Bakke reiterated his intense desire to study medicine and asked Lowrey, among other things, to "[s]uggest some other way—any way at all—that I can overcome the age factor and be allowed to study medicine."[6]

As far as the trial record revealed, UCDMS never rejected Bakke because of his age. In September 1971, responding to Bakke's inquiry about admissions policy on age, a UCDMS official noted that

> The Admissions Committee . . . has not established a fixed maximum age with respect to applicants. However, . . . when an applicant is over thirty, his age is a serious factor which must be considered. One of the major reasons . . . is that such an applicant can be expected on an actuarial basis to practice medicine for about ten years less than the applicant of average age. The Committee believes that an older applicant must be unusually highly qualified if he is to be seriously considered for [admittance.][7]

Bakke evidently met that condition because the Davis medical school gave his candidacy full and serious consideration and assigned it a high overall rating. It was entirely understandable why Bakke fastened on the age question as controlling, but that was not Dr. Lowrey's reading of the situation. At no point in the trial court proceedings did the chairman of the admissions committee suggest that Bakke's age had been the determining factor in the committee's judgment.

The First Rejection by UCDMS

Bakke began his efforts to gain entry to medical school by applying to the University of Southern California and to Northwestern University for 1972–73. Both schools rejected him and neither offered him an interview; USC wrote that his application "was not sufficiently strong" and Northwestern that his age "was above the stated limit." For 1973–74, Bakke sharply stepped up the number of applications to a total of eleven: his two alma maters (Minnesota and Stanford), three other California schools (UC Davis, UC Los Angeles, UC San Francisco), and six other out-of-state schools (Bowman-Gray, Cincinnati, Georgetown, Mayo, South Dakota, Wayne State). Four granted him interviews—Stanford, Minnesota, Mayo, and UC Davis—but none admitted him. Virtually all eleven schools sent him a formulaic rejection emphasizing the excess of qualified candidates over the number of available spaces; UC San Francisco also cited his age as a negative factor, and Minnesota noted that its primary responsibility was to in-state residents.[8]

For UCDMS's 1973 admissions, it will be recalled, 2464 applicants contested for 100 places; 2173 (88 percent) of them, including Bakke, competed for the 84 regular admission seats, which worked out to entry odds of 1 in 26 for any single applicant. Bakke's academic credentials were excellent: an undergraduate GPA of 3.5 ($B+$ to $A-$) and, on the MCAT, a score at the 97th percentile level on the science section, 96th percentile on the verbal, 94th on quantitative, and 72nd on general information. (As it turned out, Bakke's MCAT scores were well above, and his GPA was about the same as, the average of those who were accepted under the regular admissions program.) UCDMS considered his application strong enough to warrant inviting him for an interview; only about two-fifths of the "above 2.5 GPA" regular admissions applicants were granted interviews. For those invitees, the odds on entry were lowered to about 1 in 5.

Bakke's interview went very well. Theodore West, a professor of medical education and pharmacology, interviewed him and liked what he saw and heard. In his report, Professor West reviewed such matters as Bakke's age, his strong motivation for wanting to study medicine, his desire to apply his mechanical engineering expertise to improving health care, and his overall career. Among the observations made by Professor West in his 1000-word report on his March 21, 1973, interview with Bakke were the following:

> This applicant is a well-qualified candidate . . . whose main handicap is the unavoidable fact that he is now 33 years of age. . . . He is a pleasant, mature person, tall and strong and Teutonic in appearance (not surprising from his Minnesota background). A believer in personal health and fitness, he is careful about his diet and vices, runs every day and genuinely intends to improve on the actuarial statistics, as might be judged from his autobiographic remarks. . . . In his application are strong and personally-oriented letters of recommendation which help give the overall flavor of this applicant and the reaction he sparks in his associates.
>
> . . . Bakke's interview was comfortable and pleasant for both of us, I believe. He seems completely unprepossessing; he was not dynamic or aggressive and articulated well in all areas except his response to my request that he express for me some of his reasons for changing from engineering to medicine. During that phase his conversation was more halting, more introspective, and I sensed an

air of frustration and emotion which I attribute to his concern about the impact of age and the fact that this probably is about the last chance for him to apply.

At the close of this report, Professor West summed up his evaluation in a highly positive fashion:

> On the grounds of motivation, academic record, potential promise, endorsement by persons capable of reasonable judgments, personal appearance and demeanor, maturity and probable contribution to balance in the class I believe that Mr. Bakke must be considered as a very desirable applicant to this medical school and I shall so recommend him.[9]

The trial record did not reveal the individual benchmark score (overall rating, including noncognitive factors, based on the applicant's complete file) Professor West or the other four admissions committee members assigned to Bakke. Taken together, their five evaluations gave Bakke a total rating of 468 out of a possible 500. By that late time in the admissions process, however, this strong benchmark score fell just short of admission; at least a 470 score was required. Bakke was not placed on the alternate list because, according to Dr. Lowrey's written declaration entered in the trial record, "neither I nor the other members of the Admissions Committee thought that he had any personal qualities or special skills to bring diversity and interest to the class as it had developed."[10] By a form letter of May 14, 1973, Bakke received official notification of his rejection by UCDMS.

Had Bakke been able to complete his application and interview well before the close of 1972, as he had intended to, he might have been admitted on the basis of his benchmark score of 468, and there would have been no *Bakke* case or controversy. As it happened, his wife's mother became seriously ill with lung cancer, and both Bakke and his wife spent several months in Iowa looking after her. Not until January 9, 1973, therefore, was Bakke able to complete his application file, and the earliest interview scheduled in the normal course was not until March 21. Under UCDMS's "rolling admissions" procedure, much earlier in that academic year virtually automatic admission was accorded applicants with a benchmark rating of 470 and promising candidates with somewhat lower scores had been accepted. By late March and April, though, over three-quarters of total acceptances already had been extended, and the benchmark minimum of 470 was strictly enforced for regular admissions.*

Questioning the Special Admissions Program

Two weeks after Bakke received his form rejection from UCDMS, he wrote Dr. Lowrey, the admissions committee chairman, to re-emphasize his commitment to study medicine and to inquire whether there was

> . . . any possibility of my becoming a medical student at Davis in one of the following ways? 1. Place my application in a stand-by status, to be admitted should a vacancy occur at *any* time. 2. Allow me to register for courses as a special student or to audit them until a vacancy occurs in the class entering in 1973. I realize there is no assurance that such a vacancy will develop, but I desperately want to take *any* path to a medical education. . . . Dr. Lowrey, thank you for taking the time to consider this letter. I feel certain that if anyone can help me, you can. I pray that you will.[11] (Emphasis in original)

When no response from Dr. Lowrey was forthcoming, Bakke wrote him again on July 1, but this time in a greatly different tone and with a totally new message. Referring to the absence of a reply to his May 30 letter, Bakke now informed Dr. Lowrey that

> . . . I feel compelled to pursue a further course of action. . . . Applicants chosen to be our doctors should be those presenting the best qualifications, both academic and personal . . . I am convinced a significant fraction . . . is judged by a separate criterion. I am referring to quotas, open or covert, for racial minorities . . . I realize that the rationale for these quotas is that they attempt to atone for past racial discrimination. But instituting a new racial bias, in favor of minorities is not a just solution.

---

* An exception to this procedure was revealed a few years after Bakke instituted his legal challenge. It appeared that the dean of the Davis medical school was allowed to select five admittees each year without reference to the screening process. Critics attacked this practice as wrong in principle; they further complained that the dean's choices were invariably influential white applicants with ties to local or state politicians, wealthy businessmen, or campus administrators or faculty. The dean's "special admissions program" was evidently devoted to the *realpolitik* of sustaining influential support for the school. This practice was stopped in 1977.

In fact, I believe that admissions quotas based on race are illegal. For this reason I am inquiring of friends . . . about the possibility of formally challenging these quotas through the courts. My main reason . . . would be to secure admission for myself—I consider the goal worth fighting for in every legal or ethical way.

Bakke closed his letter politely, but with an unmistakable reminder of his determination: "Thank you for taking time to consider this letter. I do still hope to be admitted to medical school. I won't quit trying."[12]

Whether Bakke on his own would have acted on his stated intentions will never be known because, at this juncture, another chance occurrence (like the earlier family illness) set events in motion which increased the likelihood that Bakke would file suit. Dr. Lowrey asked one of his assistants, Peter Storandt, to reply to Bakke. A few years younger than Bakke, Storandt had joined the admissions office at UCDMS in 1972; the counseling of unhappy applicants was one of his job responsibilities. Storandt, who considered himself "stubbornly fair-minded,"[13] was disturbed by the way the special admissions program hurt the admission chances of able nonminority candidates who had worked hard to get into medical school. "We had a program with a supportable aim," he commented at a later date, "but . . . it had the effect of bringing hardships on other kinds of candidates. I couldn't be fully comfortable with that arrangement."[14] In addition, he was put off by the dean's designation of several admittees each year without regard to benchmark ratings, a practice that Storandt viewed as "an attempt to buy good will in important places."[15]

Apparently, when Storandt reviewed Bakke's application file preparatory to replying to his two letters, Bakke's situation—"a sterling record and top scores and [having to] tell him he's not admissible when I was aware of the academic difficulty of some students who had been specially admitted"[16]—brought his unease to a head. In a lengthy July 18 reply to Bakke, Storandt kicked off a correspondence between them that heavily influenced Bakke's future course of action and, perhaps, was critically decisive in Bakke's ultimate decision to file suit.

This correspondence, which was included in the trial record, was not known at the time to Storandt's superiors at UCDMS and hence should not be misconstrued as an indication of any official position of the school. After Bakke filed suit, UCDMS transferred Storandt to other duties; he subsequently left the school to take on a new job in admissions at Oberlin College. Looking back in early 1977 on the affair, Storandt reaffirmed that he continued to feel strongly about the need for a judicial resolution of the issue of preferential minority admissions and that he did not think personally "that I've done anything morally wrong. I did embarrass the university and I regret having done so."[17]

In his July 18 letter to Bakke—headed "Dear Allan"—Storandt informed him that he had been rated within the top 10 percent of "the 2,500 applicants" and included him among those "remarkably able and well-qualified individuals" who had to be turned down because of the lack of available seats. On the age question, Storandt assured Bakke that "older applicants have successfully entered . . . and that your very considerable talents can and will override any questions of age in our final determinations."

After noting that neither of the possibilities Bakke raised in his May 30 letter to Dr. Lowrey was feasible, Storandt encouraged him to reapply to UCDMS for 1974 under the Early Decision Plan. Under this procedure, advised Storandt, Bakke would complete the national medical school form that UCDMS had just begun to use, and he initially would apply only to Davis, which would let him know by no later than October 1. If UCDMS decided to defer his application for consideration under the regular admissions process, rather than to admit him, Bakke then could direct that his application be sent to other medical schools as well.

In the remaining half of his July 18 letter, Storandt took it on himself to encourage Bakke "to pursue your research into admissions policies based on quota-oriented minority recruiting." Concerning Davis's special admissions program, he observed, "I don't know whether you would consider our procedure to have the overtones of a quota or not; certainly its design has been to avoid any such designation, but the fact remains that most applicants . . . are members of ethnic minority groups." Storandt continued by calling Bakke's attention to the ongoing *DeFunis* case, and enclosed a summary of it. He then "urge[d]" Bakke to correspond with two persons, one a medical professor at the Arizona College of Medicine and the other an administrator at the New York University School of Medicine, for further information "in your research."[18]

Some two weeks later the two men met for the first time, and shortly afterward Bakke wrote Storandt of his alternative admis-

sions and litigation strategies and asked him for his advice. In that
August 7 letter, Bakke noted that "my first concern is to be allowed
to study medicine, and . . . challenging the concept of racial quotas is secondary." But he realized that others would reverse the
order of importance of the two matters and that, in any event, he
was not likely to achieve his personal goal without engaging the
larger issue. Hence the two plans he proposed included both elements.

Under either plan, Bakke would apply to UCDMS under the Early
Decision program. In Plan A, if he were admitted to Davis, he then
would sue Stanford and UC San Francisco "in order to officially
pose the legal questions involved." In Plan B, he would "confront"
Stanford in late summer, because "Stanford states categorically
that they have set aside 12 places in their entering class for racial
minorities," and attempt "to secure immediate admission [for fall
1973] as an alternative to a legal challenge of their admitted racial
quota." If Stanford admitted Bakke, he then would sue Davis and
UC San Francisco; if UCDMS admitted him also, he would "sue
only UC San Francisco."

In soliciting Storandt's advice, Bakke emphasized that he wished
to satisfy "two principles in choosing my course." The first was not
to "jeopardize my chances for admission to Davis" under the Early
Decision process. And the second was to "[a]void actions which you,
Mr. Storandt, personally or professionally oppose. My reason for
this is that you have been so responsive, concerned, and helpful to
me." A bit later in this August 7 letter, Bakke asked Storandt point-
blank: "Would Davis prefer not to be involved in any legal action
I might undertake, or would such involvement be welcomed as a
means of clarifying the legal questions involved?"[19]

Promptly replying on August 15, Storandt gently questioned the
legal feasibility of Plan A, and then suggested adoption of Plan B
for reasons that appeared to be equivalently unfeasible. (After all,
Storandt was no more a lawyer than Bakke.) Storandt appropriately
said of Plan A that in the absence of Bakke having applied to Stanford, "I wonder on what basis you could develop a case as plaintiff?"
"I prefer your Plan B," Storandt concluded, "with the proviso that
you press the suit—even if admitted—at the institution of your
choice. And there Stanford appears to have a challengeable announcement. If you are simultaneously admitted at Davis under
EDP [Early Decision Plan], you would have the security of starting

here in twelve more months."[20] But Storandt's advice on Plan B was open to the same charge that he raised about Plan A: once an applicant was admitted to a school, what legal standing would he have to challenge its special admissions program? As to which school to sue, Storandt's advice could be understood as an attempt to steer Bakke away from UCDMS and toward Stanford.

Bakke replied on August 19 and stated that "I shall proceed with Plan B . . . , but modified as you suggested." He informed Storandt that he had mailed his application to the national servicing firm a week earlier, and hoped that UCDMS would receive it, and his transcripts, soon. He then noted that his mother-in-law remained seriously ill and that he and his wife would be leaving for Iowa at the end of the month to stay with her for several weeks. Bakke requested, therefore, that the interview date in connection with his application be set before August 31 or after September 24.[21] Accommodating his request, Storandt arranged for Bakke to be interviewed on August 30.

Looking back almost four years later at his unusual relationship with Bakke, Storandt commented, "My main view is that I didn't actually encourage the suit—I suggested that it could be pursued."[22] Perhaps so, but that was a subtle difference under the best of circumstances, and surely too subtle to pick up when the person making the suggestion was an admissions official of the school that might be sued. Storandt's supportive posture doubtless helped prepare Bakke psychologically to undertake litigation, should it be required. Whether it would be required turned, at this stage, on the outcome of Bakke's application to UCDMS the second time around.

Rejection Again by UCDMS
Allan Bakke's August 1973 application for early admission for UCDMS's fall 1974 entering class looked just about the same as his application earlier that year for fall 1973 entry. His academic scores remained unchanged, of course, and even his personal statement was largely a repeat of his previous one, though perhaps even more intense in affirming his goal of studying medicine. On the school's side, the procedures for regular admissions continued as before, except that now a student member of the admissions committee also undertook to interview applicants. While the number of entering places stayed at 100, the number of candidates swelled

during the application period by more than 50 percent over the previous year, to a total of 3737. About 3100 were considered for the 84 regular admissions seats, a ratio of enrollment to applications of 1:37.

The student interviewer, Frank Gioia, reviewed Bakke's file (which contained his second letter to Dr. Lowrey concerning the illegality of special admissions for minorities) and then met with him on August 30. Gioia had formed initially unfavorable impressions of Bakke based on his reading of the file materials, but his interview session led him to a different judgment. His report on Bakke was quite favorable. On the personal dimension, Gioia indicated that he anticipated that Bakke would be "aggressive" and "self-asserting," but "I found him friendly, well-tempered, conscientious and delightful to speak with," and he noted that "throughout our conversation, Alan [sic] expressed himself in a free, articulate fashion."

Bakke's views on minority special admissions were explored for a brief time early in the interview. As Gioia reported them, "he 'was not out to sue anybody,' but . . . he simply wished to question the logic behind such policies. He simply felt that medical candidates should be selected on the basis of qualifications. I felt that he was at no time 'uppity' or threatening about the matter." Gioia also noted that Bakke's volunteer work at the hospital had convinced him to pursue a clinical rather than a medical research career and "to serve wherever he is most needed." In light of his engineering expertise, Bakke remained hopeful that he might be able to engage in "medical invention as a past-time." Overall, Gioia concluded, Bakke's "major handicap, I feel, remains his age, a factor to which he has addressed himself in last year's application. In view of my belief that age can often work for as well as against a person, I would give him a sound recommendation for [a] medical career."[23]

Bakke fared much less well in his interview that same day with the faculty member, who turned out to be the admissions committee chairman, Dr. Lowrey. In a later letter to Storandt, Bakke indicated that "I enjoyed talking to Dr. Lowrey,"[24] but Dr. Lowrey's write-up made no mention that the interview had any comparable affect for him. Dr. Lowrey characterized his report as being "in some contrast to . . . Dr. West's evaluation," which had taken place five months earlier in connection with Bakke's first application. The contrast related almost entirely to the different judgment of the interviewers and not to changes in Bakke's outlook or explanations.

On the latter, Dr. Lowrey cited only a single instance of what he took to be a shift by Bakke: "In contrast to his interview with Dr. West, he now very definitely played down the possible use of [his engineering] background in his practice of medicine. Quite surprisingly he stated that he felt there probably was little relationship between these two fields or that his background would be helpful in any way in the solution of medical problems." Otherwise, Dr. Lowrey's evaluation emphasized what he saw as Bakke's major deficiencies:

> . . . I found Mr. Bakke to be rather limited in his approach to the solution of the difficulties in improving the delivery of medical care. Part of this was undoubtedly due to lack of information but the disturbing feature of this was that he had very definite opinions which were based more on his personal viewpoints than upon a study of the whole problem. His opinion of the special selection of minority students is stated in one of his letters. He was very unsympathetic to the concept of recruiting minority students so that they hopefully would go back to practice in . . . presently neglected areas. . . . One of his main reasons . . . was that this decreased his own chances of getting into medical school. He did not have any alternative . . ., his solution would be to induce nonminority individuals to work with minority groups. Precisely how this was to be carried out he felt needed more study. . . .
>
> It may well have been the interviewer's fault, but my own impression of Mr. Bakke is that he is a rather rigidly oriented young man who has the tendency to arrive at conclusions based more upon his personal impression than upon thoughtful processes using available sources of information. This may be a rather severe criticism but I certainly felt this way about him. I do believe that his motivation is a strong one and I further believe that his academic record supports his ability to do the work in medical school. I imagine that he would be a very hard worker but that he would have a tendency to do things by the book and would have difficulty reaching independent conclusions. I would rate him acceptable but certainly not an outstanding candidate for our school.[25]

Six members of the admissions committee, including Gioia and Dr. Lowrey, assigned Bakke an overall benchmark score on a scale of 100. Each had available the two interview summaries and Bakke's file, and each arrived at his benchmark rating without knowledge of how the others scored Bakke. For 1974 admission, unlike 1973, the trial record included a tally of these individual benchmark ratings, which were as follows: 96, 94, 94, 92, 87, 86. Gioia gave Bakke a 94 and Dr. Lowrey, the 86 rating. Storandt was also one of the admissions committee members who judged Bakke's application, and he awarded him the 92 score.[26] The total benchmark rating was 549 out of a possible 600, which was weaker than Bakke's previous benchmark. (Reduced to a base of 100, Bakke's first score was 93.6 and his second 91.5; the 470 benchmark rating that was the admissions threshold in 1973 translated to a score of 94 out of 100.)

Bakke was notified in late September that UCDMS would not admit him under the Early Decision Plan and that his application had been deferred for later consideration under regular admissions. Writing Storandt in early December, Bakke indicated he was "anxiously await[ing] the committee's second and final decision" and asked when that would take place. He also informed Storandt of two personal items: his mother-in-law had died and he and his wife were expecting their first child in the summer.[27] Storandt's response in early January indicated that acceptances would be offered mid-month in January, February, and March, and

> [t]hereafter we will name a group of alternate candidates and select them individually as places open in the later spring and summer. I am unable to pinpoint the time when a decision will be made on your application; I can't yet tell when the "successful" ratings will include yours. For now, you are among a rather large group in the middle of our rated-to-date file.[28]

But Bakke was not placed on the alternate list, and under date of April 1, 1974 (April Fool's Day), UCDMS sent him a form letter of rejection identical to the one it had sent him the previous May.[29]

The evaluation process that resulted in denying entry to Bakke for the second time involved two disquieting elements. One was whether Storandt, in light of his unusual involvement with both Bakke's candidacy and his projected litigation plans, should have been among those who assigned benchmark ratings to Bakke. The other was whether Dr. Lowrey, who was a strong supporter of the special admissions program, should have so heavily and negatively emphasized in his interview report Bakke's views on that subject and should have relied mostly on that evidence in presenting a generally severe judgment on the deficiencies of Bakke's "thought processes." Of the two matters, Dr. Lowrey's involvement had the greater potential for adversely affecting Bakke's chances of admission. Lowrey's interview summary was read by the other evaluators before each made his determination of Bakke's benchmark score. And the benchmark rating of 86 Lowrey awarded Bakke was the lowest of the six ratings.

The limited evidence available in the trial record made it impossible to determine what influence, if any, Dr. Lowrey's assessment of Bakke had on the other committee members. If it was influential, the troubling possibility was raised that Bakke's second rejection might have been due in part—perhaps in significant part —to his expression of opposition to the special admissions program. That possibility was asserted during the litigation but it was never investigated any further, pro or con, than what has already been reported in this section of the study. As a consequence, it remained simply and only a possibility, neither proven nor disproven.

At the trial court stage of Bakke's suit, UC counsel argued that Bakke lacked legal standing to sue because he would not have been admitted even if the special program had not existed. For 1974 admissions, the evidence offered to support that argument consisted of Dr. Lowrey's detailed analysis that applicants with Bakke's benchmark score were too far down thc list ever to have been awarded admittance. In rebutting this line of argument, Bakke's attorney bluntly asserted:

> It becomes evident not only that Dr. Lowrey disagreed with plaintiff's [Bakke's] position regarding special admissions, but also that the dispute over the program caused Dr. Lowrey to downgrade plaintiff during the interview. Dr. Lowrey in effect penalized plaintiff for challenging the University's Special Admissions Program. . . . Dr. Lowrey's rating of plaintiff is truly self-serving to the University so far as this litigation is concerned. The University, acting through Dr. Lowrey, cannot reasonably be allowed to downgrade plaintiff for opposing a discriminatory university policy, and yet, at the same time claim that because he was thus downgraded he would not have been accepted even if there were no Special Admissions Program.[30]

This theme recurred, in more oblique form, at oral argument before the California Supreme Court, in an exchange between Justice Stanley Mosk and UC counsel:

> *Justice Mosk:* . . . for some strange reason, in reviewing Dr. Low-
> rey's evaluation of Bakke, more than half of the discussion is
> about Bakke's views on minority admissions. What does that
> have to do with Mr. Bakke's potential ability to someday remove
> my appendix?
>
> *Mr. Reidhaar:* . . . The point of Dr. Lowrey's remarks is not that
> Mr. Bakke would be disadvantaged because of his views on
> the minority admissions program, but rather, Dr. Lowrey found
> that Mr. Bakke's approach to this particular question seemed
> to involve more assertion and preconception rather than a care-
> ful analysis. . . . [A]s to the extent there is any criticism [of
> Bakke], it is criticism of process and methodology, not criticism
> of viewpoint.[31]

As of early April 1974, Allan Bakke knew nothing, of course, of
the particulars of the admissions committee's turndown of his application, since they were first revealed in the course of his subsequent litigation. All he knew was that he had been rejected again
and, consequently, that he had to decide whether to attempt, as he
had told UCDMS he might, to sue his way into the school.

Bakke Files Suit
The outcome of the Bakke-Storandt correspondence in late summer 1973, it will be recalled, was that Bakke indicated he would
consider a lawsuit if such action would not jeopardize his chances
for admission to UCDMS, which was the only school to which he
applied for 1974 admission. In early November, for reasons not
touched on in the trial record, Bakke filed a written complaint
against UCDMS and the Stanford medical school with the San
Francisco regional office of HEW–Office of Civil Rights. He alleged
that he had been "the victim of racial discrimination in medical
school admissions [in 1973]," because UCDMS had adopted "a 16%
racial quota" and he "had missed acceptance by only 2 points."
Bakke explicitly noted that "Davis officials have stated that my age
(33) was not a reason for my rejection."[32]

Nothing much came of this complaint. It was not until five
months later that the San Francisco regional office wrote the chancellor of UC Davis to inform him of Bakke's letter. Reminding the
chancellor that Title VI of the Civil Rights Act of 1964 required that
federally assisted education programs be conducted without discrimination on the basis of race, color, or national origin, the
HEW-OCR letter also noted that the Anti-Defamation League of

B'nai B'rith (a Jewish organization) had earlier complained to their office about "reverse discrimination" in admissions at various UC units. In support of its complaint B'nai B'rith had cited a mid-1972 Los Angeles newspaper editorial that referred to UC Davis as having "high quotas for minorities." The HEW-OCR letter continued:

> This latter complaint seems to reflect university policy. While it is our purpose to ensure equal opportunity, we are concerned that well-intentioned affirmative action efforts not be implemented in such a way as to promote or result in any form of discrimination prohibited by law.

The letter closed by asking for receipt by May 10 of information on several aspects of the medical school's admissions policies and practices, "in order to determine if this complaint will require an on-site investigation."[33]

This request for information was referred within the Davis campus to Dr. Lowrey in his capacity as chairman of the medical school's admissions committee. One of the questions to which he responded dealt with "the position of the University as to why Mr. Bakke was not accepted [for 1973]."[34] Dr. Lowrey wrote that

> Mr. Bakke was found by the Admissions Committee to be a highly desirable candidate and came very close to being offered a place. . . . The single reason for his non-acceptance was the lack of available space in that group; had additional places been available. individuals with Mr. Bakke's rating would likely have been admitted to the medical school as well.[35]

Presumably this response, together with the other information asked for, was sent back to HEW-OCR. The dean of the medical school, C. J. Tupper, wrote a professional colleague at the Association of American Medical Colleges in Washington, D.C., in early May that "[t]he campus is replying to HEW in general terms, and we will see what further transpires."[36]

Whatever the next move HEW might have made, it was preempted by Allan Bakke's decision to file a lawsuit. That decision had been held off for most of academic year 1973–74 for at least two practical reasons. One was Bakke's unwillingness to lessen his seemed to suggest were quite good. The other was Bakke's keen entry chances at Davis, which Storandt's January 1974 letter awareness that the U.S. Supreme Court decision in the *DeFunis* case was due at any time before mid-1974; indeed, Bakke told Storandt in December that "I have heard from Mr. DeFunis, and expect to receive some helpful information from him."[37] Both reasons were eliminated by April events, the first by UCDMS's denial of admission and the second by the Court's mooting of *DeFunis*.

In early 1974 Bakke had already begun to look seriously into the possibility of litigation. He inquired of educators and others about appropriate attorneys for his needs, and the name of Reynold Colvin turned up quite often. Colvin, fifty-seven, was a lifelong resident of San Francisco and a product of California schools, including UC Berkeley. An attorney since 1941, he was the senior partner in a small general-practice law firm whose offices were in San Francisco's financial district. From 1964 to 1970 Colvin was a member of the city's board of education, and served for a time as its president.

Through his board service Colvin got to know many school district administrators, and some of them turned to him in 1971, after he had left the board, to represent them in a suit against the school superintendent and the board. In an effort to hire and promote more minority school administrators, the local education officials voluntarily had set five-year "goals" and "targets" in such a fashion that the only way they could be met was for the school district to hire and promote only minority candidates and refuse to appoint or advance any nonminority candidates. Colvin agreed to take the case on behalf of a nonminority school administrator, and he won it handily. The federal district court held the program invalid and commented that "[p]referential treatment under the guise of 'affirmative action' is the imposition of one form of racial discrimination in place of another."[38] Colvin personally shared that view; he worried particularly that preferential treatment of minorities might result in substituting group rights for individual rights.[39]

When Bakke first met with Colvin, he was advised to await the outcome of the *DeFunis* case, which might settle the issue of the legality of preferential admission of minorities. After *DeFunis* aborted, Bakke returned to Colvin, who then agreed to represent him. It should be emphasized that Bakke's central goal was, as his August 7, 1973, letter to Storandt had stated: "My first concern is to be allowed to study medicine, and . . . challenging the concept of racial quotas is secondary."[40] As his attorney, Colvin's overriding duty was to his client, and hence Bakke's priorities became Colvin's priorities. Colvin's initial efforts, therefore, were to try to persuade the university to reconsider Bakke's application and admit him to UCDMS: "Just find another cadaver for him," it was put colloquially, "and there'll be no need for a suit." The university gave that possibility serious consideration, but rejected it on the grounds that it involved an irregular admission that would encourage other rejected applicants to sue while leaving the central legal issue unresolved.

On June 20, 1974, Bakke filed a complaint in state court against the university; it sought to compel his admission to UCDMS because the special admissions minority program had reduced the number of places for which he could compete. Cast in this form, the litigation clearly was not a class-action suit covering all others who were similarly situated, but rather a private suit solely on behalf of Allan Bakke. Moreover, the suit was narrowly focused, and there was initially an outside chance that it might have been fought out primarily on the factual issue of whether Bakke would or would not have been admitted if all 100 seats had been available to him and on the procedural issue of whether he had legal standing to sue. The university, however, because it was anxious for the legal questions surrounding preferential minority admissions to be adjudicated, filed a cross-complaint for a declaration that the special admissions program was lawful. With that, Bakke's personal quest for admission became inextricably joined with his quite secondary concern, the determination of the legality of special admissions for minorities, and *Bakke* was on its way to becoming a "big case."

Ironically, Bakke had no assurance of securing his court-ordered admission to UCDMS even if the special admissions program was invalidated. These were two separate matters; a judgment that the program was illegal would free up the 16 seats that had been set aside for disadvantaged minorities, but Bakke's claim to one of those seats would still have to be settled as an independent issue. In February 1976, for example, a California superior court (trial court) judge overturned the preferential minority admissions program at UC Davis law school on grounds that "[a]ny method that admits students solely because of . . . ethnic origin deprives a better qualified applicant of an opportunity for admission."[41] Nevertheless, the judge refused to direct the school to admit the plaintiff on the finding that he would not likely have been awarded admission in any event.

The same outcome initially befell Bakke. The trial judge, F. Leslie Manker, held to two traditional doctrines that worked against Bakke's hopes. One was that the burden of proof was on Bakke, as plaintiff, to demonstrate that he would have been admitted in the absence of the special program. The other was that judges ordinarily should not substitute their assessments for those of professional educators on so complex and judgmental a matter as school admissions decisions: "The admission of students to the Medical School is so peculiarly a discretionary function of the school that . . . it should not be interfered with by a court, absent a showing of fraud, unfairness, bad faith, arbitrariness or capriciousness, none of which has been shown."

The evidence on admissions was, of course, something that only the Davis medical school could supply; Bakke could not provide the court with it. In what is called in legal procedure the process of "discovery," Colvin asked for, and UCDMS provided, a variety of admissions data, which were entered in the trial record. In addition, Dr. Lowrey in both written declaration and under examination by Colvin and Reidhaar (UC counsel), gave further evidence on admissions. Included in Dr. Lowrey's presentation was a detailed review of how Bakke's benchmark scores in 1973 and 1974 related to decisions on admissions, rejections, and assignment to the alternate list. His conclusion from that review was that Bakke would not have been admitted even if all 100 seats had been available to him. Colvin was unable to develop either contrary evidence or argument, and that condition was almost certain to remain unless the burden of proof were shifted from Bakke to the university on the question whether or not Bakke would have been admitted.

In Judge Manker's November 1974 Notice of Intended Decision, he indicated he would hold the special program unconstitutional but would not order Bakke's admission to UCDMS. Although acknowledging that "there appears . . . to be at least a possibility that he [Bakke] might have been admitted absent the 16 favored positions on behalf of minorities," the judge considered Dr. Lowrey's conclusion to the contrary as controlling.

Confronted with this initial holding, Colvin had an uphill struggle in seeking to turn it around completely in the other direction. At this trial court stage, Colvin persuaded Judge Manker, in a March 1975 addendum to the Notice of Intended Decision, to modify his intended decision in several significant respects. The judge agreed to hold that judicial intervention on admissions decisions was warranted in the case because the unconstitutional racial quota "amounted to an unfair and arbitrary admissions procedure." In addition, Judge Manker shifted the burden of producing the evidence on the issue of Bakke's admission from Bakke to the university, though he continued to deny Colvin's request that the university be assigned the burden of proof as well (i.e., that Bakke be admitted unless the university could prove otherwise on the basis of the full evidence).

Judge Manker also granted Colvin's request for injunctive relief, which prohibited the university from considering Bakke's race or the race of any other applicant in passing upon his application to medical school. UC indicated it was willing to reactivate Bakke's 1974 application and consider him for 1975 admission, but only "under the same terms which the School of Medicine would consider any such application coming in at this late date [end of March]." Thus, Bakke could reapply at once, but he would be rejected again. The university's lack of generosity was a matter of necessity, not choice. It sought reversal by an appeals court of the trial court decision that its special program was unconstitutional, but Bakke's admission now might later result in the case being dismissed as moot because there no longer was a genuine legal controversy.*

Colvin's breakthrough came when the California Supreme Court accepted his argument that because Bakke's constitutional rights had been violated, the burden of proof was on the university to show why Bakke should not be admitted and not on Bakke to show why he should be admitted. The court therefore directed that the case be remanded to the trial court to determine, under the proper allocation of the burden of proof, the factual question of Bakke's admission. The university, however, in its petition to the court for a rehearing or a stay, suddenly conceded the issue by stipulating that "it cannot be clearly demonstrated that the special admissions program did not operate to deny Mr. Bakke admission in [1973] . . . [because he] came extremely close to admission . . . even with the special admissions program being in operation."

---

* This is precisely what happened in *DeFunis*. When the U.S. Supreme Court vacated the case as moot, Marco DeFunis was a few months away from completing his third and final year at the University of Washington law school.

What caused the university to reverse the position it had held so tenaciously up to that point? The reason suggested in the stipulation was not false, but it was hardly controlling. Because admission to UCDMS was not fixed solely in terms of a strict ranking of benchmark scores, it would be hard to demonstrate—particularly if a high level of proof was required—that any specific candidate whose benchmark was very near the admission threshold on an 84-seat basis was certain of rejection on a 100-seat basis. Still, the university had developed a detailed analysis on Bakke exactly to that effect in trial court. If UC wanted to contest Bakke's admission, it obviously could stand on that earlier analysis as a reasonable attempt to meet the burden of proof it had been assigned.

The university ceased to fight Bakke's admission after the state high court's decision for the same reason that it refused Bakke's admission after the trial court decision. As stated in UC's petition to the California Supreme Court:

> . . . the University has a strong interest in obtaining review by the United States Supreme Court of . . . whether the special admissions program at the Davis Medical School and other similar programs are, as held by the majority of this Court, unconstitutional. It is far more important for the University to obtain the most authoritative decision possible on the legality of its admissions process than to argue over whether Mr. Bakke would or would not have been admitted in the absence of its special admissions program.

Disputing Bakke's admission claim anew in trial court would have occasioned, at the least, sizable delay in UC's ability to pursue its appeal to the U.S. Supreme Court, and in the interim the constitutional invalidity of preferential minority admissions might well have taken effect for all of California public higher education.

After receiving the university's stipulation, the California Supreme Court amended its original ruling for remand and ordered Bakke's entry into UCDMS. When the U.S. Supreme Court agreed to hear the case, the California decision was stayed, including that portion of it directing Bakke's admission.

The situation now looked like this. Should the U.S. Supreme Court affirm the illegality of Davis's special program, Bakke's chances of finally gaining admission would be excellent, but still not certain. The *amicus* brief of the Justice Department urged, for example, that even if the Court overturned the particular Davis program, Davis could take race into account for admissions in other constitutional ways. The brief argued, therefore, that the case should be remanded to California to provide the university "an opportunity to establish . . . that [Bakke] would not have been admitted if the special admissions program had been administered . . . consistent with constitutional principles."[42] Invalidation of the Davis program thus remained at the end, as it had been from the outset, a necessary but not sufficient condition to ensure Bakke's admission to the Davis medical school.

Allan Bakke first sought acceptance by UCDMS in 1973 when he was thirty-three years old. He filed suit the following year and the trial court decision came a year later, shortly after he had turned thirty-five. In September 1976, another eighteen months later, the California Supreme Court ruled in his favor. Should the U.S. Supreme Court do likewise in late spring 1978, Bakke will be thirty-eight; by that time he would have completed his first year of post-M.D. residency had he been able to begin medical school back in 1973. Should the Court decide against him, presumably his quest for medical school would be ended, though the new antidiscrimination law with respect to age would enable him to keep trying if he so wished. Bakke's five-plus years of effort to gain school entry, with outcome as yet unknown, contrasted greatly with the happier fate of his predecessor, Marco DeFunis, Jr. The trial court in Washington ordered DeFunis admitted to the University of Washington law school and he was able to complete his law training there in the regular three-year period despite the ruling of the Washington Supreme Court against him.

An even more dramatic and direct contrast to Bakke's situation was provided by an episode in fall 1977, involving UCDMS and another Bakke-style rejection. Mrs. Rita Clancy, a twenty-two-year-old UCLA psychobiology major with a GPA of $A-$, applied to UCDMS. Born in Russia to Jewish parents who had survived concentration camps, Mrs. Clancy came to America at age fourteen, able to speak only Hungarian and Russian. Her lack of knowledge of English forced her to stay out of school a year. When her father became incapacitated by a brain tumor, the family went on welfare. Her mother worked, and Mrs. Clancy made her way through UCLA by working and with special aid provided by the university. She applied to the special admissions program but was denied consideration there because of her race and referred to regular admissions. (There were 4400 applicants for the 100 seats that year.) UCDMS placed her fourth on the alternate list, and she became the first alternate (but still not one of those admitted) by the time the September 1977 academic year started.* In this respect her admissions claim was stronger than Bakke's had been.

Mrs. Clancy filed suit in state court just before classes began; she requested a court-ordered admission either on *Bakke* grounds or—and here again her case was stronger than Bakke's—through the special program, which still carried the race-free label of "economically or educationally disadvantaged." When the trial judge indicated he would rule to direct her admission, UC had the case transferred to federal district court. But the university fared no better there; the district judge instructed UCDMS to admit Mrs. Clancy, partly "to give the [*Bakke*] decision respect" and partly because, in his view, until the high court settled the constitutionality of the issue, the harm to Mrs. Clancy through denial of admission was far greater than that to the university if she was admitted.[43] A federal appeals court refused to reverse that ruling, and by the close of September the judge and attorneys agreed to postpone indefinitely all further action on the Clancy suit until the *Bakke* case was decided by the U.S. Supreme Court. Mrs. Clancy remained enrolled in UCDMS; whatever the outcome of *Bakke*, there was little likelihood that the medical school would eject her. Thus Mrs. Clancy was able to make more rapid and effective use of *Bakke* for her goal than Bakke had been able to do for his.

* It is interesting to note that UC counsel Donald Reidhaar was reported as saying that Mrs. Clancy had placed that high on the alternate list in regular admissions because school officials had adjusted her ratings to take into account the fact that her native language was not English. See *Chronicle of Higher Education,* 3 October 1977.

Racial Quota?

When HEW Secretary Califano was forced by public pressure to renounce his endorsement of racial quotas (see chapter 2), his rueful observation was that "quotas" was "obviously a nerve-jangling word." He was entirely correct; the idea of racial quotas carries an intensely negative connotation for the public. As the late Yale law professor Alexander Bickel stated it:

> [A] racial quota derogates the human dignity and individuality of all to whom it is applied; it is invidious in principle as well as in practice. Moreover, it can as easily be turned against those it purports to help. The history of the racial quota is a history of subjugation, not beneficence. Its evil lies not in its name but in its effect; a quota is a divider of society, a creator of castes, and it is all the worse for its racial base, especially in a society desperately striving for an equality that will make race irrelevant.[1]

The use of negative, exclusionary, or limiting quotas against certain groups is studded throughout American history. The practice expressed the majority's effort to contain and subordinate those groups, and to impute inferiority to them. The targets of quotas included not only the racial minorities who have become the intended beneficiaries of today's affirmative action policies but white ethnics as well, such as those of Irish, Italian, or Eastern European ancestry. For Jews, perhaps more than for any other group, the quota concept was an anathema in view of their history of persecution in Europe and discrimination in the United States. In American higher education, for example, Jews were subjected to discriminatory quotas in the interwar period; not until the decade after the end of World War II did prestigious private colleges and professional schools drop these bars.

The courts' view of racial quotas, which will be discussed later in this study, was also generally hostile. This was clearly their stance on invidious quotas of the traditional sort, and the judicial overturning of the "separate but equal" doctrine and of racial discrimination generally were integral parts of the civil rights gains of minorities in the 1950s and '60s. On "benign" racial quotas, intended to bring about the inclusion rather than the exclusion of certain groups, judicial response was neither fully formed nor thoroughly consistent because of the newness and novelty of that development. (*Bakke* was a "big case" in good part because of the expectation that the U.S. Supreme Court would provide authoritative judgment on the point.) Still, a broad pattern of court reaction could be identified. Quotas were recognized as the most extreme form of minority preference, and courts reluctantly called for their imposition only in situations where racial discrimination had been demonstrated to exist and more moderate remedies were ineffective to correct the damage that had occurred. Otherwise, racial quotas generally were disallowed.

It would be appropriate, given the saliency of the quota issue to the public and its significance to the legal dimensions of the *Bakke* case, to begin our systematic inquiry into the policy problem from that same perspective. It should be noted, however, that examination of the quota question could shed only limited light on the larger policy issue of minority preferences. As the most extreme type of preference, quotas could be opposed for reasons that left open the question of whether more moderate preference devices were permissible or wise. Moreover, disputants often meant different things when they referred to "quotas," and hence they frequently talked past each other on the point. Even when they agreed on the conceptual distinctions between "quotas" and "goals," they quickly disagreed on whether goals in their actual application became de facto quotas.*

There were a few things about quotas on which all sides to the dispute saw eye to eye, and this helped to narrow the areas of dis-

---

* An example of this disagreement, relating to affirmative action programs in employment, was discussed in the second chapter of this study.

agreement a bit. First, they agreed that it would be unsound policy and also illegal to limit the admittance of highly qualified minorities to professional school when, if they had been nonminority persons, they would have been admitted. This would be, of course, the old-fashioned restrictive racial quota, outlawed by the courts. Second, they agreed that the intent of the preferential practices at issue was to expand, not constrict, minority admissions. The problem context was an affirmative desire to increase minority enrollment (At least X number wanted. Welcome!), in contrast to the negative purpose of the old-style discriminatory quota (No more than X number wanted. Keep out!). Finally, they also agreed that explicit race preference was the most direct and effective means to achieve, with predictability and certainty, designated levels of increased minority admissions.

A fourth item of seeming agreement turned out, when probed, to be the key object of dissension. Proponents and opponents alike shared the view that a positive racial quota in selective admissions voluntarily adopted by a professional school was an unwise policy and most probably illegal as well. It would constitute "reverse discrimination," which would prejudice the opportunities of nonminority students and which a school would find difficult to justify as reasonably consistent with its educational mission. Clearly, then, the position of supporters of UWLS and of UCDMS was that the admissions policies of these two institutions were quite different from an unsound and forbidden racial quota. But those who identified with Marco DeFunis, Jr., and Allan Bakke were no less adamant in asserting that the special admissions practices for minorities were variants of a racial quota, regardless of what other name they chose to go by. Both semantically and substantively, therefore, the disagreement turned on divergent conceptions of what a racial quota meant.

No, It's Not a Quota

To the advocates of preferential minority admissions, the essential attributes of a racial quota for admission were that (1) a specific number or ratio of entering places was set for minorities; (2) all these places had to be filled (a floor), and only these places had to be filled (a ceiling), by minorities; and (3) unqualified minority persons would be admitted if necessary to produce the requisite

number of minority enrollees. Under this definition, no professional school in the nation would have any difficulty in describing
its voluntary minority admissions program as sharply different
from a racial quota. In the schools' view of their own programs, no
applicants judged unqualified were admitted, the number of places
set was only a goal or target that did not have to be met, and the
target number fixed neither a floor nor a ceiling. When those opposing DeFunis and Bakke readily agreed that an affirmative racial-quota admissions policy by UWLS or UCDMS would be unjus-
tified and of dubious legality, it was to this minimal definition of a
quota they referred. In effect, then, they conceded little to nothing
by endorsing the invalidity of racial quotas.

UWLS stoutly insisted it did not operate by a quota system. As
the dean put it, the school sought a "reasonable representation" of
minorities, those who had been "historically suppressed" and "excluded from participation in . . . the mainstream . . . and certainly . . . in the legal arena."[2] (In December 1973, before oral
argument on *DeFunis* in the U.S. Supreme Court took place,
the UWLS faculty defined a "reasonable proportion" of minorities
as "15 to 20 percent . . . if there are sufficient qualified applicants available.") UWLS obtained its minority "representation" by
going down the list of minority applicants to the limit of not taking
the clearly unqualified. The dean said they were attempting to find
"the best that we can of student applicants from those groups
[minorities]."[3] "We . . . sought, within the minority category,"
stated the faculty chairman of the admissions committee, "those
persons who we thought had the highest probability of succeeding
in law school."[4]

Other law schools had minority admissions policies that, in both
form and operation, more closely approximated the minimal definition (as discussed above) of a racial quota. The law school at Rutgers University, for example, which submitted a friend-of-the-court
brief in both *DeFunis* and *Bakke*, made provision for about 40
minority enrollees. Were these minority admittees "qualified"? The
measure used by Rutgers was to consider "presumptively qualified"
any minority applicant who was in the top half of his or her college
class. UCLA law school provided another example. In April 1974,
in a *New York Times* article headed "Rise in Black Students Brings
Disputes on Law School Recruiting," the school dean candidly

acknowledged the existence of a minorities quota—"73 out of a class of 350"—and indicated his belief that his fellow law school deans around the country should admit that quotas exist.

Although in form obviously different from the practice of Rutgers or UCLA, was UWLS's talk of "reasonable representation" mostly camouflage for just about the same thing? Not so, maintained the anti-DeFunis camp, which likened the law school's pursuit of "reasonable representation" to the setting of goals in the federal government's Affirmative Action program. Recourse to that analogy, however, could only fan disagreement, not resolve it, because as noted earlier there was considerable conflict on whether Affirmative Action goals themselves were merely euphemisms for quotas.

The Davis medical school's procedure of setting aside 16 places for personally disadvantaged minorities was plainly a more rigid preferential device than that of UWLS. It also was more extreme than the practice of most other medical schools; as of the 1972–73 academic year, only about one-quarter of the nation's medical schools reported that they had adopted the goal of some stated percentage of minority students in their entering class.[5] Nor was there any analog in the employment field to UCDMS's special admissions arrangements. The chairman of the federal Equal Employment Opportunity Commission, which was no supporter of Bakke's position, noted that while the Davis method might be permissible in education, it would be "very clumsy" and unacceptable for an employer to set aside a certain number of jobs for minorities to be filled by hiring from a pool of applicants composed only of minorities.[6]

Counsel for the University of California nonetheless insisted throughout the litigation that the Davis program involved a goal and not a quota, and that it set no floor on the number of minority enrollments. "If in a given year," the argument went, "less than sixteen well-qualified [disadvantaged minority] applicants are available for admission to Davis, the goal will not be met."[7] This claim, however, could not realistically be tested because, as UC counsel acknowledged, ". . . given the current demand for medical education . . . the problem has become one of turning away qualified minority applicants rather than being unable to meet the admissions goal."[8] Without proof, the claim was subject to heavy discount.* For instance, at a moot court competition at Yale law school on the *Bakke* case, when the law student defending Davis asserted that the 16 places represented a goal, not a quota, U.S. Supreme Court Justice Byron White responded, "Every time you've had a goal of 16, you've achieved it."[9]

Much to the University of California's discomfort, it was discovered soon after the California Supreme Court's decision in *Bakke* that, in 1974, when one of the 16 special admittees decided in late summer not to enroll, the seat was transferred to regular admissions even though there was a waiting list for special admissions. This correction of the facts was made by a friend-of-the-court brief filed by sixteen organizations (mostly minority and women's groups), which unsuccessfully urged the U.S. Supreme Court not to hear the *Bakke* case.[10]† This new fact provided only weak and ambiguous evidence, however, on behalf of UC's assertion that the Davis program had a goal and not a quota. The special program enrollees initially had numbered 16, after all, and no further information was supplied on why the 85th regular admissions enrollee was preferred to the first alternate on the special admissions list. Since UC counsel saw fit not to make significant use of the event in subsequent briefs,[11] it could only be inferred that a full explanation of what had occurred would do little to bolster UC's claim and perhaps might even be embarrassing to relate if, for instance, the unexpectedly available seat had been awarded to someone on the basis of considerations having little to do with benchmark ratings.

As the defenders of preferential admissions argued it, the hallmark of a racial quota was the admission of unqualified applicants. Where such a practice was followed, it was the tipoff that a fixed number of seats were being set aside for minorities and that those places had to be filled regardless of the qualifications of the candidates. When only qualified candidates were admitted, however, no racial quota could be said to exist; even when a specific

---

* The university made a comparable argument on a related matter early in the litigation, but then abandoned the argument after it was rejected by the trial court judge. That argument, discussed in chapter 4, was that the special admissions program was open to disadvantaged whites because they would be admitted through the program if the number of minorities was less than 16.

† Why some minority organizations opposed UC's legal strategy and distrusted UC's motives are matters discussed later in this study.

number of places were set aside, that was only a "goal," and it would not be met if there were too few qualified applicants. So far as the trial record in both *DeFunis* and *Bakke* was concerned, UWLS and UCDMS appeared to be in the clear on this point. The assertion of each school that only qualified minority persons were admitted was not effectively challenged by opposing counsel, and the data needed to examine that assertion in detail were not made available. Neither school had demonstrated that the special admittees were qualified, but neither had DeFunis's or Bakke's counsel demonstrated that they were unqualified. Hence, assuming that the trial record was controlling on that question, it was not likely the issue would play a significant role in the U.S. Supreme Court's decision.

Litigation considerations aside, the question of whether all minority special admittees were minimally qualified was genuinely troubling.* Whether any applicant would be judged "unqualified," and by what measures, remained unknown because neither the Washington law school nor the Davis medical school established explicit minimum academic standards. For regular admittees, however, the procedures provided indirect but complete assurance that all would be qualified. In order to reduce the overload on the admissions review machinery, the regular applicant pool was divided into two groups, those deemed competitively eligible for admission and those not. The determination was made on the basis of academic criteria; for UWLS a predicted first-year average (PFYA) of at least 74.5 and for UCDMS a grade-point average of at least 2.5. Since admission was confined to those in the competitively eligible group, every admittee had academic credentials at or, more often, considerably higher than the stated minimum, which itself was set well above the level of minimally qualified. For those in the uncompetitively eligible group who were summarily rejected, many also were qualified and some were unqualified, but there was no need for the school to make that distinction because none would be seriously reviewed for admission in any event.

For regular admittees, then, lack of a definition of minimal qualifications was of no consequence because the only applicants reviewed and accepted had academic credentials far higher than whatever that minimum level might be. For special admittees, the

---

* The reader is reminded that aspects of this issue were discussed in the closing section of the fourth chapter of this study.

situation was altogether different. No cutoff standard was used to divide the group into those competitively eligible and those not; in effect, all were considered competitively eligible. Consequently there was no assurance that the academic qualification of all special admittees were above a designated level.

The limited data supplied in trial court showed that all the non-Asian minority enrollees in UWLS had PFYAs under 74.5 (the cutoff point for applicants reviewed under regular admissions), and about one-third had PFYAs under 71. At UCDMS, the average MCAT score of special program admittees was well below the 50th percentile nationally, and UC counsel acknowledged, in oral argument before the California Supreme Court, that there was "no absolute bottom figure" on grade-point average for special admissions.[12] That few nonminority persons with such scores would have been seriously reviewed, let alone accepted, was true but not relevant to the question under discussion: were applicants with such scores qualified? There could be no sure answer in the absence of both the requisite criteria and data, but it was understandable in the light of the available evidence why the characterization of the special admittees as "fully qualified" and "well qualified" aroused skepticism among many. In the oral argument on *DeFunis* before the U.S. Supreme Court, for example, when state attorney general Slade Gorton reiterated that "We didn't admit any of them [minorities] who weren't qualified," Justice William H. Rehnquist responded, "When you say 'qualified,' Mr. Gorton, really by the time you've diluted that phrase as much as you have in your approach to admissions, it doesn't mean a whole lot, does it? When you consider the minority applicants separately, and really don't have any base, any cutoff point on the predicted first-year average."[13]

No matter how plausible the suspicion that many minority special admittees were not "well qualified" and that some, perhaps, were unqualified, it should not lead to the conclusion that the schools knowingly enrolled unqualified students and, therefore, that they treated their goals as quotas they felt had to be met. What was at work was a more complex situation and a more subtle set of behaviors than that. The problem for most schools, once the novelty of special admissions had worn off after the first few years of operation, seldom was one of the deliberate admission of applicants thought probably unqualified and likely not to succeed as students in the school. Such a practice, whether motivated by a

genuine commitment to expand minority enrollment or by a cyni-
cal effort to achieve a specific "body count" of minorities, could
only be condemned as irresponsible; it was detrimental to the institution, to the unsuccessful students, to society, and to the cause of
minority advancement. Although there was considerable disagreement among *Bakke* disputants on the meaning and measurement
of qualifications, no one advocated that unqualified minorities
should be admitted to professional schools. The overall data on
school admissions was reassuring in this regard: for the 1976
entering class in the nation's law schools, for example, only 39 percent of black applicants were accepted, compared with 59 percent
of white applicants.[14] So sizable a difference strongly suggested
that law schools were not acting to admit as many black applicants
as possible without regard to their chances of academic success in
school.

The real problem for the professional schools was the need to
stretch their standards of qualification to satisfy their eager desire
to take in much larger numbers of minority students. How far
down those standards could be set and still remain within the
bounds of minimal qualifications was difficult to determine with
exactitude. For example, it was sound enough to believe that an
applicant's strong motivation could counterbalance to some degree
a weak academic record. But precisely how strong a motivation
was needed to offset how weak a record to ensure the candidate's
successful completion of the school program? The knowledge base
for making such fine judgments did not exist then or now. Moreover, most professional schools had little experience in evaluating
academically underprepared candidates, which required greater
attention to noncognitive factors.

In addition, the determination of whether an applicant was
qualified could not be made solely by reference to a static absolute
minimum standard independent of school norms established by its
faculty and students. It also had to take into account such shifting
relative factors as the performance standards set by the academically well-prepared regular admissions students and by the expectations of the faculty. Studies indicated, for example, that while
the average MCAT and LSAT score of blacks accepted under special admissions was well below that of white acceptees, it was
about the same, respectively, as that of medical school acceptees
in the mid-1950s and of acceptees at 80 percent of law schools in

1961.[15] Some drew the inference from these data that minority applicants whose scores came close to this average confidently could be considered clearly qualified. The inference was plausible, but the matter was not quite that simple. In this earlier period there was little competition for entering places, and national admissions standards were quite low. Over the past two decades, both medical and law training have become far more rigorous and demanding, and students much more individualistically competitive in their academic striving. In view of this upgrading of schools, curriculum, faculty, and student body, use of the average standards of the 1950s to fix minimum qualifications for the '70s was neither as sensible nor as safe as it initially seemed to be.

Given the schools' uncertainty of judgment on the one side, and their wish to enroll more minorities on the other, it was understandable why, in borderline cases, schools often might resolve their doubt by admitting the minority candidate. The risks inherent in such judgments probably were accentuated for those schools, such as UCDMS, which favored personally disadvantaged minority members, who generally had weaker academic records than middle-class minority persons. Schools learned through their experiences, however, and over the course of the 1970s they generally improved in their ability to appraise the qualifications of minority applicants with relatively weak academic credentials. In the beginning years of special admissions programs, the failure rate of enrolled minorities was greater than in recent years. Some schools began their recruitment of minorities in a spirit of misguided beneficence which misled them into thinking that the greater the person's handicap, the greater the potential for improved academic performance and, hence, the greater the "claim" on an entering seat. It was said of some medical schools, for instance, that in the late 1960s they "admitted poorly prepared black students; the effect on both students and faculties was predictably traumatic"[16] and several of these schools as a consequence kept their minority programs quite small afterward.

The improving performance of minority students during the '70s reflected not only a better applicant pool and stronger support services within schools but also the more realistic evaluation of minority candidates by the schools. Still, when the success rate of special admittees as a group was compared with regular admittees, the difference declined more slowly than was hoped for, measured by such indicators as completion of the school program or passing the state bar examination. Moreover, there was a dearth of publicly available data on minority-student performance in professional schools and on national board and bar exams, which reflected conscious policies not to release such data for fear they might be misused by partisans in the controversy over minority preferential admissions. One observer, entitling his article "The 'Gauze Curtain' at Harvard Medical School,"* complained that not only was there no information released by the school on the academic performance of its minority special admits but that the information was withheld from the school faculty as well.[17] Naturally, the absence of solid reports and hard data helped strengthen suspicions that schools were sitting on material that would lend little support to their claim that all minorities entered under special admissions were qualified.

Had the professional schools felt they could speak with candor about their special admissions, they might have said about as follows: They would have acknowledged the higher risk involved in special admissions as a group. Say, to put hypothetical numbers on it, an 80 percent probability of satisfactorily finishing the school program, meaning that about 8 of every 10 minority special admittees were expected to graduate. Their lesser rate of success as a group, however, in no way cast doubt on the integrity of the school's initial assessment that each member was deemed qualified, albeit based in part on nontraditional factors which made for less confident judgment. Since special admittees usually were less academically prepared than regular admittees, it was only to be expected that they would do less well, on the average, in school. Such a description was closer to what was actually taking place in the professional schools than either the charge that unqualified candidates were knowingly being admitted or the claim that all special admittees were "well qualified."

Yes, It's a Quota

Supporters of Bakke and DeFunis unhesitatingly granted that the purpose of the admissions practices at issue was to expand,

---

* Harvard's medical school was the site of a well-publicized controversy in 1976 in which some of its medical faculty questioned whether the qualifications standards had been lowered too far to facilitate minority admissions; the charge was vigorously rebutted by other school faculty and by the university administration.

not confine, minority enrollment; but in their view that did not change their fundamental character as a quota. Whether those practices were called affirmative, benign, remedial, or compensatory, and no matter how they differed from restrictive quotas, they shared the common characteristic of being a racial quota. To be sure, they were not quotas against whites in the sense that whites were thought to be inferior or were not wanted, or that a ceiling on their number should be imposed, no matter what. UC counsel was quite justified in dismissing that kind of charge—that the practices were antiwhite quotas in the manner of the discredited quotas of the past against blacks—as a "red herring."[18] But it did not necessarily follow, as some opponents of Bakke maintained, that because minority special admissions involved no disparagement of whites it could not appropriately be called a "quota." To the Bakke camp it was inescapably a racial quota against whites in the sense that in any situation of scarcity, such as too few entering places for applicants, the favored inclusion of some members of one group had to result in the exclusion of an equivalent number of nonmembers. Providing a floor for minorities meant, therefore, imposing a ceiling on nonminorities. Bakke's lawyer was no less justified, therefore, in insisting that his client had been prevented, "solely because of his race, from competing for the 16 quota places."[19] From that vantage point, whites had a set "racial quota of 84" at UCDMS and a variable "racial quota of from 80 to 85 percent of the entering places" at UWLS.

As the antipreferential admissions camp saw it, a quotalike situation necessarily existed whenever applicants were not allowed to compete for the full number of seats available. Whatever the name a school chose to give such a procedure, it was held to be the functional equivalent of a racial quota. And whatever its shadings— UWLS's "reasonable representation" was a "softer" variant of a quota than UCDMS's set-aside of 16 places, for example—each was solidly a quota nonetheless.

An exact number of minority admits might not be fixed, and the range might vary from year to year, but minority admissions could not be operated successfully without earlier agreement that roughly X percent of the entering class would be minorities. Otherwise, the school would be unable to assure admission for any minority candidates because of the excessive demand for the limited supply of spaces. Moreover, as Justice William O. Douglas noted in his substantive opinion in *De Funis,* which was the only opinion that dealt with the case on its merits, ". . . because the [UWLS] admissions committee compared minority applicants only with one another, it was necessary to reserve some proportion of the class for them, even if at the outset a precise number of places was not set aside." The decision of the UWLS faculty to translate "reasonable representation" of minorities into "15 to 20 percent" of the entering class provided confirmation of the point.

A reservation of places for minority special admissions was needed as a ceiling as well as a floor. In theory, under an open-ended quota, as many racially preferred candidates as possible would be admitted, with the residual number of places left to members of the unpreferred racial groups. This was not a real problem in practice, of course, because every school put boundaries around its special admissions programs. Observed UCLA law school's dean, once again with candor, "Sure we have a quota. All of the law schools do—they have to, or they won't know where to stop." At Boalt (the law school of UC at Berkeley), for example, prior to 1971 there were relatively few minority applicants, and all those who were qualified were admitted; no goal or target was set. When the number of minority candidates greatly increased in the early 1970s, that procedure had to be ended and in its place Boalt adopted a limit on its special admissions program of 25 percent of the entering class.[20]

Both sides were agreed, then, that a minority-preference program could not operate sensibly unless it was tied to a reasonably clear idea of what proportion or number of the available seats would be targeted for minorities. "Once it is decided that minorities should be preferred," one *amicus* brief bluntly commented, "the magnitude of that preference must be gauged. Once it is decided that minorities are underrepresented, the size of that underrepresentation must be assessed."[21] The interpretation of the role of such numbers or proportions provoked vehement disagreement. One side maintained that such numbers represented permissible goals; the other side insisted that "if such a number is decided upon in advance and is then striven for, a quota system is in operation."[22]

In its *amicus* brief on *Bakke* submitted to the U.S. Supreme Court, the Department of Justice argued that there was nothing inherently wrong with "reasonably selected numerical targets for minority admissions" because they could "be useful as a gauge of the [special admissions] program's effectiveness." Referring to a March 1973 joint policy statement hammered out among a number of federal executive agencies that had disagreed on what Affirmative Action entailed, the brief approvingly observed that the statement endorsed the use of flexible goals that "help measure progress in remedying discrimination." Nevertheless, the Justice Department brief continued by noting that the statement also pointed out that "[a]ny system which requires that relative abilities and qualifications be subordinated to considerations of race . . . has the attributes of a quota system which is deemed to be impermissible."[23]

In the view of the allies of DeFunis and Bakke, the quota character of the two schools' admissions procedures was revealed, above all, by the fact that in effect two separate classes were entered in each school. An exclusive and insulated admissions process, often involving minority faculty and students, was used for designated minorities, and another process obtained for all others. Two different committees, acting mostly independently of each other, made the admissions decisions separately for each group. Competition among applicants was confined to within each group; there was no intergroup competition. Different qualitative and quantitative criteria were used for the two groups, with minorities assessed by lower academic standards and a greater emphasis on noncognitive factors. Summed up one observer, who favored the consideration of race as a factor in the admissions process but considered "predetermined quotas" undesirable, "It could be argued that except for a single faculty and a common geographical location, the result [of the practices just described] is uncomfortably similar to operating two segregated schools."[24]

Advocates of minority preferential admissions countered the preceding argument by insisting that it was sensible and permissible to measure minorities separately by different criteria and by different committees and against each other. This was necessary, they urged, in order to provide for a full and fair assessment of minority applicants, whose culture and background often were considerably different from nonminorities. Similarly, a greater reliance on minority persons to appraise the qualifications of minority applicants was justifiable on the grounds that it would make for a better judgment and that the credibility of the decisions would be greater in the eyes of minority candidates. For example, the Association of American Medical Colleges noted in its *amicus* brief on *Bakke* that research was progressing on identifying non-cognitive factors useful for predicting academic success of minorities: positive self-concept, ability to understand and deal with racism, realistic self-appraisal, willingness to defer short-term gratification for long-range goals, successful leadership experience within the racial-cultural environment, and demonstrated community service.[25] The association could see nothing wrong with a separate committee using such criteria to evaluate minorities; in its view, the evaluation process would be improved and no invidious discrimination against any group would be implied.

The Justice Department's brief on *Bakke* also took the position that "the fairness of the admissions process" might be enhanced by use of "a committee with specialized knowledge of, or insights into, [the] peculiar qualifications [of minority applicants]."[26] But its approval of a separate committee covered only "the initial screening of minority applicants,"[27] not the final determination of admission. The department's brief, which opposed "rigid exclusionary quotas"[28] but did not define that term, appeared to lay considerable stress on the factor of intergroup competition. That is, a special minority-sensitive evaluation of minority candidates was proper in order to take race into account and thereby to improve the fairness of evaluation, but minority applicants then should be compared with all others and not just with one another. Applying this notion to the *Bakke* situation, the Justice Department stated that "if there was a comparison of regular and special applicants by the regular admissions committee prior to selection, this would indicate that race had not been used improperly."[29] Such a standard, it should be noted, was broadly relevant to the gamut of minority preferential admissions practices, not just to the particulars of the UCDMS device.

In advancing that position, the Justice Department was endorsing one of Justice Douglas's major points in his *DeFunis* opinion:

. . . the school [UWLS] did not choose one set of [admissions] criteria but two, and then determined which to apply to a given applicant on the basis of his race. . . . The law school presented no evidence to show that adjustments in the process employed were used in order validly to compare applicants of different races; instead it chose to avoid making such comparisons.

Most professional schools, especially in the light of Justice Douglas's views as quoted, took care to establish any separate review group used for minority applicants as a subcommittee of the regular admissions committee, rather than as an independent committee. Even back in 1972, only about one-sixth of medical schools used the latter form, and in almost all instances these were schools that had fixed numbers or percentages of minority admits as a goal.[30]

It was a necessary but hardly sufficient condition for minority and nonminority applicants to be genuinely compared that the special admissions review machinery be located within the regular admissions process and in form be accountable to the regular admissions committee. Within that formal arrangement the nature of the relationship could vary, of course, all the way from routine endorsement to independent review of the minority subcommittee's recommendations. In the instance of the Davis medical school, for example, the record adequately showed that the subcommittee's recommendations were not reviewed significantly by the regular committee, and that no attempt was made to compare regular and special admissions applicants. Nonetheless, for reasons explored later in this study, the Justice Department argued that the *Bakke* record was insufficiently clear on the point, and offered that as one of its reasons why the U.S. Supreme Court should remand the case to the California courts.

Why 16? Why Not 50?
Whether the minority admissions practices of both UCDMS and UWLS were considered goals or quotas, why did the law school faculty select 15 to 20 percent and the medical school faculty 16 percent? The trial records provided no answer. As best as could be fathomed from the briefs, several reasons seemed uppermost for deciding on that scale of minority preference. One reason was that it permitted more than tokenism, especially since a number of different minority groups had to be accommodated under the single term "minority." Another was that it represented a significant institutional commitment and contribution to reducing the underrepresentation of minority students and practitioners in law and medicine. Yet at the same time the scale was held to be "limited" and "reasonable" in that it did not require the school to allot too

much of its resources (including available first-year seats) and it was not excessive with respect to minority percentages of the national or state population. Although these after-the-fact justifications could not explain the adoption of any particular figure, they were helpful in explaining why the usual scale of preference for schools was, say, from 10 to 30 percent, rather than around the 2 percent or the 60 percent level.

Exceptions could be taken to some parts of the preceding explanations for UCDMS's 16 percent figure for special admissions. For one thing, because of the high admission rate of Asian-Americans under regular admissions, the minority proportion of the overall entering class was about 25 percent from 1970 through 1974, and reached a high of 31 percent in 1973; this compared with a California minority population of about 25 percent. The eligibility pool for medical school applicants consisted, however, of college seniors and recent college graduates who had completed premedical course prerequisites, and minorities constituted well under 16 percent of that population. Minorities were doubly advantaged, therefore, by the special program; not only were seats reserved for them but the proportion of seats was much greater than their proportion of all applicants. For example, in 1973, minorities reviewed under special admissions made up less than 9 percent of all applicants. Finally, the justifications of the 16 percent figure lumped together all the component minority groups under the single label "minority" and never dealt with them group by group. It will be recalled, from earlier discussion of the matter in chapter 4, that no adequate information was developed in the trial record to explain whether or how target numbers were developed separately for Chicanos, blacks, Asian-Americans, and American Indians or to justify the inclusion of Asian-Americans within the special program in view of their impressive acceptance rate under regular admissions.

For those who opposed minority preferential admissions on principle, the set-aside of any seats—1 or 16—was considered wrong. As a practical matter, though, the larger the proportion of seats held for minorities, the greater the exclusion of nonminorities. Hence their obvious concern, if racial preference was validated, was how the scale of such preference would be bounded and constrained. If 16 of 100 seats were allowable, then what about a school's decision to reserve 30, 50, or 80 seats out of 100 for qualified minorities on the grounds, for example, that their gross under-representation in the profession had to be reduced more rapidly? None of the pro-UC briefs spoke directly to this question because their overriding concern was to argue the validity of preferential admissions. Nevertheless, the question did come up at oral argument on *Bakke* before the U.S. Supreme Court, and the "answer" provided by UC's special counsel, Archibald Cox, did nothing to lower the opposition's anxiety on the point.

The context for Cox's answer was supplied by his earlier effort to explain the Davis medical school's 16 percent figure to the Court:

> . . . [L]et us suppose . . . that the school [Davis] was much concerned by the lack of qualified general practitioners in Northern California . . . and it told the admissions committee: "Get people who come from rural communities, if they are qualified, and who express the intention of going back there." And the Dean of Admissions might well say: "Well, how much importance do you give this?"
>
> And the . . . faculty might say, . . . "We think it's terribly important. As long as they are qualified, try to get ten in that group."
>
> . . . [W]hile [*Bakke*] involves race . . . —that's why we're here [in litigation]—[it] really is essentially the same thing. The decision of the University was that there are social purposes, or purposes aimed . . . at eliminating racial injustice . . . and bringing equality of opportunity . . . served by including minority students.
>
> Well, how important do you think it is? We think it's this important [16 places]. And that is the significance of the number. That's about the only significance.[31]

Cox's explanation was part of a broader argument that sought to persuade the Court generally to defer to the authority and judgment of educators on such key matters as whether to establish a minority preferential admissions and how to operate it, including the scale of the program. Since that argument stressed jurisdiction (who should decide?) and not substance (were some kinds of minority preferential admissions valid and others not?), Cox was in no position to distinguish sharply between a minority goal of 50 places out of 100 and UCDMS's 16 places:

> *Mr. Justice Stevens:* Can you give me a test which would differentiate the cases of 50 students from the case of 16 students? . . .
> [A]ssum[e] precisely the same motivation that is present in this

case: a desire to increase the number of black and minority doctors, and a desire to increase the mixture of the student population.

Why would not that justify the 50?

Mr. Cox: Well, if the finding is that this was reasonably adapted to the purpose of increasing the number of minority doctors, and that it was not an arbitrary, capricious, selfish setting—and that would have to be decided in the light of the other medical schools in the State and the needs in the State; but if it's solidly based, then I would say 50 is permissible.[32]

Legal Strategies

Plainly, an emphasis on quotas lay at the heart of the legal strategy employed by Reynold Colvin, Bakke's attorney. Colvin began his oral argument before the California Supreme Court with the flat assertion that "our position in this case is that what we have before us is a racial quota case."[33] And his brief to the U.S. Supreme Court reiterated the same point: "[The] special admission program is based upon race. The 16% allotment to the program of places in the first year class at the medical school constitutes a racial quota of 16%."[34] Colvin's strategy paid off handsomely in the California courts; both the trial court and the state supreme court endorsed that characterization of the Davis medical school's program. Observed the California Supreme Court:

> While a program can be damned by semantics, it is difficult to avoid considering the University scheme as a form of an education quota system, benevolent in concept perhaps, but a revival of quotas nevertheless. No college admission policy in history has been so thoroughly discredited in contemporary times as the use of racial percentages. Originated as a means of exclusion of racial and religious minorities from higher education, a quota becomes no less offensive when it serves to exclude a racial majority.

Believing that a focus on the quota question provided the best defense of Allan Bakke's interests, Colvin stressed the narrow factual situation of the particulars of UCDMS's special program and undertook little exploration of the larger legal and policy issue of whether it was permissible to use race as an admissions factor at all, and if so, how. His posture, in effect, was that whatever others might argue and decide about the proper ways, if any, race could be considered in a selective admissions process, the UCDMS practice was clearly outside those limits and illegal in any event. In keeping with that stance, Colvin took pains to distinguish sharply between the Davis program and legitimate Affirmative Action. His brief to the U.S. Supreme Court stressed that UCDMS's use of a "rigid percentage formula" made the program different from Affirmative Action and not justifiable by that concept. "The question presented [by this case] is not so broad," Colvin assured the Court, "as to involve the constitutionality of affirmative action."[35]

The *amici* briefs filed in support of Bakke's suit were not constrained by the client-centered considerations that professional ethics imposed on Colvin. These organizations voluntarily involved themselves in *Bakke* not to lend Allan Bakke a helping hand in getting into medical school but to take the opportunity presented by the *Bakke* case to urge on the Court their position on the larger issues. Hence their arguments, while advancing the same view of the Davis program as a prohibited racial quota that Colvin urged, went well beyond that theme to challenge all minority preferential admissions and race-conscious affirmative action programs as well. For example, most of the briefs called for the invalidation of the inclusion of race as a factor in selective admissions. Their strategy, consequently, was to make use of the Davis program as a good example of the infirmities that they believed generally characterized all minority special programs.

The legal strategy pursued by counsel for the University of California was just about the opposite of that employed by Colvin. As discussed earlier in this chapter, "quota" was defined in such a way as to support characterization of the Davis 16 percent figure as a "goal." Rejecting any emphasis on the quota question, counsel dismissed that concern as a "label" that "comes in on [Bakke's] side of the case for emotional, rather than analytical purposes."[36] Whereas Colvin sought to isolate the Davis program as a too extreme form of minority preferential admissions, opposing counsel denied significance to those distinctive features and justified the program as one of many permissible variants of special admissions. The latter, in turn, was justified as a voluntary form of Affirmative Action.

Variations in the form of special admissions were held to be only matters of administrative detail and strategy which raised no question of principle and provided no basis for a determination of constitutionality. Such items should be left to the informed judgment of educators to handle and decide. On the much-disputed 16 percent figure, for example, the university's brief to the U.S. Supreme Court insisted that "the choice of a particular numerical goal [instead] of a range has no independent significance. Either represents nothing more than a policy judgment . . . [on] how much of the school's limited resources should be devoted to the service of one among its many missions."[37] In case the Court attributed greater importance to the particulars of the UCDMS program than UC counsel had urged, emphasis also was given to the voluntary nature of the activity. As counsel argued it, the Court could validate such a voluntary program without implying, much less affirming, that it consequently would be permissible for government to mandate such a program under Affirmative Action.

The primary concern of the many organizations that filed *amici* briefs on UC's side was to persuade the Court to uphold voluntary minority preferential admissions in principle and to allow higher education to implement it flexibly. In pursuing that objective, most of the briefs adopted the same strategy as UC counsel had, which led them to defend the Davis program both in detail and broadly as a reasonable example of special admissions policy and practice. This was, after all, the least complicated way of making the argument, in contrast to the complex position required for arguing that the specific UCDMS program might be invalid but that other more moderate forms of preferential admission were constitutional, and then having to spell out what features distinguished proper from improper special admissions. Moreover, the California Supreme Court had set its rejection of the Davis procedures in the context of a broad repudiation of any use of race in selective admissions. Hence, the pro-UC camp was understandably fearful that if the U.S. Supreme Court affirmed the illegality of the Davis program, it also might do so on sweeping grounds that would invalidate just about any kind of minority special program.

Still, a few briefs did move a bit in the direction of the alternate strategy noted above; namely, they distanced themselves somewhat from the distinctive specifics of the Davis program in an effort to encourage the Court not to condemn special admissions per se if it chose to invalidate UCDMS's procedures. The brief submitted by the University of Washington (the defendant in *De-*

Funis) noted, for example, that "[t]here are those who have criticized the University's [UC] admission policy challenged here as
inept."[38] Similarly, the *amicus* brief submitted by several private
universities acknowledged, with respect to UCDMS's set-aside of
16 places, "we question the wisdom of this aspect of the Davis
program. . . ."[39] Both briefs urged the Court, should it decide that
Davis's admissions practices were unconstitutional, to confine its
holding to that conclusion rather than to "cast into doubt" or to
negate "other more flexible approaches."[40]

Having been exposed to all these diverse arguments on racial
quotas and goals, the U.S. Supreme Court had a number of options
if it chose to give importance to that subject. It could endorse the
view of some that the Davis program was a "crude" form of preferential admissions, and follow Colvin's tack of isolating it as impermissible. On the other hand, it could endorse the view of others
that the Davis program was "forthright," in the sense that it candidly put up front and made visible what were essential attributes
of minority special admissions in practice, regardless of form. Under the first option, the Court could stand pat and not go much
further in delineating what were legitimate and illegitimate uses of
race in selective admissions, or it could elect to come to grips with
that broader issue. Under the second option, which treated the
Davis program as representative of the larger universe of special
admissions practices, the Court's determination of its constitutionality presumably would rest on grounds applicable to the larger
problem as well. Invalidation of UCDMS's practices, in short, could
be accomplished by either a narrow or broad Court opinion, but
validation necessarily would involve a broad opinion.

In deciding *Bakke*, each of the nine justices also had the choice
of engaging with or bypassing the semantical wrangle over goals
and quotas. There was much to be said for staying out of that
thicket. The clarity of the distinction between goals and quotas
seemed to hold up only in concept. Once in operation, a committed
pursuit of goal achievement—whether the commitment was voluntary or induced by government authority—appeared to result in
what most people would call a quota. As an NAACP administrator
stated it, "Goal or quota, it's really the same thing. Blacks and
Hispanic Americans have been discriminated against. We've got
to correct the imbalance, possibly at the expense of those who have
profited from the system."[41] In view of the difficulty in distinguish-

ing between the two in practice, there seemed little substantive basis for attempting to set the constitutional boundary by drawing a line between them, assigning legitimacy to goals and outlawing quotas. Still, the Court might find it advantageous for strategic reasons to make important use of the formal distinctions between goals and quotas. If so, the intense disagreement stirred by *Bakke* and *DeFunis* over the meaning of those terms provided the Court with an extended review of alternative ways to distinguish between the two.

7 Comparative Academic Qualifications

> [t]he fact that all the minority students admitted under the special program may have been qualified to study medicine does not significantly affect our analysis of the issues. . . . Bakke was also qualified for admission, as were hundreds, if not thousands of others who were also rejected. In this context the only relevant inquiry is whether one applicant was more qualified than another. . . . Bakke alleged that he and other non-minority applicants were *better* qualified for admission than the minority students accepted . . . and the question we must decide is whether the rejection of better qualified applicants on racial grounds is constitutional. (Majority opinion, California Supreme Court, *Bakke;* emphasis in original)

A concentration on the racial-quota question, especially if quotas were narrowly defined to cover only the intentional admission of unqualified minority applicants, permitted no more than a truncated examination of minority preferential admissions. Similarly, the admissions puzzle for heavily oversubscribed medical and law schools was mostly how to choose among thoroughly qualified candidates, not how to distinguish qualified from unqualified applicants. The question of the comparative qualifications of qualified candidates, therefore, was central to both the larger policy and legal issues and the selective admissions practices of the professional schools. Some aspirants had to be judged more qualified than others and awarded admission—but more qualified relative to what and to whom? What factors in addition to academic strength should be included, and how should they be assessed? And what place, if any, should be accorded race or minority-group membership in that comparative evaluation?

Academic Criteria and Tests

A disparity in academic credentials between minority and non-minority applicants underlay higher education's turn to minority special admissions. The differences between the two groups were marked. For law schools, a representative comparison showed that 20 percent of white but only 1 percent of black applicants had a 600-plus LSAT score together with a $B+$ or higher GPA, and that two-thirds of white applicants but less than one-quarter of Chicano applicants had a 500-plus LSAT in combination with a $C+$ or higher GPA.[1] For medical schools in the mid-1970s, the average score of black acceptees on the MCAT science section was 127 points lower than that of white acceptees and 80 points less than that of white applicants.[2] The group proportions scoring under 400 on MCAT-science were 44 percent of black applicants, 13 percent of other-minority applicants, and 8 percent of white applicants.[3] If the cutoff for medical school admissions had been set at a GPA of not less than 2.5 ($B-$ to $C+$), about three-fifths of black applicants would have been excluded, one-third of other-minority members, and one-quarter of whites.[4]

Much the same contrast held for all the standardized testing so prevalent at every level of schooling in America: minority students did not score as well, on the average, as white middle-class students. And the same pattern obtained for standardized aptitude and achievement tests used in employment; generally, the higher the requirement level, the lower the proportion of minority-group members defined into the availability pool.

Explanations varied. The controversial ones advanced theories of inherent biological inferiority in intelligence, a thesis explicitly repudiated by most geneticists, anthropologists, and other scientists and no longer considered credible by most of the lay public. The prevailing explanations proffered some variant of an environmental thesis: the effects of poverty, poorer health, unstable family life, discrimination, inferior educational resources, and so forth. At the extreme, the environmentalist position asserted that had today's middle-class white students changed childhood places with today's minorities, each would now perform at the other's level on standardized tests; that is, environmental factors were everything. More moderately formulated, the thesis urged that environment was the most important single explanatory factor, but it left room for group variations reflecting differing cultural traditions, such as the importance attached to pursuit of advanced formal education. Environmental equivalency of groups, in this view, would sharply reduce though not necessarily eliminate the differences in test-score distributions among groups. Historical evidence indicated, for example, that ethnic groups in America that initially were lower class and poorly assimilated and then experienced considerable upward mobility exhibited a marked rise in their average IQ over time.[5]

Acceptance of the environmentalist explanation for the comparatively poorer performance of minorities in higher education (as in other areas of activity) inevitably raised severe moral issues. On the one side, the professional schools' heavy reliance on academic criteria disproportionately screened out minorities from admission. On the other, minorities as a group scored less well on academic measures through no fault of their own but because of a multitude of disadvantages imposed on them by society. Taken together, these considerations became the basis for minority groups to assert a strong moral claim of unfair treatment, of denial of equal educational opportunity. It was not equitable, they argued, simply to evaluate applicants as they were; one also had to consider how they got that way and what their future promise might be. To acknowledge both the deprivation and the justice of the claim was one thing. To devise effective, fair, and publicly acceptable remedies, especially for the short term, was quite another. In short, this was another way of stating the central quandary posed by *Bakke* and *DeFunis*.

Leaving aside for the moment how heavily professional schools should weigh nonacademic factors in their evaluation of candidates, it was thoroughly appropriate for them to assign prominence to academic criteria. There surely was less question about the meaningfulness and pertinence of an applicant's academic record in the case of college graduates seeking entry to a professional school than of high school graduates applying to an undergraduate college. For medical schools there was the further consideration that certain science courses had to be completed in college because they were prerequisites for the more advanced science curriculum medical students had to take. Moreover, professional schools enrolled not simply students but future practitioners who had to pass external board or bar examinations as well as the school program in order to practice their profession. While high academic competence was no guarantee a person would be an effective practitioner, neither was low academic competence, and the strong academic achiever was by far the more certain to complete the school program effectively and to pass the external licensing examinations. Finally, a profession was desirous of strengthening its knowledge and skill base, as well as its standing and prestige, which gave it further incentive to recruit academically talented applicants.

Once it was granted that a reliance on academic criteria was reasonable (again, leaving open how much to weigh other factors), the question then was whether the tests used to measure academic competence were fair. To answer this question fully and to review all the contentions on it would require a volume of its own, heavily infused with educational psychology and crammed with statistical treatment of data. Instead, some highlight observations are presented here, drawn initially from the academic tests associated with college admissions because of their greater familiarity. The interpretations also apply to such professional school tests as the LSAT and MCAT, which will be directly commented on as well.*

The standardized tests so commonplace in today's college admissions traced back to individual intelligence tests for children devised by Professor Lewis Terman of Stanford in 1916. When America mobilized for war in spring 1917, the concept was applied by the U.S. Army in the form of an Alpha examination to screen recruits. A short mental test, it was effective in identifying men who subsequently made satisfactory officers and noncoms. In the postwar period, the concept was rapidly implemented and was used more and more widely for the testing of schoolchildren. At the college level, the College Entrance Examination Board was formed in 1900 in order to develop a common entrance test for a few eastern colleges. In 1947, the nonprofit Educational Testing Service (ETS) was created to assume the research and testing functions of the CEEB, the Carnegie Foundation for the Advancement of Teaching (National Teacher Examination), and the American Council on Education (Graduate Record Examination).[6] During the 1950s, especially in response to Russia's launching into space of *Sputnik I* and to a rising imbalance between entry demand and available

---

* The reader is reminded that the origin and operation of the LSAT were briefly discussed in the third chapter.

places, many higher education institutions upgraded their entrance standards and increasingly relied on the Scholastic Aptitude Test (SAT) and comparable devices to screen candidates. These tests were on their way to national dominance during this period, and their hegemony became well established by the 1970s; 81,000 SAT exams were given in 1951, 802,000 in 1961, and 1,400,000 in 1976.

As the country's biggest testing service, ETS devised tests that affected entry into colleges, graduate and professional schools, and more than fifty professions and vocations. In the words of its current president, William Turnbull, ETS became viewed "as the nation's gate-maker" and as a "cradle to grave arbiter of social mobility in America."[7] The fundamental purpose and utility of these tests was to provide evaluators with a single standard measurement by which to assess comparative qualifications of candidates relative to the characteristics deemed most relevant to successful handling of the position in question (medical school student, insurance actuary, urban planner, etc.). At root, then, the tests were democratizing and liberalizing devices in both intent and effect; they promoted the Jeffersonian concept of an open aristocracy of talent by resting the evaluation of ability on individual performance rather than on family status or wealth or on the personal biases of administrative personnel or interviewers. Students from widely varying schools and backgrounds could be appraised by the same measure, facilitating a comparative judgment that otherwise would have been extremely difficult and often impossible to make.

It is ironic, in view of the meritocratic and egalitarian implications of standardized testing, that such tests in recent years have come under fire as inegalitarian and "elitist," and that their harshest critics have been spokesmen for minorities and the poor. Both testing and the uses of test results have been attacked, through litigation and political activity. IQ tests, for example, were banned in the schools of New York City, Washington, D.C., and Philadelphia, discontinued in California since 1974, and they will be prohibited entirely if the NAACP wins a current lawsuit which claims that such tests are intrinsically biased against minorities. The potential explosiveness of the intersection of the race issue with testing is high; the ETS, for example, refused to make annual or regular public reports on test results by race. Its concern, presumably, was not to exacerbate the already intense public conflict over minority preferential admissions nor the more fitful quarrel over intelligence and race by revealing the extent of disparity in SAT scores between minorities and nonminorities.

The Validity of Tests

What these tests showed and did not show was not well understood by the public, and the polemics surrounding the issue only added to the confusion. The tests did not measure "pure aptitude" (the meaning of which was itself a subject of disagreement) in the sense of the test taker's genetic endowment. Indeed, a person's native potential at birth could never be measured by any later test score. What the tests did reveal was a person's level of ability on certain things at the time the test was taken. On tests designed for applicants to college or postcollege professional schools, the "certain things" tested for were the abilities and skills needed to succeed in the school program. Within that compass, the SAT, LSAT, and MCAT worked well; that is, they measured the kinds of developed talents that the respective higher education units wanted in their students.

The PFYA (predicted first-year average), a measure used by UWLS and most law schools, provided a representative illustration of the broad class of academic indicators.[8] Each law school had its own formula for weighing the LSAT (law school aptitude test) and GPA (undergraduate grade-point average) of its applicants; the result was to produce a PFYA for each candidate. The formula derived from thorough statistical analysis of the accuracy of the predictors in the last few years at the particular school; it then was applied to predict the likely school performance of applicants in the upcoming year, based on each applicant's combination of LSAT and GPA scores.

The prediction (the P of PFYA) was, of necessity, only a statement of probability and hence was imperfect. For all law schools taken as a whole, the average correlation coefficient between the particular PFYA formulas used and the academic performance of first-year students was .45 (i.e., the measure accounted for about 20 percent of the variation in school performance). The range for the schools was mostly between .3 (9 percent of the variation) to .5 (25 percent) with some schools having as high as .7 (50 percent). An explanation of what a .45 correlation coefficient meant follows.

If the PFYA measure had no relationship to the students' first-year academic performance, both high-PFYA and low-PFYA students would be distributed randomly in the course grades they earned by the close of the first year; as many would exhibit low grades as high grades. At a .45 correlation level, however, a disproportionately high fraction of the top PFYA group would reappear within the ranks of those who earned the top grades, and a comparably disproportionate high fraction of the lowest PFYA group would turn up among those with the lowest grades. The higher the correlation coefficient (the closer to 1.0), the greater the predictive validity of the measure and the greater the disproportions in the direction noted in this example. A 1.0 correlation would index a perfect prediction; that is, the rank order of students in course grades would be exactly the same as that on PFYA.

Two other statistical refinements have to be understood to appreciate the usefulness of the PFYA device for comparative evaluations of law school applicants. One, termed "range restrictions," operates as follows: There is a strong correlation, for example, between the height and weight of human beings; on the average, shorter persons weigh less than taller persons. The correlation is stronger, however, for a population with a wide range of dissimilar heights (say, from 5'6" to 6'2") than with a narrow range of similar heights (say, from 5'6" to 5'7"). This meant, with respect to school admissions, that the predictive power of the PFYA was greater when evaluating the total applicant pool than just the enrollees, whose PFYA range would be much narrower. (The .45 correlation coefficient reported earlier was for enrollees, and hence the predictive value of the PFYA was considerably stronger than .45 when applied to the entire applicant pool.) Specifically, then, when there were large PFYA differences between two applicant populations, it could be predicted with confidence that the high-PFYA group was much more likely to do well in law school than the low-PFYA group.

The other statistical refinement relates to the "margin of error" or the "standard error of measurement." Say, for example, that the measurement error for the SAT-verbal section was 32 points. This meant that if a classroom of students with true scores of 500 took the test, 96 percent of them would score within 64 points, plus or minus, of 500 (i.e., from 436 to 564), with most of them much closer to the 500 mark than to either 436 or 564. In recognition of this "margin of error" phenomenon, ETS officials offered the rough rule of thumb that not too much distinction should be drawn between two students unless their difference in SAT scores was 60 points or more. Suppose, however, there were two large groups of applicants, and all that was known about them was that each of the members of group A had a 550 LSAT (or SAT) score, whereas those in group B had a 500 LSAT score. Who should be admitted, assuming that academic criteria were entirely controlling? The members of group A should be chosen because the chances were higher that their true scores were better than those in group B. Statistically, it was a matter of playing the percentages: some mistakes on individual applicants would be made, but an even higher rate of mistakes would occur if group B members were chosen instead; over the long run, the percentages would work in favor of choosing group A members.[9]

As an imperfect predictor, the PFYA could not be used to estimate with certainty the performance of every individual in each PFYA-ranked group. For example, some enrollees with high PFYAs would actually place in the low end of the class on grades, some low-PFYA students in the top tier of academic achievers. The likely proportion of "misperformers" in each group, but not the specific individuals, could be predicted by application of the PFYA. Similarly, the utility of the PFYA was much reduced for discriminating among applicants with comparable scores. These limits on what the PFYA could not predict were more than offset, however, by the value of what it could predict. The usefulness of the PFYA was established by the practical consideration that it estimated subsequent academic performance of applicants far better than any other available alternative. No other measure, whether dealing with cognitive or noncognitive factors, did that job anywhere near as reliably.

What did it mean, then, when a group scored relatively poorly on the LSAT or MCAT and had relatively low GPAs in undergraduate courses? According to the prevailing explanation, low scores revealed nothing about genuine aptitude and much about adverse environmental factors; they reflected the inadequacies of past op-

portunities to develop the academic skills emphasized in the test.*
Nevertheless, the educational deficiencies that marked the low-
scoring applicants' past were ineradicable facts not subject now to
alteration. And since the academic skills needed were of a kind
usually acquired and strengthened only over time, such as reading
comprehension and reasoning ability, how well were these applicants likely to do in the near future as students in the school?

Minorities, Tests, and School Performance

In the light of the foregoing discussion of predictive value of academic measures for professional school admission decisions, the
practice employed by UWLS and UCDMS in imposing an academic
criterion to establish a cutoff level for nonminority applicants under regular admissions programs should be more readily understandable. Each institution was playing the odds in the statistical
sense earlier explained: for UWLS, the odds that applicants with
a PFYA of 74.5 or higher were, as a group, likely to do better as
students than those with a lower PFYA; for UCDMS, the same
estimates of probability for applicants above and below the line set
by a 2.5 GPA.

Minority-group members considered under special admissions
were exempted from the cutoff levels set for other applicants. Was
this because the traditional academic measures were of significantly less predictive value for estimating their probable school performance? The answer, well researched and validated repeatedly,
was emphatically and unequivocally in the negative: the academic
indicators predicted as effectively for minorities as for nonminorities; indeed, if they erred, it was on the side of overestimating the
likely level of academic achievement of minorities. Hence it followed, despite the conspicuous absence of public systematic data
treating the school performance record of minority special admittees, that as a group they would be expected to cluster disproportionately in the lower ranks of GPA because they were disproportionately in the lower tiers of academic credentials when admitted.

---

* Much the same observation was made, it might be noted, to explain
the steady decline over the past ten years of general achievement levels
and scholastic test scores of schoolchildren all around the country.
Most of the proposed remedies moved in the direction of injecting
more rigor in the school curriculum and imposing minimum competency levels for graduation.

The requisite information on minorities in medicine was both scant and not very helpful in permitting a close appraisal of school performance. The MCAT predicted best for a student's first two years in medical school, during which basic science courses were stressed, and was much less effective in estimating student performance in the clinical training constituting the final two school years. (The curricula and teaching methods in law schools, in contrast, were primarily nonclinical.) Historically, medical schools had low attrition rates; more than 95 percent of entering medical students eventually received the M.D. degree. Not all schools required students to pass the National Board Examinations as a condition of securing their M.D. degree and, in any event, the national standard set by the exams was low. Moreover, the standard was "further lowered in recent years; National Board grades [were] normalized for each year's population, and so the absolute norm for passing [was] necessarily lowered by any nationwide increase in admission of students with substandard academic qualifications."[10]

No new data on minority performance in medical schools were contained in the *amici* briefs submitted on *Bakke*; a handful of earlier published studies were cited as the information base. The general pattern of their findings was similar. Compared with nonminority students, minorities had a somewhat higher attrition rate, and a considerably higher proportion of them took three years to complete the two-year science curriculum. The major study relied on showed an attrition rate for blacks triple that for whites among entrants in 1970 (about 5.0 percent compared with 1.7 percent) and in 1971 (about 7.5 to 2.5 percent). The same study indicated that one in six black entrants in 1970 and one in ten in 1971 repeated all or a part of the year's science courses, in contrast to less than one in a hundred for whites. In absolute numbers, there were more black than white repeaters, although there were sixteen white entrants for every black entrant. Over 95 percent of whites were promoted with their class, together with about 80 percent of blacks; most of the balance of the black entrants had decelerated the rate of their program completion, in effect taking a five-year rather than a four-year M.D. degree.[11]

Attrition rates for minority students who entered law school from 1971 through 1975 were revealed in the *amicus* brief submitted in *Bakke* by the Association of American Law Schools. For the five-year period overall, the rate for minorities was about double that for nonminorities, 19 percent to 10 percent;* annually, minority attrition ranged from 16 to 23 percent, that of nonminorities from 9 to 13 percent.[12] At Boalt (the law school of UC Berkeley), where special admissions was conducted with considerable care, the minority attrition rate for that same five-year period was about 18 percent.[13]

On state bar examinations, national statistics on pass/fail rates were not available by race or ethnic group. Most states, including all the big ones except New York, participated in the Multistate Bar Examination, a nationwide multiple-choice exam that tested knowledge of six areas of law. It was known, however, that LSAT scores correlated more strongly with bar-passing rates than with law school graduation rates. The failure rate of minorities was much higher for the bar than for law school, and the difference in passing rates between minorities and nonminorities was far greater for the bar than for completion of law school.[14]

In New York, for example, state bar examination data became publicly available after five black law school graduates who failed the exam claimed in a petition to the state's highest court, which had jurisdiction over the tests, that the tests, although not intended to be racially discriminatory, had a discriminatory impact on minorities. From 1969 to 1975, the petitioners said, only 18 percent (26 of 148) of black students who took the bar exam in the Fourth Department passed, compared to a statewide passing rate of 72 percent for all applicants. Citing specific figures by school based on their own survey, the student petitioners noted that for the July 1975 bar exam only 7 of 13 blacks from the Columbia University Law School passed, 5 of 9 from New York University, 6 of 15 from Harvard, and at the extreme, none of 8 from Brooklyn Law School.[15] It was thought likely, in response to this petition and for other reasons, that New York might decide to adopt the Multistate Bar Examination instead of continuing to devise its own exams.

---

* The attrition rate was measured by comparing the second-year total minority enrollment with that of the preceding first year; it did not include, therefore, attrition that occurred during the course of the second year or the third year. A reasonable estimate would be that about 6 percent of second-year minority students did not re-enroll as third-year students; this meant that another 5 percent of minority admittees failed to complete the law school program. Hence the attrition rate was about one in four.

In California, relevant data for the early 1970s became a matter of public record because of legislative concern about high failure rates on the state bar exam of minority graduates of the four state law schools (Boalt, Davis, Hastings, and Los Angeles), all part of the University of California system.[16] Among those taking the bar exam for the first time, the overall passing rate was 78 percent (2010 of 2588) but only 36 percent (100 of 277) for minorities. School rates varied greatly: Boalt had the highest passing rates for both groups (87 percent for all graduates and 49 percent for minorities), while at Davis and Los Angeles about three-quarters of all graduates and from one-quarter to one-third of minority graduates passed. After retaking the exams one or more times, minorities upped their eventual passing rate to 39 percent (UCLA) and 53 percent (UC Davis).

The academic performance of minorities at Boalt, which was unusually strong compared with the other state law schools, was described as follows in an *amicus* brief by the deans of the University of California's four law schools filed in support of the university's petition to the U.S. Supreme Court to consent to hear *Bakke*.

> The students within the group specially admitted do have predicted grade point averages below almost all of those with whom they would have to compete in the absence of the program. And, when admitted and enrolled, they do tend to cluster toward the lower part of the class. The range of possible error in the predictor as applied to individual cases is such that some of them, it is impossible to predict which in advance, will fall into academic difficulty or fail to pass the bar. On the other hand, most do satisfactory work and a number of them outperform regular admissions students whose records appeared much better.[17]

In contrast to this rather reassuring description, there was considerable basis for concern in the disparity between the number of minorities initially enrolled in the California public law schools and the number actually admitted to the practice of law. If UCLA's figures were used, and the national minority attrition rate of 25 percent factored in, the loss rate went about as follows: for every 100 minorities admitted, 25 did not complete law school and 46 of the remaining 75 failed the bar exam, which left only 29 of the original 100 who succeeded.* For Boalt, which had a minority attrition rate of about 18 percent and for which the eventual bar-passing rate of minorities was not reported, it could reasonably be estimated that about 60 of the original 100 succeeded. The Office of Legislative Analyst, which investigated the matter for the legislature, expressed particular worry over the bar exam failure rates at Davis and Los Angeles. Since the state bar had concluded on the basis of careful study that the bar exams were not biased against minorities, the Legislative Analyst's recommendations stressed the need for strengthening the support services for minority students in the two law schools.

Attacking the Tests

In the absence of publicly available racial breakdowns of standardized test scores, educators estimated that whites averaged more than 100 points higher on the SAT and similar tests than minorities.[18] In response, some minority spokesmen and others frontally attacked traditional testing as "culturally biased" and "inherently racist." Some drew the inference that the tests were constructed in such a way as to make minorities do poorly on them, and hence they concluded that the minority-nonminority differences in average scores proved nothing except the bias of the tests themselves. To demonstrate that contention a black psychology professor, Robert L. Williams, developed a test called BITCH (Black Intelligence Test Counterbalanced for Honkies; later renamed Black Intelligence Test of Cultural Homogeneity).† It consisted of multiple-choice questions stressing black argot: Blood means (a) a vampire, (b) a dependent individual, (c) an injured person, (d) a brother of color. When administered in the early 1970s, the test typically resulted in a bimodal distribution, with almost all blacks scoring higher than whites.

The BITCH test demonstrated great cleverness, but what else it demonstrated, in view of its concentration on ghetto slang vocabulary, was open to dispute. Professor Williams claimed that "a person who scores well on the test has demonstrated an ability to cope

---

* UCLA law school, it may be recalled from the last chapter, was described by its dean as operating a quotalike minority admissions program in the early 1970s.
† In keeping with the wit displayed in the test's concept and execution, Professor Williams named its later variants the S.O.B. test.

in one environment and, by extension, shows that he can cope and learn in any environment." But a rather different interpretation could be placed on the test, as suggested by the rejoinder of a black journalist, William Raspberry:

> . . . it strikes me that coping involves a good deal more than learning slang. . . . It is no solution to devise a test whose only virtue is that inner-city blacks can pass it more easily than whites. Unless, of course, the idea is to certify applicants as residents in the inner-city ghetto.

The journalist continued by deploring both the misuse of tests (attempting to measure qualifications not needed for the position being applied for) and the excessive reliance on tests as "keepers of the gate to the decent colleges, the preferred professions, the better jobs." He observed, however, that as long as tests "hold such sway we'd better teach our kids to pass them." He concluded by endorsing the following judgment of a minority educator:

> To dismiss mathematics and reading achievement test scores as irrelevant to black children is to do these children a disservice. It is like responding to a fire by putting out the alarm instead of the fire.[19]

If the BITCH test was intended to prove that the inherent aptitude of blacks was greater than their standardized test scores implied, it was simply fighting one wrong inference with another. The tests, to underscore the point again, measured current ability in specific areas and not native aptitude; and they did that reasonably well or, in any event, better than any other available alternative. To accuse the tests of being "culturally biased" because of the large divergence of average scores between minorities and nonminorities was, at bottom, to blame the messenger for the unhappy message.

To be effective in its purpose, a test of education qualifications was supposed to be more difficult for educationally disadvantaged than for advantaged persons. Low scores by minorities were the result of their unequal educational opportunities, broadly defined, which the tests appropriately reflected. For example, it made little sense to brand the tests as culturally biased because they stressed reading ability. Rather, if there was cultural bias, it was the "bias" resulting from a society that stressed reading ability and in which reading was a skill developed in school and nurtured at home, and hence related to educational and economic opportunity.

The tests relied on by professional schools in evaluating applicants measured various kinds of "learned ability" (studentship skills) developed over many years of past schooling. These were the skills that medical and law schools—and they were *schools*—assumed its students possessed and would apply effectively to complete a demanding program of study. It was highly misleading to suggest, therefore, that LSAT and MCAT scores were not relevant to appraising minority applicants and their *academic* promise. The evidence (incomplete as it was) was decisively in the other direction, and it provided no basis for the hope or assumption that most applicants whose previous adverse environments had left them with thinly developed studentship skills nevertheless would be able to pick them up quickly after entering medical or law school.

It followed that the relative academic qualifications of groups of applicants could be addressed confidently, especially when those groups greatly differed in their average test scores. Specifically, it was both accurate and realistic to characterize minority applicants, as a group, as markedly less qualified *academically* than nonminorities. And it was no less realistic to acknowledge that, as with any group having comparable low scores, minorities would be expected to do relatively poorer in school and on the postgraduation external licensing examination.

Nevertheless, just because comparative academic qualifications could be determined with some precision, it did not follow that admission decisions should turn solely or even primarily on the use of such measures. Even when academic criteria were given heavy emphasis, the limits and imperfections of the standard academic indicators had to be kept in mind; other factors, although not well understood and to date even less capable of measurement, also shaped academic performance. Moreover, the data on test scores were often misused by overliteral interpretation of small differences in scores as "proof" of better academic credentials or capabilities. Most important, the availability of good measures of academic ability said nothing by itself about how determinative academic criteria should be for the admissions judgment. What else should be included, and what weight should be assigned these other factors, remained an open and hotly disputed question.

A Better Matching of Minority Students and Schools?

One important concern not given adequate attention in either the *Bakke* or *DeFunis* controversy was the closeness of fit between the academic credentials of minority students and the academic standards of the particular school in which they enrolled. This neglect was curious because the relevance of this factor to the central issue was direct and obvious. After all, it was reasonable to suppose that the problems posed for a professional school by academically underqualified minority students were a function in part of how underqualified they were, and that in turn depended on the size of the difference in average scores between its minority and nonminority entrants. The closer the match in academic credentials, presumably the more moderate the problems; the greater the mismatch, the more severe the problems for both the minority students and the institution. For example, minority persons who had an average LSAT score of 470 could be enrolled in a law school whose white entrants averaged 525 or in another law school where the average was 670. An academic disparity between the groups was present in either case, but the first situation was close to a match, whereas the second represented a severe mismatch.

Professor Thomas Sowell, a black economist at UCLA, was a leading exponent of the argument that excessive mismatching of minority students and higher education institutions aggravated the difficulties associated with recruiting and enrolling minority students through "special" rather than regular admissions.[20] Although his argument dealt largely with college admissions, its logic was no less applicable to professional school admissions. In Sowell's view, the push for increased minority enrollment too often resulted in a mismatching upward—that is, many minority students entered institutions geared to students with much stronger academic qualifications. This mismatch was most pronounced for the prestige colleges and universities (though present elsewhere as well), which for a variety of reasons enrolled sizable numbers of minority students.

The mismatch of student ability to institutional norms was, as Sowell saw it, systematic and not accidental, because it proceeded from deliberate policy. Many advocates of minority advancement shared the assumption that it was desirable for prestige units to have significant numbers of minority students, even if they were greatly underqualified and the institution was required to make "special" accommodations for them, such as separate admissions criteria or revised course loads and curricula. The universities themselves embraced the same assumption; they were eager to attract minority students—but not nonminority students—who did not meet the usual academic standards. Philanthropic foundations and the government promoted the same bias, often reserving special training and financial assistance for those with academically substandard performances in high school or college.

Because Sowell's argument was easy to mishear or misinterpret, it would be useful to restate it at this point. Although on the average minority students were academically underqualified when compared to white students, the members of each group exhibited a wide range of test scores, with considerable overlap. Some minorities had good test scores and some nonminorities had mediocre test scores. For any specific school, the magnitude of the disparity in academic credentials between its minority and nonminority enrollees could be greater or less than the national average, depending upon the particular mix of students it admitted. It was Sowell's contention that because of a mismatching upward, too many minority students were located at the "wrong" schools, that is, at schools whose high academic standards were too distant from their present academic capabilities.

For example, probably most of the minority students in a prestige higher education unit had academic records better than the national average for minorities and nonminorities alike; but their records often were well below the average of the nonminority students at that institution, who came mostly from the top tier of all students. (At UC Berkeley's law school, for instance, the median LSAT score for enrolled minorities was near 575, which was about the upper 30 percent level, but that for white entrants was 700, which was the top 3 percent.) Hence these minority students were "underqualified" only because of the school they were at, not by national standards. Furthermore, the problem of "underqualified students" at such places became virtually synonymous with the presence of minority students because those schools rejected nearly all academically underqualified nonminority applicants. Had these minority students located at schools with a broader cross section of nonminorities, they would have been as fully qualified as their fellow students.

Why, Sowell bluntly asked, should minority students be channeled to schools for which they were underprepared in order to get slower-paced curricula and remedial work and, in general, to be treated as less than adequate and as requiring a range of special treatment and services? Rather, he urged, the emphasis should be much more on matching student and institution, so that minority students could perform positively in institutions whose normal academic standards they already met. Sowell was quite aware that the "mismatch policy" reflected in large part well-meaning commitments on behalf of minority gains. But good intentions, whether stemming from moral imperatives, racial guilt, or desire to remedy past injustice, were no offset to bad policy. In the professor's judgment, the harm of the unintended effects of mismatching far outweighed whatever its intended benefits achieved. Perhaps the major damage was the inadvertent reinforcement of the stereotypes of minorities as incapable of "making it" by the usual rules of the game and, instead, requiring preferential treatment.

Another important benefit would follow from reduction of the rate of upward mismatching. First-class schools would have greater incentive to search earlier and more diligently for high-quality minority students who were fully qualified for their level of instruction but who, in the absence of such efforts, settled for enrolling in mediocre or poor colleges whose standards were below their abilities. As a result, many able minority students never got to connect with the kind of first-quality institutions their talents merited. At the outset of the 1972–73 year, for example, 75 percent of black students classified as having medium ability (measured by composite test scores) and 52 percent of those with high ability were attending relatively unselective undergraduate institutions in which the average academic ability level of the entering freshman class was lower than theirs; the counterpart figures for white students were, respectively, 55 and 44 percent.[21]

In sum, the argument was that the common-sense standard used for nonminorities also should be applied to minority students: the academic qualifications of the applicant should be roughly matched to the academic norms of the institution. Where a reasonably close fit obtained, the acceptance of minority applicants could be accomplished mostly or entirely by regular admissions; where mismatching prevailed, the route of entry for minorities became special admissions. If Sowell's prescription were followed, its main effect at present and for the foreseeable future would be to distribute minority enrollees away from the prestigious professional schools and concentrate them more in the less selective ones. In 1975, for example, the 12 most selective law schools enrolled 1250 minority students, some 15 percent of the national total. Had those schools insisted on admitting only those minority students whose academic scores exactly matched those of their white admittees, they would have enrolled little better than a token number of minorities.[22]

The following account of practices at Stanford's law school, which moved in the direction of reducing mismatch, provides a less extreme illustration of what would ensue. At Stanford, the number of minority admittees varied each year, and, as it happened, the number of black applicants accepted by the school fell from 26 in 1975 to 17 in 1977. What explained the drop? The first reason, according to the faculty chairman of the admissions committee, was that the school was not admitting students "with as weak records" as it did during the late 1960s and early '70s. "We dug deep [then] to get minority students. We're not digging as deep now." He added that in the past, there was often a "huge gap" between minority and white students, which "created problems for everybody." The second reason offered by the admissions committee chairman related to trends among nonminority students. Stanford's recent procedure was to take the predicted GPA of the 10 lowest nonminority admittees of the previous year and then "substantially admit any minority student within three-tenths of that grade point average." As the predicted GPA of the 10 lowest whites went up in 1976 and 1977, fewer minority applicants were able to meet the rising minimum standard.[23]

If a larger proportion of enrolled minorities were located in the less selective schools, new sources of funding would have to be found to provide the financial assistance needed by these students. The chances of getting better jobs might also be reduced for minority graduates, although mere graduation from an elite school gave no assurance of securing a good job. "Many placement officers [in law schools] admit privately," commented a spokesman for the American Bar Association in late 1977, "that they are having trouble placing their 'average' and 'marginal' black students, particularly since many of them were specially admitted. They simply do not have the same quality academic records the white students do."[24]

How would the promotion of a closer academic match between

minority students and schools affect the total number of minority admissions? The answer is not clear. A cutback of special admissions programs likely would reduce the number of minority applicants because the programs served to stimulate minority applications and, perhaps, to increase the number who were accepted. However, effective implementation of a strategy of matching presupposed a more coordinated national effort by the professional schools, including better school placement for academically able minority students—and these new activities also would be likely to stimulate interest among minorities. Moreover, there remained possibilities worth exploring that would enable students with modest academic qualifications who demonstrated high academic competence in a less selective professional school to transfer to, and complete their program at, a more selective school.

Overall, then, the "mismatch" thesis and the remedy it proposes are obviously of direct relevance to any search for alternate admissions processes. As such, it warrants serious and close review. Its core virtue is its emphasis on enrolling minorities mostly through regular rather than special admissions, which would result in greatly reducing the whole range of problems associated with minority preferential admissions. Its chief deficiency is its assignment of the large majority of minority students, because of their weaker academic credentials relative to whites, to less prestigious professional schools. It is a measure of the extraordinary sensitivity attaching to the race issue that no serious public discussion of the mismatch thesis has been undertaken because the deficiency just noted has been deemed an unacceptable outcome no matter what the offsetting benefits might be.

The political vulnerability of the mismatch argument is all too evident: it is open to attack as offensive to minorities and as an act of selfishness by prestige universities. Because of this vulnerability, the argument is not likely to be considered on its merits but to be discounted and dismissed as an arrogant claim put forward by "elitist" schools to protect their status, to excuse their lesser efforts on behalf of minority advancement, and to shoulder onto others the burden of doing what is necessary to promote minority gains. So cavalier a treatment of what is a genuine policy alternative is both odd and unfortunate. It is odd because a remedy that is seen as fatally offensive proposes nothing more than to treat minority applicants in the manner of nonminority applicants, that is, it simply encourages minorities to apply to schools that would accept rather than reject similarly qualified whites. And it is unfortunate because the argument represents a fresh way of seeing an important part of the problem, and unconventional approaches to *Bakke* and *DeFunis* disputes are in no danger of oversupply.

Taking Race into Account for a Fairer Evaluation of Minority Academic Qualifications

In both principle and practice, there was little justification for a professional school to assign the same meaning to academic scores regardless of the background of the applicant. Suppose, to take an obvious example, two candidates had comparable academic qualifications, but one had worked on a job twenty hours a week and full-time every summer throughout the four college years and the other had not taken any employment during that time. It would be reasonable for a school to take that difference into account in making a more refined interpretation of the comparative academic credentials of the two; indeed, many would argue that it would be unreasonable or unfair for the school not to do so. Plainly, a school's reliance on the predictive value of academic indicators presents no bar to its use of such additional information. Academic measures are understood to be imperfect predictors, which means that the actual school performance of some admittees will deviate significantly from what has been predicted for them. And, as previously noted, the helpfulness of test scores in estimating probable academic achievement is greatly reduced when applied to a population with a limited range of scores.

In his *DeFunis* opinion, Justice William O. Douglas eloquently endorsed the idea that a fair appraisal of candidates required attention to their background:

> The Equal Protection Clause did not enact a requirement that law schools employ as the sole criterion for admissions a formula based upon the LSAT and undergraduate grades, nor does it proscribe law schools from evaluating an applicant's prior achievements in light of the barriers that he had to overcome. A Black applicant who pulled himself out of the ghetto into a junior college may thereby demonstrate a level of motivation, perseverance and ability that would lead a fairminded admissions committee to conclude that he shows more promise for law study than the son of a rich alumnus who achieved better grades at Harvard.

That applicant would not be offered admission because he is Black, but because as an individual he has shown he has the potential, while the Harvard man may have taken less advantage of the vastly superior opportunities offered him. Because of the weight of the prior handicaps, that Black applicant may not realize his full potential in the first year of law school, or even in the full three years, but in the long pull of a legal career his achievements may far outstrip those of his classmates whose earlier records appeared superior by conventional criteria.

There is currently no test available to the admissions committee that can predict such possibilities with assurance, but the committee may nevertheless seek to gauge it as best as it can, and weigh this factor in its decisions.

As Justice Douglas formulated it, however, an admissions committee's consideration of the personal backgrounds of applicants was only partly for the purpose of clarifying or correcting their test scores; it also was to give greater emphasis to background factors and potential for postdegree achievements, and less to test scores and expected school performance. What he appeared to be urging, therefore, was both a significant supplement and a refinement of academic criteria in the admissions review process.

Much the same dual focus marked the core argument advanced by the Department of Justice in its *amicus* brief on *Bakke*. The department's broad position was that consideration of an applicant's past and present circumstances was necessary for fair assessment of candidates. Applied to *Bakke* and minorities, this position meant that "in order fairly to compare minority and non-minority applicants," the Davis medical school could—indeed, should—"tak[e] race into account."[25] "[R]ace may be useful to provide more complete information about the meaning of credentials that, standing by themselves, do not fully reveal the applicant's abilities and potential."[26] "[C]onsideration of the race of professional school applicants . . . [enables the schools to] adjust for differences in credentials that may be caused by race but have little or nothing to do with the ability to succeed."[27] Although the Justice Department appeared to mean academic qualifications when it referred to "credentials," it had something in addition to, or other than, school performance in mind when it spoke of an applicant's "abilities and potential" and "ability to succeed."

Broadly speaking, what both Justice Douglas and the Justice Department were singling out for disapproval was the tendency of too many professional schools—law schools perhaps more than medical schools, but evident in both—to rest their admissions decisions solely or primarily on test-score results, treating that partial evidence as a valid substitute for faculty judgment of the larger and more complex package of relevant applicant characteristics. It was within that context that their shared prescription of "pay less attention to raw test scores" had to be understood. Otherwise, their argument could be misheard as advocating that little attention should be paid to academic criteria in general, or to the traditional academic measures relied on in particular. Both had incentives to take the latter position, Justice Douglas because he mistrusted the uses made of standardized testing and the Department of Justice because it was keenly aware that minority applicants were uncompetitive with whites with respect to academic credentials. Yet neither chose to deny the importance of academic criteria and measures, even as they urged avoidance of excessive dependence on them.

It was highly instructive, in this regard, to note that in the examples presented in their arguments for consideration of background factors, the hypothesized differences in academic credentials between the applicants were relatively modest. On the LSAT, for instance, Justice Douglas conceded that in its predictive value it did "seem to do better than chance. But [the tests] do not have the value that their deceptively precise scoring system suggests." Still, Douglas stated without qualification:

> The school can safely conclude that the applicant with a score of 750 should be admitted before one with a score of 500. The problem is that in many cases the choice will be between 643 and 602 or 574 and 528. The numbers create an illusion of difference tending to overwhelm other factors.

Douglas's two examples involved test-score disparities of 41 and 46 points. Recall, however, that much larger differences characterized *DeFunis*. At least ten of the minority admittees to UWLS in 1971 had a PFYA under 71, which represented a combination of scores such as 469 on the LSAT and a 2.7 GPA (this resulted in a PFYA of 70.2). In contrast, DeFunis—along with two-thirds of the other white applicants who also had a PFYA between 76.0 and 76.9—was rejected, despite an LSAT of 582 and a GPA of 3.7.

The Justice Department, in a draft brief, had no difficulty in resolving a situation in which a disadvantaged black applicant and an advantaged middle-class white applicant had the same academic credentials. "It would obviously be reasonable," the department commented, "to conclude that . . . [the] black applicant . . . has shown more motivation and determination to succeed . . . and is therefore more deserving of admission."[28] But when the department went on to discuss a tougher choice that was closer to the actual problem facing schools in reviewing minority applicants, it only raised questions and provided no answers.

> [What should happen] when the admissions committee must choose between a disadvantaged minority applicant with a 3.0 [B] average and a [middle-class] white applicant with a 3.5 [B+ to A−] average? It may be fair to conclude that the minority applicant has shown great determination and ability to overcome hurdles placed in his path. But what weight should the admissions committee give to this in determining which of the two to admit?[29]

When the brief appeared in its final form, however, the example was recast to help make the point that significant differences in background factors among applicants should be considered to evaluate test-score differences more accurately, and that race was one of those background factors that could (and should) be taken into account.

> A grade point average of 2.6 [B−] produced by a minority applicant may indicate every bit as much potential to be a physician as a 3.0 [B] average by a white applicant, because the minority applicant has demonstrated not only the ability to succeed in obtaining grades but also the determination and ability to overcome non-academic hurdles. The evaluation of the meaning of the 2.6 average is assisted by cognizance of color.[30]

The contrast in academic credentials in *Bakke* was far greater than the examples put forward by the Justice Department. For 1973 admission to UCDMS, regular admittees averaged a 3.5 (B+ to A−) GPA and special admittees 2.6 (B−); on the MCAT-science they averaged, respectively, 83rd and 35th percentile and on MCAT-verbal, 81st and 46th percentile. Allan Bakke's GPA, it may be recalled, was the same as, and his MCAT scores were stronger than, the average for regular admittees. For all medical schools in 1975–76, the average MCAT-science score of black admittees was 127 points lower than that of white admittees, 80 points less than that of white applicants, and 52 points below that of rejected white applicants.[31]

It surely was no accident that Justice Douglas and the Department of Justice chose the examples they did to illustrate how academic credentials could appropriately be "adjusted" or "reevaluated" in recognition of background differences among applicants. The former's examples involved differences in academic qualifications between applicants that were much less than what obtained in *DeFunis,* and the latter's examples did likewise vis-à-vis both *Bakke* and *DeFunis.* It was reasonable to infer, therefore, that the reach of their thesis—major disparities in applicant background could counterbalance disparities in academic scores—was limited: it applied only when the academic credentials of the competing applicants were not too dissimilar. Because of this limiting condition, fewer minority students would be admitted under this standard than were being enrolled through special admissions, even if lower academic credentials were "corrected" solely for minority applicants rather than for all applicants whose background was disadvantaged.

Advocates of minority preferential admissions had more fundamental reasons to oppose the standard under discussion than simply dissatisfaction with its practical effects. The context for Justice Douglas's advocacy of the thesis was his insistence that admissions decisions had to be "racially neutral." Thus, immediately after Douglas discussed why it would be fair to admit the black applicant from a ghetto background over the Harvard man (as quoted earlier in this chapter), he continued:

> Such a policy would not be limited to Blacks, or Chicanos or Filipinos or American Indians, although undoubtedly groups such as these may in practice be the principal beneficiaries of it. But a poor Appalachian white, or a second-generation Chinese in San Francisco, or some other American whose lineage is so diverse as to defy ethnic labels, may demonstrate similar potential and thus be accorded favorable consideration by the [admissions] committee.
>
> The difference between such a policy and the one presented by this case is that the committee would be making decisions on the basis of individual attributes, rather than according a preference solely on the basis of race.

Douglas faulted UWLS precisely because of its failure to rest its admission of minorities on the basis of a review of the "individual attributes" of the candidates:

> [A]lthough the [admissions] committee did consider other information in the files of all applicants, the law school has made no effort to show that it was because of these additional factors that it admitted minority applicants who would otherwise have been rejected. To the contrary, the school appears to have conceded that by its own assessment—taking all factors into account—it admitted minority applicants who would have been rejected had they been white. We have no choice but to evaluate the law school's case as it has [been] made.

As Justice Douglas applied the standard he put forward in *De-Funis*, it was not only antithetical to preferential admissions based on race categories but also to any comparable preference, even for those with disadvantaged backgrounds. At bottom, his argument had nothing to do with "preference" as that term is ordinarily used and understood. Rather, it implicitly reaffirmed that law schools should admit the "best qualified" applicants by comparing individual applicants, and then called upon the schools to make that determination by "put[ting] more effort into assessing each individual than is required when LSAT scores and undergraduate grades dominate the selection process." In particular, Douglas urged, information on the personal background of applicants should be considered to facilitate more realistic appraisals of academic credentials and career promise. The purpose of this fuller and more judgmental inquiry was to make the evaluation of candidates fairer and to give greater assurance that the genuinely "best qualified" were selected, not to extend "preference" to any group.

The Justice Department's brief was an uneasy hybrid of themes, in part supportive of Douglas's standard and in part seeking to wed it to a more explicit emphasis on race.* The factor of race should be considered in selective admissions evaluations of applicants, the department argued, because its inclusion "enhance[d] the fairness of the admissions process."[32] To its credit, the department's concept of a fair process cut in both directions, not just in

---

* The tensions evident in the department's brief probably reflected in good part the politics that surrounded its development, which is discussed later in this study.

favor of minorities. From the concerns the brief expressed about UCDMS's admissions practices, it could be inferred that in the department's view a fair process required, at the least, a comparative evaluation of all applicants with each other. Without this, the department's argument implied, the process shifted heavily toward "rigid exclusionary quotas," which the department opposed and held illegal. It was only when this basic characteristic of a fair process was maintained that the department considered permissible any practice that contributed to a fuller and more accurate evaluation of minority applicants (e.g., separate committee review of their applications and their exemption from the academic cutoff level applied to nonminorities). Thus far, then, the department's views were broadly in accord with the standard enunciated by Justice Douglas in *DeFunis*.

The department did not follow Douglas's emphasis on a "racially neutral process," however, because of its anxious concern to sanction "minority-sensitive" actions that sought "to remedy the lingering effects of past discrimination." Thus, for example, the setting of numerical goals by schools was approved to guide and encourage them in their efforts to increase minority enrollment.[33] In addition, it was held to be proper for a school to consider every minority applicant to be disadvantaged, without having to inquire into the individual circumstances of each.[34] And it was appropriate for schools to treat race as a special disadvantage, independent of economic disadvantage; the department explicitly rejected the California Supreme Court's suggestion in *Bakke* that UCDMS consider substituting a preference to all disadvantaged applicants for its minority-preference policy.[35]

Precisely what kind of admissions process the Justice Department favored could only be conjectured by putting all these bits and pieces together; it was nowhere tidily laid out in the brief. On the one side, it had some of the trappings that would be expected of extreme race-preference programs, such as numerical goals, higher minimum academic standards for nonminorities, separate review of the qualifications of minorities, the ascription of disadvantage to all minorities per se, and the use of disadvantage to offset lower academic credentials. On the other side, the department endorsed as fundamental to a fair admissions process a competitive evaluation of each applicant compared to all others and it appeared to condemn arrangements, such as that of

UCDMS, which eliminated competition between minority and non-minority applicants. Furthermore, from the examples it offered on the extent to which disadvantage could counterbalance lesser academic qualifications, the department seemed ready to support that practice only when the disparity in academic credentials was relatively small.

As often happens to compromises, the Justice Department's attempted "middle-ground" position between the opposing poles of the dispute displeased partisans more than it pleased them. Many Bakke supporters took it to be a cosmetic version of UCDMS's practices and hence only a better disguised quota system. It was, in any event, too distant from a race-neutral process for them to support. For advocates of minority preferential admissions, on the other hand, the department's position was deficient theoretically and practically. It cast admissions decisions in the frame of comparing minority and nonminority candidates individually and assigned a significant, albeit reduced, role to academic credentials in making that comparison. In practice, a school would have to choose between conducting such a process honestly and reducing the number of minority admittees or operating it deceitfully and keeping those numbers up. Rather than accept so discomforting a choice, the anti-Bakke forces advanced an alternate view of qualifications that was free from the defects they attributed to the Justice Department's position.

Another View of Qualifications

[B]y adopting the special admission program, the medical school has indicated that in its judgment differences in academic credentials among qualified applicants are not the sole nor best criterion for judging how qualified an applicant is in terms of his potential to make a contribution to the medical profession or to satisfy needs of both the medical school and the medical profession that are not being met by other students. (Dissenting opinion, California Supreme Court, *Bakke*)

Proponents of minority special admissions recognized that a precondition for the justification of widespread use of explicit race preference in admissions was the demonstration that no alternative method would produce as large a number of minority enrollees. Chief among those alternative methods was the traditional one of resting a significant part of the decision to admit on a comparison of an applicant's academic qualifications with those of all other applicants. What would happen to minority enrollment if the nation's professional schools evaluated all applicants entirely or mostly by academic criteria and in a race-free manner? The difference between the number of minority applicants who would have been admitted under this race-blind process and the number who were actually admitted provided a rough but credible measure of the effects of race-conscious admissions programs.

To be sure, such an analysis would furnish the opposition with evidence of what they were sure to interpret as the alarming spread of unfair and impermissible race favoritism. But that was already a well-established theme among Bakke supporters; the findings would not expose the anti-Bakke side to any new vulnerability. The analysis *would* provide something of distinctive value to the allies of the University of California, namely, part of the indispensable evidence they needed to make the argument that nothing less than race preference would bring about the results wanted. Hence it should occasion no surprise to learn that the friends of special admissions, not its foes, presented the most thorough documentation of the inability of minorities to compete effectively with non-minorities for admission on the basis of academic credentials.

Academic Criteria Squeeze Out Minorities

The analysis under discussion was commissioned by the Law School Admissions Council, which was greatly concerned about the impact on minority enrollments in legal education if the California Supreme Court's decision on *Bakke*—especially its emphasis on race-neutral evaluations of applicants—was affirmed by the U.S. Supreme Court. Franklin R. Evans, a researcher at the Educational Testing Service, was asked to do the study, which was released in May 1977. Its findings provided the empirical underpinnings of the *amicus* brief the council filed on *Bakke* with the U.S. Supreme Court; the brief supported the University of California's position on minority preferential admissions.[1]

The Evans study concentrated on a comparison of blacks and Chicanos (Mexican-Americans) with whites for fall 1976 law school admission. The actual admissions results that year for the two minority groups were analyzed in the following way. To begin with, blacks comprised 12.7 percent and Chicanos 2.8 percent of the national population in the 21–25 age range appropriate for entry into law school. Compared with whites, however, blacks and Chicanos had much lower rates of high school graduation, college entry, and completion of college degree. As a consequence, their share of college degree recipients—the potential eligibility pool for law schools—was only 5.3 percent for blacks and 1.3 percent for Chicanos. The law school acceptance rate for the two groups was exactly the same—5.3 and 1.3 percent—as their proportion of the potential eligibility pool.

This result reflected two opposing patterns that canceled each other out: a somewhat larger percentage of blacks and minorities applied to law schools than did white college graduates, but white applicants had a higher acceptance rate (59 percent) than either blacks (39 percent) or Chicanos (47 percent). At *any* specific level of LSAT/GPA qualifications, however, members of the two minority groups were accepted at a higher rate than whites. For example, of all applicants who had an LSAT score within 550–599 range and a GPA between 3.0 and 3.24 (*B* and *B*+), 96 percent of blacks, 95 percent of Chicanos, and 69 percent of whites were accepted by at least one law school; for those applicants with an LSAT score of 450 or higher and a GPA of 2.5 (*B*− to *C*+) or better, the acceptance rate was respectively 83, 79, and 69 percent. Black and Chicano applicants had a lower overall acceptance rate, therefore, because disproportionately so many of them were located at the lower levels of LSAT/GPA scores.

Against this backdrop of the actual admissions data for 1976, Evans constructed two different projections for minority enrollment under race-free admissions processes. The first projection was the less realistic of the two and, therefore, produced the more extreme findings. It posited that school admissions decisions would be made solely on the basis of LSAT/GPA scores. Combining all law schools for statistical purposes as if they constituted one great law school, Evans devised a weighting formula for the LSAT and GPA (multiply GPA by 135 and add LSAT score) that was the average of the validated formulas actually used by the nation's ABA-accredited law schools, and applied that formula to all applicants for whom LSAT and GPA data were available. In effect, this method ranked 76,000 applicants by their predicted first-year average (the formula that weighed the LSAT and GPA), then examined the white, black, and Chicano composition of the top 41,500 candidates whose acceptance would have filled all the available spaces, assuming that every acceptance resulted in an enrollee. Two key findings emerged. Compared with the actual 1976 enrollments, overall black enrollment would have been reduced by slightly more than three-quarters; Chicano enrollment would have been reduced by nearly half. The reduction would have been even more severe for the most selective law schools, leaving only a token presence of a minor fraction of 1 percent for the two minorities.

Evans's second method of projection more closely reflected the actual admissions criteria of law schools, which combined a heavy emphasis on academic qualifications with attention to a wide range of other factors. For example, for white applicants in 1976 admissions, 81 percent of those with an LSAT score range of 600–649 were accepted, 67 percent of those between 550–559, and 47 percent between 500–549. Obviously, the higher the LSAT score range, the higher the acceptance rate. But no less obviously, something more than LSAT score range was considered; otherwise, for example, 100 percent of the 550–559 range would have been accepted before any of those in the 500–549 range were. Although there was no way of knowing the weighting each school gave to these other factors, the nationally aggregated results of their decisions could be developed in the manner illustrated by the data just cited (e.g., the proportion of white applicants, classified by range brackets of combined LSAT/GPA scores, who were actually accepted by one or more law schools for fall 1976). The assumption then could be made, as Evans did, that "applications of minorities would be affected by such factors in precisely the same way as those of whites."

In sum, the second projection asked: how would minority enrollment have been affected if blacks and Chicanos were accepted at the rates for nonminorities at the same levels of LSAT/GPA? The answer: black enrollment would have declined by 60 percent and Chicano enrollment by 40 percent. They would have constituted, respectively, only about 2 percent and three-quarters of 1 percent of total first-year students at the nation's law schools, instead of the 5.3 and 1.3 percent they actually constituted. And, as would be expected, the enrollment decline would have been relatively much greater at the most selective law schools, each of which would have accepted on the average no more than a handful of blacks and Chicanos.

As a check on his statistical analyses, Evans sent a questionnaire to all 163 ABA-approved law schools, asking them "How many minorities do you have in your present first-year class?" and "Assuming that it were *impossible to identify the racial background of applicants*, how many of the above would have been admitted?" For each question, the minority groups specified were "Black Americans, Chicano (Mexican Americans), Puerto Ricans, Other Hispanic Americans, American Indians, Asian Americans, Other." A total of 129 schools, which enrolled about three-quarters of all first-year minority law students in the nation, responded to both questions. They reported that, overall, a race-blind admissions process would have resulted in a 73 percent decline in minority enrollment, from 2810 to 774. For blacks, the drop would have been 82 percent (from 1539 to 285), and for Chicanos 73 percent (from 462 to 126). The smallest reduction would have been for Asian-Americans (only 40 percent), the largest for Puerto Ricans (87 percent).

The admissions data for Boalt (UC Berkeley), a highly selective law school, was representative of the overall findings provided by Evans's study. To begin with, white applicants at the lower range of academic qualifications were intentionally discouraged from applying because Boalt publicized that the median GPA for those accepted was about 3.5 ($B+$ to $A-$) and the median LSAT about 700; by Boalt's formula, this came out to a 75.5 predicted first-year grade average. For minority applicants, however, Boalt publicized that those not meeting this academic standard could be admitted under the special admissions program and that the school sought actively to recruit applications from minorities. For fall 1974 entry, 574 of 2830 (20 percent) white applicants had a predicted average in the top tier of 78.0 or higher, as compared with only 1 of 373 black and Chicano applicants. Had Boalt wished, it could have used up virtually all its acceptances by extending admission invitations just to these 574 top white applicants; as it happened, 70 percent of the group was accepted. At the other end, 94 percent of black and Chicano but only 36 percent of white applicants had a predicted first-year average of less than 75.0. On acceptances, then, 85 percent of the white admittees came from the top category of predicted grade average (78.0 and over) and only 1 percent from the under-75.0 level; the counterpart figures for blacks and Chicano admittees were exactly reversed, namely, 1 percent and 88 percent.[2]

The analysis available on medical school admissions, though less extensive than the Evans report on law schools, led to much the same conclusions. Making use of a study it had commissioned, the Association of American Medical Colleges observed in its *amicus* brief on *Bakke:*

> Without special admissions programs it is not unrealistic to assume that minority enrollments could return to the distressingly low levels of the early 1960's. This would mean a drop from the present level of 8.2 percent enrollment . . . to slightly over 2 percent.[3]

For fall 1973 admissions, for example, the mean MCAT scores for white, black, and Chicano admittees were, respectively, 604, 472, and 521 on the science section and 576, 471, and 510 on the verbal; the mean undergraduate GPAs in science were 3.43 ($B+$), 2.64 ($B-$), and 2.96 (B).[4] Plainly, then, the greater the emphasis on academic credentials in admissions decisions, the lower the proportion of minorities among those accepted. This was particularly true for blacks, the largest minority group; their academic credentials for either law or medicine were below those of most other minorities. In that regard, it was instructive to note that the medical schools' acceptance rate for minorities, unlike the pattern for law schools, was higher than that for whites; for example, in the first half of the 1970s, slightly under 50 percent of black applicants were admitted, compared to 40 percent of whites.[5]

For both medical and law schools, the gap in academic credentials between minority and nonminority candidates was greater on standardized test scores (LSAT, MCAT) than on undergraduate grade-point averages (GPA). It followed, therefore, that when the two measures were combined by some formula, the greater the weight accorded the test-score component rather than the GPA, the larger the average difference between the two groups of applicants. Typically, schools gave greater weight to the LSAT or MCAT over the GPA; the averaged formula used by Evans in his first projection (GPA multiplied by 135; add LSAT score) did exactly that.

Not surprisingly, spokesmen for minorities often argued that, if academic criteria were relied on heavily, the GPA figure should be assigned predominance and the test-score result downgraded in importance. Such a change, however, would markedly reduce the predictive value of academic indicators and would undercut the purpose for which the standardized test was developed in the first place. Statistically, a composite measure such as predicted law school first-year averages had greater predictive values than either LSAT or GPA taken alone, and the decision on what weight to give each of the two factors reflected a purely statistical conclusion on what correlated most strongly with actual first-year course grades. Moreover, the tests were highly useful precisely because there was no other feasible way to assess the meaning of GPAs earned in different colleges and in different courses. This need was even more pronounced in an era when instructors' evaluations of student course work had become less reliable because of grade inflation.

Of the several analyses summarized here, Evans's second projection—which assumed that minority applicants would have been accepted at the rate of white applicants at the same level of LSAT/ GPA—seemed to provide the best estimate of the loss rate for minority admissions if race-blind processes displaced special admissions. By that estimate, only 40 percent of the black candidates who were in fact admitted to law school in fall 1976 would have been admitted under race-free procedures. Presumably this proportion might have been increased had law schools been more inclined to offset moderate differences in academic credentials by consideration of personal disadvantage, in the manner urged by Justice Douglas and the Department of Justice (as discussed in the preceding chapter).

Most critically, the qualitative meaning of Evans's finding was nowhere as clear as its quantitative meaning. Certainly the number of minority admittees would drop greatly, but how much would the number of new minority lawyers three to five years later be affected? Black applicants who were actually admitted but who would have been rejected under a race-blind process were disproportionately located at low LSAT/GPA levels; statistically, such persons would be expected to have higher school attrition and bar-exam failure rates than those with stronger academic credentials. Recall, from the previous chapter, that the national attrition rate for minority law students was 25 percent and that, for example, no better than about 29 of 100 minority enrollees at UCLA and about 60 of 100 at Boalt completed law school and passed the bar. In short, what was needed to make full sense of Evans's analysis was, once again, counterpart data on the school completion and bar-exam passing rates of minority law students. As noted earlier, although the collection and analysis of such data were entirely feasible tasks and their relevance to the controversy could not be more direct, the information was not forthcoming. Without it, there was no way of telling just how serious the actual loss to minority groups would be if the number of minorities entering law school were to drop in line with Evans's estimate.

Another aspect of Evans's study worth noting was the overestimate of law schools of the proportion of black and Chicano admittees they would have rejected under strictly race-blind procedures. Overall, their estimates added up to a drop of 82 percent for blacks and 70 percent for Chicanos; Evans's projection, you will recall, was respectively 60 and 40 percent. No confident explanation for the schools' exaggerated figures could be offered in the absence of more detailed data, including information on what proportion of schools were accurate in their estimates or underestimated the drop that would occur. Still, two possibilities warrant mention. "Mismatch" between minority applicant and school, a pattern discussed in the preceding chapter, could account for part of the discrepancy (i.e., minorities were encouraged to apply to schools that would reject whites with comparable academic qualifications). In addition, the broad association of minorities with weak academic credentials and with race-conscious admissions programs could easily have resulted in a general misperception of how many minority applicants would have been admitted under regular procedures and without reference to race. To the extent this latter explanation was true, it underscored one of the high prices paid by the reiterated argument that only through race preference could adequate numbers of minorities be enrolled.

The pro-Bakke groups offered neither significant comment nor challenge to Evans's study, and they raised none of the questions or qualifications discussed here. The anti-Bakke camp, obviously, had no reason to respond critically to the study. Hence Evans's analysis was generally accepted as providing the fullest documentation of the proposition that the combination of a race-free admissions process and an emphasis on a ranking of applicants by academic credentials would lead to a substantial decline in minority enrollments. Because that result was thoroughly unacceptable to the allies of the University of California, they used the Evans report as additional evidence for their argument that one or both of the minority-limiting attributes—the race-blind process and the stress on comparative academic qualifications—had to be severely modified.

Admissions Viewed as a School's Discretionary Selection
Neither Reynold Colvin (Bakke's attorney) nor the organizations that filed briefs supporting Bakke insisted that professional schools had to rely primarily on academic criteria in their admissions judgments. Even those who strongly believed that a strict meritocratic process defined by academic credentials was the "best" system recognized that a school was under no constitutional obligation to define its admissions criteria in accord with that model.

Similarly, everyone agreed that Allan Bakke had no constitutional right to be accepted by a California medical school, nor to have his application judged solely by his ranking among applicants on academic criteria. For example, it was considered unquestionably permissible for a school to include noncognitive criteria in admissions, to reinterpret an applicant's academic qualifications in light of his or her disadvantaged background, and the like. When, therefore, the University of California's brief characterized medical schools' admissions as involving a "tempered reliance on numerical indicators,"[6] Bakke partisans did not dispute this formula.

Although they were open to any reasonable and relevant admissions criteria a school elected to use, Bakke's supporters did insist that the criteria neither recognize, represent, nor give preference to race as a positive (or negative) factor in itself. They believed, for example, that the permissible way to take applicant background into account was for the school to review all applicants individually by applying the same or equivalent indicators, and not by employing racial group categories. The same requirement held, in their view, for the incorporation of noncognitive factors into the applicant evaluation process. Admittedly, as Justice Douglas had noted in his *DeFunis* opinion, there were no satisfactory measures of these noncognitive factors, but the admissions committee was entitled to exercise its best judgment—on a comparative application-by-application basis and without explicit preference to race.

To the University of California and its supporters in the *Bakke* controversy, the choice offered by the pro-Bakke camp was thoroughly unpalatable. On the one side, schools could continue to stress mostly academic criteria, but at the price of sharply reducing their intake of minorities. On the other, schools could experiment with new criteria with an eye to maintaining the scale of minority enrollment at present or higher levels, but at the price of having to determine the admission of all students by these new criteria. Even if the latter option were seriously to be considered, what would those "new criteria" be? In short, the one choice denied the university their objective; the other choice made achievement of their objective uncertain or too costly. To escape from this bind, the anti-Bakke camp had to reject this frame of choice altogether. They did this by presenting a different conception of admissions, one that, if accepted by the Court, would enable them to have the best of both worlds: schools would be able to continue to apply largely academic criteria to evaluate nonminority applicants, but would treat minority applicants separately and differently to assure the desired scale of minority enrollment.

The starting point for this alternate view was the unexceptionable proposition that school admissions policy was properly conceptualized as a selection process controlled by those best able to judge merit among competing applicants: the school faculty. In deciding admission or rejection for each applicant, the faculty determined both who was qualified and, within those ranks, who should be admitted to meet a wide variety of institutional, educational, professional, and societal needs. This concept of admissions contrasted with another view, held by many students (and often by the parents of applicants), that admissions was a contest to be won by the applicant's own efforts, especially by his or her hard-earned academic credentials.[7] Of course, as school admissions programs actually worked out, much of the second concept was accommodated by the first, because schools typically chose to emphasize academic criteria in their comparative assessment of applicants. Still, the distinction between the two alternate concepts remained important. For example, professional schools varied in the extent to which they relied on academic criteria to judge admission—law schools generally did so more heavily than medical schools—but none totally excluded consideration of other factors and criteria.

From the perspective of minority-group spokesmen, schools generally remained too wedded to academic criteria and were insufficiently flexible in the exercise of their admissions authority. These spokesmen argued that such a policy was especially wrongheaded for professional schools, which were not merely schools but also gatekeepers to their respective professions. Control over admission to law or medical school constituted, in reality, effective control over admission to the practice of the profession. It followed, went their argument, that admissions criteria should reflect that fact.

They urged, specifically, that too many admissions decisions were measured by who was likely to get the best grades in law or medical school. Instead, admissions qualifications should also reflect the needs of the profession and of society. This required taking into account the greatly varied tasks members of the profession did, and the even more varied tasks the public wanted them to do. A large range of factors contributed to the successful handling of those tasks—for attorneys one could cite motivation, commitment, maturity, advocacy skills, client empathy, ability to cope with uncertainty, and so on—and these factors should be incorporated within the admissions criteria. Similarly, urgent needs of society were underserved, and applicants also should be appraised with respect to their capacity to meet those needs.

Professional schools were legitimately open to such criticisms because, generally speaking, they had not shown adequate concern to produce a wide variety of professionals who would offer a balanced set of services to society.[8] In medicine, for instance, the model of the student as "potential research medical scientist" had dominated since 1958;[9] there were too many surgeons and too few primary-care physicians, and the medical needs of rural and inner-city residents remained poorly met. It was unquestionably true, moreover, that professional schools characteristically had responded to the oversize demand for entry by setting minimum academic qualifications for admissions higher and higher, at levels well above the minimum academic credentials needed to complete the school program satisfactorily. This admissions pattern, more than any other factor, froze out minorities from regular admissions and led schools to develop "special" criteria to ensure their admission. In the words of one education specialist:

> The inflation of minimal standards has a particularly unfortunate effect upon the educationally disadvantaged student, who is often poor and also a member of an ethnic or racial minority. "Minimal" standards that are set at artificially high levels have the effect of screening out very high proportions of these students, and consequently can be perceived by them as arbitrary and unreasonable barriers. Likewise the faculty, having created an artificial "floor" that is too high by far, is tempted then to waive or alter such standards on the basis of race or disadvantaged status—creating thereby potential dissension, and sometimes causing understandable resentment on the part of minority students for the paternalism that such actions may imply, as well as accusations of unfairness voiced by majority students.[10]

The opponents of Bakke pulled these threads together—admissions as a selection process controlled by faculty, the inflation of minimum academic standards for admission, the overreliance on academic criteria for an excessive share of total admissions—to proffer a conception of admissions designed to justify minority preference. They held, in essence, that admissions was properly understood as a distinctive two-stage process under the control of the faculty: the first stage was to decide which applicants were at least minimally qualified to complete school successfully; the second selected from that large pool those who were to be admitted because they best satisfied various needs of the school, profession, or society.

The president of the University of California, David S. Saxon, set forth the official version of this position in January 1978, in a public release that explained the importance of the *Bakke* case, why UC was committed to pressing for the U.S. Supreme Court to hear the case, and UC's position on the core issues concerning admissions.[11]

> Admissions committees are . . . faced with two tasks: first, to determine which of the many applicants are *qualified,* and then to determine which of those qualified should be *selected* for the relatively few available spaces.
>
> A student is considered qualified who is judged likely to succeed in professional school and in the entry testing for professional practice. To make this judgment, admissions committees look at past grade point averages, professional school entrance test scores, and evidence of motivation and persistence. Those applicants identified as qualified will naturally have a spread of grade point averages and test scores; nevertheless, all will be considered fully qualified. . . . [N]o student will be admitted who is thought unlikely to succeed. . . .
>
> The final selection of students from among the qualified applicants is the crux of the issue. For many years, the selection was based primarily on [academic credentials] . . . [which resulted in giving] preference to students with the best educational opportunities and the most academically supportive family and cultural backgrounds—in short, middle- and upper-class white students. Although no one intended it that way, it produced in the medical field, for example, a generally segregated body of medical students and a profession with severe shortages of minority physicians and severe maldistribution of medical services favoring wealthier, largely white communities. This maldistribution contributes to the significantly shorter life spans and infant mortality rates for some minorities in this country.
>
> And so a number of schools have been reconsidering their method of deciding which qualified applicants to admit. They may select some for their outstanding academic records, others for evidence of broad rapport with people or of commitments to public

service, and still others for their expressed interest in certain medical specialties or for service in certain geographical areas. And some may be chosen to redress the high degree of segregation of the medical profession or because of their declared intent to bring medical services to people and communities now grossly undeserved, including the ghettos and barrios.

This two-stage admissions model was applied immediately to rebut the argument that minority admittees were inferior in qualifications to white rejectees. In his official statement, President Saxon went on to fault the majority opinion of the California Supreme Court for "not grasp[ing] the essential difference between *qualification* and *selection* of applicants" and thus wrongly concluding that the Davis medical school had enrolled minority students who were "not as qualified" as Allan Bakke.[12] In terms of the university's conception of admissions, minority admittees were at least as qualified as Bakke, though on different grounds and for different needs and purposes of the medical school. Saxon commended Justice Tobriner for his "eloquent and well-reasoned dissent,"[13] which adopted UC's admissions rationale on this key point.*

In commenting on this alternative view of admissions, it first should be noted that it was developed "after the fact." No such coherent rationale accompanied the introduction of special admissions programs or their public explanation; it emerged from the necessities of litigation. Second, the implication that a school, when admitting applicants for primarily nonacademic reasons, was indifferent to their relative ranking on academic credentials as long as they were judged admissible, was misleading. As discussed in the third chapter, the willingness of schools to give preference for some of their entering places to "out-of-staters" or "those likely to become primary-care physicians" was implicitly conditioned on a rough parity of academic credentials among applicants with and without the preferred characteristic. Once academic indicators did not discriminate significantly among candidates within a given subset of the qualified pool, other criteria could be used to admit particular applicants from that subset. It was inaccurate, therefore, to analogize minority admissions to these other categories of admissions

---

* The relevant extract from this dissenting opinion is presented at the outset of this chapter.

preference; no other sizable group regularly preferred for admissions had average academic qualifications that were as low.

The persistent question of the meaning of "qualified" was raised anew by UC's concept of admissions, which appeared to collapse the differences between "minimally qualified" and "fully qualified" and to give schools maximum discretion to select whom they wanted, ruling out only the "unqualified" as inadmissible but leaving it to each school to define and apply that term. Since President Saxon's statement was carefully drawn to be consonant with the arguments of UC counsel in their *Bakke* brief, it was not surprising that it affirmed rather than resolved the ambiguity surrounding UCDMS's determination of minimum qualifications. Thus, for example, Saxon indicated that "evidence of motivation and persistence" was reviewed along with academic scores, but no minimum academic qualifications were specified to set a clear line between those deemed admissible and those not.

Indeed, Saxon added to the uncertainty by commenting as follows on the "checks [that] are essential to prevent unfair treatment and invidious discrimination [by schools in the exercise of their admissions authority]":

> For *qualification,* the major test is whether all or almost all students do succeed. One other question remains: are there students with still lower formal academic credentials who also could succeed and so have a right to be in the pool of qualified applicants? Admissions committees are aware of the need to take cautious risks in order to check on the proper cutoff points.[14]

Unfortunately, professional schools had released little data on the success rate of minority admittees, and the data that had become available by other means, such as those earlier reported for California public law schools, revealed that far fewer than "all or almost all students" had succeeded. Moreover, Saxon's observation that students with even lower academic qualifications might be judged admissible and hence would have a *right* to be in the qualified pool, together with his approval of expanding the limits of admissibility, seemed to dilute even further whatever substantive meaning UC would otherwise attach to the term "qualified." Saxon's statement also left unclear whether explicit considerations of race would enter into the determination of minimum qualifications, and if so, whether racial considerations would figure as prominently as in the second-stage selection process. It could plausibly be inferred that UC's position was designed more to enlarge the number of minority applicants who would be considered fully admissible than to establish, without regard to race, reasonable and firm minimum academic qualifications.

Finally, nothing in UC's view of a two-stage admissions process provided new or independent justification for adopting an explicit race preference. It was quite acceptable to affirm a school's right to apply multiple criteria flexibly in behalf of diverse admissions objectives, but it was a different matter to assert that right as a blanket justification for a school to prefer members of one race over members of another for a share of the available spaces. The latter attempt served only to raise yet again, not to resolve, all the basic questions about whether and how race could be recognized in admissions decisions.

Similarly, little was gained by positing, as justification for minority preference, certain school and societal needs that could be met only by minorities (e.g., the need for an integrated student body, for more minority professionals, for positive role models to motivate minority youth). These reasons simply restated rather than answered the essential question, which was the appropriateness of the means used to achieve a broadly desired end. For instance, since racial integration was an important objective everywhere in the nation, did that mean that any institution at its discretion could reserve positions or places for minorities and exclude nonminorities from them?

Leave It to the Educators?

In its assignment of effective control over admissions practices to higher education units, UC's two-stage admissions model affirmed the widely endorsed view that admissions policy was traditionally reserved for university and faculty determination—and jealously guarded by them against invasion. It was clear to everyone, for instance, that no candidate (of whatever race) had a right to direct a school to use a particular method of evaluation for his or her application. Moreover, the factors involved in admissions and in the human judgments on applicants were so many and diffuse, and so dependent on professional expertise for their sound application, as to make such decisions generally unsuited for litigation. Judicial intercession on such matters, therefore, was generally deemed unwise and unmanageable. In addition, judicial restraint was necessary to avoid undercutting the vitality and diversity of higher education and the capacity of schools to develop different admissions processes. And, not least, continued recognition of state authority in a federal system also called for avoidance of extensive monitoring or intervention by the national judiciary on questions of admissions policy.

Since their strategic needs in the litigation dovetailed with their deeply held beliefs on this theme, many supporters of minority preference in admissions emphasized the importance of maintaining autonomy for professional schools to control their own admissions policies. The point was well taken, but often much overdone. Harvard's President Derek Bok, for example, decried the turn to litigation as the mode of settlement for the issues raised by *Bakke:* "To many universities, the effort to resolve such matters through constitutional litigation represents a dangerous threat of government intrusion into academic processes that should be left in the hands of educational institutions."[15] To encourage the Court to defer to university decisions, an *amicus* brief on *DeFunis* insisted that "the root issues . . . are educational, not legal."[16] In its *amicus* brief on *Bakke,* the NAACP framed a stark choice:

> [T]he question, on a policy basis, is . . . whether a court or the university should determine priority in the acceptance of students from the pool of qualified applicants. In a constitutional sense, the question is whether the Fourteenth Amendment somehow dictates the order in which qualified applicants must be admitted to a state university's medical school.[17]

The *Bakke* brief submitted by several private universities advanced a considerably more moderate formulation of the same general concern:

> When . . . the problem is central to the educational process as is the determination of the qualifications of students, when educators are searching in good faith for solutions, and when applicable legal norms are in doubt, we believe that the cause of education, and hence the welfare of our society, are best served by judicial restraint.[18]

It was neither reasonable nor realistic to escalate a legitimate concern about possibly excessive judicial interference into a call for a hands-off policy by courts. Because responsibility and fairness were the re~·isite companions of discretion, law and medical schools could not be given immunity from accountability should they choose to exercise their admissions authority unfairly or capriciously. Moreover, deference to the expertise of educators was a more persuasive thesis for such matters as courses of study, requirements for graduation, and evaluations of student performance in courses than for general admissions policy, which necessarily involved resource allocation in a setting of scarcity and exclusion of qualified applicants. (In some states and cities, admissions policy was set by political bodies and not by the higher education institutions.) Above all, when the issues of race and the constitutional rights of equal protection were inextricably intertwined with admissions policy, no blanket exemption of such a controversy from court adjudication was warranted. In his *DeFunis* opinion, Justice Douglas struck an appropriate balance:

> The educational policy choices confronting a University Admissions Committee are not ordinarily a subject for judicial oversight; clearly it is not for us but for the law school to decide which tests to employ, how heavily to weigh recommendations from professors or undergraduate grades, and what level of achievement on the chosen criteria are sufficient to demonstrate that the candidate is qualified for admission. What places this case [*DeFunis*] in a special category is the fact that the school [UWLS] did not choose one set of criteria but two, and then determined which to apply to a given applicant on the basis of his race.

Even the reiterated fear of undue judicial intervention, though usefully serving as a reminder to the judges, seemed exaggerated in light of the Court's clear reluctance to become intimately involved in the details of admissions policy. If the Court decided to bar positive race discrimination in admissions, it was not readily apparent why that would be a significantly greater incursion on university autonomy than the earlier Court-ordered ban on negative race discrimination in school admissions. A Court ruling in favor of Allan Bakke could easily be formulated so as to leave to the professional schools virtually undiminished authority over admissions standards and practices. Schools could continue to use and experiment with whatever mix of objective and subjective criteria they wished; indeed, they presumably could avoid having to choose altogether (other than determining who was admissible) by selecting among their qualified applicants randomly or by lottery. To a considerable degree, therefore, the vocal anxiety of anti-*Bakke* spokesmen about the dangers of "rigidifying the admissions process," "judicializing or constitutionalizing the question of admissions," or "imposing a single, uniform rule on admissions" was best understood as a strategy of litigation rather than a realistic prediction of what was likely to occur if *Bakke* was affirmed by the Court.

When viewed as a strategy, an emphasis on the importance of preserving university autonomy was neither the monopoly of the anti-Bakke forces nor did it automatically call for a rejection of the California high court's *Bakke* decision. Nathan Glazer, a sociologist and long-time student of race and ethnicity in America, provocatively argued precisely the opposite position: affirmance of *Bakke*, not its overturn, would serve to protect the faculty's ability to experiment with different admissions policies and procedures. The issue in *Bakke*, as Professor Glazer saw it, was "whether it is constitutional for a state-supported medical school to reserve a number of places for the exclusive use of minority-group applicants." Hence, Glazer argued,

> If [Allan Bakke] loses, we can be sure that the Department of Health, Education and Welfare will fasten a quota for race and minorities on every medical school in the country, and on every institution of higher education that is within its reach, which is almost all of them.

In short, Glazer asserted, "a judgment against Mr. Bakke *reduces* university freedom and leads to [governmental] imposition of quotas."[19]

Much the same boomerang effect could result from UC's insistence that admissible minority applicants were not only as "fully qualified" as nonminorities with superior academic records but were uniquely qualified (hence better qualified) to satisfy race-related admissions objectives. As the *amicus* brief on *Bakke* of the National Association of Minority Contractors observed:

> . . . Davis [medical school] has sought to integrate the profession racially and to contribute to the solution of California's and the country's racial problems. When matched against this objective, black Davis applicants are superbly competent and white Davis applicants are entirely incompetent.[20]

If the Court were to endorse UC's argument that minority enrollees were needed in order to satisfy compelling educational, professional, and societal requirements, would minority admissions continue to be considered a matter entirely within a school's discretion to offer or not, to shape as it wished? Or would it become a school's obligation to ensure minority entry? And would minority applicants come to see themselves as having an enforceable claim or right to be accepted in significant numbers? Once minority admittees were deemed better qualified than nonminorities by some admissions criteria, would a school still be able to impose whatever numerical limit on minority admissions it chose? Or would it have to provide persuasive justification for that limit, to avoid being charged with setting a discriminatory ceiling that worked against better-qualified minorities and favored less-qualified nonminorities? In sum, even if the Court's reversal of *Bakke* did not lead to the HEW actions predicted by Glazer, it could set in motion other changes that would reduce the present level of university discretionary authority with respect to minority admissions.

Compared to the larger landscape of Affirmative Action positions, there was at least a surface irony in the insistence by the anti-*Bakke* and anti-*DeFunis* camp that professional schools should have virtually unfettered admissions discretion; that admissions criteria could appropriately be multiple, diffuse, and often unmeasurable; that subjective judgment was an essential ingredient of an effective admissions process; and, not least, that medical and law schools should be trusted to exercise their authority in these matters fairly and responsibly. In other problem areas, in contrast, advocates of minority advancement often spoke of the need to reduce discretion and subjectivity. In employment programs, for example, standardized, objective evaluation processes (validated for job relevance, to be sure) were frequently prescribed for firms. This seeming contradiction was easily explained: it reflected a flexible strategy on behalf of the constant objective of aiding minorities. In employment, the problem was seen as preventing discrimination against minorities; in school admissions, the problem was one of promoting discrimination for minorities. The means, accordingly, were tailored to match each of these different contexts. Such a result-oriented approach scored high on effectiveness, but it ran the risk of appearing to others as treating means strategically at the expense of normative considerations—that is, simply whether they worked rather than whether they were good or bad in themselves or consistent with some larger principle.

If significant changes in the control of admissions by educators were to come about in the near future, the likeliest impetus would not be the issues of race preference central to *Bakke* and *DeFunis* but rather a rising concern for strengthening procedural due process. Ours is a time when institutional legitimacy and discretion have become somewhat suspect, and the remedies typically offered have gone in the direction of regularizing, standardizing, reducing subjectivity, and providing explicit, objective, and uniform measures. Looked at from this vantage point, there was considerable room for improvement in admissions processes.

For one thing, much too little was publicly available or known about the details of admissions practices in higher education institutions. Most schools felt that such disclosure would confine their flexibility and exercise of judgment. As a consequence, "[d]etailed information on the practices of institutions has come more out of litigation than out of any other source."[21] The glimpses afforded by *Bakke* and *DeFunis* were not reassuring with regard to the overall systematic quality of admissions practices. Neither the Davis medical school nor the Washington law school came close to offering their evaluators any uniform set of admissions criteria. Nowhere was each major factor quantified and assigned a relative weight as its contribution to an overall judgment of an applicant's qualifications.

It would be unfortunate if the due process deficiencies associated with unnecessarily loose, unsystematic, and unreliable admissions procedures were to result in a turning away from the increasing use of subjective judgment in candidate evaluations. In order to appraise applicants more fully and hence more fairly, schools should be encouraged to go well beyond an uncritical reliance on traditional academic measures, especially for that large portion of applicants who fall between top and bottom academic tiers. To continue to be able to exercise discretion in this regard, educators would be wise to develop ways of enhancing the procedural fairness of the applicant review process. Neglect of that task could invite the imposition of "reforms" embodying formalistic due process notions that, far more than the *Bakke* case about which universities expressed great worry, could bring about an unwelcome rigidifying of the admissions process.

Increasing the Supply of Qualified Minority Applicants

A concentration on questions of proper admissions criteria and processes and how to evaluate applicant qualifications in highly selective admissions, although inescapable when dealing with *Bakke* and *DeFunis,* obscured a larger problem. The ability of schools to admit larger proportions of minorities hinged only in part on validation of their authority to proffer race preference; it turned, most basically, on the number of qualified minority applicants available for school consideration and acceptance. On that critical dimension, the hard truth was that existing special admissions programs already were accepting as many minority students, if not more, as could be admitted in light of the available supply of adequately qualified minorities.

For medical schools in the 1970–76 period, 5.0 to 6.6 percent of applicants were blacks, and because schools accepted them at a higher rate than nonminorities, they constituted from 6.1 to 7.5 percent of the entering class.[22] In order for blacks to have constituted about 12 percent of fall 1975 new enrollees—to match their proportion of the national population—80 percent of all black applicants would have had to be admitted.[23] Plainly, then, medical schools had exhausted the available supply, and their ability to move significantly beyond the static level of black enrollment in the '70s depended upon a step-up in the number of qualified black candidates.

Given the college science course prerequisites that all medical school applicants had to meet, however, any effective effort to produce the larger numbers desired had to reach down to the precollege stage, and to be sustained without interruption for many years. The following two accounts indicated the scale of school initiative, commitment, and involvement required.

Recruiters [from the University of Southern California medical school] blitz predominantly black and chicano high schools in Los Angeles to identify sophomores with interest and aptitude in medicine. The university helps tutor them through college and provides jobs as orderlies and assistants. "We put a lot motivation into getting to know them," [said a school official]. "And when it's time to apply for medical school, we have them right here."[24]

The University of Arkansas . . . has devised an "all-out game plan" for medical education that first identifies promising youngsters in high school and prepares them for college. Then they receive advice and encouragement about premedical courses, are helped to find summer work in health-related fields, and go through an orientation program before entering medical school.[25]

To date, few medical schools have chosen to engage themselves in so extensive and long-term an involvement to increase the number and quality of minority applicants.

The situation facing law schools was essentially comparable to the experience of medical schools. In rebutting the California Supreme Court's suggestion in its *Bakke* decision that more aggressive recruiting of minorities was a feasible alternative to preferential admissions, the Law School Admissions Council noted that recruiting by law schools was already at the maximum. In 1975–76, for example, 8.3 percent of college-graduating blacks applied to law school, as compared to 7.3 percent of whites. Other graduate disciplines complained, the council observed, that active recruitment by law schools had "skimmed the cream from the pool of most promising minority students."[26]

Notwithstanding these recruitment activities—or perhaps in part because of them—the academic qualifications of black applicants were not commensurate with their numbers. For 1976, as noted earlier in this chapter, the nation's law schools accepted only 39 percent of black applicants as compared to 59 percent of whites. And to get that 39 percent, schools had to go well down the LSAT score range (e.g., 63 percent of black candidates with an LSAT score between 450 and 499 were accepted as compared with 27 percent of whites; for those in the 350–399 range, 25 and 6 percent[27]). School attrition and bar-exam failure rates, both high for blacks, further underscored the need to increase the number of academically better qualified black applicants. To achieve that objective required, as with medical education, that the schools extend their recruiting and involvement to the college and precollege phases of minority education.

For many minority students who entered under special admissions, an understandably difficult period of transition and adjustment followed, especially during the critical first year of law or medical school. Few schools were so indifferent as to apply a sink-or-swim policy, but not many provided effective, timely, broad-ranging assistance. Most schools were oriented toward their better academic students, and hence their ability and sometimes their interest in identifying and responding to students who needed additional help was low. Then too, if the provision of special assistance was associated mostly with minorities, it ran the risk of being resented as condescending and paternalistic, or as assigning minorities to an inferior "track" within the school. No matter how real the difficulties, however, it made little sense for a school that admitted minorities preferentially not to follow through supportively after their minority students began the school program.

Moreover, there was little justifiable reason for schools to limit their supporting activities to facilitate the adjustment of minority students to the existing curriculum. The presence of a new and different student group gave opportunity for program innovation and adaptation, the benefits of which would be available to all students, not just to minorities. Thus, for example, law schools could offer students more clinical, applied, and client-oriented training, stressing negotiating and interactive skills, problem solving, oral communication, and the like. Once this took hold, the LSAT and bar examinations would presumably reflect this development and modify their present emphasis on legal analysis and written communication skills. Medical schools, similarly, could complement or reduce their emphasis on the training of researchers and specialists and undertake new activities designed to serve the needs of poor urban communities, such as running inner-city clinics or developing programs in health education, nutrition, and disease prevention. In these regards, law and medical schools possessed a large potential for varied activities, which they had scarcely begun to tap.

Until professional schools invested greater initiative and resources in these other minority-supporting activities, the genuineness of their commitment to minority advancement remained open to question. When a school confined its effort almost entirely to offering minorities special entry, this meant that the major cost was borne neither by the school as an institution nor by its faculty.

Rather, the school imposed the cost on those white applicants it rejected, but otherwise would have accepted, in order to keep entering places for minorities. In their public position, the schools claimed that the objectives of increasing minority representation in the schools and professions and of improving the professional services available to minority communities were as compelling for them as for the nation. It was reasonable to expect, therefore, that their institutional efforts would be commensurate with their claim. Nothing less would suffice, it was clear, to bring about a marked improvement in the quantity and quality of minority applicants and in the school performance of minority students.

Equal Protection of the Laws and Racial Classifications

The admissions procedures of the Davis medical school and the University of Washington law school represented variations of a race-preference policy: both schools treated applicants differently by race in a deliberate, positive effort to secure a larger number of minority enrollees. As was evident from the eagerness with which first the *DeFunis* and then the *Bakke* case was awaited, such a preferential admissions policy had yet to be tested by the highest court in the land. Further, lower federal courts had divergent holdings on diverse preferential employment actions; it was hoped that, through *Bakke*, the Court might help settle that contentious and confused problem area also.

Clearly, the final character of the law on preferential racial treatment would likely not be known for many years; it would depend on a succession of judicial, bureaucratic, and legislative actions on different kinds of preferences reflecting a variety of contexts and circumstances. Nonetheless, few doubted that the judiciary's contribution would be anything less than influential, and perhaps decisive. *Bakke* gave the Court the opportunity for a precedent-setting ruling that could establish the framework for subsequent policy resolution of the controversy. To provide a basis for understanding the choices before the Court in *Bakke*, this chapter highlights current doctrine on legitimate and illegitimate use of racial classification by government and also explores some related legal and policy questions.

Standards of Review for Equal Protection Challenges

"No state shall . . . deny to any person within its jurisdiction the equal protection of the laws." This protection against state action, set forth in Section 1 of the Fourteenth Amendment, had as its counterpart the Due Process Clause of the Fifth Amendment, which imposed similar requirements on the federal government. Because these constitutional strictures applied to governments and governmental action, private colleges and universities were not covered by them. Technically, therefore, judicial invalidation of minority-preferential admissions on constitutional grounds (as a violation of the Equal Protection Clause) would still permit the private sector of higher education to continue the practice. Nevertheless, virtually all private colleges and universities have significant financial and other relationships with federal or state agencies or both, through which they have become subject to governmental regulation in the discrimination area. (Title VI of the Civil Rights Act of 1964, for example, forbids discrimination in any program receiving federal financial assistance under penalty of withdrawal of federal funds.) As a result, *Bakke* and *DeFunis* were of direct concern to nonpublic higher education units as well as to the public sector, and the *amici* briefs in both cases included some substantial ones submitted by private colleges and universities on the side of UCDMS and UWLS.

In its origins, the Fourteenth Amendment was one of three post–Civil War constitutional amendments designed to gain freedom for Negroes and to ensure certain equal rights that attached to all persons as free persons. Because of the historic tie between the amendment and the protection of Negro rights, some argued that while equal protection of the laws* clearly barred negative racial classifications, it justified "benign" race preferences intended to aid minorities.[1] Similarly, a recurrent theme in the anti-Bakke briefs was that it would "stand the equal protection clause on its head" to use it as the basis for invalidating minority preference in admissions.[2] But over the more than one hundred years since the Fourteenth Amendment was adopted, the courts have interpreted Equal Protection to cover all persons, not just Negroes or other minorities, and to do so in their personal and individual capacity, not as a member of a group.

For many years the U.S. Supreme Court chose not to countenance use of the Fourteenth Amendment on behalf of the protection of Negro rights; as a result, state-enforced racial segrega-

* Hereafter called Equal Protection.

tion was permitted to develop without effective judicial challenge. During this lengthy period the Court elected to assert its authority as the interpreter of the Constitution on another section of the amendment and for quite different purposes. The Due Process Clause was given a meaning by the Court that enabled it to provide business with broad protection from regulation by state and national governments. What became known as the "substantive due process" doctrine held sway until midway into the New Deal, but by the latter 1930s it was decisively abandoned by the Court. Since that time Equal Protection has come into its own, and its interpretation has been the basis of major constitutional litigation. For example, the watershed *Brown* case of 1954–55, overturning racial segregation in education, rested on Equal Protection rights. With reference to race, the contemporary reading of Equal Protection was, broadly, that race was an arbitrary and hence invalid basis on which to distribute governmental benefits or burdens.

Unequal treatment by government was not in itself a violation of one's right to equal protection of the laws. Governments routinely classified their citizens for various purposes and treated some differently from others; indeed, governments could not sensibly carry on much of their activity without making such distinctions. Some examples: setting a speed limit of 55 mph for autos and 50 mph for trucks; imposing more severe punishment for a violent crime when the victim is elderly or a police officer; requiring job retirement at a certain age or reducing social security benefits in the light of the amount of earned income; allowing blind persons to bring guide dogs into areas where animals are otherwise forbidden.

What Equal Protection required was that governments treat similarly all who were similarly situated. So broad a formulation left open, as the central question in disputes, whether those who received different treatment were similarly situated or were different in ways that justified treating them differently. Not all governmental acts that treated some persons differently from others were open to legal challenge under Equal Protection; for example, governmental policies in promoting the general welfare, such as a decision to concentrate public medical research funds on cancer and not heart disease, were matters to be decided by the political process. When conferring benefits, however, governments were bound by the Equal Protection requirement; they could not award them as they pleased on the argument that because no person had a right to a gratuitous benefit, no one could challenge its distribution. A state did not have to provide a law school or medical school; but once it did, the school's admissions policies could not violate Equal Protection rights.

For most types of state classification, the courts operated by a traditional standard of review known as the "rational basis" test: if the purpose was legitimate and within the powers of the state, and if the classification was reasonably or rationally related to that purpose and treated all persons alike who were similarly situated, the courts would uphold the classification as legal. This was a deliberately slack standard of review, designed to give considerable latitude to state policy makers and prevent the courts from taking on the role of superlegislature. Reflective of that purpose, the courts were often willing to accept as justification for the classification any means-end relationship that could be thought of, even one that the state probably did not have in mind. Further, the means did not have to fit the end as tightly or precisely as possible; some slippage could result without danger of a means being held invalid. In effect, then, court use of the rational-basis standard signaled a noninterventionist posture that almost always resulted in judicial affirmation of the state's action.

For certain categories of Equal Protection challenges, however, the U.S. Supreme Court developed a more stringent standard of judicial review, one that virtually reversed the ordinary presumption of constitutionality accorded to legislation whose validity was attacked in the courts. These categories were characterized by either or both of the following:

1. Where the individual interest affected was deemed "fundamental" by the Court, such as the right to vote, to travel from state to state, and to a criminal appeal. In a 1973 case, the Court declined to include primary-secondary education as a "fundamental interest,"[3] and hence no serious attempt was made in *DeFunis* or *Bakke* to persuade the Court that postcollege education merited inclusion in this special category.

2. Where the basis for a classification was deemed "inherently suspect" by the Court, such as race (at least for classifications seen as constituting negative discrimination), national origin, alienage, and perhaps illegitimacy as well. (Classifications based on sex were in an in-between status, one that is still in the process of

development by the Court.) The origin and justification of this category of special exception lay in Justice Harlan F. Stone's observation in a 1938 case that

> . . . prejudice against discrete and insular minorities may be a special condition, which tends seriously to curtail the operation of those political processes ordinarily to be relied on to protect minorities, and which may call for a correspondingly more searching judicial inquiry.[4]

In 1973, the Court laid out "the traditional indicia of suspectness" in terms of a class of the population that was saddled with such disabilities, or subjected to such a history of purposeful unequal treatment, or relegated to such a position of political powerlessness, as to command extraordinary protection from the majoritarian political process.[5] A year later, in a ruling that conscientious objectors did not constitute a "suspect" class, the Court reiterated the preceding characteristics and added one more, namely, possession of "an immutable characteristic determined solely by the accident of birth."[6]

For either of these two categories of Equal Protection cases, the Court's standard of review was one of "strict scrutiny," also termed "more exacting," "more searching," or "heightened" scrutiny in various case decisions. This meant that the classification was treated as constitutionally suspect under Equal Protection, and that the statute was closely reviewed in the light of the purpose it asserted; the Court would not think up plausible purposes in behalf of the state, as it might under the rational basis test. The Court weighed the validity of the government's substantive purpose, with the state assigned the burden of proof of demonstrating a "compelling state interest" in using such a classification. In addition, and no less important, the necessity of the particular classification was reviewed. The state had to show that the classification was absolutely necessary to carry out its permissible objectives, that there was a "tight fit" between the means and the allowable end. If other available means could substantially accomplish the objective and were, as the Court variously expressed it, less "intrusive," "onerous," "restrictive," "burdensome," or "drastic" than the challenged classification with respect to encroaching on valid interests or rights, then the classification was invalid.

An example of strict scrutiny on a nonracial matter should

help clarify how the doctrine was applied. Tennessee enacted durational residence requirements for the ostensible purposes, among other objectives, of protecting against vote fraud and providing for an informed electorate. Because constitutional rights to vote and travel were affected, and these were "fundamental interests," the Court applied the strict scrutiny standard of review. Although the Court acknowledged the importance of the law's objectives, it held the statute invalid because the means were too "attenuated" to achieve the objectives. In pursuing a compelling interest, the Court stated that

> . . . the State cannot choose means that unnecessarily burden or restrict constitutionally protected activity. Statutes affecting constitutional rights must be drawn with "precision," and must be "tailored" to serve their legitimate objectives. And if there are other, reasonable ways to achieve these goals with a lesser burden on constitutionally protected activity, a State may not choose the way of greater interference. If it acts at all, it must choose "less drastic means."[7]

An Equal Protection challenge of a racial classification came under strict scrutiny by the courts, then, as an instance of an "inherently suspect" class; the classification was subjected to the rigorous test of whether it was "necessary to promote a compelling state interest." Assignment of racial classifications to a special category warranting stringent review originated, of course, in the Court's dealings with racial discrimination of the traditional negative, exclusionary, invidious, stigmatizing sort. To date, when the strict scrutiny test has been applied, no state government has been able to justify to the Court's satisfaction that it had a compelling state interest warranting adoption of a negative racial classification.

At the federal governmental level, however, the Court upheld such a classification and, ironically, did so at the same time that it first explicitly made race a suspect classification subject to exacting review. The setting was World War II, and the issue was the exclusion of Japanese-Americans and Japanese aliens from the West Coast and their forced relocation and lengthy internment. With three justices dissenting, the Court in effect accepted the military's rationale as meeting the high level of justification required: the prevention of sabotage and espionage during an invasion constituted a compelling government interest in wartime and the difficulty of distinguishing on an individual basis between loyal and disloyal persons of Japanese ancestry necessitated applying the measures to the entire group.[8] Since few commentators, especially in recent years, found much to praise either in the military orders or in the Court's acquiescence in them, this case became in effect a reverse precedent, a basic lesson in what not to repeat.

As a practical matter, then, just as invocation of the rational basis standard of review ordinarily signified judicial upholding of the governmental classification in question, so the use of the strict scrutiny standard signaled its invalidation. Because of this pattern of judicial decision making, it was not clear what sort of "compelling state interest" a state would have to demonstrate as an essential part of justifying its use of a racial classification—or whether the Court would find any state interest sufficiently compelling to warrant a turn to racial classification as the means of achieving it. On the other hand, the anti-Bakke camp hoped that the Court would accept its argument that the positive purposes served by minority preferential admissions thoroughly satisfied the "compelling state interest" criterion and that no other admissions method could accomplish those purposes. But did every important social objective qualify as a compelling state interest? And was race preference automatically permissible when wedded to minority-promoting goals? "If discrimination based on race is constitutionally permissible when those who hold the reins can come up with 'compelling' reasons to justify it," observed Justice Douglas in his *DeFunis* opinion, "then constitutional guarantees acquire an accordionlike quality."

There was a real question, in sum, about the usefulness of the strict scrutiny standard, which historically was associated with evaluating negative racial discrimination, as the basis for dealing with the contemporary phenomenon of positive racial discrimination. More generally, there was also a question of whether the "two-tier" approach to Equal Protection challenges—the either/or use of the rational basis or the strict scrutiny test—was not too simple and too rigid a framework for judicial review. As an answer to both questions, some law commentators suggested the addition of a "middle-ground" standard of review, one that would involve the Court more actively than the rational basis test but without the automatic overturn of the governmental classification that was associated with the strict scrutiny test.[9]

A recent Supreme Court case dealing with an Oklahoma drinking law provided a good illustration of such an intermediate review standard. In that state, males under age twenty-one were prohibited from drinking 3.2 percent beer; females were allowed to do so at age eighteen. Clearly this was unequal treatment, but because a state had the authority to draw proper legal distinctions between men and women, the question was whether this particular distinction was or was not proper. Oklahoma said it had a rational basis for making the sex-based age distinction: statistics showed that men were more likely than women to drink beer, to drive after drinking, and to be arrested for drunkenness. Proponents for women's rights argued that the state should have to demonstrate a "compelling state interest," not merely a "rational basis," for the statute to be allowed to stand. The women's rights group was not concerned about the lack of young male beer-drinking partners; rather, they wanted to establish the much tougher of the two review standards for determining the validity of government policy that discriminated between the sexes.

All nine members of the Court agreed that sex classifications should not be subject to the review standard of strict scrutiny. Three of them applied the rational basis test and found the Oklahoma law valid. Five justices, in an opinion written by Justice Brennan, endorsed a middle-ground review standard for determining Equal Protection challenges to sex classifications:

> To withstand constitutional challenge, . . . classifications by gender must serve important governmental objectives and be substantially related to the achievement of those objectives.

Applying this *"important state interest/substantial relation"* standard, the Court majority struck down the Oklahoma statute because it was not substantially related to the achievement of its purported objectives, the regulation of driving and drinking.[10]

The same intermediate review standard was applied by a Court majority, again speaking through Justice Brennan, in a subsequent case treating the equal protection guarantees against federal government action of the Fifth Amendment's Due Process Clause. A "dependency" requirement of the Social Security Act sharply discriminated between the sexes: widowers, but not widows, had to show they had been receiving at least one-half of their support from their deceased spouse's work in order to collect survivor's benefits based on the spouse's lifetime of work. Advocates of women's rights

attacked this provision because it resulted in giving less protection
to the family of a female wage earner than to that of a male wage
earner. The Court overturned the provision by finding it wanting
when measured by the test set forth in the earlier Oklahoma case.[11]

It should be apparent from even this brief account of Court doctrine that the question of standards of judicial review might well be
controlling for the legal disposition of *Bakke* and the larger issues
of race preference policy it raised. Faced with the novel development of affirmative racial classifications, the Court could try to
fit it within the existing dual formulas for handling Equal Protection challenges—rational basis or strict scrutiny. Or it could devise a review standard between those two, as it had for dealing
with gender classifications by government. Or it could develop an
entirely new and different approach for evaluating minority preferential admissions in particular or race preference in general.

The standard of review the Court chose also would determine
the extent of its own continuing involvement in the resolution of
the controversy. The two older standards were so closely associated
with predictable outcomes—the rational basis test with judicial affirmation and the strict scrutiny test with judicial invalidation—
as to leave little effective discretion in the hands of the Court. The
use of other review standards, in contrast, would leave the Court
at the center of the task of defining, delimiting, and shaping what
sorts of positive racial classifications were permissible and which
were not.

As these comments imply, in considering what review standard
to adopt the Court was not likely to treat the problem abstractly or
simply as an intellectual puzzle divorced from a practical context.
Almost certainly, the justices would remain mindful of the effects
of alternative standards on their judgment of affirmative racial discrimination and on the Court's continuing role in settling the conflict—and the choice of a review standard would follow accordingly.

Racial Remedies for Racial Wrongs

In some circumstances, nonnegative racial classifications were endorsed or imposed by the courts without reference to the strict scrutiny standard. Two such categories merit discussion, with special
attention to their fit to the *Bakke* problem.

The first class of exceptions was the use of racial classification
as a specific remedy for specific cases of past racial discrimination.

When, for example, a firm was shown to have discriminated against hiring blacks or promoting those black employees it had, a court might impose race-specific remedies. (The determination of employment discrimination and its remedies ordinarily would come about through enforcement of statutes or administrative regulations, not as an Equal Protection proceeding as such.) On hiring, the court-imposed remedy might go so far as to require the firm to assign a fixed percentage of new hires over a given period to qualified black job applicants. On promotion, the remedies might include requiring the firm to upgrade or promote all qualified black employees, to extend them compensatory back pay, and to give them seniority in their new positions equal to the seniority they would have had if they had been promoted at the appropriate earlier time.*

Court-directed desegregation of public education provides another illustration of the deliberate use of racial categories to counter the effects of previous racial discrimination. For example, in holding unconstitutional a North Carolina antibusing law that prohibited the assignment of students to public schools on the basis of their race, the Court observed:

> Just as the race of students must be considered in determining whether a constitutional violation has occurred, so also must race be considered in formulating a remedy. To forbid, at this stage, all assignments made on the basis of race would deprive school authorities of the one tool absolutely essential to fulfillment of their constitutional obligation to eliminate existing dual school systems.[12]

Moreover, federal courts could order school districts to provide remedial education programs for children from illegally segregated schools, on the grounds that the reassignment of children, black and white, might not be enough to erase the effects of segregation.

Could the admissions practices challenged by DeFunis and Bakke be placed in this category of exceptions to the strict scrutiny rule (i.e., as being a racial remedy for a specific racial wrong)? Under the customary meaning of a "specific racial wrong," the answer

---

* The Supreme Court has not yet reviewed the full range of racial remedies that lower federal courts and administrative agencies have imposed. For example, the Court has approved compensation, including the award of retroactive seniority, for identifiable victims of specific discrimination, but it has not decided the legality of procedures requiring employers who previously had discriminated to hire or promote a certain ratio of qualified minorities or women into their next openings.

had to be unequivocally in the negative. No anti-DeFunis or anti-Bakke brief alleged, much less demonstrated, that the school had engaged in overt discrimination against minorities. Neither school sought to explain its preferential admissions in those terms, and the trial records were devoid of any evidence to that effect. Minority spokesmen were correct in complaining that none of the direct litigants could reasonably be expected to charge or acknowledge negative racial discrimination, but even so there appeared to be no grounds for attributing such discriminatory behavior either to UWLS or to UCDMS.

But even if neither school had practiced invidious discrimination against minorities, weren't both schools integral parts of a larger educational system, and of a society, that had? And since professional schools could offer a remedy for the racial wrongs suffered by some minority persons, why should they be barred from doing so? Using arguments like these, supporters of special admissions sought to expand—really, to alter—the concept of racial remedies for racial wrongs. Thus, for example, it was emphasized that as late as 1948 one-third of approved medical schools in the nation officially denied black applicants admission solely on the basis of race. Minorities were greatly underrepresented within the undergraduate ranks in the University of California system. Many of California's school districts had been found guilty of de jure discrimination, and a large majority of minority students in the nation attended public schools in districts where unlawful school segregation existed.

Public medical schools in California had at no time prior to special admissions programs enrolled significant numbers of Chicanos or blacks. Even if minority applicants generally were competitively weaker than nonminorities, it was argued that medical schools had acted simply to perpetuate, and not to offset, the effects of past and continuing discrimination against minorities elsewhere in the educational system. Anti-Bakke advocates urged, therefore, that at the least those professional schools which wished to rectify the situation by preferentially admitting qualified minority candidates should be allowed to do so.

The broadest formulation of this argument implicated all institutions in the persistent societal discrimination that had been visited on minorities, and imposed on these institutions, especially those in the public sector, an affirmative duty to provide the remedies they could. On the first leg of that argument, UC's *Bakke* brief referred to "unequal education . . . [as] but one facet of a much more pervasive pattern of discrimination against minority persons in this country. . . . Growing up black, Chicano, Asian, or Indian in America is itself an experience which transcends the particular fact of segregated education. . . . The difficulties inherent in growing up as a member of a discrete and insular minority are encountered throughout society."[13] On the second leg, the *amicus* brief on *DeFunis* submitted by Rutgers University made the point squarely:

> [T]he nation's law schools must bear a substantial part of the collective social responsibility for the general exclusion of non-whites from the legal profession and legal institutions as a result of myriad legal, social and educational discriminations over hundreds of years. If these myriad social inequities and injustices have left disproportionate numbers of non-whites ill-equipped to compete in a strict credentials contest, then the law schools must reject strict credentialism in favor of a system which guarantees admission to a substantial number of otherwise qualified non-white applicants.[14]

The most troubling feature of these otherwise plausible arguments was the unrestrained approval they gave for any institution at its own discretion to develop and apply "remedial" race-preference policies. "Racial remedies for racial wrongs" was a sound and workable approach only to the extent that it was carefully circumscribed and monitored; as an open-ended grant of authority to all institutions, its potential for in effect suspending Equal Protection for nonminorities was all too obvious.

In their handling of employment discrimination, for example, the courts considered explicit race preference and racial quotas as extreme forms of relief that were not to be routinely required. Courts imposed such remedies only reluctantly, and then with a pronounced concern to shape them to constrain their harmful effects on nonminorities. Courts were sensitive to the need to tailor the remedy for victims of proven discrimination in terms of a specific, identifiable wrong, and to avoid setting indiscriminate or oversize racial preferences. The purpose of the remedy was "to make persons whole"—not "wholer"—"for injuries suffered on account of unlawful employment discrimination."[15]

It was this judicial structure of constraints that anchored and made feasible limited use of race-based remedies as specific relief for specific, definable, and proven wrongs. What the proponents of special admissions proposed, therefore, was no mere extension of the racial remedies/racial wrongs approach. It was, instead, its transformation from a mode of legal relief that was practical and equitable because it was delimited into a runaway doctrine that gave blanket endorsement for the proliferation of racial preferences throughout the society.

Add-On Benefits
Another category of racial classifications not subject to the strict scrutiny review standard consisted of "add-on benefits" that did not significantly deprive others of benefits or rights. In the area of political rights, for instance, it was permissible to require foreign-language ballots for sizable minorities who were literate in that language but not in English. Viewed narrowly as a matter of voting rights and equality (and without reference to larger issues of ethnic pluralism, Americanization, etc.), this was obviously a facilitative measure for some that did not deny anyone else's voting rights. In the field of education, the Court held that the Civil Rights Act of 1964 required school districts to provide English-language instruction to students of foreign ancestry who spoke no English. This was upheld as an application of the federal government's obligation, through the Due Process Clause of the Fifth Amendment, to provide Equal Protection. Hence the states were instructed to employ certain race or national-origin classifications, not as a remedy for past official discrimination and without any application of the strict scrutiny test.[16] Here, too, a basically add-on benefit was involved, allowing for some small effect on the allocation of a school district's educational resources.

In a sense, school desegregation fit this category as well as the previous one. Race classification in assignment to schools was for the purpose of achieving integration and better racial balance, from which all students, nonminority and minority alike, were presumed to benefit. Even if the benefits were said to be primarily for minorities, Court doctrine made it impossible to claim that pupil assignment by race significantly deprived nonminority students of a right. A school-age child had only the right to attend a public school in his or her district, not to attend a particular school in the district. Hence the school reassignment within the district of a white (or minority) student to promote desegregation violated no one's rights.

There appeared to be no way that preferential admissions for minorities in professional schools could be brought under the protective umbrella of an add-on benefit. Logically, this required that specially admitted minority applicants would be enrolled in addition to all other applicants who would have been admitted in the absence of that program. For the Davis medical school, for example, 84 or 100 seats would have had to be available for regular admissions and an add-on of 16 seats assigned to special admissions. Even in this situation, however, if a school could accommodate 100 rather than 84 new entrants (or 116 rather than 100), and there were 30 to 40 applicants for every available place, the reservation of 16 seats for minorities could hardly be considered an add-on without effect on the admissions chances of others.

Nevertheless, anti-*Bakke* groups attempted to justify minority preferential admissions by analogizing it to educational desegregation, partly on the argument that special admissions was much the same kind of add-on benefit and partly on the previously discussed argument that racial wrongs warranted voluntary racial remedies. A 1971 case, *Swann* v. *Charlotte-Mecklenburg Board of Education*, was given special emphasis because it included the following dictum by Chief Justice Warren Burger, as part of a unanimous Court decision:

> School authorities are traditionally charged with broad power to formulate and implement educational policy and might well conclude, for example, that in order to prepare students to live in a pluralistic society each school should have a prescribed ratio of Negro to white students reflecting the proportion for the district as a whole. To do this as an educational policy is within the broad discretionary powers of school authorities; absent a finding of constitutional violation, however, that would not be within the authority of a federal court.[17]

According to this dictum, it was permissible for a local community, on its own initiative, to make school assignments by race and to require concomitant busing in order to remedy school segregation caused by de facto residential segregation. The authority exercised in this voluntary fashion exceeded that available to the courts, which were restricted to framing such remedies for situations of demonstrated de jure segregation. Moreover, the Court in *Swann* said nothing about racial classifications as suspect or as requiring the strict scrutiny test.

Not surprisingly, supporters of special admissions pressed the *Swann* dictum into service in their behalf, arguing by analogy that voluntary race preference in admissions was equivalently allowable. In rejecting that argument, the partisans of Bakke and DeFunis stressed several themes. One theme was that education desegregation cases stood for the proposition that race distinctions in education were illegal, not that race preference was valid. The purpose was to secure equal benefits to all through racial integration, the achievement of which required equal treatment of all with respect to school assignments. Another theme was to note that constitutional justification for voluntary busing for desegregation had never been made very clear by the Court, that the *Swann* comments were only dicta and hence neither essential to the decision nor binding on the Court, and that *Swann* actually dealt with court-ordered desegregation of a school system in North Carolina that had been guilty of de jure segregation. The final theme, and the one most emphasized, sharply distinguished preferential admissions from education desegregation on the grounds that it inescapably involved a major deprivation of nonminority rights or benefits, namely, exclusion from the professional school.

This last argument—the exclusion factor—was the most damaging to the hopes of those favoring special admissions that the race preferences they sought could be justified by linkage to education desegregation doctrines. There were only two ways to try to neutralize that key argument, and both were tried. The first, which was much the less credible and estimable of the two, sought to escape the problem by minimizing the adverse effect of preferential admissions on nonminority applicants who were rejected. For example, one otherwise sensible study of the special admissions problem concluded on the following note:

". . . if expansion of opportunity for blacks from Seattle's center city means that Marco DeFunis will have to attend law school in Oregon rather than remaining at home, that seems not too heavy a price for a result that can be achieved in no other way.[18]

The other side of this coin was the argument that a nonminority applicant who was not accepted at some school of his choice probably was not deserving of admission (e.g., Allan Bakke and his string of rejections by medical schools for 1973, followed by his applying only to UCDMS for 1974 admission).

Another point often made was that no nonminority applicant had a constitutional right to go to medical or law school, as if somehow that minimized the deprivation of being rejected on illegitimate grounds. The obvious response was that no one, nonminority or minority, had a right to be admitted under selective admissions and that the issue in contention was precisely what role, if any, race could play in admissions decisions. Finally, some applied a group measure to admissions and concluded that nonminorities as a class had not been hurt by the advent of special admissions in the late 1960s. Most of the entry places, taking into account the additional first-year places opened by expansion of existing schools and establishment of new ones, still went disproportionately and overwhelmingly to nonminorities. The ready answer to this was that Equal Protection was an individual right, not one conditioned on group membership; consequently, white applicants who were rejected because of minority preference could not be expected to feel less harmed because other whites who were admitted constituted the large majority of the entering class.

The second line of argument that sought to connect special admissions to education desegregation took a direction exactly opposite to the first. If it could not be demonstrated that the adverse effects of preferential admissions on nonminorities were much less than supposed, then perhaps it could be shown that the deprivations caused by school desegregation were much greater than supposed. To support that thesis, it was argued that forced busing to nonneighborhood schools "hurt" or "harmed" some children (and their parents) in psychological and other ways. And when they were hurt, it was because of their race, which was the basis for their school assignment.* Yet these adverse consequences had not been recognized by the Court as a barrier to school desegregation; they were simply unavoidable side effects of the necessity to achieve a constitutional objective.

The situation in preferential admissions, the argument concluded, closely paralleled that in education desegregation. Affected nonminorities were injured in both instances because of their race. Nevertheless, just as no child had a right to attend a segregated school, so no one had a right to go to a lily-white professional

---

* It might be noted, in passing, that this sort of argument, when advanced by opponents of busing, was often dismissed as a cloak for simple racism.

school. When, therefore, school desegregation was treated as an add-on benefit involving no deprivation of anyone's rights, special admissions was entitled to the same characterization and legal status. "The school desegregation cases," asserted UC's *Bakke* brief, "stand for the proposition that injury to some whites unavoidably prompted by the pursuit of race-conscious remedial ends does not contravene the Equal Protection Clause."[19]

There was always the possibility that the U.S. Supreme Court might accept in some important degree the parallelism between preferential admissions and education desegregation vigorously pressed by the anti-Bakke side. It appeared to be a slim chance at best. For one thing, the analogy seemed forced because the exclusion factor remained as an obvious differentiation between the two areas; even if the harm occasioned by school desegregation was acknowledged, it was not comparable to the damage wrought by denial of entry to a professional school. For another, if the deprivation of rights or benefits of nonminorities was to be treated as "unavoidable" and of no legal importance, such an approach in effect became indistinguishable from the previously discussed position that sought to justify voluntary race preference as a remedial response to societal discrimination.

Finally, and by no means least, the asserted analogy between the two areas had twice been explicitly rejected in the litigation. In *DeFunis*, Justice Douglas dismissed the argument with the footnote comment that

> . . . there is a crucial difference between the policy suggested in *Swann* and that under consideration here [UWLS's special admissions]: the *Swann* policy would impinge on no person's constitutional rights, because no one would be excluded from a public school and no one has the right to attend a segregated public school.

In *Bakke,* the rejection of the argument by the California Supreme Court was all the more significant because that court had gone even further than the U.S. Supreme Court in promoting and requiring education desegregation within the state.

> Whatever the inconveniences and whatever the techniques employed to achieve integration, no child is totally deprived of an education because he cannot attend a neighborhood school, and all students, whether or not they are members of a minority race, are

subject to equivalent burdens. . . . The disadvantages suffered by a child who must attend school some distance from his home or is transferred to a school not of his qualitative choice cannot be equated with the absolute denial of a professional education, as occurred in the present case.

Was Regular Admissions Racially Discriminatory?

Under the regular admissions program, stated the professional schools over and over again, they would be able to accept only a fraction of the qualified minority applicants they actually accepted under special admissions. Could this be taken to mean that regular admissions, precisely because it disproportionately excluded qualified minorities, was itself racially discriminatory? If that interpretation was endorsed, preferential admissions would be solidly vindicated: it could be said that UCDMS and UWLS had simply adopted the kind of minority-favoring program a court or an administrative agency would have ordered them to adopt once the discriminatory character of their regular process had been demonstrated. Surely a professional school, knowing it was but one step ahead of a formal finding that it practiced racial discrimination, could correct its behavior earlier and voluntarily?

For obvious reasons, the direct litigants had no interest in even touching on such a claim, let alone subscribing to it. Neither the Davis medical school nor the Washington law school believed their regular admissions program was discriminatory, and they could not be expected to plead otherwise for the sake of presenting another line of justification for special admissions. As for Bakke and DeFunis, they could only harm their own cause by such an allegation. As a consequence, the trial records are bare of any inquiry or airing of charges about a racially discriminatory reliance on academic criteria for admissions. What Justice Douglas said about UWLS in *DeFunis* applied, therefore, to UCDMS in *Bakke* as well: "There was . . . no showing that the purpose of the school's policy was to eliminate arbitrary and irrelevant barriers to entry by certain racial groups into the . . . profession."

The claim under discussion was advanced by some of the *amici* briefs filed in support of UWLS or UCDMS; it stood little chance of being accorded serious attention by the Court, much less of being accepted as dispositive of the key question of the legality of minority preferential admissions. Without exploration of the claim in trial court, the Supreme Court had no way of evaluating it on its merits; to do this, the Court would have to remand *Bakke* to the California courts with instructions to that effect. In addition, the claim rested on no federal statute or enforcement program that sought to promote minority enrollment in higher education. No such statute or program existed; colleges and universities were accountable to the federal government, as were other contractors, for their employment practices, but the government's authority did not extend to student admissions. The argument that regular admissions involved racial discrimination was based, rather, on analogizing it to administrative and judicial treatment of employment discrimination.

Notwithstanding the probable lack of impact of this line of argument on the *Bakke* outcome, it warrants discussion in its own right. For one thing, it constituted a major theme of some minority and other organizations that was frozen out of the litigation because minorities were not a direct party to the lawsuit. For another, attention should be paid to any serious argument that sought to topple the primary barrier to sizable minority enrollments in professional schools, namely, the heavy reliance on evaluating applicants by their academic credentials. Finally, looking to the future, there was always the possibility that an argument found unpersuasive today could become tomorrow's conventional wisdom.

In the area of government regulation of employment practices, the concept of discrimination was expanded to cover situations where job qualifications or tests had "adverse effects" on minorities. This occurred frequently when the definition of job eligibility disproportionately excluded minorities from the eligibility pool in the first place (e.g., requiring job applicants to have a high school degree) or disproportionately rejected minorities included in the eligibility pool (requiring a minimum score on a general intelligence test). In either situation, the employer was then obligated to demonstrate that the qualifications set for the job were closely related to actual job performance and to validate whatever tests and procedures were used to measure those qualifications. Failing such a demonstration or validation, the qualifications and/or measures had to be altered or dropped, thus modifying or eliminating their adverse effects on minorities.

The foregoing doctrine was established in 1971 by a unanimous Court (Justice Brennan not participating) in *Griggs* v. *Duke Power Company,* which was a landmark case for the field of employment discrimination.[20] Blacks were employed within only one department, which involved primarily manual labor, in the power plant. For new hirings or transfers to better jobs in other departments, possession of a high school diploma and/or the passing of certain tests was required. Blacks failed to meet these requirements at a much higher rate than whites, and a group of black workers brought suit to challenge them as discriminatory.

These requirements were race-neutral on their face and race-related in their effects. The importance of the *Griggs* holding lay in the Court's adoption of the latter standard: where adverse racial effects obtained, and regardless of intent, the job qualifications and tests used were deemed racially discriminatory unless the employer could validate them as accurate indicators of actual job performance. Declared Chief Justice Burger:

> . . . the act [Civil Rights Act of 1964] proscribes not only overt discrimination but also practices that are fair in form but discriminatory in operation. . . . Congress directed the thrust of the act to the consequences of employment practices, not simply the motivations. . . . [G]ood intent . . . does not redeem employment procedures or testing mechanisms that operate as "built-in headwinds" for minority groups and are unrelated to job capability.

This adoption of an effects test for discrimination represented the Court's acceptance of the Equal Employment Opportunity Commission's aggressive and debatable interpretation of congressional intent on Title VII of the Civil Rights Act. The act explicitly permitted employers to make use of "any professionally developed ability test" in their employment practices, provided they were not intended or used for the purpose of discriminating on the basis of race. And there was little evidence that the act sought to buffer any person or group from the effects of color-blind and uniformly applied standards. Nevertheless, the EEOC insisted, and the Court concurred, that such testing mechanisms could not be given

> controlling force unless they are *demonstrably* a reasonable measure of job performance. . . . What Congress has commanded is that any tests used must measure the person for the job and not the person in the abstract. . . . The touchstone is business necessity. If an employment practice which operates to exclude Negroes cannot be shown to be related to job performance, the practice is prohibited.

Title VII also explicitly prohibited requiring an employer to grant preferential hiring or advancement to any individual or group in order to maintain a racial balance in his work force. As part of its *Griggs* decision, the Court took pains to emphasize that it was neither advocating nor countenancing racial preference in employment:

> Congress did not intend . . . to guarantee a job to every person regardless of qualifications. . . . [Title VII] does not command that any person be hired simply because he was formerly the subject of discrimination, or because he is a member of a minority group. Discriminatory preference for any group, minority or majority, is precisely and only what Congress has proscribed. . . . Congress has not commanded that the less qualified be preferred over the better qualified simply because of minority origins. Far from disparaging job qualifications as such, Congress has made such qualifications the controlling factor, so that race, religion, nationality, and sex become irrelevant.

There could be little doubt of the soundness of the general direction set by what came to be called the "*Griggs* doctrine": an insistence on the job-relatedness of job qualifications spurred the removal of artificial and unnecessary barriers to hiring and promotion which, however unintendedly, operated to disadvantage minorities. Yet, like the controversy that developed over Affirmative Action, considerable dispute followed in the wake of *Griggs* over alleged divergence between principle and practice, notwithstanding the Court's ringing declarations (as quoted above) against race-based preferential hiring in neglect of comparative qualifications and for race-free individual hiring in accord with proper job qualifications.

As it happened, although the "science" of setting standards for job qualifications and performance was practiced by a multimillion-dollar industry and appeared sophisticated, it was in fact rather primitive. Often, companies could not meet the burden of proof assigned to them to demonstrate job qualifications or validate tests. Moreover, the enforcing federal bureaucracies could, if they wished, make the standards for validation onerous and virtually impossible to satisfy. Then, too, the same confusion marked the thinking about job qualifications and tests as was earlier noted in connection with attitudes toward SAT, LSAT, and MCAT requirements for higher education admissions. Because many wrongly assumed that a fair test was one that did not distinguish between disadvantaged minorities and others, any standards or measures that led to such distinctions became automatically suspect. Indeed, at the extreme, there were those who dismissed the whole business of standards as nothing but a power play by white (male) insiders designed to keep minorities (and women) on the outside.

As one group saw it, overzealous administrative and lower-court enforcement violated the intent of Title VII and the Supreme Court's clear directive. As another and opposed group saw it, vigorous implementation fulfilled the law's purpose; indeed, as EEOC and the Civil Rights Commission told it, the trouble was that enforcement was not energetic enough. Whatever the truth of these conflicting views, it appeared that many firms chose neither to risk litigation, bad publicity, or contract cancellation nor to engage in the difficult, expensive, and uncertain task of seeking to validate their job tests. "The legal status of employment tests has become so complicated now," reported a close observer in late 1977, "that many employers have taken the easy road and suspended their use even before the tests have been challenged."[21] With lower job qualifications, the minorities' proportion of the eligibility pool increased, which in turn set larger Affirmative Action goals for minority employment.

The *Griggs* doctrine, in short, became the foundation for subsequent enforcement of equal employment objectives because it approached racial discrimination in terms of the effects of employment practices rather than their intent or purpose. Earlier, when official racial segregation had been rampant, its discriminatory purposes and consequences were so flagrant as to obviate any need to distinguish sharply between intent and effect. As blatant forms of race discrimination disappeared, it was no longer easy to infer racist intent from a reading of a statute or administrative regulation on its face. Instead, inquiry focused on whether the effects of a given law or policy were distinctively disadvantageous to minorities. In a sense, intent was inferred when pronounced adverse effects were found, but the language used was that of an "effects" test of discrimination. Administrators and judges made frequent use of this approach in the policy fields of housing, urban renewal, education, and the like.

Griggs, then, both contributed to and reflected this development with respect to equal opportunity in employment. But the *Griggs* doctrine was the Court's reading of Title VII of the Civil Rights Act, not of the Equal Protection Clause of the Constitution. In mid-1976 the Court addressed the latter subject, and it came out with another approach to racial discrimination that introduced (or reintroduced) the dimension of intent.

The case centered on the use of a federal civil service exam of verbal ability, vocabulary, reading, and comprehension for police training applicants in Washington, D.C.[22] Blacks failed the exam at four times the rate of whites (57 to 13 percent), and a suit was filed in 1970 based solely on that statistical evidence. Because the litigation began before the Civil Rights Act was extended to cover public employees in 1972, the exam was challenged on Equal Protection rather than Title VII grounds. In a 7–2 decision, with Justice White writing the majority opinion, the Court held that

> Disproportionate impact is not irrelevant, but it is not the sole touchstone of an invidious racial discrimination forbidden by the Constitution. . . . [T]he invidious quality of a law claimed to be racially discriminatory must ultimately be traced to a discriminatory purpose.

To prove discriminatory intent was a more stringent standard than to demonstrate disproportionate impact and then to assign the employer the burden of proving the validity of the job qualifications set and the job tests used. Hence Justices Brennan and Marshall warned in their dissent that the Court's holding had "the potential of significantly weakening statutory safeguards against discrimination in employment." Indeed, in their decision the Court majority criticized but did not overturn some sixteen recent lower federal court rulings won by minorities on the basis of the "disproportional racial effects" standard. And in two subsequent cases, the Court's decisions gave substance to the anxiety that underlay the dissenters' warning.

In the first of these two cases, decided in mid-1977 by 7–2 vote, the Court held that seniority systems perpetuating the effects of past discrimination that occurred before July 2, 1965 (the date Title VII of the Civil Rights Act went into effect), were legal unless it could be shown they were set up for discriminatory purposes.[23] (In this same case the Court also reiterated its earlier ruling that retroactive seniority had to be granted workers who could prove job bias in violation of Title VII after the effective date of July 2,

1965.) The opinion indicated that the *Griggs* doctrine would have been applied but for a specific exception for "bona fide" seniority systems Congress had put into Title VII. It was not the intent of Congress, stated Justice Potter Stewart for the majority, "to destroy or water down the vested seniority rights of employees simply because their employer had engaged in discrimination prior to the passage of the [Civil Rights Act]."

Nevertheless, the lower courts had consistently read that provision oppositely to the high court's interpretation; if a seniority system had the effect of locking minorities into less desirable jobs, it was deemed to be discriminatory in intent and not bona fide. Justices Brennan and Marshall, who dissented once again, termed the majority opinion "devastating" and predicted that because of it ". . . equal opportunity will remain a distant dream for all incumbent employees."

The second case, decided in early 1978, dealt with a familiar sort of question: was the use of standardized tests for the hiring and promotion of teachers presumptively discriminatory because the results demonstrated disproportionate racial impact?[24] The setting was South Carolina, which at the time spent the least amount of money per capita for public education of the 50 states. As part of an effort to upgrade the educational performance of its students, the state began to tighten its teacher certification through use of two tests prepared by the Educational Testing Service. In 1975, the year the suit was filed, the passing level was set at the fifth percentile nationally; that is, 95 percent of those who took the test nationally averaged higher scores. Even at this low minimum level, however, less than one-fifth of the black test takers passed, compared with over four-fifths of the whites who took the tests. Acting on a complaint by the Equal Employment Opportunity Commission, the Justice Department (joined by the National Education Association, a teachers' union) filed suit to invalidate the tests.

A federal appeals court held the tests not to be discriminatory, despite their stark racial impact, because no intent to discriminate was shown. The U.S. Supreme Court, without hearing oral argument and without issuing a written opinion, summarily affirmed by 5–2 vote the decision of the appeals court. Justice White sharply dissented on the grounds that the appeals court had slighted the *Griggs* doctrine and had misunderstood the Court's decision in the

District of Columbia police applicants case that he had written. Justice Brennan joined him in an unsuccessful call for the Court to hear the case and provide a written opinion; Justices Harry Blackmun and Marshall did not participate in this decision.

In sum, the Court developed different standards for determining whether employment discrimination existed. Starting from *Griggs* in 1971, the one standard was an "adverse racial effects" test for enforcement of Title VII. From the Washington, D.C., police applicants case in mid-1976, the other and much tougher standard was a "discriminatory intent" test for application of Equal Protection rights. The two standards could coexist because each derived from a different source of authority, the one statutory and the other constitutional. But it was an uneasy coexistence, productive of tension and ambiguity, as indicated by the two recent cases just discussed. The Court still had some distance to go to provide a unified standard for determining when employment discrimination existed.

For reasons earlier explored, the attempt to defend minority preferential admissions by likening it to employment nondiscrimination regulation had little chance of directly affecting *DeFunis* or *Bakke*. The introduction of the argument was best understood as an effort by concerned organizations to lay the groundwork for a possibly useful approach in future litigation and to test the waters for Court receptivity to that approach. Viewed in these terms, it appeared unlikely that the argument would prove persuasive or helpful to the anti-Bakke cause.

One version of the argument called for treating admissions decisions to professional schools as the initial, critical stage of employment for prospective attorneys and doctors (i.e., admission was not analogous to employment, it was employment).[25] In its usual formulation, however, the argument emphasized the disproportionate racial impact that resulted from school dependency on academic criteria for their regular admissions decisions, and then insisted that the schools be required, as would employers in a comparable situation, to validate their regular admissions standards:

Where utilization of ability tests has the effect of excluding minority applicants, those tests become themselves "suspect" and the proponent of relying solely on testing bears the burden. Since it is the petitioners [DeFunis] who seek here to base admission solely on tests and grades, it is *their classification* that is "suspect," not that of the law school.[26] (Emphasis in original)

Yet another variant, discussed in chapter 8, urged that professional schools should prepare persons for varied professional careers and not just for good school performance as students. Hence UWLS and UCDMS should be assigned the burden of demonstrating that its admissions criteria were closely related to the skills needed for employment as a lawyer or doctor.[27]

Even if the debatable premise that admission was analogous to employment were accepted, effective response to the argument was not hard to come by. On the one side, nothing predicted school performance better than the academic measures that were used. And on the other, no one as yet knew what other factors to measure, or how to measure them, that would reliably predict successful postschool professional careers. Hence it surely was reasonable —and permissible—to make considerable use of the proven indicators of superior school performance.

Furthermore, a justification for race preference did not automatically follow from a sharply lessened dependence on academic criteria for admissions decisions. All that followed was that other criteria would be accorded greater influence or, at the extreme, that the choice of which qualified applicants to admit would be accomplished by random selection or lottery. Whether preference could be given to minorities, in other words, would still remain the key disputed issue requiring resolution.

The chief stumbling block to the anti-Bakke side's profitable use of the employment analogy was the hard fact that the traditional academic indices predicted as accurately for minority applicants as for nonminorities. Given that condition, a reliance on the model of employment discrimination regulation could actually be turned to the benefit of the supporters of Allan Bakke. Qualifications that led to adverse racial impact had to be validated, but once validated they were legitimately in place and controlling for the selection among competitive applicants. The *Griggs* doctrine, after all, established the primacy of validated job qualifications and tests, not of race preference; indeed, as quoted earlier, the

Court in that case flatly declared that Congress intended in Title VII to proscribe "discriminatory preference for any group, minority or majority. . . ."

Moreover, when in mid-1976 the Court adopted discriminatory intent as the hallmark of employment discrimination in violation of Equal Protection, the change tipped the analogy even farther in Bakke's direction. By the test of intent, the Davis medical school plainly was innocent of racial discrimination in resting its regular admissions on academic criteria. The same could not be said about the special admissions program. On that, UCDMS's intent to discriminate racially was readily inferable from the fact that the set-aside of 16 seats inescapably limited white enrollees to no more than 84.

The Available Equal Protection Formulas
In considering the constitutionality of positive racial classifications challenged under Equal Protection, lower federal courts and state courts had to operate within a framework provided by U.S. Supreme Court holdings on the subject. This framework could be altered, of course, by the Court's own decision in *Bakke,* but until that happened the other courts remained bound by previous Court interpretations. As this chapter's commentary on Court doctrine has indicated, the available legal formulas had not been developed with race-preference policies in mind and, consequently, they generally were not well suited for the handling of that new phenomenon.

If treated as just another form of racial classification, minority preferential admissions at UWLS and UCDMS would have to meet the strict scrutiny test as to both ends and means. The exceptions to that review standard would not apply: neither school's special admissions program was justifiable as a racial remedy to correct past overt race discrimination by the institution or as an add-on benefit without effect on the rights or benefits of others. Similarly, extending the *Griggs* doctrine from employment to admissions provided no exception; preferential admissions was not adopted to modify academic criteria that had been shown to be unrelated to qualifications for effective school performance. When a racial classification was assessed by strict scrutiny criteria, the classification typically was held unconstitutional. Since strict scrutiny was not the same as a flat prohibition of racial classifications, however, there remained a chance that race preference, in contrast to negative race discrimination, might pass the strict scrutiny test.

There were other ways to use the available formulas in behalf of a judgment that special admissions was a constitutionally permissible form of racial classification. The exception to strict scrutiny that allowed racial remedies for racial wrongs could be held to apply, on the arguable grounds that professional schools could act to offset the effects of extensive past discrimination against minorities by other institutions of education and of the larger society. Much less persuasive, but still available for a court determined to use it, was the argument that preferential admissions was as much an add-on benefit as education desegregation, to which strict scrutiny did not apply. Finally, positive and negative race discrimination could be deemed sufficiently dissimilar for the former to warrant a less stringent review standard than strict scrutiny, such as the rational basis test or a special intermediate standard.

DeFunis in the Courts

Both sides to the *DeFunis* and *Bakke* controversies agreed on a number of important matters concerning racial classification. For one thing, invidious race discrimination against minorities was uniformly condemned as a violation of Equal Protection. For another, it was felt proper for a court or administrative agency to use racial classification as part of a remedy to correct for specific past discrimination. A third item of consensus was that positive and negative racial classification shared the common feature of being classification by race. Finally, except for a few dissenting voices, there was agreement that Equal Protection covered an individual's claim to fair treatment and was not solely a group right.

The gulf dividing the disputants related to their divergent views on how positive racial classifications should be treated. Race preference and race discrimination were alike in some respects and different in others. Did what they shared outweigh what differentiated them? Should they be judged by the same constitutional criteria and tests? If not, what standards should be used to distinguish permissible race preferences?

What Review Standard for Race Preferences?

The allies of Marco DeFunis and Allan Bakke were essentially wedded to the wisdom and necessity of holding fast to nonracial policy (allowing for the few exceptions noted earlier) as the standard for constitutionality. Their touchstone was Justice Harlan's dissent in the turn-of-the-century case in which the Court approved separate-but-equal racial segregation: "The Constitution is color-blind and neither knows nor tolerates classes among its citizens."[1] In their view, race preference was well-intentioned racism at best;

obviously better than malevolent racism, it was racism nonetheless.

Just as the antipreferential admissions spokesmen would have outlawed negative race discrimination on a per se basis, so they considered race preference unconstitutional. Argued one pro-Bakke *amicus* brief:

> A difference in race cannot be an appropriate justification for different treatment by the state. . . . [The] Equal Protection Clause means that the constitutional rights of a person cannot depend on his race, or it means nothing.[2]

They realized that this was likely to be too flatfooted a position for the Court to adopt, especially since it had not done so for invidious racial discrimination against minorities. After all, might there not be some circumstances when a race classification, positive or negative, would be tolerable?

In terms of the feasible legal formulas available, then, the closest to the per se invalidity standard that could be had was the application of the strict scrutiny standard—and that was exactly what the supporters of Bakke and DeFunis emphasized. By requiring a close review of both ends and means, and especially by insisting on rigorous use of the "less onerous means" test, it was anticipated that race-preference policies would be invalidated as invariably as negative race discrimination had been. More precisely stated, the expectation was that all race preferences which deprived others of benefits or rights (and which were not properly imposed racial remedies for specific racial wrongs) would be routinely held unconstitutional.

Not surprisingly, most proponents of preferential admissions took a comparably extreme position on the other side. The differences in purpose and effects between positive and negative racial classification were so clear-cut, they argued, that the latter's review standard was entirely inappropriate for the former. True, race preferences imposed some costs on some nonminority persons. But these costs, being unavoidable and relatively small, were offset by the important benefits achieved in promoting minority equality of opportunity and social-racial integration. Moreover, went the argument, the political process provided ample safeguards against excessive race preferences because nonminorities controlled the process and hence could alter the preferences as they wished.* Unlike the need for special judicial protection under the strict scrutiny test for "discrete and insular" minorities, there was no need for the courts to protect the interests of the majority. The only review standard required, concluded this argument, was the rational basis test.

Considerably more than preferential admissions would be permissible under so unexacting a review standard. Broadly, any policy could be adopted whose intent or effect was to assist minorities and for which there was some plausible justification. On the rationale of providing minorities with sensitive support, for example, a school could arrange for racially separate residence units or special curricular and grading systems. There would be no need, as far as the rational basis standard was concerned, to take into account the effect of such policies on others or the availability of less extreme actions. All varieties of special admissions would be equivalently lawful; their differences in concept and operation would be matters of detail entirely within the discretion of each school.

Nevertheless, it was apparent that race-preference polices called for a more substantial review standard than the rational basis test, which in effect neutered the courts.[3] Race was inherently too dangerous and divisive a category, and one that was too liable to misuse, to be exempted from effective judicial monitoring and genuine review. Since the granting of race preference in any competitive situation necessarily involved some degree of reverse discrimination, a significant judicial role was required. Moreover, the argument's premise—that one could confidently and easily distinguish between "good" and "bad" racial discrimination—was unsound. Gauging a policy's legislative or administrative intent was subject to uncertainty; relying on an assessment of effects also provided no sure guide between the two categories of discrimination. For example, in public housing units an upper limit on the proportion of blacks often was set below the "tipping" point when whites would leave the area, in order that the housing would remain integrated rather than become predominantly black. The effect was to reduce the amount of housing available to blacks. For those who equated promotion of racial integration with minority advancement, the intent was benignly pro-minority; for those who preferred minorities

---

* This line of argument is discussed in chapter 13.

to have more resources, even at the expense of integration, the intent was not benign.

Why did so many briefs argue for so inadequate a review standard as the rational basis test? For some, there was a genuine belief in the compelling need for compensatory and remedial policies in behalf of long-disadvantaged minorities, which would often involve some burdens on nonminorities, and a corresponding disposition to provide maximum discretion to government to enact such policies. For most, the emphasis on the rational basis standard was an appropriate adversarial strategy for the litigation at hand. It underscored the proposition that positive race classification was so different from negative race classification that the Court should not apply to the former the approach it had developed for the latter. The objective, in short, was not so much to get the rational basis standard adopted as to secure a standard less severe than strict scrutiny.

One example of an intermediate review standard was the important state interest/substantial relation test the Court had applied to sex discrimination, as in the case of the Oklahoma drinking law (see chapter 9). Another possibility was a "balancing of interests" test, involving the weighing of costs and benefits, which will be discussed later in this chapter. Still another was suggested by the University of California's counsel:

> No race-conscious admission program should be wholly free from constitutional scrutiny. When race is taken into account, the federal courts, upon a proper showing, have a duty to inquire (1) whether the use is noninvidious, (2) whether the program was adopted to counter the effects of past societal discrimination and secure the educational, professional and social benefits of racial diversity, and (3) whether the program is tailored to such objectives. Once these criteria are satisfied, as in the present case, the judicial function is discharged.[4]

There could be no assurance, of course, that the Court would agree with UC's position that "[w]hatever standard of review properly controls in this case [*Bakke*], it is not strict scrutiny."[5] Hence the university's brief, and virtually all the anti-Bakke *amici* briefs, laid considerable stress on the argument that the special admissions program at Davis was constitutional under that exacting review standard. Its objectives clearly met the test of compelling state interest, and the means chosen were the most precise, tailored, and effective means to reach the permitted objectives. "Under any standard of strict scrutiny which does not require the impossible," declared the UC brief, "the Davis program is valid."[6]

From this bewildering array of conflicting arguments, the courts had to determine what justifications to require to validate positive racial classifications. Until the U.S. Supreme Court acted definitively on that issue, however, other courts had no sure guidelines for coming to grips with it. In these circumstances, it should not surprise that the state courts of Washington and California came to opposite conclusions about the legitimacy of minority preferential admissions.

DeFunis in the Washington Courts

The trial court judge, Lloyd Shorett, fully upheld Marco DeFunis's Equal Protection claim.[7] As Judge Shorett viewed UWLS's special admissions program, it involved "the admission of less qualified" persons on racial grounds, which then resulted in "a denial of places" to those better qualified. The judge based his decision on his understanding that the *Brown* case of 1954 (the watershed education desegregation case) held that "public education must be equally available to all regardless of race." After that 1954 ruling, Judge Shorett concluded, "the Fourteenth Amendment could no longer be stretched to accommodate the needs of any race. . . . [T]he only safe rule is to treat all races alike. . . ."

Believing "there should be a remedy for the wrong," Judge Shorett instructed UWLS to enroll DeFunis in time to begin the 1971–72 academic year; he carefully excluded from that ruling all other applicants UWLS had rejected, none of whom had filed suit, to ensure that no rash of litigation by them would follow. Complying, UWLS allowed DeFunis to enter, but at the same time it appealed the ruling directly to the state supreme court, being able to bypass the court of appeals because a constitutional claim was involved. The case was argued before the state's high court in mid-May 1972; in March 1973, by a 6–2 vote, the Washington Supreme Court reversed the lower court and held for UWLS.[8]

The first question for the court was whether Marco DeFunis had "standing" to sue (i.e., was he a proper party to bring the case?). The doctrine of standing set mutually reinforcing limits on the extent of court intervention and on who could challenge a law or other government action in the courts. Under the Constitution, the jurisdiction of the judiciary extends only to a genuine "case or controversy," and the U.S. Supreme Court has consistently held that "federal courts are without power to decide questions that cannot affect the rights of the litigants before them." The requirement that a litigant have standing meant that the courts would consider only concrete cases involving specific litigants with real interests at stake, not friendly nonadversary proceedings or requests for advisory opinions.

When applied to the issue of minority preferential admissions in professional schools, the doctrine of standing resulted in few persons being able to challenge that practice. Only those applicants who might have been admitted in the absence of the special admissions program were eligible; the extent to which such plaintiffs would have to demonstrate the probability of their admission depended on how stringently the particular court chose to apply the requirement of standing. Several *amici* briefs of minority organizations, for example, urged that DeFunis had no standing and that his suit should be dismissed accordingly. The Washington Supreme Court felt otherwise. Although acknowledging that "[t]here is no way of knowing that plaintiff would have been admitted to the law school," the court held that DeFunis's personal stake in the outcome of the case was sufficient to establish his standing to sue.

On the substance of the case, the court began by rejecting the trial court's view that Equal Protection or the *Brown* case required color-blind admissions. It held, instead, that a denial of a benefit on the basis of race alone was not, in itself, a violation of Equal Protection "if the racial classification is used in a compensatory way to promote integration." The court read *Brown* as barring racial classifications that "stigmatize a racial group with the stamp of inferiority," and it judged UWLS's special admissions program to be free from that defect.

Having accepted the UWLS policy as a special type of racial classification, the court nonetheless rejected the school's contention that "its purpose and effect . . . both dispense with the need for the strict scrutiny required where 'suspect classification' of state action impinging on 'fundamental interests' is concerned." The court insisted, rather, that the review standard of strict judicial scrutiny was necessary. In rejecting the argument that because affirmative discrimination was "benign" it merited the more permissive rational basis test, the court noted that "the minority admissions policy is certainly not benign with respect to nonminority students who are displaced by it." Once having used that theme to justify adoption of the more stringent rule, however, the court did not return to it again.

Applying the strict scrutiny test, the court held that UWLS had demonstrated a "compelling state interest." The key elements of that demonstration, in the court's view, were the elimination of "racial imbalance within public legal education," hinged in part on the argument that minority persons were taxed along with everyone else to pay for public education; the production of "a racially balanced student body at the Law School," for educational needs and to train lawyers fully competent to practice in the American multiracial society; and the alleviation of a nationwide "shortage of minority attorneys," a need that was linked to the benefits of fuller participation by minorities in political and economic leadership—because lawyers made up a high percentage of public and corporate officials. As to the "less restrictive means" component of the strict scrutiny standard, the court observed that admissions policies such as that of UWLS were the only feasible means that "promises realistically to work now" to reduce the "gross underrepresentation" of minorities in law schools.

The court majority made several other key points in their opinion. It was emphasized that the Equal Protection issue was whether the law school was permitted to take voluntary action to remedy racial imbalance, not whether it was required to do so. In that context, the court rejected the argument that the school was confined to providing remedies only for its own previous racial discrimination and could not try to offset the effects of societal discrimination against minorities. The court also saw no need for UWLS to review each minority applicant's record to determine the extent of personal disadvantagement. Membership in a minority group was felt to be sufficient to establish the likelihood of having suffered psychological harm and, besides, the question of personal disadvantage was irrelevant to satisfying the state's compelling interest in having more minority lawyers. Finally, three majority justices in a brief concurring opinion added a comment on procedural due process. They urged UWLS to provide "more complete published standards for admission" in order to ensure "not only the complete fairness of the process, but also the appearance of fairness."

In sum, although a court's use of strict scrutiny was ordinarily fatal for the challenged measure, the Washington Supreme Court made an exception for the special admissions program because it was an instance of positive racial classification. While the spine of the court's argument was clear enough, the quality of its reasoning left something to be desired because it proceeded more by assertion than by thorough review of the problem. No effort was made, for example, to explore the key elements of a "compelling state interest" or how it differed from just any important governmental objective. Nor was there a careful review of a possible range of nonracial alternatives; the "less onerous means" aspect of strict scrutiny generally was given short shrift. In relying on *Swann* for their justification of special admissions, the court majority neglected its obligation to deal with the racial-exclusion factor inherent in preferential admissions; the entire question of using education desegregation as an analogy to special admissions turned on resolving that issue. Moreover, although the court often spoke of the validity of race as "one factor" in admissions decisions, UWLS's practices—in common with race preference in admissions generally—made race *the* dispositive factor with respect to a share of the available entry places.

The chief justice, joined by another justice, dissented from the majority opinion. They held education desegregation cases to be inapposite because they lacked the element of exclusion of whites that was central to the *DeFunis* problem. As they saw it, Equal Protection meant color-blind policy, hence the UWLS program was unconstitutional and the judgment of the trial court should be affirmed. "Racial bigotry . . . will never be ended," declared the chief justice, "by exalting the political rights of one group or class over that of another. The circle of inequality cannot be broken by shifting the inequities from one man to his neighbor."

Interestingly, the dissent made considerable use of a recent federal district court decision upholding the Equal Protection claims of San Francisco white school administrators against a voluntarily adopted affirmative action plan that excessively favored minorities at the expense of nonminorities.[9] This was the case, discussed in chapter 5, that Reynold Colvin (Bakke's attorney) had successfully argued on behalf of the white administrators. The dissent quoted approvingly from the San Francisco decision that "[n]o one race or ethnic group should ever be accorded preferential treatment over the other" and that "[p]referential treatment under the guise of 'affirmative action' is the imposition of one form of racial discrimination in place of another."

The dissenters also suggested several nonracial means that might be considered in lieu of special admissions. One suggestion was for a set of "comprehensive competitive examinations in predesignated courses" in a variety of disciplines, with the top scorers awarded admission. Another possibility was to "work out a reasonably accurate mathematical correlation between grade values from different colleges . . . in preannounced prelaw courses and to compute those equivalent grades with admission granted the 150 students with the highest grades." Although both methods involved ending the reliance on LSAT scores, their continued emphasis on high academic performance promised to do little, if anything, to bring about increased minority enrollment in law schools.

Chief Justice Hale's third suggestion, perhaps tongue-in-cheek, would revive a method once used by most law schools:

> . . . the fairest way of all—but I doubt its efficacy—[is to] admit all applicants possessing a minimum prerequisite grade point in prescribed courses, conduct the law classes in the field house or stadium, if necessary, give frequent examinations, and let the better qualified few survive on the basis of their grades in law school.

This policy combined a modified version of "open admissions" with a subsequent pruning of the oversize student body by applying the single measure of competitive academic achievement at the close of the first year. For many law students it would set into dizzying motion a revolving door of admission followed by dismissal or withdrawal. The attrition rate for academically underprepared students, such as minorities, would be markedly higher than for students who already had strongly developed academic skills. In effect, this method was also but a variant of academic merit criteria, one that was simply shifted in application from the admissions stage to the end of the initial school year.

The fourth possibility raised by the dissenters was to "prescribe a sound but not extraordinarily high prelaw standard and make a random selection by lot and chance of the 275 applicants to be admitted from among those qualifying." Few schools would find this an attractive option because it would deprive them of an adequate proportion of top-tier applicants and generally would reduce the academic quality of their entering class. Every school would have strong incentives to modify selection by lottery in two complementary directions. One modification would be to exempt those with the strongest academic credentials from the lottery and admit them directly. The other would be to raise the standards for defining minimally qualified so as to reduce the number of low academic achievers who qualified for the lottery. Both modifications, note, would have disproportionate adverse effect on minority applicants.

Finally, the dissenting opinion encouraged the state of Washington to provide special training and financial assistance to students "whose domestic environment has deprived them of a fair chance to compete." But, continued the dissenters, "once these students have reached the point of seeking admission to a professional or graduate school, no preference or partiality can or should . . . be shown them." Read one way, this position could be interpreted to mean that the disadvantagement associated with minority-group membership was an insufficient reason to justify race preference in admissions. Read another way, it could be said to argue that even a race-free preferential admissions program for personally disadvantaged applicants would not pass constitutional muster. In the light of the dissent's heavy emphasis on the use of academic merit criteria for competitive selection among applicants, it was entirely possible that the more stringent second interpretation was the correct one.

Marco DeFunis was about midway through his three-year program at UWLS when the Washington Supreme Court ruled against his claim, and he was almost through with his second year when, in May, the court denied his petition for a rehearing. Since the university made no effort to oust him, DeFunis had no pressing need to appeal the state high court's decision. Moreover, his litigation had led some of his fellow law students to treat him as the "house bigot." DeFunis was not inclined, therefore, to pursue an appeal of the state supreme court ruling, but he was persuaded to do so by his attorney's reminder that he remained at UWLS only by sufferance, and that the university was legally free to dismiss him at any time.

On to the U.S. Supreme Court

Many Americans believe that the U.S. Supreme Court must pass on the constitutionality of all national laws, or of all decisions by state high courts, or of all rulings by lower federal courts. None of these beliefs is true. Statutes take effect without the involvement either

of the Court or courts, and official actions are presumed constitutional unless they are successfully challenged in the courts—but
relatively few are challenged and even fewer are invalidated. Recall,
further, that the Court is limited to dealing with genuine cases or
controversies, with suits brought by litigants who have a clear stake
in the outcome of the case. The Court's basic posture is reactive, not
initiatory. Moreover, the Court is confined by its jurisdiction; virtually all the Court's business is done under its appellate jurisdiction,
which is controlled by the Congress. Because of federalism, for example, the Court has no authority to review a challenge to a state
court's interpretation of the state's own constitution. The Court is
the ultimate judicial interpreter of the meaning of the U.S. Constitution, however, and the interpretations of the Constitution it de-
velops through case decisions are controlling for all other courts and
all public officials, state and federal.

Equally mistaken is the popular notion that any loser in litigation
who is willing to expend the time and money can ultimately have
the Supreme Court decide his or her case. In practice, the overwhelming majority of cases are disposed of at the state trial court or
federal district court level; only a small percentage of cases are
appealed in either jurisdiction. Further, nearly all litigation begun
within the state court system is settled within that system and never
comes before the federal judiciary. The root error of the popular
notion is the supposition that the Court must agree to hear and resolve every case appealed to it that lies within its proper jurisdiction.
Actually, the Court determines which cases, from among the oversupply asking to be heard, it will hear and decide.

The Court, in other words, has its own version of selective admissions; with many more applicant cases than docket places, it must
exercise discretionary judgment on what cases to accept. In recent
years the Court has received annually about 2500 petitions for review involving substantial questions of law or constitutionality. Of
these, the Court has accepted and decided about 150 with full
written opinion. Another 200 or so were accepted and handled on a
per curiam basis (i.e., a short, unsigned opinion "by the Court" that
stated the disposition of the case without elaborating details). The
balance of 2150 cases, representing about 85 percent of the
petitions, were denied review by the Court.

Thus, when Josef Diamond (DeFunis's attorney) sought to have
the Court review the state high court's decision for UWLS, there

was no assurance that the Court would accept his petition. The following brief discussion of the Court's concept of its review function should be helpful in explaining why the Court found the *DeFunis* case worthy of its acceptance.

Nearly all cases filed in the Supreme Court for its consideration for review are brought by petitions for a writ of *certiorari,* which is a Latin term for an old writ that was used to call up the record of a case from an inferior court for prompt review by a superior court. In deciding whether to grant certiorari, the Court's concern is whether the case involves serious and important questions of law or constitutionality whose resolution would be of public benefit. For example, has a lower court decided a substantial federal question inconsistent with, or in advance of, the Court's rulings? Or have federal courts come up with divergent holdings that require reconciliation by the Court? If the petition is supported by at least four of the nine justices, the Court will grant certiorari. When certiorari is denied, the Court ordinarily provides no reason. Since considerable public confusion exists over the meaning of a denial of certiorari, it warrants emphasis that it does not signify Court approval of the lower court's decision. By refusing review, the Court simply leaves standing the decision of the lower court, which remains effective only within that court's geographic area. Hence, even when the Court thinks a lower-court opinion is mistaken, it may deny certiorari if the case is otherwise deemed not important enough for review. It follows that the Court's own positions may reliably be found only in its own decisions, not in lower-court decisions the Court declines to review.

Promptly after the Washington Supreme Court turned down DeFunis's request for a rehearing, his counsel took action to petition the U.S. Supreme Court to hear the case. In early June, Justice Douglas agreed to stay the execution of the state high court's decision, pending the Court's disposition of DeFunis's writ of certiorari.* One *amicus* brief, that of the Anti-Defamation League

---

* Each justice oversees one or more of the eleven U.S. judicial circuits and their courts of appeals. The particular circuit assigned to a justice usually reflected his geographic background; Douglas, from Oregon, had the Northwest. Because the Court closed its term in June, it could not decide on certiorari for *DeFunis* until the fall. Hence it was appropriate for DeFunis to request Justice Douglas to act on behalf of the Court.

of B'nai B'rith, was filed on the issue of certiorari; it urged the Court
to accept the case because of the new and substantial Equal Protection question it raised. UWLS opposed certiorari, of course,
primarily on the grounds that the case was properly decided on the
basis of *Swann* and, therefore, no significant federal question was
involved. In October, the Court requested each side to provide a
memorandum on the question of mootness, i.e., would a Court decision really have any effect on DeFunis's completion of the program at UWLS? Although both sides agreed it was unlikely that
UWLS would dismiss DeFunis if the Court affirmed the state high
court's opinion, they also agreed the case was not moot because
technically the law school would have the right to deny DeFunis's
petition to continue at the school. In November 1973, the Court
granted certiorari.

The Court Moots DeFunis

Well before the Court agreed to hear *DeFunis*, the case had already
aroused considerable interest because it promised to deal for the
first time with the controversial question of the legality of race-
preference policies in the absence of demonstrated overt racial discrimination. Thirteen *amici* briefs were filed in the state supreme
court; eight supported UWLS and five backed DeFunis. (Included
in the eight were several national law school organizations, the
American Bar Association, the American Civil Liberties Union, and
two associations of minority law students. The five pro-DeFunis
briefs were submitted by two Jewish organizations and three individual attorneys.) After the Court announced it would accept
DeFunis for review, over 60 organizations allied themselves with
one or another of 30 *amici* briefs, which was an unusually large
number to be submitted. Once again, the briefs were distributed un-
evenly; 22 were for the university and the remaining 8 for DeFunis.

In theory, *amici* briefs have a distinctively useful function in
helping the Court come to its decision. Even though only cases involving substantial federal questions are accepted for review, the
attorneys for the direct litigants may be unable to present a full
range of argumentation because their overriding obligation is to
their client's needs, not to an examination of the larger issues as
such. Originally, *amici* were disinterested friends of the court who
were not personally involved in the lawsuit, and who could offer the
court legal arguments on the issues different from those stressed by

the litigants. As the practice evolved, however, groups or organizations whose policy, ideological, or material interests were likely to be affected by the Court's decision took over and changed the *amici* role. They submitted briefs as advocates, not as neutrals, and aligned themselves on one side or the other of the legal dispute at issue. Their briefs mostly duplicated the arguments of the litigant they favored; seldom did they present new arguments of potential interest to the Court.

The one general exception to this picture was the *amicus* role of the U.S. government. At present, for example, the solicitor general appears as *amicus*, on behalf of the United States, in any case in which the federal government declares an interest. In addition, the Court frequently invites the solicitor general to participate in nongovernment cases as a valued source of expertise and as representing a breadth of outlook different from the private litigants in the case.

Because of the way *amici* briefs changed, they are often more useful to the organizations submitting them than to the Court. An *amicus* brief serves to meet various needs of an organization, such as demonstrating its activism and status, cementing its alliances with other groups, and reinforcing the policy inclinations and loyalty of its members. Since these objectives obviously have nothing directly to do with the Court, *amici* briefs have been dismissed by some as "show biz," of little value to the judicial process. At the least, however, the opportunity to file *amici* briefs provides a public indicator for both Court and nation of which cases are socially divisive, of which interests line up on what side, and of the extensiveness of group and organizational concern about the outcome.

In *DeFunis*, for instance, if the justices were unaware from other sources about the importance major interests attached to the case, the oversize number of *amici* briefs, together with the twofold number of organizations associated with the briefs, brought home the point to them most forcefully. And the diverse alignments of the briefs on the issues told the Court something of the complexity of the central questions up for resolution.

There were instances of unusual, if not strange, bedfellows: the AFL-CIO and the National Association of Manufacturers submitted separate pro-DeFunis briefs, reflecting their shared fear that a precedent in public education might sanction a racial-quota system in private employment. (Some individual labor unions, such as the United Auto Workers, the United Mine Workers, the United Farm Workers, and the American Federation of State, County, and Municipal Employees, filed briefs on the other side.) Dissension within the liberal and civil rights coalitions was evident, especially among Jewish groups. The leading *amicus* brief for DeFunis was that of the Anti-Defamation League of B'nai B'rith, long active on behalf of civil rights; the American Jewish Committee, the American Jewish Congress, and the Jewish Rights Council also filed pro-DeFunis briefs. On the other hand, one of the outstanding briefs on the anti-DeFunis side was that of the National Organization of Jewish Women, which the Commission on Social Action of the Union of American Hebrew Congregations endorsed.

Although many civil rights and liberal organizations came out in opposition to DeFunis, that position often papered over extensive disagreement within the group on the controversial issues involved. The government exhibited the same tensions. It was said that Solicitor General Robert Bork wanted to file a brief for DeFunis, but was vetoed by the White House on grounds that the case was a "hot potato." The Civil Service Commission, advocate of the merit system, was also understood to have pushed, in vain, for submission of a Department of Justice brief in support of DeFunis. In contrast, the Equal Employment Opportunity Commission, one of the two most aggressive public agencies promoting the interests of minorities (the other was the Civil Rights Commission), actually filed an anti-DeFunis brief in the Court. In a most unusual move, Bork requested the Court not to accept the EEOC brief, and the Court obliged his request.

Briefs on the side of UWLS were submitted also by Harvard, MIT, and Rutgers; by the American Bar Association and various national organizations of law schools; by the Association of American Medical Colleges; and by a variety of black, Mexican-American, Puerto Rican, and Japanese-American organizations, including the NAACP Legal Defense and Educational Fund and the National Urban League. Included within the ranks of the pro-DeFunis camp were organizations of "white ethnics," such as Polish-American and Italo-American groups. These nationality groups, also underrepresented in the professions and generally in the higher occupations, resented what they took to be governmental neglect of their needs and governmental favoritism of blacks and other racial minorities. Because many white ethnics had just begun to "make it" in terms of upward mobility, they felt threatened by the minority-preference policies proliferating in higher education and the public and private employment sectors.

Broadly, the major themes advanced in the *amici* briefs paralleled those emphasized by the direct parties to the case. Josef Diamond argued on behalf of DeFunis that UWLS's minority admissions program involved an invalid special privilege based explicitly on race—"they admitted two classes, not one"[10]—that "classified" DeFunis out of his Equal Protection rights. The decision of the Washington Supreme Court was attacked as a novel and untenable interpretation of Equal Protection; Diamond particularly stressed that the court had made no demonstration of a compelling state interest, which was a prerequisite for any possibility of sustaining a racial classification under the strict scrutiny test.

In arguing for UWLS, Slade Gorton, the attorney general of the state of Washington, essentially reiterated the key points of the state high court's decision. The *Swann* case was held to be controlling for UWLS's admissions policies—"he [DeFunis] was in exactly the same position as the school children in *Swann*"[11]—and hence the strict scrutiny test was unsuitable. Even if strict scrutiny were used (as the Washington Supreme Court had done), Gorton urged that the special admissions program was valid because it met the two tests: there was a compelling state interest to reduce minority underrepresentation in the law school and the law profession, and preferential minority admissions was the only precise and effective way to realize that objective.

Oral argument in *DeFunis* was held on February 26, 1974. With but four months of the Court's term remaining, the media geared to forewarn their readers and viewers of the importance of the forthcoming decision. To the extent this whetted the public's appetite, the disappointment that followed was all the greater. In late April, a bare majority of five justices (Stewart and the four Nixon appointees, Blackmun, Burger, Powell, and Rehnquist) held the case moot because DeFunis would be graduating from UWLS in any event; hence there no longer was any genuine legal controversy before the Court.[12] Justice Brennan, in a forceful dissent concurred in by Douglas, Marshall, and White, characterized the majority as "straining to rid itself of this dispute." In view of how fully the case had been argued, the dissenters complained, and of the tremendous public interest and *amici* participation the case had generated, the Court's disposition of *DeFunis* as moot "clearly disserves the public interest." Moreover, predicted Brennan, the central legal issue would soon be back for Court resolution.* Going further than his fellow dissenters, Justice Douglas delivered a full opinion and thus was the only member of the Court to provide a substantive judgment on the case.

Technically, what the Court had done was to vacate the judgment of the Washington Supreme Court, to which it remanded the case. Because *DeFunis* was a state case, this meant that it provided no precedent for the federal court system but only for the state of Washington. On remand, however, the Washington Supreme Court split so badly that a stalemate resulted: three justices voted for dismissal of the case and of the six who again voted on its merits, four reaffirmed the court's original judgment and two stood by their initial dissent. There was no majority, in other words, for any of the three positions.

Justice Douglas's Opinion

Two themes were uneasily joined in Justice Douglas's opinion; although they were not contradictory, the tension evident in their combination suggested that Douglas had divided views on *DeFunis*.

The first theme was in effect a declaration of the per se invalidity of race preference in competitive admissions. "A finding that the state school employed a racial classification in selecting its students," asserted Douglas, "subjects it to the strictest scrutiny under the Equal Protection Clause." Unlike Washington's high court, Justice Douglas was not disposed to justify preferential admissions by that review standard because it allegedly served a "compelling state interest." "[C]onstitutional guarantees acquire an accordion-like quality," he warned, "[i]f discrimination based on race is constitutionally permissible when those who hold the reins can come up with 'compelling' reasons to justify it." Noting that there might be a few "extreme" situations (such as "racial susceptibility to certain diseases") in which differences in racial treatment would not be

---

* See the opening page of this study for an excerpt from Justice Brennan's opinion.

considered "invidious" discrimination by anyone, Justice Douglas concluded

> Mental ability is not in that category. All races can compete fairly at all professional levels. So far as race is concerned, any state sponsored preference to one race over another in that competition is in my view "invidious" and violative of the Equal Protection Clause.

Race neutrality was the touchstone of constitutionality for Justice Douglas. It was also, in his view, the "key to the problem":

> There is no constitutional right for any race to be preferred. . . . There is no superior person by constitutional standards. A DeFunis who is white is entitled to no advantage by reason of that fact; nor is he subject to any disability, no matter his race or color. Whatever his race, he had a constitutional right to have his application considered on its individual merits in a racially neutral manner.

Justice Douglas's second theme was to suggest admissions policies that were different from minority preferential admissions and from a primary reliance on traditional academic criteria and that might still accomplish much of what law schools wanted. Starting with the premise that tests like the LSAT might be culturally biased against minorities, Douglas concluded that it was appropriate for a school to treat minority applicants separately as a class and evaluate them by a range of criteria in addition to college grades. For example, personal interviews might be stressed, with an emphasis on determining the applicant's motivation, perseverance, and other dimensions of his or her full potential. Summer prelaw programs could be set up, and performance in such programs could be weighed heavily in the admissions decision. Favorable consideration could be given to candidates who were likely to apply their legal skills to service underserved communities. Above all, schools could reassess an applicant's prior achievements in the light of his or her disadvantaged background, which could include taking racial discrimination into account.

All these permissible alternatives to UWLS's special admissions program, it should be emphasized, were set within the frame of racial neutrality. "The reason for the separate treatment of minorities as a class," Douglas noted, "is to make more certain that racial factors do not militate *against an applicant or on his behalf.*" The purpose, in short, was to make possible a fairer assessment of minority applicants, not to prefer minority applicants. Nonminority candidates also would be included within, and could benefit from, these expanded admissions practices, thus enlarging opportunities for all deserving applicants.

The critical difference between the admissions practices suggested by Douglas and that used by UWLS was that admissions decisions would be made "on the basis of individual attributes, rather than according a preference solely on the basis of race." It was because UWLS applied a race-preference policy, argued Douglas, that minority applicants were admitted "who, in the school's own judgment, were less promising than other applicants who were rejected." Under the alternatives proposed by Douglas—assuming they actually worked in the race-neutral manner intended—only the most promising applicants would be accepted, though the measurement of promise would differ for some individual admittees (minority and nonminority) whose overall potential had been understated by conventional academic criteria.

The themes stressed by Justice Douglas plainly led to the conclusion that the Washington high court's decision should be overturned. But Douglas's concern about possible cultural biases in the ordinary admissions criteria led him to a different conclusion. His decision called for vacating the judgment of the state court and remanding the case for a new trial, to consider the impact of objective testing procedures on minorities and whether the LSAT should be eliminated in the evaluation of minority applicants. With this fuller trial record in hand, Douglas would then be able to determine whether "the law school's selection was racially neutral," which in turn would determine his judgment of the constitutionality of UWLS's program.

Justice Douglas's odd disposition of *DeFunis* was of a piece with the generally conflicted and somewhat ambiguous character of his opinion. His major themes comprised a curious duo: on the one side, a condemnation of race preference and an insistence on race-neutral evaluations of competing applicants; on the other, an emphasis on the need to process minority applicants separately and evaluate them by special criteria. The theoretical consistency of the two positions was ostensibly established by Douglas's argument that admissions committees would then be able to compare fairly evalu-

ated minority applicants with fairly evaluated nonminority applicants. The committee's selection would turn on assessing each
candidate's individual promise with respect to meeting a variety of
school objectives, none of which could be defined in racial terms nor
used to justify preference to any racial group, minority or majority.

Douglas's two themes were fully consistent only if they meant
simply that every applicant's personal disadvantagement should be
taken into account to ensure a fairer evaluation of past performance
and future promise. If, however, they meant that primarily minority
applicants should be weighed by different criteria, then the fit between that and race-neutral selection obviously became problematic.
How could applicants be equitably compared on an individual basis
by reliance on noncomparable criteria? In such circumstances, was
it likely in practice—regardless of what the theory said—that the
race of minority applicants would be kept a neutral factor in the
admissions decision? Consider the example offered by Justice
Douglas that was discussed in chapter 7, in which an admissions
committee chose a strongly motivated black applicant with a ghetto
background over a Harvard man from an affluent Harvard family
who had much better, but not top, academic credentials. Douglas
endorsed this hypothetical admissions decision as an instance of
the committee making a judgment on the "individual attributes" of
the two applicants, without reference to race. To be sure, the decision could have come about for that reason, but clearly it also
could have reflected mostly a positive awareness of race.

Justice Douglas's dissent could be read, therefore, as prescribing
an idealized color-blind admissions process within which considerable opportunity existed to exercise race preference quietly to ensure
significant minority enrollment. Almost surely, this was not
Douglas's intent or design. Rather, the tension between the two key
themes of his opinion reflected either Douglas's empathy with both
DeFunis's situation and that of minorities or the intrinsic difficulty
of the policy dilemma, or both. On the former, Douglas was a strong
supporter of minority civil rights, pluralism, diversity, and noncon-
formity. As he saw it, excellence and ability came in many different
forms and were not indexed solely by high LSAT scores. At the same
time, Douglas was himself an outstanding example of a poor boy
who had succeeded by hard work and earned merit; he had worked
his way through college and law school (as Marco DeFunis had
done), and had capped an impressive career by his appointment to

the Supreme Court at the tender age of forty-one. On the second reason for Douglas's conflict, the policy quandary was no easier for him to resolve than for anyone else: was it possible to have genuinely color-blind admissions procedures and sizable minority enrollment; if not, what then could be done?

The Alevy Case

The possibility that the Court might moot *DeFunis* did not lack advance warning. In late 1973 the Court requested each side to submit a memorandum on the issue of mootness. The subject arose again at oral argument in February, and the opposing counsel (Diamond and Gorton) were questioned closely for their views, especially since Marco DeFunis was then in the process of registering for his final term.[13] Still, the question of *DeFunis*'s mootness appeared to be arguable either way; it presented no real bar to any Court majority that was strongly disposed to decide the case on the merits. Hence it was reasonable to speculate, when a case originally accepted on certiorari and argued before the Court was subsequently mooted on technical grounds, that the Court was divided on its substantive issues. It was also probable that *DeFunis* was mooted because the majority of the justices believed it might be useful for the Court to buy time before it had to reconfront the contentious problem of minority preferential admissions.

What might the Court gain by buying time? For one thing, *DeFunis* might stimulate professional schools to experiment with significantly different mechanisms for admitting minorities. This could transform the problem the Court would be asked to resolve, especially if newer mechanisms moved closer to racial neutrality and downplayed race preference. (Justice Douglas's dissent could be helpful in this regard because, as one of the most liberal members of the Court, he would have been expected to support minority preferential admissions, not to oppose it as unconstitutional.) No widespread change in minority admissions practices developed, however, in the three years between the Court's mooting of *DeFunis* and its acceptance of *Bakke* for review.

Another possible benefit of buying time was that the Court might avoid being in the exposed position of having to dispose of a new, controversial problem entirely on its own action. By giving lower courts a chance to work the problem over more, the Court would be better buffered and could profit from their experiences. The Court had a bit better luck with this possibility. In April 1976, several months before the California Supreme Court announced its *Bakke* decision, the highest state court of New York decided a comparable case.

Martin Alevy, a *magna cum laude* graduate of Brooklyn College and a resident of Brooklyn, was denied admission in 1974 to the Downstate Medical Center, a part of the New York State University system. (At the time he applied, Alevy was a second-year microbiology student at the University of Southern California School of Medicine; his GPA was straight *A.*) Alevy filed suit to gain admission, charging that his Equal Protection rights had been violated because less qualified minority applicants were admitted under the school's race-preference policies. The school conceded that it gave special preference to disadvantaged members of certain minority groups and to minority applicants from "the ghetto area of Brooklyn," and that the academic scores (GPA and MCAT) of Alevy were superior to all 66 minority candidates the school had accepted.

In its review of the case, the New York high court dismissed Alevy's petition for relief on the grounds that he failed to show that he would have been admitted in the absence of the minority preferential admissions program.[14] Nonetheless, the court took the opportunity to present its unanimous view of what review standard was appropriate for positive race discrimination. By the standard it offered, "reverse discrimination" (a term deliberately used by the court) was constitutional "in proper circumstances."

For "benign discrimination," the court held, neither of the two prevailing review standards was satisfactory. Strict scrutiny was inappropriate because it "could cut against the very grain of the [Fourteenth] Amendment were the Equal Protection Clause used to strike down measures designed to achieve real equality for persons whom it was intended to aid." The rational basis standard was also unsuitable because of the "untoward consequences" inherent in race-preference policies and practices. Hence some in-between criterion was required, one that would recognize both the benign and the discriminatory features of race preference.

The standard proposed by the court represented a significant modification of the strict scrutiny rule. To be valid, preferential treatment would have to meet two conditions. First, it had to satisfy "a substantial state interest," meaning a legitimate objective that was based on "actuality, and [was] not merely conjectural," and that was clearly articulated by the state. Nevertheless, the interest did not have to be "urgent, paramount, or compelling." The test, ultimately, was one of balancing gains against costs: "to satisfy the substantial interest requirement, it need be found that, on balance, the gain to be derived from the preferential policy outweighs its possible detrimental effects."[15] Based on the example of harmful effects cited by the court, it appeared to refer mostly to social and group consequences rather than to the admissions chances of rejected white applicants. The second condition related to the means used to achieve a racial objective validated by the "substantial state interest" criterion. It had to be shown that "no nonracial, or less objectionable racial, classification [would] serve the same purpose," such as reducing the size of the preference or limiting the time span of its operation.

In anwer, then, to the blunt question it posed for itself—"Is 'reverse' discrimination constitutional?"—the New York court said that race preference could be upheld if it met the ends and means requirements set forth in the court's "balancing" test. Since the court did not apply its test to the particulars of the preferential admissions program of the Downstate Medical Center, the practical effects of the test were as yet unknown. On its face, however, the *Alevy* test differed enough from strict scrutiny to provide the U.S. Supreme Court with another possible way to consider the *Bakke* case and the general problem of affirmative racial discrimination.

Bakke in the California Courts

It was early April 1974 when Allan Bakke received the second and final turndown on his application for 1974 admission to the Davis medical school. One last hope remained for him: the Supreme Court in its *DeFunis* decision might rule against the University of Washington law school in terms that would also invalidate UCDMS's special admissions program. That hope ended later in April, with the announcement of the mooting of *DeFunis*. Recontacting Reynold Colvin, Bakke made preparations to sue UCDMS. After Colvin's efforts to persuade the university to reconsider Bakke's candidacy favorably proved fruitless, the suit was filed in late June. With that action, Bakke took the first step in the fulfillment of Justice Brennan's prediction that the critical questions raised by *DeFunis* would soon be back for the Court's resolution.

The Trial Court
UC Davis is located in Yolo County; Colvin filed Bakke's suit there in order to secure a quicker trial schedule for his client. He also hoped that a "country judge" might be more willing than a big-city judge to grant the injunctive relief Bakke sought, i.e., a court order directing UCDMS to admit Bakke, in exactly the manner that the Washington trial court judge, Lloyd Shorett, had ordered Marco DeFunis's admission to UWLS three years earlier. F. Leslie Manker, a retired superior court (trial court) judge, presided over Bakke's case, which was heard without jury in the old county courthouse in rural Woodland. Since much of Judge Manker's decision has been noted earlier in this study (see chapters 5 and 6), the following summary account merely highlights its major themes.

At issue were two matters: whether the medical school's special admissions program for "economically and/or educationally disadvantaged persons" was legal, and whether Allan Bakke should be admitted to the school. For Bakke, the two matters were necessarily joined. With no basis for claiming one of the 84 regular admissions seats, for which he had competed unsuccessfully, his only chance of gaining admission was to lay claim to one of the 16 seats for which the school had not allowed him to compete because of his race. In short, Bakke had to attack the legality of minority preferential admissions.

For the University of California, on the other hand, the two matters at issue were separable, at least in theory. The university initially had the option of trying to confine the case to the narrow factual question whether Bakke would have been accepted if the 16 seats held for special admissions had been available to him. The regents, however, were primarily concerned about getting an authoritative judicial determination of the validity of minority special admissions; such practices by many of the professional schools on UC campuses had subjected the regents to angry and opposing complaints and pressures. Consequently, UC countered Bakke's suit by filing a cross-complaint for a declaration that the special admissions program was lawful. Once that occurred, the court had no choice but to focus its attention on the program's legality as the paramount issue (which it might have done, in any event) and treat the question of Bakke's admission as secondary.

Judge Manker's Notice of Intended Decision appeared in late November 1974. It included a review of a large number of education desegregation and affirmative action cases (most of which had been cited by Reynold Colvin or Donald Reidhaar, UC's counsel), on the basis of which the judge concluded that "there could be said to be support for either position which the Court might take upon this issue." Nonetheless, Judge Manker came out on the larger of the two questions as firmly against UCDMS as Judge Shorett had earlier ruled against UWLS.

Since no whites had ever been accepted under special admissions, the court held that the program discriminated against white applicants on the basis of race. Characterizing the program as a racial quota (which is what Colvin had emphasized), the judge ruled that it violated Bakke's rights under Equal Protection:

> This Court cannot conclude that there is any compelling or even legitimate public purpose to be served in granting preference to minority students in admission to medical school when to do so denies white persons an equal opportunity for admittance.

Intimating that any use of race was impermissible in admissions decisions, Judge Manker rested his judgment on the Supreme Court's observation in *Brown* (the landmark education desegregation case) that "[s]uch an opportunity [for an education] where the State has undertaken to provide it is a right which must be made available to all on equal terms." In addition, the judge quoted approvingly from the federal district court decision in the San Francisco administrators' case that Colvin had earlier argued successfully:

> No race or ethnic group should ever be granted privileges or immunities not given to every other race. . . . Only in individual accomplishment can equality be achieved.[1]

On the question of the plaintiff's standing to sue, the trial court judge noted that Bakke's claim would have been stronger if he had been eligible for consideration under special admissions and had been denied consideration under that program because of his race. Still, because the special admissions program "reduced his chances of admission by 16 percent," Judge Manker affirmed Bakke's standing as a litigant entitled to object to UCDMS's admissions practices.

The judge did not instruct the Davis medical school to admit Bakke because Dr. Lowrey's review of 1973 and 1974 admissions indicated that Bakke would not have been accepted even if all 100 seats had been available. The process by which Colvin ultimately secured Bakke's admission by judicial order has been fully described earlier in this study; it culminated, it will be recalled, with the California Supreme Court shifting the burden of proof from Bakke to the university, and with UC then stipulating that it could not demonstrate that Bakke would have been rejected in 1973 if there had been no special admissions program.

The Trial Record and the Department of Justice

The record of a case as developed in trial court, especially with respect to establishing the facts of the situation and the major lines of legal argument, is often critical to the disposition of the case at all appellate levels, at which no witnesses are heard. Since the *Bakke* record was alleged to be seriously deficient by the Department of Justice and by some pro-minority organizations, a review of that issue would be appropriate at this point. Some general observations and a discussion of the Justice Department's assertions follow immediately below; the charges of the pro-minority organizations are treated in the next chapter.

To begin with, it would be both unrealistic and unfair to appraise the quality of the *Bakke* record by the inflated standard whether it was fully "worthy" of a U.S. Supreme Court case, or, even more demandingly, of a landmark case. That was not how the case could have been perceived at the trial court stage, albeit both sides to the litigation were aware they were involved in something potentially of considerable importance. Cases that eventually are taken up by the Supreme Court are not flagged as such in advance; in the American judicial system, many important cases accepted by the Court start off as "ordinary" cases, without expectation by the litigants that the case will ultimately go before the Court. The proper standard of judgment, therefore, is whether the *Bakke* record was adequate, not whether it was as close to perfection as possible.

Moreover, as noted earlier, an attorney's professional and ethical obligation is to concentrate on arguments designed to benefit the client, not to argue "big" points of law or constitutionality as such. Adversary-based justice is primarily client-centered justice; although it results in considerable exploration of larger and disputed issues, the explorations remain anchored in the interests of the litigants. "There are few things Supreme Court justices like less," Anthony Lewis has observed, "than a lawyer who puts his client's interest aside in the zeal to make some great change in the law."[2]

As Reynold Colvin saw his client's interests, there was little need (and probably much risk) in using Bakke's claim as the occasion to open a broad inquiry into positive racial discrimination, reverse discrimination, or the permissible and impermissible uses of race in selective admissions. The more effective strategy was to concentrate on the distinctive particulars of UCDMS's admissions practices, especially the explicit reservation of 16 places for minorities, and to hammer home the thesis that it constituted an invalid racial quota. Colvin's objective in trial court, therefore, was to build a record that would document the "narrow factual situation" argument that the special admissions program was in reality a disguised quota system for minority admissions. Since Bakke's goal was to secure entry to Davis medical school, it would be met even if the court chose to respond narrowly to Colvin's argument by overturning UCDMS's program and leaving unanswered the larger question of what race-related admissions practices might be allowable.

The strategy Colvin chose also enabled him to lead from his strength as an accomplished trial lawyer, one who was comfortable with, and skilled at, the task of developing facts and evidence at trial court. As Colvin said of himself when preparing for oral argument on *Bakke* before the U.S. Supreme Court:

> I would be a fool to pretend I'm a great constitutional lawyer or a social philosopher. But the facts of this particular case are very, very strong facts, and as long as I remember my place somehow I'll get through.[3]

While Colvin's public self-appraisals tended to understate his talents—he was fond of describing himself to reporters as "just a country lawyer from San Francisco"—he sought throughout the litigation to stay focused on the facts of the Davis admissions program and to reiterate his core argument: however else race might legitimately be taken into account in admissions decisions, it could not be done by means of a racial quota.

In the trial record he helped develop, Colvin certainly met the essentials of his strategic objective. Considerable detail on UCDMS's regular and special admissions processes was elicited. He established that only minority applicants had been accepted under special admissions and that they were evaluated separately and not in competition with applicants for regular admissions. And he secured evidence to confirm that special admittees had weaker academic credentials than regular admittees. These were the most important characteristics of the Davis program to set in the record, as far as Colvin's needs went, and they provided the factual basis for the decision by both the trial court and the California Supreme Court.

There was room for improvement, nonetheless, in the quality of the data Colvin settled for in trial court. The *DeFunis* record, for instance, included a listing of every candidate accepted for the fall 1974 entering class, with the following data on each: GPA, LSAT score, predicted first-year average, resident/nonresident status, and minority/nonminority status. Equivalent individualized admittee data for 1973 and 1974 admissions at the Davis medical school were not developed in the *Bakke* record; in its place was a relatively slim amount of information reported largely on a group basis (e.g., the averaged academic scores of regular and special admittees). In the absence of specific data on minority candidates actually admitted to UCDMS, Colvin was never able to pinpoint their academic qualifications or establish how the school had determined that each admittee was "fully qualified." Similarly, Colvin chose not to call for the submission of data that would enable him to review how the school decided whether a minority applicant was sufficiently "personally disadvantaged" to be considered under special admissions.

As these comments imply, the burden of developing an adequate trial record fell mostly on Colvin as the attorney for the plaintiff. Broadly speaking, the university as defendant had little interest in presenting a data base on applicants and admissions any fuller than the materials it provided in response to Colvin's requests. Nonetheless, UC did have an obvious need to enter in the record an account of the school's admissions practices from its viewpoint. On the whole, this was done satisfactorily though somewhat thinly, because the views and judgment of only one person (Dr. Lowrey) were elicited. (In *DeFunis*, the participants in trial court included, in addition to the faculty chairman of the admissions committee, the president of the university, the dean of the law school, an expert on the LSAT from the Educational Testing Service, and another outside expert on summer prelaw programs for minorities). To judge by what followed in the California court decisions on *Bakke*, UC's contribution to the trial record was weaker than it might have been in providing a fuller explanation why the "16 seats" constituted a goal, not a quota, and why there were no feasible alternatives to a race-preference policy.

The Department of Justice took a different view of the adequacy of the trial record and the trial court's findings of fact. Asserting that "the findings of the trial court leave unresolved serious questions concerning operation of the special admissions program at Davis in 1973 and 1974,"[4] the department's *amicus* brief advised the Court to vacate the judgment of the California Supreme Court and to remand the case for further proceedings in California that would provide the answers to those questions. What were the alleged deficiencies of the record that led the Justice Department to take so extreme a position?

The department's adverse judgment of the trial record's adequacy derived from its fundamental position on the *Bakke* litigation. The department argued that both the litigants and the California courts had concentrated on the wrong issue, namely, whether race could be taken into account in selective admissions. The answer to that question was in the affirmative, said the department. The real issue, neglected in the litigation, was how race might *permissibly* be taken into account. When the trial record was looked at to determine how UCDMS used race, not simply whether it used race, as an admissions factor, the record's "unresolved serious questions" became apparent. The department's identification of "serious" and "unresolved" questions derived from its own prescription for the proper consideration of race in admissions decisions. This prescription, you will recall, was that race could be used for the purpose of improving the fairness of the evaluation of the prior record and likely potential of minority applicants. The context, however, was one of comparing minority and nonminority applicants competitively for scarce places; the absence of such competition indexed the existence of "rigid exclusionary quotas," which the department held were illegal.

The critical question for the Department of Justice, therefore, was whether the Davis medical school had compared special applicants with regular applicants. If it had, "this would indicate that race had not been used improperly."[5] (And if it had not, the clear implication was that UCDMS had used race improperly.) It was exactly this factual question, the department stated, that the trial record left unresolved. As the department interpreted it, the evidence in the record indicated "that the regular admissions committee played some role in the selection of all 100 students, but it does not indicate what the role was."[6] In like manner, "it also is unclear whether and how the benchmark ratings of special applicants were compared against the benchmark ratings of regular applicants."[7]

It was nothing short of incredible for the Department of Justice to maintain that these factual questions remained unresolved, in view of the fact (duly noted in its brief) that the trial court had found no comparative evaluation of special and regular applicants had taken place and that the university had not challenged the trial court's finding on appeal. It was unthinkable that the university would have failed to make so critical a point, were it true. Independent of what the trial record revealed, absolutely nothing about

UCDMS's admissions program would have led anyone to expect non-minority and disadvantaged minority candidates to have been comparatively evaluated. Quite the contrary. The whole point of the program was to enroll 16 minority persons through special admissions because they were unable to compete effectively against regular applicants by the usual criteria. In sum, there could be no reasonable doubt that the Davis program—in intent, structure, and practice—involved no comparison between the two admissions groups.

The department's questions about the two specific factual matters—comparative benchmark ratings and the role of the regular admissions committee—were no less insubstantial. On the first matter, the trial record did leave unclear such things as whether applicants in special admissions were rated on the same standards as those in regular admissions or whether anything was added to the former's benchmark ratings because of their minority status. But such questions were important only if benchmark ratings were to be used comparatively across the two groups and were so used. Neither in fact was the case, which in itself explained why no one thought to enter into the trial record a detailed account of how the benchmark ratings of special applicants were derived.*

On the second matter, the role of the regular admissions committee, the implication of Dr. Lowrey's testimony (discussed in chapter 4) was that the committee routinely approved recommendees of the special admissions committee, checking only to be sure that each had satisfied formal entrance requirements. So passive a role for the regular committee was thoroughly consistent with the workings of the Davis special program. Plainly, then, there was no reason to suppose that the compiling of a fuller record upon remand of *Bakke* might reveal that the regular committee had actively reviewed minority admittees, much less that it had compared minority and nonminority recommendees.

At oral argument before the U.S. Supreme Court, which occurred after the department's *amicus* brief was submitted, Archibald Cox (UC's special counsel) was asked by Justice Brennan whether "the benchmark ratings in the two programs were comparable?" Cox's reply verified, if further proof were needed, that the department's claims for more information than the trial record provided were without merit.

There wasn't any occasion to put them [special admissions applicants] on the same scale [as regular applicants]. . . . [I]f you were qualified, minority, and disadvantaged, then you were eligible for one of the 16 places and there was no occasion for you to be compared with anyone in the general pool. . . . It [the special admissions committee] wasn't comparing them, it wasn't charged with comparing them with anyone else, and therefore the benchmarks it put on them were only for the purpose of comparing them with each other.[8]

As additional justification of its recommendation for remand, the Justice Department brief offered a grab bag of items on which it said more complete information was necessary. One item was the need to clarify what Judge Manker meant by his use of the term "quota"; perhaps he had confused it with a goal, which also involved a numerical designation?[9] This was a somewhat curious argument for the department to advance; its own brief made only passing mention of "rigid exclusionary quotas," which it then carefully refused to define. In any event, by the department's standards the determination of whether the set-aside of 16 seats represented a goal or a quota appeared to turn on whether applicants to special admissions were evaluated against each other only or against regular applicants as well. This first item, in other words, was a derivative of the larger question just examined, without independent importance.

A second item was that "the record contains no explanation for the selection of the number 16."[10] This complaint was true, but the size of UCDMS's preference program was well in line with that of other schools and required no more than the standard explanation (as discussed in chapter 6). Yet another complaint, also true, was that the record did not explain "why Asian-American persons are included in the special program."[11] The data in the record did indicate, however, that only 2 of the special admissions enrollees in 1973 were Asian-Americans and that members of that minority

---

* Reynold Colvin was mistaken to use as part of his argument that minority special admittees were less qualified than Allan Bakke the fact that some of those admittees had benchmark scores as much as 30 points lower than Bakke. In the absence of the comparability of the ratings, the comparison had no meaning.

group made up less than one-fifth (12 of 63) of all special enrollees in the 1971–74 period. More broadly, it was difficult to understand in what way the Court's determination of the legality of the Davis program might be so dependent on this information as to require remand of the case to provide the explanation before a judicial decision could be reached.

In sum, the Department of Justice failed completely to substantiate its idiosyncratic judgment that the trial record was fatally deficient, which was the ostensible reason it offered for recommending remand of the case to the California courts. The evident flimsiness of its argument on this subject suggested that the department was unwilling to follow through to where its core position obviously led. If, as the Justice Department said, the insulation of minority special admissions applicants from competition with regular applicants was the hallmark of "rigid exclusionary quotas," and such quotas were invalid, then the conclusion followed that the Davis program was unconstitutional. Why the department chose not to adopt that conclusion but to argue unconvincingly for remand will be discussed in the next chapter.

The California Supreme Court

Both parties promptly appealed from Judge Manker's judgment, which was officially entered in early March 1975. Bakke's appeal was from that part of the judgment that denied him admission to UCDMS; the university appealed the trial court's holding that the special admissions program was unconstitutional and that Allan Bakke was entitled to have his application considered without regard to his race or the race of any other applicant. Because of the importance of the issues involved, the state supreme court responded favorably to UC's petition and in June transferred the appeals directly to itself, thereby enabling *Bakke* to bypass the court of appeals.

Since the *Bakke* litigation had begun soon after the unexpected demise of *DeFunis*, it was evident early on that it might turn out to be the successor case on the controversial issue of preferential admissions for minorities. Hence the beginnings of national attention were apparent even at the trial court stage. In mid-January 1975, for instance, the *New York Times* carried an account of Judge Manker's intended decision and noted that legal experts saw in *Bakke* the possibility of a landmark case.[12] It was no surprise, there-

fore, that a sizable number of *amici* briefs on the case were submitted to the state's high court. Six were aligned with the University
of California and two with Allan Bakke, which was just about the
same imbalance that had occurred on *amici* briefs for *DeFunis*. Of
the six for the university, three were from the legal profession (including the Association of American Law Schools), two from the
medical profession (including the Association of American Medical
Colleges), and the remaining one was from the Mexican American
Legal Defense and Educational Fund. The two pro-Bakke briefs
came from the Anti-Defamation League of B'nai B'rith and the
American Federation of Teachers. Yet another indicator of high
interest in *Bakke* was the fact that the court chamber was packed
at oral argument on the case, held March 18, 1976.

The California Supreme Court delivered its decision in mid-
September 1976; the seven-member court divided 6–1.[13] Justice
Stanley Mosk, a former attorney general of the state and a twelve-
year veteran on the court, wrote the majority opinion, which
strongly rejected the University of California's position and struck
down minority preferential admissions as unconstitutional under
Equal Protection. Stated the court:

> We conclude that the program, as administered by the University,
> violates the constitutional rights of nonminority applicants because it
> affords preference on the basis of race to persons who, by the Uni-
> versity's own standards, are not as qualified for the study of medicine
> as nonminority applicants denied admission.

The court began its opinion by recognizing that race classification
by itself was not unconstitutional, and that the positive use of racial
categories had been upheld both in school integration and as an
add-on benefit. But these instances differed from UCDMS's program
in "one critical aspect": "[i]n none of them did the extension of a
right or benefit to a minority have the effect of depriving persons
who were not members of a minority group of benefits which they
would otherwise have enjoyed." Moreover, two things were plain
about the deprivation occasioned by the school's preferential admissions program: (1) some white applicants were denied admission "solely because of their race," and (2) the deprivation involved "the absolute denial of a professional education." Because of
the severity of the Davis program's harmful effects on whites—the
exclusion factor, as this study has called it—the court found un-

acceptable the university's contention that preferential admissions deserved to be treated by the courts in the same manner as school desegregation.

The court also found unpersuasive the asserted analogy of special admissions to employment cases and Title VII. Although preferential treatment of minorities was an allowable remedy, it customarily came into play only with a specific finding of past discriminatory practices by the employer. Rejecting an argument raised in two *amici* briefs, the court noted that the medical school's reliance on academic criteria for its admissions decisions could not be considered as a racially discriminatory practice for which a Title VII remedy was appropriate. For one thing, the Supreme Court had recently read the Equal Protection Clause to require proof of discriminatory intent, not simply of disproportionate racial impact, to demonstrate the existence of racial discrimination. (This referred to the Washington, D.C., police training case, discussed in chapter 9.) For another, the argument raised by *amici* was inappropriate to the case since the trial record contained neither charge nor evidence that the Davis medical school had engaged in past discriminatory conduct.

With respect to the contention that the university's program should be accorded greater toleration because it was undertaken voluntarily, the court noted that voluntary reverse discrimination practices had been overturned in several federal district court cases and rejected the argument that a voluntary program warranted any different treatment than an imposed one. Observed the court:

> [T]here is no merit in the assertion . . . that there is some undefined constitutional significance to the fact that the University elected to adopt the special admission program and was not compelled to do so by court order. To the victim of racial discrimination the result is not noticeably different under either circumstance.

Having established that whites were excluded from the 16 places set aside for disadvantaged minorities, the court majority next looked into the relative qualifications of special applicants and regular applicants. Since special admissions applicants competed only with one another for the 16 seats, "it is obvious," the court stated, "that this procedure may result in acceptance of minority students whose qualifications for medical study, under the standards adopted by the University itself, are inferior to those of some white applicants who are rejected." That is exactly what occurred in 1973 and 1974 admissions (the entering classes for which Bakke was rejected), declared the court, citing the lower GPA and benchmark scores of special applicants. That all special admittees "may have been qualified to study medicine" did not change the problem; most rejected applicants also were qualified and hence "the only revelant inquiry is whether one applicant was more qualified than another."*

The way the court formulated the *Bakke* issue, therefore, was as follows: "whether a racial classification which is intended to assist minorities, but which also has the effect of depriving those who are not so classified of benefits they would enjoy but for their race [i.e., the better-qualified whites who were rejected], violates the constitutional rights of the majority."

The first step was to decide the critical question of the review standard to be used for a racial classification that favored minorities but harmed nonminorities. The court emphatically turned down the notion that anything less than strict scrutiny was appropriate simply because the classification at issue was not anti-minority in intent and did not stigmatize or impute inferiority to the rejected white applicants hurt by special admissions. In the majority's view, strict scrutiny was required "where the [racial] classification results in detriment to a person because of his race." In one of its more eloquent passages, the opinion declared:

> We cannot agree with the proposition that deprivation based upon race is subject to a less demanding standard of review under the Fourteenth Amendment if the race discriminated against is the majority rather than a minority. . . . [W]e do not hesitate to reject the notion that racial discrimination may be more easily justified against one race rather than another, nor can we permit the validity of such discrimination to be determined by a mere census count of the races. . . . [T]he equal protection clause . . . applies to "any person," and its lofty purpose, to secure equality of treatment to all, is incompatible with the premise that some races may be afforded a higher degree of protection against unequal treatment than others.

---

* For a fuller exposition of this point, see the excerpt from the court's opinion presented at the outset of chapter 7 of this study.

The strict scrutiny standard involved two criteria, the first of which was whether the purpose served by the racial classification represented a "compelling state interest." The court identified the following objectives as the university's justification for the Davis program: to integrate the medical school and the medical profession; to provide role models to motivate minority youth; to increase the number of doctors willing to serve the minority community; to enable minority patients to have better rapport with their physicians; and to promote greater interest in treating diseases prevalent among blacks, such as sickle cell anemia and hypertension. Of these five objectives, the court assumed at least for the purposes of argument (*arguendo*) that the first three objectives established a compelling governmental interest. The latter two were rejected, the "rapport" thesis because "racial exclusivity" was an unsound doctrine and the "racial disease" thesis because it was "parochial" and lacked any supporting evidence in the trial record.

After assuming *arguendo* that the Davis program met the first of the two tests under strict scrutiny, the court went on to invalidate special admissions because it failed the second test, i.e., the "less onerous means" requirement. In the view of the majority, the University of California had not demonstrated that its compelling objectives could not be achieved by means less burdensome to the rights of nonminorities. In explicating that judgment, the court developed a position akin to that earlier presented by Justice Douglas in his *DeFunis* opinion, especially his insistence on racially neutral admissions practices as the touchstone of constitutionality and his encouragement of the use of flexible admissions criteria.

The opinion stressed that the requirement of racially neutral admissions standards did not confine the university to conventional academic criteria in evaluating candidates. Encouraging the medical school to apply "flexible admission standards," the court flatly stated:

> The University is entitled to consider, as it does with respect to applicants in the special program, that low grades and test scores may not accurately reflect the abilities of some disadvantaged students; and it may reasonably conclude that although their academic scores are lower, their potential for success in the school and the profession is equal to or greater than that of an applicant with higher grades who has not been similarly handicapped.

The court also endorsed as proper the university's inclusion of such other factors when appraising applicants as the "personal interview, recommendations, character, and matters relating to the needs of the profession and society, such as applicant's professional goals."

As a secondary line of suggestions, the court invited the university to "increase minority enrollment" through "aggressive programs to identify, recruit, and provide remedial schooling for disadvantaged students of all races who are interested in pursuing a medical career and have an evident talent for doing so." The last of the "ameliorative" measures named by the court was to increase the number of entering places in medical schools as they existed or expand the number of medical schools.

The context for applying these court-proposed means, it should be reemphasized, was neutrality on race: "[n]one of the foregoing measures can be related to race, but they will provide for consideration and assistance to individual applicants who have suffered previous disabilities, regardless of their surname or color." The essence of the court's doctrinal position was as follows:

> [T]he standards for admission employed by the University are not constitutionally infirm except to the extent that they are utilized in a racially discriminatory manner. Disadvantaged applicants of all races must be eligible for sympathetic consideration, and no applicant may be rejected because of his race, in favor of another who is less qualified, as measured by standards applied without regard to race.

How would using these racially neutral measures affect the number of minority enrollees? No one could predict the results, said the court; perhaps more than 16 in some years, less than that number in other years. But, even with fewer minority admittees, "without a program which focuses on race," UCDMS's paramount objective would not be "appreciably impaired." That objective, as the court majority saw it, was "the need for more doctors to serve the minority community." To achieve that goal, preferential admissions was not the least intrusive means; indeed, it was not even an effective means. Allowing for the probability that a somewhat higher proportion of disadvantaged minority than of white admittees would later choose to practice in minority communities, the court urged the use of more reliable indicators than race and disadvantage. For example, has the applicant (of whatever race) demonstrated concern for disadvantaged minorities in the past, and has he or she indicated the intention to serve a minority community after earning the medical degree? Furthermore, noted the court, if the medical school desired to persuade white medical students to help in meeting the health needs of minority communities, there obviously were better and more direct methods available than to depend on "the influence exerted by [minority medical students] upon the student body." The curriculum could include training directed to the medical needs of minorities, and greater emphasis could be given to producing general practitioners to serve "the basic needs of the poor."

In the closing section of its opinion, the court majority affirmed its awareness that the issue in *Bakke* was sensitive and complex and that legal commentators were genuinely troubled, divided, and ambivalent about how best to resolve it. The "persuasiveness" of various arguments that preferential treatment of minorities was necessary to promote true equality of opportunity was acknowledged; "the ends sought by such programs are clearly just if the benefit to minorities is viewed in isolation." "But there are more forceful policy reasons against preferential admissions based on race," declared the court, stressing such effects as damage to racial harmony, overemphasis on racial definition of individuals, conflict in determining which groups should be preferred and how large the preferences should be, and difficulty in altering or ending preferences once they became established. "Perhaps most important," the court asserted, "the principle that the Constitution sanctions racial discrimination against a race—any race—is a dangerous concept fraught with potential for misuse in situations which involve far less laudable objectives than are manifest in the present case."

The court continued by characterizing UCDMS's program as "a form of an education quota system, benevolent in concept perhaps, but a revival of quotas nevertheless." Repudiating such a quota as a "thoroughly discredited" college admissions policy, the court reiterated that "a quota becomes no less offensive when it serves to exclude a racial majority." "To uphold the University," stated the court, "would call for the sacrifice of principle for the sake of dubious expediency. . . ." Persons should be judged "on the basis of individual merit alone," and hence

the safest course, the one most consistent with the fundamental interests of all races and with the design of the Constitution is to hold

. . . that the special admission program is unconstitutional because it violates the rights guaranteed to the majority by the equal protection clause. . . .

The lone dissenter was Justice Mathew O. Tobriner, who was viewed as the court's staunchest defender of individual rights and civil rights. Initially a successful labor trial lawyer in San Francisco, he had been appointed to the state court of appeals in the late 1950s and to the state's high court several years later. In his dissent, Justice Tobriner disputed the court's opinion on every major point.

Benign racial classifications were not presumptively unconstitutional or suspect, insisted the dissent; hence the strict scrutiny review standard was not applicable. In its place Justice Tobriner advanced a new standard: the ends had to be compelling, but the means had only to be rationally related to those ends. Since "a good faith attempt to promote integration" met the ends test and preferential admissions met the means test, the Davis program was permissible. Under the review standard applied by the dissenting opinion, the medical school was not required to demonstrate that no means less onerous than preferential admissions would achieve the compelling objective.

Matching the court's interpretation of case law by his different reading, Justice Tobriner argued that both the school desegregation and the Title VII employment cases provided suitable analogies for judicial treatment of minority preferential admissions. In addition, urged the dissent, the university should be given greater latitude of action because its pro-minority efforts were voluntary, not mandated by administrative or court orders. It was an entirely reasonable exercise of the medical school's educational judgment, as Justice Tobriner saw it, to decide that "the attainment of a racially integrated, diverse . . . student body, made up of qualified students of all races, is more important than the perpetuation of a segregated medical school composed of students with the highest objective academic credentials." Moreover, since the school considered all special admittees "fully qualified" to complete the degree program successfully, they were no less qualified for admission than regular admittees with higher test scores and grades.*

---

* Justice Tobriner's position on the relative qualifications of special and regular admittees is set forth in the excerpt at the outset of chapter 8.

Moving on to the alternate means put forward by the court majority, Justice Tobriner characterized them as "either disingenuous or impractical or both." From the dissent's viewpoint, the school's dominant objective was to secure a racially integrated student body. How could a racially neutral practice achieve a racial end without being disingenuous?

> . . . any nonracial classification will achieve the medical school's objective only to the extent that such nonracial classification in fact correlates with minority race. . . . Thus, the process of selecting a racially neutral criterion to promote integration cannot honestly be described as a "nonracial" decision. Yet the majority [opinion] commands just such a manipulation of labels, so that the perfectly proper purposes of the program must be concealed by subterfuge. I do not concur in this retreat into obfuscating terminology.

Furthermore, commented Justice Tobriner, expanding the special admissions program to disadvantaged applicants of all races would inevitably result in reducing the number of minority enrollees; disadvantaged persons required extensive financial aid, and medical schools lacked the monetary resources to admit much larger numbers of them.

The dissent continued by chastising the majority for indulging their policy judgments on whether, on balance, the costs of preferential treatment of minorities outweighed its benefits. As a policy problem, Justice Tobriner noted, the *Bakke* issue had provoked profound disagreement, and each side had strong arguments. But such policy judgments should be left to the educational authorities to exercise; the courts should confine themselves to the question of lawfulness.

Commenting that "affirmative action" programs had resulted "in at least some degree of integration in many of our institutions," Justice Tobriner spoke of the "sad irony" of using the Fourteenth Amendment to strike down the Davis program and concluded by indicating his unhappiness with his brethren's decision:

> Two centuries of slavery and racial discrimination have left our nation an awful legacy, a largely separated society in which wealth, educational resources, employment opportunities—indeed all of society's benefits—remain largely the preserve of the white-Anglo majority. . . . By today's decision, the majority deliver a severe, hopefully not fatal, blow to these voluntary efforts to integrate our

society's institutions and to ameliorate the continuing effects of
past discrimination.

Understanding the California Court's Decision

In the light of the California Supreme Court's reputation for lib-
eralism, its 6–1 decision against the Davis program surprised many;
and surprise deepened as the breadth of the ruling became evident.
The decision was not narrowly confined to any particular infirmities
of UCDMS's version of special admissions; it dealt broadly with
minority preferential admissions in all forms. Yet, as Justice Stanley
Mosk told it,* the court did not find itself sorely divided on resolving
the key issues.[14] The court majority "had very little difficulty" reaching a decision, he observed. "The court saw quite clearly that this
was a case of racial discrimination, and it was our feeling that discrimination against a person of any race is just bad." Justice Mosk
also commented that the legal issues of the case would have changed
had the situation involved previous discrimination against minorities by the medical school; by analogy to the Title VII employment
cases, minorities would then "be entitled to some kind of preference."

It was clear from Justice Mosk's comments at oral argument and
from the majority opinion he authored that the court found no merit
in the proposition (discussed in chapter 9) that voluntary preferential admissions was equivalent to, and therefore just as lawful as,
a school district's voluntary efforts to achieve racial integration.
This turndown was of more than ordinary importance because the
California court was second to none in its commitment to fostering
education desegregation. Whereas the U.S. Supreme Court had
neither recognized nor imposed an affirmative duty to remedy de
facto school segregation, the California high court since the 1960s
had obligated education officials to eradicate school segregation regardless of its cause.† The court's rejection of the proposition under
discussion could not be ascribed, therefore, to its unfamiliarity with

---

* The occasion that gave the public a rare glimpse into the workings of
the court was an interview with Justice Mosk conducted by an educational television station in mid-June 1977. By that time the *Bakke* case
was well on the way to achieving celebrity status; Justice Mosk, as the
author of the court's opinion, naturally was asked several questions
about it.
† The state court accomplished this by relying on its interpretation of

the extensiveness of public school segregation around the state or its lack of zeal in pursuing racial integration in public elementary and secondary education. Rather, the exclusion factor inherent in preferential admissions explained the court's unwillingness to transfer to that area the strong pro-integration stance it took on school desegregation.

In their conclusion that special admittees were less qualified, by the school's own standards, than some white applicants who were rejected, the court majority cited the lower benchmark ratings of minority enrollees as part of the supporting evidence. This simply repeated Colvin's mistake, discussed earlier, which was to misconstrue the benchmark scores as a uniform measure suitable for comparing special and regular admittees. These scores were never designed for intergroup comparative evaluations, but only to assess individual candidates within each separate group.

The heart of the quarrel between majority and dissent on the relative qualifications of minority enrollees turned on the question whether race itself was a substantive qualification. Following up on the university's argument that a diverse student body contributed greatly to improving education at the medical school, Justice Tobriner noted that "minority applicants possess a distinct qualification for medical school simply by virtue of their ability to enhance the diversity of the student body." But that kind of tautological justification for race preference, as the majority opinion observed, "simply assumes the answer to the question at issue. . . . To accept at the outset the premise that a minority applicant may be better qualified *because* of his race would foreclose consideration of the constitutional issue raised by [Bakke's] complaint."

The court majority's handling of the central issue produced its own set of problems, however. For one thing, the California court provided even less enlightenment than the Washington state court had in *DeFunis* on what made certain government objectives "com-

---

the California constitution, which enabled the court to protect individual rights beyond the limit set by the U.S. Supreme Court's reading of the national Constitution. By this method, the California court pioneered in decisions that invalidated the death penalty and that prohibited inequitable financing of schools caused by variations in the taxable wealth of school districts.

pelling." The Mosk opinion simply assumed for the purpose of argument that several of the Davis school's goals met the first part of the strict scrutiny standard (i.e., it did not actually decide the matter one way or the other). Since the issue was thus disposed of by assumption and not decision, it was unnecessary, and therefore odd, for the court to have gone on nevertheless to reject two of the objectives as insufficient to satisfy the "compelling state interest" test. What all this said about the distinguishing characteristics of compelling and uncompelling objectives, other than that they were labels readily available for a court to use as it saw fit, remained unclear.

The chief difficulty with the court opinion was that its central holding—only racially neutral means could be used to achieve racial ends—invited divergent interpretation, and the invitation did not lack for takers. It would be helpful, therefore, to try to clarify what the California court's decision probably meant and what it probably did not mean.

The central holding could be read as a conditional rather than a flat ban on the use of racial means in school admissions. Under this interpretation, the court was saying that no racial quota could be employed until the Davis medical school had first tried a variety of nonracial measures to achieve the objective of sizable minority enrollment. Should these other measures prove ineffective, adoption of race preference in admissions would be acceptable as a last resort.

There was some support, though slim, for this reading of the opinion. One of Colvin's themes was that UCDMS had been "quota happy," by which he meant that the school in its second year of operations had jumped immediately into special admissions without attempting to increase minority enrollment by more moderate devices. The court opinion also noted, after suggesting several means other than preferential admissions, that "[s]o far as the [trial] record discloses, the University has not considered the adoption of these or other nonracial alternatives to the special admission program." And one of the *amici* briefs submitted to the U.S. Supreme Court expressed its worry on exactly the point under discussion:

The Court's rationale leaves open the door for an institution to prove that no other means but racially preferential admissions would suffice to achieve one or more allegedly "compelling state interests"—and

thus to convince a court of the constitutional validity of that school's
discriminatory policies.[15]

Seeing this as a loophole that should be closed, the *amicus* brief
urged the prohibition of reverse discrimination in all circumstances
except when required of an institution as a remedy for its proven
past racial discrimination.

The probability was greater that the court holding meant an un-
conditional proscription of racial means because to do otherwise
would violate the constitutional rights of nonminorities. If that reading was accurate, the seeming anomaly in the court's holding was
its acquiescence in the validity of the school's racial objectives as it
simultaneously forbade the school from using race-based measures
to accomplish those racial objectives. Justice Mosk saw no inconsistency or contradiction in this regard; in the mid-1977 television
interview mentioned earlier, he stated that the court's suggestion
for admissions criteria that would enable the university to enroll disadvantaged students of any race "gives the university plenty of leeway."[16] But that assessment was strongly disputed by Justice
Tobriner and by many *amici* briefs; they insisted that racially neutral means would be either ineffective or effective only to the degree
racial criteria were covertly applied. The University of California's
brief to the U.S. Supreme Court, for example, argued the California
court had said, in reality, that "the state may recognize compelling
ends, but it may not vindicate them."[17]

Whether significant minority enrollment could be produced by
racially neutral means depended, of course, on how one defined the
latter standard. On this crucial question, the court's position was
only thinly elaborated, which made it vulnerable to hostile interpretation. The anti-Bakke side, in particular, had the greatest stake
in discrediting the feasibility of the nonracial alternatives proposed
by the court, since their discrediting would bolster the case for preferential admissions as the only available effective method. Hence
they interpreted the court's prescription tightly, as if racial neutrality ruled out any consideration of race. For different reasons, the
Department of Justice took much the same tack; this reflected its
concern that if the Supreme Court upheld Allan Bakke's complaint,
it should do so on a rationale that protected the concept of affirmative action and permitted race "to be taken into account."

The court majority surely had in mind a much more expansive

view of what racial neutrality permitted than the partisans of the university claimed. The court opinion told the university, in effect, that "race-based programs are too extreme, so try something else that you will find gets you most of what you want anyway." What was not tolerable, then, were explicit racial criteria, minority status per se as a positive qualification, racial quotas, seats reserved for minorities, evaluation of minority candidates in isolation from non-minority applicants, disqualifications of whites by race, and other like devices associated with race-preference policy. While racial neutrality thus precluded making race the dispositive factor in admissions, it left considerable room for taking race into account in connection with general admissions criteria applied to all applicants—which is undoubtedly what Justice Mosk meant by his comment that the court's suggestion for the admission of disadvantaged persons of all races left the university "plenty of leeway" to accomplish all or most of its racial objectives. For example, the court's standard presumably would permit a school, when determining on an individual basis the extent of each applicant's disadvantaged background, to consider the race of the applicant as a relevant datum.

Unfortunately, the clarity and persuasiveness of the majority opinion suffered from the absence of adequate detail on how far and in what ways race could be taken into account, and how all that related to the results desired for minority enrollment. To the extent this deficiency was remediable by the court, it was regrettable that the majority did not provide more specific guidance by amplifying its position. If the court's critics were right, however, it was understandable why the court avoided spelling out how nonracial means might be used to meet racial goals. The only effective way that could be done, maintained the critics, was to apply racial criteria to some degree and under the protective cover of ostensible racial neutrality. The court could hardly be expected to enumerate publicly the various "subterfuges," to use Justice Tobriner's term, professional schools might employ to meet their minority admissions needs. Alternatively, said the critics, a fully honest racially neutral program would not produce the requisite number of minority admittees—and here, too, the court could not be expected to lay out in detail a set of unfeasible criteria that schools might unprofitably employ.

Bakke Goes to the Supreme Court

Soon after the California Supreme Court announced its decision, the University of California requested the court to rehear the case or, alternatively, to stay the case pending the U.S. Supreme Court's review and disposition of it. As expected, the state court in late October declined to do either; the vote was again 6–1, with Justice Tobriner in dissent. As part of these proceedings, UC stipulated that it was unable to sustain the burden of proving that Allan Bakke would not have been accepted in 1973 if no special admissions program had been in effect. The court then modified its original opinion and directed UCDMS to admit Bakke. The university promptly applied to the U.S. Supreme Court for a stay of execution and a stay of enforcement of the California decision. In mid-November 1976, the Court granted a 30-day stay pending the filing of a petition for a writ of certiorari. One month later, UC filed the petition. The Court granted certiorari in late February 1977; the time for submission of briefs was set and it was anticipated that oral argument would be scheduled early in the fall, when the Court began another term.

Opposition to Appealing the Case

These cut-and-dried legal steps were played out against an unexpected backdrop. A sizable number of minority organizations intervened to try to convince the university not to appeal *Bakke* to the Supreme Court and, after UC filed its certiorari petition, to persuade the Court not to accept *Bakke* for review. Included among these groups were the National Urban League, the Mexican American Legal Defense and Educational Fund, the National Conference of Black Lawyers, and the National Organization for Women. Some of these organizations' concerns about *Bakke* had earlier been expressed in several substantive *amici* briefs submitted to the California court before it decided *Bakke* and in the NAACP's *amicus* brief urging the court to rehear Bakke and remand the case for a new trial in order that more evidence could be presented. (Even after the Court agreed to review *Bakke,* these concerns were again voiced in *amici* briefs filed by minority organizations and more bluntly by anti-Bakke student groups in their public demonstrations and occasional confrontations with UC regents.) What moved these groups to ally with Allan Bakke's attorney in opposition to Supreme Court review of the *Bakke* case?

To begin with, the basic structure of the litigation set the stage for uneasiness and resentment among minority organizations. "For minorities," observed a black law professor, "the *Bakke* case was a classic instance of litigation without representation."[1] Minorities had the greatest stake in the outcome of the case, but they had no direct role as participants because the parties to the lawsuit were a white and the university. In contrast, the civil rights cases productive of minority gains characteristically involved either a minority litigant (with proven counsel such as the NAACP Legal Defense and Educational Fund or the American Civil Liberties Union) or the federal government acting on behalf of minority rights. Still, the change in identity of the litigants obviously reflected the change in direction of the litigation, namely, a reverse discrimination suit by an aggrieved white instead of a traditional antidiscrimination suit by an aggrieved minority person. In this respect the lineup of direct litigants in *Bakke* was to be expected, and it was exactly the same as that in *DeFunis.* Although it was understandable why some minority groups chafed when, as they saw it, they were kept on the sidelines while others disposed of their fate, more particular reasons explained their resistance to having *Bakke* reviewed by the Supreme Court.

At bottom, the position of these minority organizations rested on their suspicious perception of the University of California as an unreliable advocate of their cause and on their worried strategic estimate that the *Bakke* case was a poor vehicle for conducting a major, and perhaps landmark, test of minority-preference policy and affirmative action. It was a measure of the strength of these concerns that these groups indicated they preferred to live with the California court's decision rather than challenge it anew at the Supreme Court.

The University of California had been for some time the target of complaints and attacks by minority organizations and their allies within the legislature and around the state. The dispute centered on a variant of a familiar problem: selective admissions on the one side, and disproportionately low minority enrollment on the other. Under the state's master plan for higher education, the nine-campus university system was committed to academic excellence in much the manner of the most prestigious private universities in the nation. On the undergraduate level, for instance, the plan restricted enrollment at UC campuses to the top 12.5 percent of California high school graduates. (Overall, the public higher education system included over 100 junior colleges and 19 colleges in addition to the university system; students were able to transfer to a UC campus from these other units, subject to their having met certain academic standards.)

As a consequence, even with a special admissions program that was heavily but not exclusively a route of minority entry, black and Chicano students were underrepresented at UC relative to their proportion of high school graduates; Asian-Americans were overrepresented by this standard. Note that this statistical imbalance was the result of high admissions standards, which minority (and low-income) students met at only one-third the rate of their more advantaged counterparts; the imbalance at the undergraduate level was not caused by too few places for too many applicants. The undergraduate special admissions program raised no *Bakke*-style problem because it was mostly an add-on benefit with no effect on anyone else's admission to the university system, though it could affect the entry chances of applicants who wished to go to a specific UC campus.

Building on their view of UC as an elitist institution insufficiently hospitable to increased minority access, minority groups also considered the university to be at best a lukewarm supporter of affirmative action. Some, but by no means all, of the professional schools on the UC campuses had adopted a special admissions arrangement to increase minority enrollment. The regents of the university had taken no public leadership role in articulating the university's commitment to affirmative action or in encouraging campuses or schools in that regard. And UC Berkeley, the most prestigious of the campuses, had engaged in a lengthy hassle with HEW during the mid-1970s over an acceptable affirmative action plan for the hiring of faculty members.

Whatever their doubts about UC's commitment to their cause, minority organizations would have insisted that *Bakke* be appealed had they felt it was a good case with a reasonable prospect of victory for the university. But the Davis program, already a two-time loser in the California courts, could easily be seen as having special disabilities from a legal viewpoint because of its distinctive characteristics: e.g., its quota character; its entirely separate treatment of special and regular applicants; and the newness of the school, which precluded it from having any history of past discrimination against minorities. In addition, and no less important, the Burger Court would decide the case, and minority groups viewed that court as less supportive of their interests than its predecessor, the Warren Court. The net of this strategic thinking was to urge that *Bakke* not be appealed: "Why push a bad case? Wait for a better one."

For some who were convinced that UC was no friend of minorities, it was but a short step to call into question UC's motives in wanting to pursue a "poor case." One accusation was that the university had "fabricated" the case. Events were cited that, when read with the requisite suspicion, could support the accusation, even though each event was explainable in terms other than "fabrication," e.g., Storandt's role in encouraging Bakke to sue, UC's insistence that the legality of the Davis program be at issue in the trial court, and UC's stipulation that it could not prove Bakke would not have been admitted in 1973. As to why the university should want to "fabricate" a case, some went so far as to suggest the regents were pleased with the *Bakke* case because they did not want preferential admissions in the first place. When anti-Bakke student advocates hit hard on this theme, in an open debate with several regents on the Berkeley campus in May 1977, one regent lost his temper and responded, "It makes me damn mad to . . . hear these paranoid rantings and ravings that are totally inaccurate."[2]

Although the *amici* briefs and the public statements of minority organizations varied greatly in the extent to which they openly expressed mistrust of the university, they all maintained that the *Bakke* trial record and UC's legal defense were inadequate. What those claims boiled down to was that the minority organizations would have argued the case differently from the university, which was only to be expected. For example, minority groups would have pressed the *Griggs*-based claim that UCDMS's reliance on academic criteria, because it had a disproportionate racial impact, required validation in the manner of job tests. UC, for obvious reasons, would never advance such an argument. For the most part, however, minority complaints were addressed to matters of relative emphasis, such as whether the racially discriminatory patterns in California public education had been stressed enough, rather than to sins of omission or commission. While such considerations were important, they concerned litigation strategy more than any inadequacies of the record, and hence they could be taken into account, if thought desirable, in the design of UC's brief to the Supreme Court. (As it turned out, the latter brief did cover much more fully the history and legacy of past discrimination in the nation and in California.)

Within the sector of minority organizations that opposed Court review of *Bakke,* opinion was divided on the likely consequences of the California court's ruling. Some thought that significant levels of minority enrollment could be gotten under the court's concept of a racially neutral preference for disadvantaged persons. Others disagreed, but they still preferred to limit the damage to California rather than extend it to the entire country through an unfavorable Supreme Court ruling. Even the California effects might be short-lived, because three of the state's six high court justices who composed the *Bakke* majority were to retire soon; new members appointed by Governor Jerry Brown might tip the balance in the other direction on the issue of preferential admissions.

There was little chance the regents could be dissuaded from petitioning the Court to review *Bakke.* Had the California court simply struck down the Davis program and left all else unresolved, or had the regents been assured that racially neutral admissions policies would result in considerable minority enrollment, they might well have chosen not to appeal *Bakke.* Neither condition obtained, however, and with both the president of the university and the general counsel strongly urging the regents to press for Supreme Court review, they voted in mid-November 1976 to do so. The consequences of accepting the California court's ruling, they felt, were too severe for the state and, because of the influence the ruling might have on universities and courts in other states, for the rest of the nation as well.

It would be hard to fault the university for deciding to appeal

Bakke. UC would have been attacked even more severely, by minority organizations as well as by countless others, had it not sought review of the case. If blame attached to UC, it likely was for its apparent willingness at the outset to let *Bakke* become the test case—but even that judgment could not be made confidently. True, the possible liabilities of the Davis program as an object of litigation were highly visible. It was not unreasonable to argue, however, that the differences between the Davis program and others were more in form than in practice, and hence the Davis setup adequately represented the run of minority admissions programs. If the regents were overly receptive to the latter of these two views of UCDMS's program, it was not because they secretly wanted to press a losing case to secure broad invalidation of special admissions for minorities, as their extreme detractors charged. It probably reflected their overanxious desire to have the minority admissions controversy settled by the courts once and for all, a desire sharply intensified by their several years of waiting in vain for *DeFunis* to do that job. In short, the regents' rush to secure judgment on *Bakke* reflected, at worst, their deeply felt need for a judgment, not their covert plan to get minority admissions outlawed.

The Amici Briefs
Until the time of the California Supreme Court decision, UC was represented by its general counsel, Donald Reidhaar, and three other lawyers from its in-house legal office. Within ten days after the state court's ruling, Reidhaar and the regents assembled a special team to handle subsequent litigation. Paul Mishkin, a professor at UC Berkeley's law school (Boalt) and an expert on constitutional law and federal court practice, took on the primary responsibility for preparing UC's brief. Assisting him was Jack Owens, who had recently clerked for the U.S. Supreme Court and had later taught at Boalt, where he had become familiar with that school's minority special admissions program.

When the minority organizations that unsuccessfully opposed UC's move to appeal *Bakke* called for the addition of a minority co-counsel to the team, the regents countered in mid-March 1977 by securing the services of Archibald Cox to present the oral argument before the Supreme Court and to assist in the preparation of the brief. Cox, a Harvard law professor, was a strong supporter of affirmative action and was the principal author of Harvard's *amicus* brief in *DeFunis*. A noted advocacy lawyer, he had served as solicitor general from 1961 to 1965; in that role he argued the national government's cases before the Supreme Court. Cox was best known, of course, as a hero of the Watergate period. As the first Watergate special prosecutor, Cox gained national fame as the target of the "Saturday night massacre" of October 21, 1973, when President Nixon ordered his dismissal after he had sued the President for access to the White House tapes.

Since Allan Bakke's legal resources stayed unchanged, the university's strengthening of its litigation team gave it a further edge. For Bakke, there remained Reynold Colvin, head of a small general-practice firm, who had never argued a case before the U.S. Supreme Court and who readied himself for his first appearance there by becoming admitted, in January 1977, to practice before the Court. His young assistant, Robert Links, a recent graduate of UCLA law school, was not eligible to apply for admission to practice before the Supreme Court; Links was still two months short of the minimum requirement of three years experience in legal practice when oral argument was held in mid-October 1977. Links had joined Colvin in working on the case when the brief for the California high court was being prepared, and together they carried the case to its conclusion in mid-1978. When Bakke was no longer able to pay for the extended litigation, Colvin continued to represent him without further fee. "I couldn't leave a case of this type," Colvin commented, "and Allan wouldn't drop it."[3]

The university also enjoyed a comparable advantage with respect to the division of the *amici* briefs that came pouring into the Court. Although apparently no one keeps such records, it was widely reported that *Bakke* attracted a larger number of *amici* briefs by organizations and individuals—57 in all—than any case in the remembered past.* Almost three-fourths of the *amici* briefs submitted by organizations were aligned against Allan Bakke and with UC. This percentage also held true for the more than one hundred organizations that sponsored or endorsed an *amicus* brief.

---

* Some 50 *amici* briefs were submitted in the 1954 *Brown* case on education desegregation and 40 in the 1950 case of the "Hollywood 10," which dealt with contempt convictions of motion picture writers and directors who refused to answer congressional committee questions about alleged communist activity.

The lineup of interests on *Bakke* in the *amici* briefs of 1977 was basically the same as that on *DeFunis* in 1973. Thirty-six of the organizations that filed or endorsed *amici* briefs in *DeFunis* did so again in *Bakke*, and not one of them changed sides. In support of the University of California's position were many other universities, minority organizations, civil rights groups, and professional and school associations in law and medicine. On Bakke's side there were Jewish organizations; white ethnic groups of Italian, Polish, or Ukrainian ancestry; business interests; and conservatives. Marco DeFunis, who was a practicing lawyer by this time, accepted the invitation of Young Americans for Freedom, a conservative group, to write their *amicus* brief in support of Allan Bakke. Of several pro-Bakke briefs submitted by individuals, one was by a junior at Oberlin College who felt strongly, both in principle and as a prospective law school applicant, that it was wrong "that I should suffer a burden as great as possible denial of admission to law school for past racial discrimination I did not commit."[4] Another personal brief was filed by an Italo-American of disadvantaged background who had been rejected as ineligible for special admission to the University of Florida law school because of "his not being a minority conspicuous to the State of Florida"; his *amicus* brief was, in effect, his brief against the Florida law school.[5]

Worth noting were two small but significant differences in the configuration of *amici* groups on *Bakke* as compared with those on *DeFunis*. The first was that the open division of Jewish organizations on *DeFunis* did not reappear on *Bakke*. All seven Jewish groups that entered *amici* briefs sided with Allan Bakke; two groups that had submitted anti-*DeFunis* briefs did not file any brief on the *Bakke* case. This display of greater organizational unity reflected the rising disenchantment of many Jews with Affirmative Action over the course of the '70s.[6] As they saw it, the "something more" they initially had strongly supported as a fair and effective way to promote equal opportunity for minorities was in danger of being transformed into race preferences and quotas, which they felt were wrong in principle and threatened the welfare of their own group. Having themselves benefited greatly from the meritocratic definition of equal opportunity, Jews generally were strong advocates of evaluating persons by standards of individual performance, divorced from considerations of racial or ethnic group membership. Hence they were dismayed and alarmed by the increasing respectability given to redefining equality, equity, and individual achievement in terms of groups and the group identity of the individual. The *Bakke* controversy brought these anxieties to a head; the *amici* briefs filed by Jewish organizations represented the prevailing sentiments of their members in the firm opposition they expressed to racial preferences and quotas.

The second difference meriting comment was that the AFL-CIO, which had filed a pro-DeFunis brief, chose not to submit a brief on *Bakke*. The ostensible reason was disagreement within the federated organization; four member unions (together with the United Automobile Workers) submitted a joint brief in support of the university, while one union (American Federation of Teachers) filed for Bakke. Nevertheless, much the same split had occurred on *DeFunis*, and it had not stopped the AFL-CIO from submitting its own *amicus* brief. Nor had the dominant sentiment against preferential admissions of either the federation hierarchy or the rank-and-file members changed. It seemed that the AFL-CIO's decision to stay neutral on *Bakke* reflected the desire of George Meany, its president, not to exacerbate already strained relationships between minority groups and organized labor.[7] Nonetheless, within the leadership conference on civil rights (an umbrella organization of some 100 organizations), organized labor and Jewish groups lined up on one side, with minority and civil rights groups on the other; as a result, the conference was unable to take any position on *Bakke*.

The quality of the 57 *amici* briefs varied greatly, and the same arguments repetitively appeared in many of them, but on balance they provided a richer and deeper understanding of the legal and policy issues confronting the Court. Most of the pro-Bakke briefs, for example, went well beyond Colvin's focus on racial quotas to review more broadly the use of race in the admissions process and elsewhere; several of them explored parallel problems in the employment field. On the university's side, one *amicus* brief developed an interpretive history of the Thirteenth and Fourteenth amendments and another (discussed in chapter 8) empirically tested what would happen to minority admissions if academic criteria were controlling. Still others, most notably the joint brief submitted by eleven private universities, fully developed the thesis of the importance of protecting university autonomy in admissions. And many minority organization briefs, as previously noted, advanced legal arguments that UC could not be expected to make. In sum, the *amici* briefs on

Bakke made a substantive contribution to the case, as well as demonstrating to the Court the intensity and division of opinion on the issues.

A "mini-*amicus* brief" was submitted by the *New York Times;* it took the form of an uncommonly lengthy editorial (one half of a full page) on *Bakke* in its Sunday, June 19, 1977, issue. Titled "Reparation, American Style," the editorial reviewed the problem, the case, and the choices before the Court and the public. Characterizing the problem as one that "touches the central nervous system of American democratic ideology," the *Times* recognized that "wise and generous people disagree profoundly" on how best to resolve it. Moreover, "both sides are right," the newspaper commented, and "the law, without too much difficulty, could resolve this case either way." For the *Times*, the need for minority professionals and the justice of offsetting previous racial deprivation tipped the scales. "It is in the national interest," the editorial declared, "that Mr. Bakke should lose the case."

Another and quite different source of information for the Court was the variety of peaceful collective activities—rallies, protest meetings, talk-ins, demonstrations, picketing—that took place episodically from spring 1977 to midsummer 1978. The participants were mostly students, minorities, and civil rights activists. Their message to the Court was uniform: overturn the California high court's *Bakke* ruling and uphold Davis's special admissions program. Established organizations did not involve themselves in these ad hoc activities, and efforts to arouse the larger public on the *Bakke* issue—in the manner of the earlier anti-Vietnam war protest and the civil rights movement—never caught fire.

Allan Bakke—as a flesh-and-blood person—was never the vilified target of anti-Bakke partisans nor the lionized hero of pro-Bakke adherents. The extensive discussion of *Bakke,* whatever the source and no matter how intense the disagreement, focused on the issues and not on the man. This was exactly as Allan Bakke wanted it. He resolutely kept himself and his life private, made no public appearances or statements, consistently refused to talk to reporters, and otherwise made sure that he would not be conscripted into the role of personal spokesman for a cause. As a consequence of Bakke's avoidance of any public role, the *Bakke* controversy proceeded under its own steam, without either the distraction or the stimulation his personal involvement might have caused.

The Politics of the Justice Department's Brief

The Department of Justice stayed out of *DeFunis*, it will be recalled, partly because several agencies disagreed on what position the government should take but mostly because intervention was thought to be too risky politically. On *Bakke*, though, the department submitted an *amicus* brief on behalf of the U.S. government. The brief it filed with the Court differed in important respects from earlier department drafts, however, and the changes reflected the outcome of a short but intense political struggle in which the White House was directly involved. An account of what transpired to alter the department's brief should help to illuminate some of the politics of the *Bakke* controversy and to explain why the Justice Department's brief took the positions it did.[8]

The official most directly responsible for deciding in which cases the government would intervene by filing an *amicus* brief was Wade McCree, Jr., the solicitor general. McCree was the first black elected to a judgeship in Michigan; he was appointed a federal district judge by President Kennedy in 1961 and, five years later, President Johnson appointed him to a federal court of appeals judgeship. When named by President Carter to be solicitor general, McCree became the second black to hold that important post; the first was Thurgood Marshall. On *Bakke*, as on other cases affecting civil rights, McCree worked closely with Drew Days III, assistant attorney general in charge of the civil rights division, who was also a black.

While the solicitor general has the authority to determine whether to intervene and how best to argue the government's brief, his office normally seeks advice on those matters from agencies directly concerned with the particular case. McCree and Days followed this procedure on *Bakke;* they sought the views of HEW, HUD, EEOC, the Civil Service Commission, the Department of Labor, and the U.S. Civil Rights Commission. All the responses favored intervention. By mid-June, Department of Justice officials affirmed that course of action and noted what they took to be agreement among the agencies on the broad position the government's brief should take: strong support for affirmative action and condemnation of rigid racial quotas.[9] At a press conference in July, however, after endorsing affirmative action in principle, President Carter indicated he would defend the Davis minority admissions program even though, he noted, the program might "contravene the concept of merit selection."[10]

The government's brief had to be submitted, at the latest, a decent interval before October 12, when oral argument was scheduled. Unexpected difficulties arose in its preparation, and as late as the close of August a final brief had not yet emerged; the latest draft was still circulating in the relevant agencies for their reaction. About this time, outside groups had gotten wind of the complexion of the various draft briefs. The anti-Bakke camp took alarm at what they heard, and their expressions of concern caught the attention of key presidential aides. The intervention of those aides, and of President Carter himself, in the drafting process ultimately resulted in a significant alteration of the brief.

There was nothing very novel, much less sinister, about White House intervention in the brief-drafting process. Presidents do not routinely concern themselves with the Justice Department's position in a case before the Court, but their occasional involvement in specific cases is a practice common enough to raise no eyebrows. In like manner, there was nothing unusual or surprising in the efforts of various agencies to shape the department's brief more to their liking. What is submitted to the Court, after all, is the brief of the U.S. government, not narrowly that of the Department of Justice. This distinction was recognized in the regular procedures by which the solicitor general's office consulted with agencies affected by a case, as McCree and Days did on *Bakke*.

What *was* unusual about what followed in the wake of White House intervention was that the public was let in on why and how the *Bakke* brief was changed. From September 1 to 19 (the day the Justice Department filed its brief with the Court), the press ran almost daily accounts of sharp disagreements within the Carter administration over what position to take on *Bakke* and of the lobbying, pressure, and conflict of agencies and interest groups on the issue. Copies of the draft brief, and information on major changes made in it, were leaked to the press; it was not clear whether that was done to promote an agency's position, to mobilize outside allies, or to test interest-group reaction to one or another position.

Why the press avidly covered these events required no special explanation; *Bakke's* status as the biggest case of the Court's term was reason enough. The puzzle was why the Carter administration was so ineffective in insulating the brief-drafting process from excessive public disclosure. Perhaps the inexperience of key officials provided the explanation; the President and his team, barely nine months in office, were still green to the ways of Washington, bureaucrats, and the press. Whatever the reason, the exposure to the public of how the final brief was written worked against its credibility as a legal document. The Court took offense as well; it was reported that Chief Justice Burger told Solicitor General McCree that the entire Court "was offended . . . by the numerous news leaks of early drafts of the brief [and] that the justices felt the resultant uproar had subjected them to improper public pressure when they were about to hear oral arguments" in the case.[11]

White House intervention, to return to the story of what happened, was predicated on an entirely reasonable proposition: the Justice Department's brief on *Bakke* would be seen by many as expressing the Carter administration's position on affirmative action, minority advance, and reverse discrimination. It was felt, therefore, that the brief should be reviewed by the President to ensure that it was consistent with his views on these sensitive and contentious issues. If there were inconsistencies, the President had the right to correct them; in accord with proper procedure, his suggestions would be made to the attorney general and not directly to the solicitor general. It seemed that four key officials held these views strongly, and they were instrumental in alerting the President to the politically explosive potential of the *Bakke* brief: Hamilton Jordan, Carter's de facto chief of staff; Fritz Mondale, the vice-president; Stuart Eizenstat, the head of Carter's domestic policy staff; and Robert Lipshutz, the President's counsel.[12]

These views—on the President's stake in the brief and his authority to determine the position it took—were not disputed by the Justice Department. Attorney General Griffin Bell felt, however, that the White House staff was overly anxious on the matter and that it should hold off reviewing the brief until it was close to, or in, its final form. Bell saw little to worry about. For one thing, the brief reflected the consensus of the affected agencies. For another, the two men responsible for the brief's drafting, McCree and Days, were not only able and respected professionals but were also among the top black appointees of the Carter administration. Surely, then, the brief they would produce and sign would be satisfactory to the White House, as well as to civil rights and minority groups.[13]

By means of such arguments, Bell was able to avoid having to turn over to presidential aides for their review any of the successive drafts that appeared over the course of the summer. But in late

August the aides became aware of the dissatisfaction of minority and civil rights groups with the draft briefs and insisted on seeing the current brief. Acceding to their request, Bell brought over a copy of the latest draft on September 1, handing it to the President in the presence of Eizenstat and Lipshutz.[14] With that, direct connection between the brief-drafting process and the White House was made.

The 88-page September 1 draft brief on *Bakke* urged the Court to confine its ruling to the selective admissions problem and not use the case as the occasion to review broadly the whole run of affirmative action policies and practices. In the event the Court chose to deal with a larger compass than school admissions, much of the brief was spent on arguments and evidence on behalf of the constitutionality of affirmative action principles and programs. On the admissions problem, the draft advanced two positions for its resolution: race could be taken into account in selective admissions decisions, but not to the extent of instituting a racial quota of reserved seats for minorities. This "middle-way" stance called for partial affirmation and partial reversal of the California high court's holding: the unconstitutionality of the Davis program and the order to admit Allan Bakke to the medical school would be upheld, but the ruling that race had to be excluded as a factor in admissions would be rejected.

In the light of subsequent events, it should be noted that the antiquota position was clearly and emphatically communicated in the draft. "Affirmative action programs," it stated, "must use race as a way of eliminating unfairness, not perpetuating it." "We doubt," the brief observed, "that it is ever proper to use race to close any portion of the class for competition by members of all races." And at another point the draft held that precise racial quotas amounted to "using race as a tool of exclusion" against whites.[15]

After close review of the draft brief, Eizenstat advised the President of his serious misgivings. In Eizenstat's judgment the brief had been formulated without adequate recognition that the public and affected interest groups would read it as presidential policy. Among Eizenstat's major concerns was that the draft's language against fixed quotas might be used to oppose some government activities on behalf of affirmative action.[16] Objections by others to the draft were soon forthcoming; they also concentrated on, but were not limited to, the issue of repudiating quotas.

President Carter was reported to be undecided whether to accept the key themes of the Justice Department's position, and White House aides let it be known that a range of options still remained open. With that, the political pressures mounted. Civil rights activists voiced their disapproval of the draft, and warned that it would be taken as a signal that the Carter administration was not fully committed to Affirmative Action. The congressional Black Caucus expressed its displeasure with the draft and met with President Carter on September 7 to press their criticisms. A few days later the black congressmen warned the President that if the Court were to act in accord with the draft brief, it would have the effect of "irretrievably undermining the affirmative action programs of public and private entities."[17] A lukewarm brief, asserted Representative Louis Stokes, a black congressman, would be "an indelible blot on the Administration's record."[18] Within the executive branch, several agency heads—notably Joseph Califano of HEW, Eleanor Holmes Norton of EEOC, and Patricia Harris of HUD—strongly advocated revision of the brief; Andrew Young, U.S. representative to the United Nations, was also of that view.

On September 10, Solicitor General McCree told Eizenstat that he had decided the final draft should take a strong position in favor of broad affirmative action programs and a stand against rigid quota systems. After checking with the President, Eizenstat informed McCree that his position was "not inconsistent with the President's policy."[19] On September 11, White House officials informed the media that President Carter had decided not to alter the general themes of the draft brief, though he might suggest some "substantive" changes in the wording.[20] At the meeting with his Cabinet on September 12, the President assured those who had pressed for change in the brief that they would not be displeased with the final brief.[21] Later that day, a Justice Department attorney stated that the wording of the new brief might be softened to give greater weight to the position of civil rights groups, but that the basic argument would not be changed, that is, the Carter administration planned to stand by the department's position that racial quotas were unconstitutional.[22]

McCree, Days, and other Justice Department officials completed the writing of the final brief over the next six days. The department submitted its 74-page *amicus* brief to the Court on September 19, some three months after the initial deadline and a scant three weeks before oral argument was to be heard. Commenting on what had changed in the brief, Attorney General Bell stated: "We didn't shift. It is a matter of emphasis. . . ."[23] Minority and civil rights groups, though indicating the final brief was not the one they would have written, considered it markedly better than its predecessor and one with which they could live.[24]

Compared with the September 1 draft, the final brief was far from a total transformation; the two documents were recognizably related on many points. Nonetheless, what they did differ on was so substantial that "turnabout" rather than Bell's "a matter of emphasis" provided a better description of the changes that had taken place.

Two critical differences were immediately evident. The first was the absence of the previous brief's full and explicit condemnation of racial quotas as illegal; in its place was a single passing mention of "rigid exclusionary quotas," its meaning left undefined and the significance of the mention left equivocal. The antiquota position that the Justice Department spokesman had said a week earlier would be maintained (though perhaps "softened") by the Carter administration was not eliminated entirely—but it was thoroughly downgraded in visibility and importance, to the point of virtual obscurity. Only a few traces remained in the brief, and these were scattered about in the manner of clues that might be uncovered and then put together—as has been done in this study—to reconstruct some part of the antiquota position. Thus, for example, it could still be inferred from the final brief that a key test for the department on the "goal" or "quota" character of the Davis program was whether or not special and regular admissions applicants were compared with each other.

The second difference between the briefs was the logical complement of the change just discussed. To maintain the inconspicuousness of the antiquota position, the brief had to avoid coming to grips with the particulars of the Davis program. Otherwise, it would have to hold the program unconstitutional and support Allan Bakke's admission to the medical school; these judgments, in turn, could be explained only by fully developing the antiquota argument. But how could the quota character of the Davis program, which was the most prominent feature of the *Bakke* case, not be dealt with? One way was to put forward a forced and insubstantial argument that more information was needed to determine whether it really was a quota, and hence the case should be remanded to the California courts. Another way was to say, as Attorney General Bell did on the day the department's brief was submitted to the Court, "We do not think . . . this case concerns quotas, . . . except in a secondary way."[25]

Understandably incensed by the Justice Department's dismissal of the core of Bakke's claim, Reynold Colvin responded in his reply brief that the government's brief was "a make-believe effort to avoid the direct question at hand."[26] Elaborating that position in biting fashion, Bakke's attorney asserted:

> The issues raised in the government's brief are not matters of sub-stance. They are only desperate attempts to find some trap doors in the record. It does not matter that these secret escape hatches are only a fiction. It is sufficient that they seem to fulfill the government's daydream: the fantasy that they will magically open, and through them the government's political problems will miraculously dis-appear.[27]

Shorn of its antiquota emphasis, the brief filed with the Court was mostly a lengthy defense of the necessity, wisdom, and con-stitutionality of the principle of affirmative action and of the wide range of "minority-sensitive" programs and procedures undertaken under that principle. On selective admissions, the Justice Depart-ment's position was that universities could "take race into account" as one of a number of admissions factors. In justifying that prac-tice, the brief stressed the broad ground of counteracting the effects of societal discrimination against minorities; this would enable all universities to consider race as an admissions factor, if they wished, and not just those universities with a record of antiminority dis-crimination.

In sum, what the government's brief asked the Supreme Court to do was to use the *Bakke* case to legitimate Affirmative Action and the use of race-conscious admissions procedures. The brief advised the Court not to go beyond that because *Bakke* was not a good vehicle for determining the permissible and impermissible ways for universities to take race into account on admissions. The trial record, argued the brief, did not adequately reveal "how race was used" by the Davis medical school; that was why *Bakke* should be remanded to the California courts.

Partisans of Affirmative Action had good reason to be pleased with the substantial alterations of the government's brief brought about by their criticisms and pressures. Less satisfaction might

have been taken had they fully realized that a key legal position that
could not have been much to their liking had survived intact in the
final brief. This position constituted, ironically, the department's
answer to the question it urged the Court not to address in *Bakke,*
namely, how race could permissibly be taken into account in determining admissions. "Race should be used in making admissions decisions," stated the early-September draft, "only to assist in promoting the fairness of an evaluation that is otherwise racially
neutral."[28] The final brief left that position substantially unchanged: "We argued in our principal brief," the Justice Department said, "that the Constitution does not bar [Davis medical school]
from taking race into account in order fairly to compare minority
and non-minority applicants."[29] As discussed in chapter 7, this position allowed for only a modest, limited use of race as an admissions
factor; the constitutional boundary it marked out was much closer
to Justice Douglas's insistence on racially neutral standards (in
DeFunis) than to the race-preference policy underlying Davis's
special admissions program.

The Justice Department's brief thus bore the marks of the conflict that produced it. A draft brief developed for one legal/political
position (affirmative action and Bakke, yes; quotas and the Davis
program, no) had to be reworked on a crash basis to sustain a different legal/presidential position (affirmative action, yes; Bakke
and the Davis program, remand). Not unexpectedly under such circumstances, the resulting brief exhibited an odd mixture of old and
new positions that did not fully cohere, whether viewed as a legal
argument for the Court or as a presidential policy statement for the
public.

Oral Argument
The presentation of oral argument by opposing counsel is an integral part of the process by which the Court makes up its mind. The
Court hears oral argument four hours a day, Monday through Thurs-
day; about an hour is assigned to each case, so that some dozen-plus
cases are heard each oral-argument week. The format is not one of
lectures by the two attorneys or direct debate between them, but of
a succession of exchanges and dialogues between individual justices
and counsel conducted in a conversational question-and-response
fashion. Having read the principal briefs and perhaps some of the

amici briefs (if any have been filed) in advance, the justices use the occasion to satisfy their informational and analytical needs on the case, and especially to explore the implications and limits of the various lines of argument counsel have urged on the Court. From the attorneys' perspective, the oral-argument stage provides the opportunity to underscore points of argument, to persuade the members of the Court, and to reassure individual justices on specific questions troubling to them.

Normally, Supreme Court oral argument attracts little public attention even though it is the only other major part of the Court's operation, in addition to the written opinions themselves, open to public view. *Bakke* was no ordinary case, however, and the scene at the Supreme Court building on the day of oral argument (Wednesday, October 12, 1977) was reminiscent of the dramatic time three years earlier when the Court sealed President Nixon's fate by ruling that he had to turn over key White House tapes that implicated him in the Watergate coverup. The 500-seat chamber was filled well before the *Bakke* proceedings began promptly at 10 A.M.; additional chairs had to be placed in the aisles to accommodate the crush. To handle the overflow of reporters—nearly one hundred of them—extra chairs were also set up behind the regular press section. Security precautions were unusually tight; guards checked the overcoats and purses of entrants to the courtroom.

Most of those seated in the courtroom were guests, special visitors, or public officials who had put in for a seat well in advance. About one hundred places were available to members of the general public, who would be permitted to sit through the entire session on *Bakke;* in addition, ten spectators as a group were to be allowed into the courtroom for three minutes at a time to observe the proceedings. The line of hopefuls for spaces allocated to the general public began to form in late afternoon of the preceding day; by midnight Court police were informing newcomers to the line that they had little chance of getting into the courtroom. Many chose to join the queue anyway. The police estimate was accurate; about 250 of those in line were admitted for either a regular seat or a three-minute glimpse, but among those unable to get in were many who had been there for most of the night. Throughout the morning, across the street from the Supreme Court building, a group of minority and nonminority young men and women "serenaded" those in line with their view of how *Bakke* should be decided. In repetitive refrain, the women chanted, "We won't go back." "Send Bakke back," responded the men.[30]

Inside the courtroom, things proceeded on schedule. *Bakke* was the first case to be heard that day; at exactly 10 A.M. Chief Justice Burger called for "No. 76-811, *Regents of the University of California* against *Bakke*." Although most cases are allotted one hour for oral argument, the Court granted *Bakke* two hours: 45 minutes apiece to Archibald Cox and Reynold Colvin, and 30 minutes to Solicitor General Wade McCree. As counsel for the party that lost in the lower court—"the moving party"—Cox spoke first; McCree came next, then Colvin. Each attorney, standing behind a lectern on a small rostrum between the two counsel tables, faced the members of the Court, with his back to the audience. The justices were seated in their traditional seniority-based order, with the chief justice as the pivot point in the center; clockwise from the spectators' perspective, the seating was as follows: Rehnquist (7th in seniority), Blackmun (5th), White (3rd), Brennan (1st, most senior), Burger (chief justice), Stewart (2nd), Marshall (4th), Powell (6th), and Stevens (8th, most junior). The use of recessed microphones by counsel and by each of the justices enabled the attentive audience to hear the proceedings clearly.

Obviously at home in the Court, Cox cast the case in broad social and constitutional terms and underscored its gravity at the outset of his presentation:

> The answer which the Court gives will determine, perhaps for decades, whether members of those minorities are to have the kind of meaningful access to higher education in the professions, which the universities have accorded them in recent years, or are to be reduced to the trivial numbers which they were prior to the adoption of minority admissions programs.[31]

Following the lines of argument set by UC's written briefs, Cox argued for the validity of the Davis program by emphasizing two themes: (1) it was legal for admissions decisions to take race into account for pro-minority purposes; and (2) how a university took race into account was an administrative option not of constitutional significance, for that decision was properly one educators should make.

During the 45 minutes available to him, Cox also initiated arguments intended to show that special admittees were not less qualified than regular admittees, that nonracial means were ineffective to achieve the objectives sought, and that the reservation of 16 seats constituted a goal and not a quota. Of those three themes, the last attracted the largest amount of questions from the justices. For their part, Court members initiated exploration of the following themes: the meaning of the benchmark ratings for special admittees compared to those assigned regular admittees; the scale of preference (exchanges between Rehnquist and Cox, and between Stevens and Cox, on whether a set-aside of 50 seats would be allowable); why Asian-Americans were included in the special admissions program; the relevance to the case of Title VI of the Civil Rights Act; and the origins of the Davis program (who authorized it and what was its rationale?). In fielding these inquiries, Cox was able to respond with greater fullness and certainty on the first two, less conclusively on the others.

Reynold Colvin's approach contrasted greatly with that of Cox, which reflected in part his inexperience in the Court as compared with the former solicitor general, but mostly their differences in legal strategy on the case. As counsel for UC, Cox had no choice but to argue in large constitutional and policy terms about the need for, and the validity of, race-conscious admissions. Colvin, however, had emphasized throughout the litigation the particulars of the Davis program and, in effect, had staked the case for Allan Bakke on the proposition that the program was an illegal racial quota. In making his maiden argument before the Supreme Court, Colvin saw little reason to veer from that emphasis, which had clearly been a winner in the California courts.

"I am Allan Bakke's attorney," Colvin began his presentation to the Court, "and Allan Bakke is my client."[32] Staying within this frame of the case as a private lawsuit brought to secure one person's admission to medical school, Colvin spent most of his first twenty minutes recapitulating the facts and the sequence of developments at each stage of the lawsuit. Although Colvin touched on themes of interest to the Court—six justices questioned him further about particular items—the approach he took was unsuitable if it was intended to constitute the whole of his presentation. Expressing the impatience of the Court, Justice Powell pointedly commented to Colvin:

. . . the University doesn't deny or dispute the basic facts. We are
here . . . primarily to hear a constitutional argument. . . . I would
like help, I really would, on the constitutional issues. Would you address that?[33]

On these larger issues, Colvin was pressed hard for his position
on whether race could be considered in any way in choosing
students for a professional school. Justice Marshall, probing
whether the scale of preference was critical to Colvin's argument,
asked him whether the reservation of only one seat for a minority
person was allowable. "Numbers are unimportant," responded Colvin. "It is the principle of keeping a man out because of his race
that is important."[34] In a set of exchanges with Justices White and
Rehnquist, Colvin had some difficulty formulating his position, but
he ultimately asserted what seemed to be the view that Davis's use
of racial classification was invalid per se, even if it were granted
that the Davis program fully satisfied the strict scrutiny test (compelling ends, necessary means).[35] Colvin also argued, however, that
the California court's suggested alternative means, a race-neutral
program for disadvantaged persons, was feasible and that it was
constitutionally sound because it focused on the individual and his
personal circumstances, not on generalizations or preferences based
on racial groups. In determining the disadvantage of an individual
applicant, race could be taken into account among many other factors, but "race itself is an improper ground for selection or rejection
for the medical school."[36]

Members of the Court queried Colvin, as they had Cox, on the
origins and rationale of the Davis program and on the relevance of
Title VI to the possible disposition of the case. Finally, Colvin
initiated a theme that found no receptivity from those justices who
responded to it. To bolster his argument that the set-aside of 16
seats was a quota, Bakke's attorney questioned whether all special
admittees were really qualified in terms of the school's standards for
incoming students. Justice Stevens noted that the trial record failed
to demonstrate that any special admittee was unqualified.[37] And
Justice White suggested that the question of the qualifications of
special admittees was not necessarily central to the core of Colvin's
argument, which was, in White's words, "[that Bakke was] deprived
of an opportunity to compete for one of the sixteen seats because
of his race."[38]

Solicitor General McCree's turn at argument came between that of Cox and Colvin, and it proved uneventful; if the justices were resentful of the manner in which the Justice Department's brief had been developed, none gave evidence of it during the half hour. McCree's basic theme was that institutions could voluntarily adopt minority-sensitive programs that sought to remedy the pervasive effects of societal discrimination. He made no mention of any anti-quota argument and liberally sprinkled his comments with references to the "sparseness of the [trial] record." Few questions were asked of him, and these related mostly to the record's adequacy on why Asian-Americans were included in the Davis program and McCree's views on the relationship of Title VI to the case.

The Court's session ended on schedule, promptly at noon. Oral arguments are carefully watched for hints as to the thinking of individual justices on the case or on some particular line of argument, but the *Bakke* proceedings revealed no reliable clues. Colvin had come in for more critical questioning than Cox, but that was no indicator of anything about the Court's leanings. Overall, the session had covered—in typical fragmented fashion—a large number of topics and had engaged the active participation of most of the justices (Blackmun and Brennan were less active). But no pattern was evident nor could even be confidently guessed at, though the Court's questioning of Cox, Colvin, and McCree on Title VI was suggestive. What the Court might likely decide on *Bakke* thus remained as undecipherable after oral argument as before.

Title VI of the Civil Rights Act
On Friday of each week in which oral arguments have been held, the Court meets in private conference to vote on the cases heard during the preceding four days. On *Bakke,* the Court conference of October 14 came to an unusual, though not unprecedented, decision. It requested the parties to the case and the Justice Department to submit supplemental briefs within thirty days on Title VI of the Civil Rights Act of 1964 "as it applies to this case." Section 601 of Title VI required that

> No person in the United States shall, on the ground of race, color, or national origin, be excluded from participation in, be denied the benefits of, or be subjected to discrimination under any program or activity receiving Federal financial assistance.

At oral argument, the Court had learned that the university's counsel believed that the Court could not ground its decision on Title VI, that Solicitor General McCree believed it could, and that Bakke's attorney was entirely willing to have the Court order his client's admission to the medical school on Title VI or Equal Protection grounds, or both. What the Court felt it now needed was a more careful review of whether it could decide *Bakke* on the basis of Title VI and, if so, was the Davis program valid or invalid under Title VI?

Title VI had related to the litigation in the following manner. Bakke's original complaint had cited three grounds—Equal Protection, the privileges and immunities clause of the California constitution, and Title VI of the Civil Rights Act of 1964—and the trial court had based its decision against the Davis program on all three grounds. In their briefs to the California Supreme Court, UC counsel mentioned Title VI only briefly; Colvin also concentrated on Equal Protection, with no separate treatment of Title VI. The California high court held for Allan Bakke on Equal Protection grounds exclusively. In their briefs to the U.S. Supreme Court, the university did not present the Title VI issue and Bakke did not rely on Title VI as a distinct ground for affirmance of the lower court's judgment. (Two *amici* briefs did argue a Title VI position, both on behalf of UC's position; one was filed by Howard University and the other by the NAACP.)

On the threshold question whether the Court could resolve *Bakke* on the basis of Title VI, if it chose, the supplemental briefs filed in mid-November went their expected different ways. The Justice Department said the Court could do so because the Title VI issue had been sufficiently present during the California court stages of the case; but since the state courts had not really explored the issue, *Bakke* should be remanded for that purpose. Colvin agreed that the Court could appropriately settle *Bakke* on Title VI grounds, but argued there was no need for remand. UC counsel agreed with Colvin that remand was inappropriate, but disagreed with both Colvin and the department by insisting that the Title VI issue had appeared in the case in only a technical formal sense and thus represented a new ground not open for the Court's use.

Another technical threshold question was involved. Could the antidiscrimination provisions of Title VI be enforced by means of a lawsuit brought by an aggrieved private person, or only by a federal administrative agency? The Department of Justice acknowledged it was arguable either way, but urged the Court to decide in favor of allowing individuals to sue. For *Bakke,* however, the department took the position that because UC had not argued against Bakke's use of Title VI in the California courts, it was precluded from raising that objection at the Supreme Court. Colvin and university counsel advanced opposing views, of course, on this question.*

On the substance of the issue, the blunt truth was that when the Civil Rights Act of 1964 was discussed and adopted, no one had been thinking about the exercise of positive race preference by institutions receiving federal funding. The chief concern then was the establishment of the antidiscrimination principle, which was embodied in Section 601 of Title VI, as quoted earlier. At the same time, language in other sections of Title VI, together with subsequent HEW implementing regulations, authorized affirmative action to correct conditions that limited the participation of minorities. Voluntary activities by institutions were especially encouraged, independent of the question whether the institution had engaged in antiminority discrimination. In Title VI, then, as elsewhere in antibias policy, nondiscrimination and affirmative action were intermixed uneasily, providing a basis of argument for each side of the *Bakke* dispute.

It was likely, though hardly certain, that if the Court chose to treat *Bakke* as a Title VI problem, the outcome would favor Allan Bakke rather than the University of California. The opposition of UC counsel to disposing of the case on Title VI grounds suggested this, as did the worry openly expressed by some civil rights and minority activists when the Court called for supplemental briefs on the issue. It provided an ironic reminder of how far current conceptions of equal opportunity had traveled since the mid-'60s to note the fears of pro-minority advocates that the Civil Rights Act of 1964 might be used as the basis for deciding the merits of Allan Bakke's claim.

Both UC and the Department of Justice argued strongly that Title VI permitted an institution receiving federal funds to engage voluntarily in any form of affirmative action that the Equal Protection Clause would permit. That is, there was no difference between Title

---

* Still another technical question, the details of which need not be discussed here, was whether a private person, assuming he had the right to sue, first had to exhaust all available administrative remedies.

VI and Equal Protection in the circumstances presented by the *Bakke* case. But Congress unquestionably could proscribe what the Constitution merely permitted, and many observers felt that Title VI was more restrictive than the Equal Protection Clause. If that estimate was correct, a Court majority would be expected to hold, at the least, that the antidiscrimination standard in Title VI prohibited preferential racial quotas when adopted without reference to an official finding of institutional discrimination against minorities.

Would the Court use Title VI rather than the Constitution to settle the case? Such a shift would conform to the Court's general "rule" to decide cases, when possible, narrowly rather than broadly, and on statutory rather than on constitutional grounds. If Title VI was used to dispose of *Bakke* by deciding against the Davis program, the scope of the ruling would be broader in the sense that it would directly cover private as well as public colleges and universities (as recipients of federal funds) and not be confined to the public sector of higher education (as governed by Equal Protection requirements). In all other respects, however, a Court interpretation of a provision of the Constitution—whether used to decide for or against the Davis program—would be more sweeping in its potential scope and less open to change than if the decision was based on the Court's reading of a law. To the extent, then, that the Court preferred to give the political process another chance to grapple with the vexing problem of reconciling nondiscrimination and affirmative action, rather than to keep the burden, responsibility, and power to itself, deciding *Bakke* on Title VI grounds might prove an irresistibly attractive option.

Ends and Means

The public attention lavished on *Bakke* (and earlier on *DeFunis*) reflected intense concern with a larger question than the problem of minority admissions to highly selective professional schools. This question was nothing less than the central civil rights issue of our time: how can affirmative action programs promote equal opportunity for minorities in ways that are consistent with other key objectives and values of our society? In turning to race preferences in admissions, the Davis medical school and the University of Washington law school provided one possible answer. Before concluding this study with a review of the Court's decision on *Bakke*, therefore, it would be appropriate to examine the adequacy of race-preference policy as the means to reach the agreed-on end of greater equality of opportunity.

Explicit Race Preferences: A "Temporary Deviation"?
Enthusiastic advocates of positive discrimination in behalf of minorities did not lack an intellectual defense of their position; over the course of the 1970s themes of justification developed for compensatory justice, racial quotas, and redefinitions of equal opportunity. Most of those who supported minority preferences, however, did so ambivalently and uneasily, which reflected the tug of competing values inherent in the problem. Many resolved their doubts by embracing the comforting belief that preferential treatment of disadvantaged minorities represented transient, short-lived remedies for past discrimination. In this view, the irrelevancy of race and the traditional idea of equal opportunity embodied the proper values; the present exceptions were temporary deviations required by short-term circumstances and needs. At some future time, when the cur-

rently preferred minorities had "made it" into the mainstream of American life, group preferments would be eliminated. How persuasive was this view?

The more realistic prognosis was that the dynamics of the positive discrimination process would go in a direction opposite to that of a self-destruct mechanism. Newly acquired benefits create their own vested interests. Those interests would come to see the benefits as just and earned, as durable entitlements and not as a temporary redress subject to later withdrawal. Society's values and beliefs also would change, initially to allow for the deviations but ultimately to justify their continuance. There was no reason to suppose that either minority-preference policies or their supporters' behavior would constitute an exception in these regards. The standard anti-Bakke position on this question was, therefore, something less than persuasive:

> [Special admissions programs] are . . . transitional steps, pending the achievement of a more complete racial equality in the professions, which the political process can be counted on to abolish when the felt need for them no longer exists.[1]

When would the "felt need" for minority preferential admissions no longer exist? "We hope," said the Carnegie Council on Policy Studies in Higher Education, "that the current period of transition will not last longer than until the end of the current century—less than one generation."[2] In "a generation or two from now," suggested the University of California's counsel.[3] Others avoided any time estimates but set conditions that, when achieved, would supposedly cause the policy "to expire of its own force."[4] One such condition, which fixed "its own time limitation" for preferential admissions, was offered by the Law School Admissions Council: "when the applicants coming to the graduate and professional schools are no longer the products of segregated elementary and high schools."[5]

UC's brief implied that special admissions programs might be ended, some decades from now, if they were considered to have failed. One measure of the programs' failure would be if the academic scores of the various minorities "continue[d] to lag behind other groups."[6] Yet, that finding would undoubtedly be interpreted by others as demonstrating precisely the opposite conclusion. By the present thinking of partisans of positive discrimination, the finding would indicate that equal opportunity had still not been achieved and, therefore, that special admissions should be continued and perhaps enlarged—but surely not dropped. The Department of Justice was plainly of that view: "As long as prior discrimination has present effects, mere neutrality to race is insufficient. As long as the effects of past racial discrimination persist, the employment of race-consciousness in rectifying that discrimination should not be abandoned."[7]

Under the department's formulation, preferential treatment would be broadly justified until such time—however long it might be—as minorities achieved an approximate parity with whites. That position was the complement of the premise underlying the government's Affirmative Action programs (discussed in chapter 2), namely, that disproportional nonemployment of members of minority groups within the availability pool constituted a condition of underutilization that had to be corrected. The assumption was made that if a variety of barriers, roughly equated with systemic/societal/institutional discrimination, were removed, the occupational distribution of racial groups would be approximately the same. So, too, with regular admissions to highly selective professional schools. It followed, therefore, that the continued failure of minorities to meet regular admissions requirements in about the same proportions as whites constituted the standing justification for their special admissions under, to use the Justice Department's term, "minority-sensitive" policies and procedures.

The notion of equality of opportunity embraced by this position was that of group proportionality of results (discussed in chapter 2), which diverged greatly from the traditional view and which was not subscribed to by most of the nation. No anti-Bakke brief openly argued this view; some, indeed, denied their support of it. Nonetheless, all the briefs that spoke to the problem of minority underrepresentation in the professions or of assessing the effects of past discrimination on minorities addressed those issues by making proportional comparisons between minority and majority populations and numbers of professionals—and in a context of urging that the state had a compelling interest in solving those problems through minority preferential admissions. Whether intentionally or not, this common emphasis on securing minority parity with whites in terms of group outcomes gave credibility and respectability to that alternate view of equal opportunity.

From the viewpoint of any individual law school or medical school, there was no set formula for determining what degree of minority representation was "reasonable," to use UWLS's term. It seemed to depend on who was asked and on who made the decision, rather than on any consensus as to the proper base for representation. For example, UWLS favored a national population base because that would yield a higher percentage as a target level for admission of blacks than would the use of the state of Washington's population as the base. But black spokesmen in New York City or in Newark, New Jersey, would push for a local population base for higher education units in that area because it would produce a higher percentage than the counterpart national or state data. Another example: In 1972, minority-student caucuses at Boalt law school (UC Berkeley) demanded, in total, about half the entering places. Each minority group pressed a different formula: blacks insisted on a national population base, Chicanos on a California base, and Asian-Americans on a local San Francisco Bay Area base. In each case, the base sought would have resulted in a larger group claim than the alternate bases. In short, how the base was determined in turn fixed the proportion of the scarce resource (entering places) the group could get. Hence the process of deciding what base to use was typically a highly political and disputed affair.

In Affirmative Action programs in employment, for example, the determination of whether underutilization existed turned on comparing detailed data on a firm's employment of minority-group members, by job categories and rank, with the proportion of minority-group members that "would reasonably be expected by their availability." An inexact standard to begin with, its slipperiness was increased by inadequate data on who was "available" and by extensive disagreement over determining availability "to do what." Because how a job was defined obviously directly affected who was included as being available for the job, the setting of job qualifications became an object of political and administrative conflict.

In admissions to selective professional schools, use of the "wrong base" would exacerbate the problem of how qualified some minority admittees were likely to be. If one assumed the existence of such a thing as a minority group's "fair share" of school admissions, why should it have any relationship to the proportion of a minority-group's population to total population, local, state, or national? Professional schools admitted only college graduates who applied, not members of the adult population in general. Hence the appropriate base was the total of school applicants, and a minority group's fair share would be its proportion of that base. Suppose, then, a professional school set a 10 percent target for minority admissions, based on national population data, but minorities comprised only 5 percent of its applicants. If the school was determined to reach its 10 percent goal, it would have to go much farther down the list of minority applicants—with presumably some decline in student qualifications—than if it had opted for the more appropriate 5 percent base.

Once race preferences became legitimated and widely applied, the conferring of governmental benefits to favored racial groups would whet the appetite of other groups for comparable advantages. If the ticket of entry to the roster of preferred minorities was the statistical underrepresentation of a group in a given profession, occupation, or industry, then virtually any number of ethnic groups could join today's governmentally designated list. And the dynamics of the political process would promote the expansion of the number of group beneficiaries, which in turn would help assure that the new patterns of group claims would become a durable feature of policy making and the social landscape.

Jano F. Paulucci, national chairman of the Italian American Foundation, made some observations in late 1977 on affirmative action and *Bakke* that aptly indicated how a new group basis of politics would develop once government-sanctioned group preferment took hold.[8] Paulucci strongly favored affirmative action, but wanted it extended to members of white nationality groups from Southern and Eastern European stock who also were underrepresented in higher education (Italians, Greeks, Poles, Slavs, Hungarians, and others). "To do anything less," he asserted, "is to promote racism, not to eradicate it." Paulucci called for every college and university to analyze the general population from which it drew its applicants "to assure that no significant group in that population [was] being systematically excluded by its admission procedures." Providing a broad clue as to what would happen to university autonomy on admissions policy under the new system of group representation, Paulucci blamed the inadequate representation of white ethnics on "the fact that colleges want to decide for themselves what situations they will consider special, subject to no one's scrutiny but their own." In concluding his comments, the head of the Italian-

American group expressed his hope that the Court would decide *Bakke* on statutory rather than constitutional grounds, so that the political process would be able to expand affirmative action to cover the white ethnic groups his organization represented.

By these observations, the Italian-American spokesman unwittingly confirmed what Justice Douglas had foreseen in his *DeFunis* opinion. As other claimant groups demanded their equivalent share of admissions, Douglas said, "first the [law] schools, and then the courts, will be buffeted with the competing claims." And once the Court sanctioned racial preferences like those at UWLS, Douglas observed, "it could not then wash its hands of the matter, leaving it entirely in the discretion of the school." But there was no accepted or acceptable standard the Court (or any other agency) could apply to determine how "fair shares" should be allocated to the rival groups. Nor, in Justice Douglas's view, was there any legitimate state interest, much less a compelling state interest, in achieving group "fair shares":

> The state, however, may not proceed by racial classification to force strict population equivalencies for every group in every occupation, overriding individual preferences. The Equal Protection Clause commands the elimination of racial barriers, not their creation in order to satisfy our theory as to how society ought to be organized.

Sociologist Nathan Glazer suggested what the unwelcome consequences would be once the proliferation of racial preferences got underway:

> Thus the nation is by government action increasingly divided into racial and ethnic categories with differential rights. The Orwellian nightmare ". . . all animals are equal, but some animals are more equal than others, . . ." comes closer. Individuals find subtle pressures to make use of their group affiliation not necessarily because of any desire to be associated with a group but because groups become the basis for rights, and those who want to claim certain rights must do so as a member of an affected or protected class. New lines of conflict are created, by government action. New resentments are created; new turfs are to be protected; new angers arise; and one sees them on both sides of the line that divides protected and affected from unprotected and nonaffected.[9]

Perhaps the most distasteful aspect of the foregoing developments would be the necessity of government having to monitor, detect, and reject false claims by individuals who would assert they were members of a favored group or not members of a disfavored group. Government would be forced into the ugly business of defining and applying standards for race and ethnicity.

The surest casualty in the different America depicted above would be public confidence in the integrity of government, as it was seen to deviate openly from its ostensible principles of race neutrality and fairness to all citizens as individuals, irrespective of racial or ethnic group membership. Once that confidence had been destroyed, the next likeliest casualty, ironically enough, might be the minority groups that were initially the subject of favor. The disadvantaged character of these groups, which led to their being awarded preferential treatment, might handicap them in any persistent scramble by diverse groups for special advantage. The best protection for today's minority groups, in other words, lay in a combination of race neutrality and affirmative action that stayed well clear of outright preferential treatment.

How the Court would decide the *Bakke* case was, therefore, of fundamental importance to the issue discussed in this section. The Davis special admissions program was, despite all legal arguments to the contrary, a racial quota or, if that semantical quagmire is avoided, it was an explicit race preference. Moreover, the Davis preference was so rigidly structured that if it met with the Court's approval it would be hard to imagine what kind of "affirmative action" plan for school admissions (or new hiring) would be considered impermissible. Consequently, in view of the dangers and divisiveness inherent in extensive governmental use of racial or ethnic preferences, what was called for was the Court's resolute rejection of Davis's minority preferential admissions program.

Stigmatizing Minorities

Would a minority-preference policy be acceptable if it were assumed, contrary to the discussion in the preceding section, that an intense racial and ethnic group rivalry for special advantage would not develop? Even under these circumstances, the policy would be fatally flawed. The gains of minorities would rest precariously on the capacity of government to maintain preferential programs in the face not merely of their unpopularity but of widespread resentment of them as unfair favoritism. Beyond the question of group divisiveness, political retaliation, and backlash, however, the fundamental rationale for extending minority preferences was open to the greatest doubt. It was urged that a "temporary" period of racial preferences was needed in order to advance minorities into a position of parity with whites, at which time the entire society would return to the race-blind perceptions and policies that was everyone's stated objective. But the idea of ultimately promoting racial neutrality by engaging in an extended period of racial emphasis and preference was dubious as a concept and virtually certain to fail in the real world of government, politics, bureaucracy, and citizen attitudes.

Above all, confinement of preferential treatment to minorities would aggravate the problem that the policy was supposed to alleviate: it would stigmatize the favored groups and thus deny to them any genuine benefits from the material gains the policy afforded. Arguments expressing that belief angered and alarmed advocates of preferential treatment. Such arguments were irresponsible and dangerous, it was felt; their repetition and widespread circulation could make them self-fulfilling judgments if accepted. Some also felt it was presumptuous (and perhaps racist?) for whites to make such arguments; complaints about stigmatization should properly come from those alleged to be stigmatized, namely, the minorities. It was self-deceiving, however, to dismiss the question of minority stigmatization as a nonissue manufactured by misguided or malevolent supporters of Allan Bakke's claims. Rather than being exorcised from the debate, the question deserved the fullest airing because it dealt with a deeply troubling and fundamental problem, one that inhered in the concept of minority preferences.

The built-in risk of racial preferences was their potential for instilling or reinforcing the negative stereotype of the lesser competence of minorities. The risk was greater when minority preferences were applied to areas concerned with intellectual competency and capacity, and when individuals were awarded favored treatment essentially on the basis of their membership in a racial group, without having to compete with nonminorities. In his *DeFunis* opinion, Justice Douglas underscored how racial preferences could stigmatize minorities in the legal profession:

A segregated admissions process creates suggestions of stigma and caste no less than a segregated classroom, and in the end it may produce that result despite its contrary intentions. One other assump-

tion must be clearly disapproved, that Blacks or Browns cannot make
it on their individual merit. That is a stamp of inferiority that a State
is not permitted to place on any lawyer.

If preferential treatment created nagging doubts for minority
persons about the meaning of their personal accomplishment—had
it come about by individual merit measured by the customary performance criteria or by an artificial race preference measured by
lower standards?—their sense of self-worth and drive to achievement could not help but be harmed. In this sense, minority preferences would work against the development of the motivations and
capabilities that everyone agreed were indispensable to sustained
and genuine minority advance. The point was angrily made by
Thomas Sowell, a black economist:

> What all the arguments and campaigns for quotas are really saying,
> loud and clear, is that *black people just don't have it,* and that they
> will have to be *given* something in order to have something. The
> devastating impact of this message on black people—particularly
> black young people—will outweigh any few extra jobs that may result
> from this strategy. Those black people who are already competent,
> and who could be instrumental in producing more competence
> among this rising generation, will be completely undermined, as
> black becomes synonymous—in the minds of black and white alike
> —with incompetence, and black achievement becomes synonymous
> with charity or payoffs.[10] (Emphasis in original)

Some minority spokesmen, suspicious of white support of preferential treatment, went even further and charged that the policy was
a "Trojan horse." Asserted a black psychiatrist,

> I wouldn't hit a dog with some of the minority students I've seen,
> and I have an idea that you honkies are taking in these dummies so
> that eight years from now you'll be able to turn around and say,
> "Look how bad they all turned out."[11]

Even among those opposed to preferential treatment, however, it
was generally understood that the support of the policy by white
elites derived from the best, not the worst, of motives. This meant,
of course, that the policy was far more resistant to change than if
it had been identified with opponents of minority advance. Precisely
because the policy was well-intentioned and linked to humane and

urgent social objectives, its adherents were less receptive to considering the possibility that it might be self-defeating. Still less were they open to the thought that their insistence on the necessity and rightness of racial preferences might reflect condescension and subtle racism on their part. To be sure, if racism were present it was a "liberal racism" ostensibly dedicated to the welfare of minority groups. Nonetheless, it often appeared to be predicated on a paternalistic outlook that stripped minority persons of their individuality and individual responsibility for their own actions and that used the themes of race, discrimination, and poverty as blanket justifications for exempting minorities from the customary standards applied to everyone else.[12]

Whatever the hold of the foregoing ideas on some white political elites, they had much less attraction to the broad public. The great majority of Americans continued to subscribe to traditional views of equal opportunity and the individualistic work ethic. One core belief was that a person should get ahead on ability, persistence, hard work, and initiative and that a person's own efforts were the major force in shaping his or her future.[13] Its corollary belief was that lesser success was attributable primarily to one's own actions, not to social conditions or luck.[14] When applied to minority groups that had been severely discriminated against, these beliefs were modified in recognition of the appropriateness of compensatory measures to enable individual minority persons to overcome the effects of previous discrimination. Preferential treatment was not acceptable, however, because that awarded advantage based solely on group membership and implied that minority persons were incapable of developing themselves to meet the ordinary standards of qualification and performance.[15]

Since the public discussion of race was surrounded by too many taboos to permit either white or minority leaders to talk candidly about it, the world of private discourse was undoubtedly more critical of the stigmatizing implications of race preferences than was revealed in the public debate. In professional schools, for example, where academic merit was the standard currency, the broad association of minority special admittees with poorer academic performance could not be totally obscured from other students or the faculty, even if the institution released no data on the subject and implied otherwise in its public pronouncements. All too often, there was a marked divergence between private and official views of racial preferences and the relationship of such preferences to minority competency. Whereas the institution typically gave repeated public assurance that all minority special admittees were fully qualified and that the usual high standards were being maintained, the school insiders' impressions were that many of those students were only marginally qualified and that the institution's standards were being bent, if not broken.

If this private view were to harden into an unofficial national consensus, the damage to the objectives racial preferences were intended to serve could scarcely be exaggerated. Nothing could undercut minority interests more severely than the widespread belief that the progress of minorities, because they were seen as less competent, required society to choose between equality and quality rather than to promote both at the same time.

The core counter-argument to the thesis that racial preferences promoted minority stigmatization was the insistence that even greater stigmatization would result from racial exclusion. As expressed in the *amicus* brief of the Association of American Law Schools:

> There is, concededly, a danger that the consequence of these [special admissions] programs may be to reinforce adverse stereotypes regarding intellectual capability and thus retard continued development toward the goal of equality. On balance, however, the law schools . . . have concluded that this danger is far smaller than the danger that these misperceptions will persist as the result of exclusion of minorities from the profession.[16]

The University of California's brief asserted the same view:

> If the choice is between a concern for a purported stigma and essentially all-white medical schools, the answer is obvious. The most damaging stigma derives from total exclusion or a merely token admission. It reinforces the notion that minorities have no place in medical schools, or in the "best" medical schools, or in the profession.[17]

Contrary to the foregoing arguments, it was not "obvious" that the higher minority enrollments in professional schools under special admissions were less stigmatizing than the hypothesized low enrollments for regular admissions would be. Under the former situation—but not the latter—*all* minority enrollment could come to be perceived as unearned by individual ability and conferred as a group benefit for reasons unrelated to the achievement standards that nonminorities were required to meet. The stigma imposed by that judgment would consign minorities to second-class status indefinitely. In the words of a close observer of minority preferential admissions:

> [D]oubts about minority professional competence are now widespread and openly voiced. There seems to be no hesitation in saying that one would not choose a minority doctor or lawyer—as one friend put it to me, a bit owlishly, "not for anything serious." If that attitude were to become entrenched, we would have the most serious consequence of all. The era of affirmative action would leave as its legacy the belief that all minority professionals, including the most competent, are not to be trusted with anything "serious."[18]

The alternatives set forth in the excerpt from the UC brief quoted above could be restated as follows: "If the choice is between a much larger number of minority professionals about whose competence the public has considerable uncertainty and suspicion, and a much smaller number whose competence is unquestioned, the answer is obvious."

In sum, by overemphasizing the need for numbers and slighting the even greater need for quality, professional schools unintentionally contributed to undermining the integrity of minority achievement in their professions. In their quest for greater numbers, schools admitted minorities who were greatly underqualified relative to white enrollees and whose school performance, as a group, could be expected to be much lower than that of better-qualified nonminorities. The stigma question was further aggravated by the schools' unwillingness to communicate credibly with the public or the campus about the ongoing operations and results of special admissions programs. Moreover, the schools' preoccupation with preferential admissions deflected them from dealing with the heart of the problem, which was the need to develop larger numbers of more strongly qualified minority applicants. That objective (discussed in chapter 8 of this study) was admittedly more difficult to achieve than instituting a special admissions program, but only through its accomplishment could the stigma question be put to rest firmly and durably. In addition, once schools adopted as their top priority the necessity of enlarging the pool of minority talent, they would be more willing to tackle the stigma problem unnecessarily created by extensive mismatching of minority students and schools (as discussed in chapter 7).

A Stringent Review Standard

The high courts of Washington and California applied the same review standard of strict scrutiny but came to opposite conclusions on the constitutionality of minority preferential admissions. Since one of the key questions for the Court was the appropriate review standard to apply to positive racial classifications, the state court opinions provided the Court with both guidance and problems in coming to its decision.

Neither in *DeFunis* nor *Bakke* did the state supreme court use the concept of a "compelling state interest" in a manner that clarified its meaning or that permitted ready identification of which governmental objectives fell within or outside that category. Nor did either state court address the question whether, in the absence of state legislative confirmation, an educational institution could appropriately claim that the political objective it pursued (such as providing compensatory justice to minorities) was a compelling state interest.

As to the "less intrusive means" prong of the strict scrutiny test, the courts' decisions conflicted on how rapidly and fully the means should satisfy the compelling objective. Was the Washington court right in its *DeFunis* decision that a race-based method was permissible when it was the fastest and most efficient way to achieve the purpose? Or was the California court correct in its *Bakke* holding that if nonracial methods could help achieve the objective, even though much less efficiently, they had to be chosen instead of racial classifications? Use of the strict scrutiny standard as the basis for delimiting allowable and forbidden race-conscious measures for positive pro-minority purposes required, then, that both its ends and means components be refined by the Court.

Despite the different conclusions the two courts drew, their common use of strict scrutiny affirmed that the validity of positive racial classifications should be determined by a stringent standard permitting close judicial review. This was a sound position to take: the

costs and problems associated with governmental racial classifications made the term "benign" discrimination a dangerously de-
ceptive misnomer. On selective admissions to professional schools,
for instance, an appropriately rigorous review standard would insist that the school carefully delineate the ends for which it alleged
its employment of racial classifications was necessary. All too often
—and UWLS and UCDMS were no exceptions in this regard—the
school cited in buckshot fashion a number of diverse purposes and
then applied them piecemeal as part of a loose defense of race preferences.

A suitably tough review standard would also insist that racial
categories could not be justified when they were used simply as
imperfect indicators of an admissions criterion valued by the school.
Considerations of administrative convenience typically buttressed
such an overinclusive use of race; the school found it easier to treat
the desired factor as group-related than to undertake case-by-case
review of all applicants to determine which individuals actually
satisfied the characteristic in question. An example: because the
academic scores of whites as a group were much higher than those
of minorities, no school would be justified in eliminating all minorities from consideration and confining attention only to whites. The
error was obvious—not every member of a group could be assumed
to possess a characteristic that was true of a large majority of the
group—but the error nonetheless appeared with some frequency in
connection with justifying minority preferences.

Consider, for example, the policy objective of meeting better the
medical needs of underserved minority communities. Although data
relating the race of applicants to the objective were fragmentary,
they suggested that a significantly higher proportion of minority
than of nonminority applicants was likely to practice in minority
areas. Supposing, then, that a medical school wanted to assure that
20 percent of its incoming students would meet the stated objective,
could it use this racial correlation to justify a racial classification of
its applicants? In seeking to meet its 20 percent target, could the
school review only minority applicants, on grounds of statistical
probability and administrative convenience? Given the special
dangers inherent in the use of race classifications, a negative answer
was required. An individualized assessment of all applicants was
called for; the expected result would be an eligible pool consisting
of both minorities and nonminorities.

A Racially Neutral Program for Disadvantaged Persons?

The ends-means tensions in using strict scrutiny to determine the legality of pro-minority racial classifications were conspicuous in the California court's *Bakke* decision. The shotgun marriage of racial ends and racially neutral means—which led the court to recommend a racially neutral program for disadvantaged persons—was, to understate the matter, problematic in logic and unstable in practice. Nonetheless, it would have been a thoroughly acceptable solution in political terms if it could be demonstrated that such a program was capable of producing a sizable minority enrollment in professional schools.

Hard evidence was not available because the professional schools had not operated their special admissions programs in accord with this model. For example, after the California court's *Bakke* decision, Boalt law school sought to gather evidence on "constitutionally safe approaches to special admissions programs"; their inquiries to forty law schools revealed that there was no "real body of experience in dealing with a disadvantagement approach to special admissions."[19] The extensive quarrel over the feasibility of this alternative thus took the form of rival estimates of its likely ability to produce adequate minority enrollment.

The University of California and its allies clearly won that quarrel. Their critique of the disadvantagement thesis went as follows: In terms of economic disadvantage (defined in terms of low family income) minorities were disproportionately more disadvantaged than whites; but, in actual numbers, some two-thirds of the economically disadvantaged were white persons. Moreover, disadvantaged whites had higher average academic scores than their minority counterparts. Were admissions for disadvantaged persons governed by their comparative academic credentials, only 10 to 15 percent of those admitted under this program would be minorities. To secure a much larger minority enrollment, schools would have to expand the disadvantaged program's share of total seats to 50 percent and more, which was unfeasible. In sum, a disadvantagement program would benefit a class of whites at present underrepresented in the professional schools, but it would not result in a scale of minority enrollment anywhere near current levels.[20]

Without any hard numbers of their own to offer, the Bakke camp was at a considerable handicap in countering the opposition's grim projections. They insisted that disadvantagement programs should actually be tried and not rejected beforehand by statistical estimates based on faulty assumptions. The concept of disadvantagement, they noted, was far more complex than that of family income levels, upon which the opposition's analyses were based. And why assume that applicants assigned to the disadvantagement pool would be reviewed only by academic criteria, and not by a wide range of other criteria as well? Once disadvantagement programs were adopted by professional schools, they urged, the resulting experimentation would produce better measures of prior educational and economic disadvantage and of identifying ability and potential in minority students.

At bottom, however, advocates of the disadvantagement position could offer no credible "guarantee" of adequate proportions of minority admittees. The position's commitment was to racial neutrality, not to racial results. Logically, how could a genuinely race-neutral process (even fully allowing for the use of race as one measure of disadvantage) promise a satisfactory level of minority admissions, especially in view of the comparative data on disadvantaged white and minority groups presented by the anti-Bakke side? Given the whites' edge in numbers and academic credentials, what race-neutral criteria would enable minority candidates to win out in the competition? And if minorities did succeed in securing a major share of admissions under the disadvantaged program, would this not lead to the suspicion that race preference had been used? The disadvantagement approach thus continued to be vulnerable to Justice Tobriner's charge (in his *Bakke* dissent) that it could meet the need for minority professionals only to the extent that it covertly deviated from racial neutrality.

Any Middle Ground?
If the more extreme forms of race-conscious activities were prohibited as suggested in this chapter, was there any middle ground left to consider? Neither the *Bakke* nor *DeFunis* debates generated much information on more moderate admissions practices. One reason was that the cases focused on the explicit race preferences used by each school, and neither the parties to the lawsuit nor their supporting *amici* had any incentive to explicate more modest ways that professional schools could, or did, consider race. In the *Bakke* dispute, for instance, both sides adopted the strategy of minimizing differences between the Davis program and less rigid uses of race.

By this strategy, the university's side sought to insulate the program from any special vulnerability arising out of its quota character, and Bakke's side sought to demonstrate that the use of race had to be forbidden because otherwise it would lead to race preferences.

This litigation strategy was more a reflection than a cause of the absence of a middle ground. From the perspective of principle and logic, the *Bakke* problem invited either/or answers: was race preference permissible or not, rather than how much race preference was permissible. In-between, middle-ground positions were easier to defend on political than on legal grounds. For example, it was not difficult to think up admissions procedures that would give minority applicants an offset for their racial handicap yet would still require them to compete with nonminority applicants for admission and not guarantee them entry places (in the manner of Davis's reservation of 16 seats). Even such limited racial assistance, though, was in principle a form of preference, as the following comment by Justice White, made at oral argument on *Bakke,* indicated: "[i]f taking race into account increases a person's chances of getting in, it is inevitable that it is going to be crucial at some point, or at any point."[21] In deciding *Bakke,* therefore, one of the Court's greatest difficulties was likely to be whether to draw the constitutional line on race preference per se or between allowable and forbidden forms of race preference—and if the latter, by what persuasive rationale?

Connecting Bakke to the Political Process

In *Bakke* (as in *DeFunis*), the Court was called on to settle a hotly disputed social policy initiated by educators. Conspicuously missing from that lineup was any input from the state's political process. For example, how would the California legislature have resolved the problem of increasing the number of minority doctors produced by the state's medical schools? Because the legislature was a public, representative, and politically accountable body—which the UCDMS faculty was not—would its decision have been different from the minority preferential admissions program the faculty chose?

Should the Court concern itself with what the California legislature might have decided? Clearly, the Court was under no obligation to do so; by conventional legal doctrine the Court could determine the validity of voluntary racial preferences (or any other means) per se, without regard to what state authority had instituted the policy. On *Bakke*-type problems, however, the clash of values and the conflict of needs and rights were every bit as much political as legal in character. Consequently, the Court might find it of special value to have available a record of what the state's political process had earlier decided to do about the problem. Once possessed of that information, the Court could then decide whether and to what degree it wished to defer to the earlier state action. What follows is a review of this approach to the problem and its implications for disposition of the *Bakke* case.

Had the preferential programs adopted by UCDMS and UWLS dealt primarily with educational matters, it would have been appropriate for education officials to have made the decision entirely on their own and, by extension, for the Court to have given considerable weight to that decision. Although that argument was set forth in some anti-Bakke and anti-DeFunis briefs, it was evident that many of the objectives cited to justify special admissions programs were more political-social than educational in character (e.g., reducing minority underrepresentation in the professions, increasing the number of positive role models for minority youth, providing "compensatory" justice for past discrimination). Something other than an educational judgment, for instance, explained the following defense of special admissions programs by the chairman of the UC board of regents:

> It's Bakke and these other fellows who are going to have to look elsewhere to other schools perhaps for their education. . . . In the past it was others who had to look elsewhere and couldn't find those schools. . . . What we're saying is we can and should be allowed to discriminate to allow those who have suffered inequities in the past to gain admissions at this time.[22]

In short, the "stark question" posed by *Bakke*, as the *New York Times* put it, was essentially a political, not educational, question: "[s]hould we reduce opportunity for some whites—somewhat—so as to accelerate opportunity for some blacks and other victims of pervasive discrimination?"[23]

If the problem was basically political, there was little reason to give considerable deference to educators' judgments on it. To counteract that conclusion, the anti-Bakke side urged that the faculty decisional process on whether to extend preferences to minorities should be accepted as a microcosm of the political process; its outcome, therefore, should be treated with comparable respect. But no matter how full and thoughtful the deliberative process of the Davis faculty might have been (and the trial record revealed nothing about the process), it could not serve as a surrogate for the political process. The factors affecting a medical (or law) faculty's decision whether to adopt minority preferential admissions neither mirrored nor even approximated the range and intensity of the factors that would envelop and affect a state legislature, a governor, or other politically accountable body. The considerations and incentives most salient for faculty and university officials were skewed in favor of preferential treatment of minority-student applicants, with the result that nearly all medical and law schools chose to institute some form of special admissions.

If educators constituted no proxy for politically accountable public officials, was there some other way that minority preferential admissions could be said to have been reviewed by the political process? If such review could be shown, then the Court might choose to give it heavy weight in coming to its judgment on the legality of special admissions. Proponents of special admissions made an imaginative attempt to present such a case. Although their argument was ultimately unconvincing, careful examination of it is warranted because of its ambitious scope and because its failings help illuminate the theme under discussion.

What the argument proposed was nothing less than a broad justification of all racial discrimination favoring minorities.[24] The justification rested on two basic premises. One was that a cohesive white majority fully controlled the state political process, and the other was that pro-minority discrimination reflected the decision of the white majority to disadvantage itself in order to benefit minorities. Whites who disagreed with that decision could easily challenge it through the state political process, which was dominated by fellow whites and to which they had ready access. Race-preference policies that remained in force did so only with the implicit approval or consent of the state political process (i.e., of the white majority); at any time they wished the white majority could put an end to minority-preference programs. Since these policies were sanctioned by the political process on the one side, and involved majority discrimination against itself on the other, it followed that the Court should defer to the state's decision and uphold the policy.

The major practical application of this argument made by the pro-UC side in *Bakke* was in connection with differentiating positive from negative racial discrimination, especially with respect to urging—in the words of the UC brief—that "whatever standard of review properly controls in this case, it is not strict scrutiny."[25] "The majority, or . . . groups that historically have commonly coalesced into political majorities," the brief continued, "have a life-or-death control over special admissions programs. . . . [Bakke's] group has control over its own political destiny."[26] An *amicus* brief offered a comparable position: "Strict scrutiny would be appropriate if California's population were made up of a majority of Blacks and Chicanos, its legislators were controlled by them, and they predominated on the board of regents, and the complaint still were made by a white person. . . ."[27] Close judicial review of pro-minority discrimination was unnecessary, in other words, because whites were well able to protect their racial interests through their control of the political process; by this means they could easily get rid of any minority-preference policy that displeased or threatened them. The proper forum for resolving the complaints of Allan Bakke and other whites who believed they were victims of reverse discrimination, this argument suggested, was the legislature, not the courts.

This argument made better sense as a theoretical perspective on the problem than as a description of the actual political world. It was one thing to emphasize, as a relevant distinction between new and old forms of racial discrimination, that a political process controlled by a self-conscious white majority provided a more effective potential source of constraint for pro-minority preferences than for anti-minority discrimination. It was quite another thing to argue as if the simplifying assumptions underlying this abstract thesis characterized political reality. Whites made up a numerical majority, to be sure, but they constituted no monolithic group, nor were they cohesive in political outlook and behavior on matters of race. It was equally unrealistic to portray the political process as automatically and accurately reflecting the wishes of the so-called white majority on racial policy; neither the legislative nor administrative process worked that simplistically.

Since the political world functioned differently from the logical model, the argument's conclusion fitted its theory better than it did the California facts. The conclusion that the political process had "approved" the Davis program derived from the logic of the thesis, which equated nonrejection with approval. But all that had actually happened in California was that no political judgment, approving or disapproving, had been passed on the issue. Because the non-involvement of the political process was explainable on a variety of grounds, it provided only ambiguous and inconclusive evidence on how that process really viewed the issue. In sum, the argument provided no reliable way of knowing how California's political institutions would have handled the problem of promoting greater minority enrollment in the public professional schools of the state.

The situation in California, where the policy of minority preferences in admissions was set by educators and not by the legislature, matched the experience of other states. Consequently, if the Court felt strongly that the political process should have the opportunity to address that issue before the question of its legality was decided, it fell to the Court to bring about that sequence. This meant that the Court would have to make use of the *Bakke* case to formulate a new general rule that assigned the state legislature an essential role in the resolution of the problem. For example, the Court could require legislative endorsement of minority preferences in selective admissions as a necessary but not sufficient condition of judicial affirmation of the legality of the practice. The rule might stipulate that any university policy that lacked explicit legislative approval was automatically invalid and that only legislatively sanctioned racial preferences would be substantively reviewed by the courts as to their legality. Alternatively, the Court's holding might affirm preferential treatment as legal, but require that the legislature explicitly approve the principle before it could be validly applied within the state.[28]

Was it likely that the Court would assign so high a priority to state legislative involvement that it would be willing to frame its decision on *Bakke* along the lines just discussed? The chances were exceedingly low. For one thing, it would require the Court to accept constriction of its own role in favor of a "partnership" with the state political process. For another, the approach was highly vulnerable to public misperception of it as judicial abdication or as "passing the buck" back to the states. Most crucially, there was no evidence throughout the *Bakke* and *DeFunis* public debate of widespread concern about what this approach identified as an important problem or about the prospect of the Court's resolution of the disputed issues without reference to state legislative action. The *Bakke* decision, therefore, was almost certain to leave uncorrected what was perhaps the most anomalous feature of the controversy: resolution of a fundamentally political problem without direct, meaningful involvement of the political process at any stage.

Although there was no way of knowing with certainty how state legislatures would have handled the problem of increasing minority enrollments in professional schools, the indirect evidence plainly suggested that the kind of overt and rigid race-preference policy exemplified by the Davis special admissions program would not have been approved. In California, for instance, the legislature in 1974 enacted a concurrent resolution that requested all institutions of public higher education (community colleges, state colleges, and the University of California) to do the following:[29]

> [P]repare a plan that will provide for addressing and overcoming, by 1980, ethnic, economic and sexual underrepresentation in the make-up of the student bodies . . . as compared to the general ethnic, economic and sexual composition of recent California high school graduates.

The context the legislature set for this effort, it was highly instructive to note, eliminated the exclusion factor so central to the *Bakke* problem: "It is the intent of the legislature that this underrepresentation be eliminated by providing additional student spaces rather than by rejecting any qualified student." Moreover, the methods the resolution directed the higher education units to consider were moderate and provided not even a hint of preferential admissions: affirmative action searches and contacts, experimentation to discover alternate means of evaluating student potential, increased financial aid, and improved counseling for disadvantaged students.

In Congress, the House in 1976 passed an amendment (to an education bill) that would have prohibited the HEW secretary from requiring "the imposition of quotas, goals, or any other numerical requirements on the student admission practice of an institution of higher education . . . receiving Federal funds."[30] The Senate had no comparable provision, and the amendment, after being changed in conference committee, was adopted by Congress in the following form:

> It shall be unlawful for the Secretary [of HEW] to defer or limit any Federal financial assistance on the basis of any failure to comply with the imposition of quotas (or any other numerical requirements

which have the effect of imposing quotas) on the student admission
practices of an institution of higher education. . . .[31]

In 1977, the House voted to prohibit the use of HEW funds to enforce "ratios, quotas, or other numerical requirements" involving
race, sex, creed, color, or national origin in admissions or hiring;
the Senate rejected the provision.[32]

Public sentiment supported compensatory assistance to enable
disadvantaged minorities to catch up and compete effectively, but
was antiquota and generally opposed to preferential treatment.
"Every major national study shows," concluded two specialists, "that
a sizable majority of Americans are . . . opposed to remedying the
effects of past discrimination by giving any special consideration in
hiring or school admissions."[33] Two weeks after the *New York Times*
presented a lengthy editorial favoring the university's side in the
Bakke case, the newspaper reported that the flood of letters it had
received on the subject ran 15 to 1 against its position.[34] And on
seven of the University of California's nine campuses, including
Davis, the student newspaper endorsed Allan Bakke's claim that the
medical school's special admissions program was illegal.[35]

Judged by the foregoing evidence on legislative actions and public
opinion, the involvement of the political process in the problem of
minority admissions to highly selective professional schools would
not have resulted in sanctioning explicit racial preferences, much
less quotas. The adoption of minority preferential admissions was
accomplished, therefore, not with the "implicit approval" of the
political process (as argued by the abstract thesis discussed earlier
in this section), but outside the political process. Educators decided
to extend preferences to minorities not because they were operating
within and were reflecting a widespread political consensus on the
issue but precisely because they were insulated from, and not much
accountable to, the political process. Would the Court, which also
was insulated from the political process, be more sensitive than the
Davis educators had been to public sentiments on race preferences?

14 The Supreme Court Decides

The U.S. Supreme Court has a distinctive place in the design and operation of American government. Americans take it for granted that some of the most difficult and disputed policy questions of every era will be cast in the form of legal challenges and referred to the Court for resolution. Over the past twenty-five years, the Court has led in defining policy on such divisive social issues as education desegregation, racial balance in schools, and busing; obscenity; capital punishment; legislative apportionment; abortion; religious exercises in schools; and the rights of the accused in criminal procedures. Controversial Court decisions may stimulate resistance, protest, or political opposition; but seldom does the Court's role in the constitutional system come under sustained attack.

Indeed, the public's stance toward the Court usually goes in the opposite direction, perhaps too much so. When the Court upholds a challenged action, many Americans interpret that judgment as certifying not simply the legality of the action, but its wisdom and often its morality as well. Yet a measure deemed permissible by the Court need not be even a good policy choice, let alone the best choice. The broad effect of this misperception, however, is to increase the public's disposition to accept Court rulings not merely as establishing a framework of legality within which a large variety of policies may be considered, but as the soundest policy.

This was the public mood of anticipation in which the nation awaited the Court's decision in the *Bakke* controversy. It was to be a long wait. The Court had granted certiorari in early 1977, oral argument had been held during the second week of the Court's October–

June term, and the ruling was generally not expected until late in the term. During this eighteen-month period, those concerned about the disposition of *Bakke* watched the Court closely.

Watching the Court for Clues

The Burger Court, although considered more conservative than the preceding Warren Court, could not be labeled too accurately. Broadly speaking, it had kept faith with its predecessor's principles in the areas of education desegregation and legislative apportionment (the equal-population standard for legislative districts). In addition, the Burger Court had taken action to protect the rights of prisoners, aliens, and the mentally ill and to expand the reach of the free speech guarantees of the First Amendment. It was also developing review standards for sex discrimination challenges, though its efforts here appeared uneven in case outcomes and inclined to ad hoc decision making at the expense of consistent principle. Nevertheless, the Burger Court was much more disposed than the Warren Court had been to reduce access to the federal courts by civil rights and public-interest plaintiffs; in placing procedural roadblocks to easy use of the federal courts, the Court sought to encourage more reliance on state courts and to discourage excessive litigation as a substitute for resolving problems by the political process. Finally, the Court under Burger was more supportive of law-enforcement agencies in criminal procedure cases than it had been under Warren.

Because *Bakke* was the precedent-setting case in an area of law yet to be developed by the Court, there was no satisfactory way of estimating how the Court as a whole or its individual members would line up on the key issues. Prediction was made more difficult by the lessened cohesion of the Burger bloc—the Chief Justice plus the three other Nixon appointees, Blackmun, Powell, and Rehnquist. The "hard core" of allied justices, statistically speaking, consisted of Brennan and Marshall on the "left" and Burger and Rehnquist on the "right"; the other five members were less reliably identifiable in bloc terms, though they voted more with Burger than with Brennan. When the four-member Burger bloc voted together, which occurred from about two-thirds to three-quarters of the time through mid-1977, they almost always were on the majority side in Court decisions.[1] For the 1977–78 term, however, the Burger bloc was unified in only about one-third of the cases.*

The most detailed public prediction on the Court and *Bakke* was offered by Harold Spaeth, a political scientist at Michigan State University, who operated with a computerized data bank in forecasting Court decisions.[2] On the cases he predicted, Professor Spaeth claimed a success rate of 93 percent on the Court decision and 86 percent on the votes of individual justices. Spaeth's predictions were based on the assumption that a justice's voting pattern on an issue was usually consistent; thus the chief difficulty in prediction lay in identifying what issue in a case each justice would see as paramount. His willingness to forecast *Bakke* was venturesome since the only data bases available for his use consisted of Court decisions on school desegregation and employment discrimination, problem areas that were unreliable surrogates for the *Bakke* issue of minority preferential admissions in the absence of institutional discrimination. Spaeth's prediction for *Bakke* was: a unanimous Court decision, probably written by Justice Marshall; in favor of Allan Bakke and holding reverse discrimination unconstitutional; and suggesting a program of racially neutral admission of disadvantaged persons as the permissible way to increase minority enrollment.

The informal corps of Court-watchers searched for evidence in the Court's 1977–78 decisions of lines of argument or doctrine that might be applicable to *Bakke*. One case, decided around the time the Court granted certiorari to *Bakke*, involved the use of race in state legislative redistricting.[3] Kings County (Brooklyn), New York, had become subject to a provision of the federal Voting Rights Act that required the attorney general to approve any legislative reapportionment within the county. In an effort to comply with the act and secure the approval, the state legislature redrew assembly and senate district lines within Brooklyn so as to leave unchanged the number of districts with nonwhite (black and Puerto Rican) majorities but to increase the size of the nonwhite majorities to at least 65 percent of the district population. Prior to this new districting, the Hasidic Jewish community of Williamsburgh (a section of

---

* Since the Court's deliberations are secret, statistical analyses of alignments among the justices on the cases (together with qualitative analysis of the written opinions) provide the only available evidence for gauging Court patterns. Such analyses are helpful, but they should not be misinterpreted to suggest that justices see themselves as members of a bloc or faction; each justice votes independently on each case argued.

Brooklyn) was located entirely within one assembly and one senate district; although Jews comprised a minority of the district, they had effective political control because their voter turnout rate was much higher than that of blacks or Puerto Ricans. As a result of the new districting, the Hasidic community was distributed between two districts. They filed suit to challenge the redistricting, claiming that the value of their franchise had been diluted solely to achieve a racial quota and that they had been assigned to voting districts solely on the basis of race. The suit lost in the federal district court, but was upheld by divided vote in the appellate court.

The U.S. Supreme Court upheld the constitutionality of the redistricting plan, 7–1 (Justice Marshall not participating). A multiplicity of opinions emerged, however, and no more than four justices subscribed to any single line of reasoning. At one extreme was the Chief Justice, who was the lone dissenter; his opinion opposed "racial gerrymandering" and implied that racial preferences were necessarily unconstitutional. The validity of the redistricting measure was supported by Justices Brennan and Blackmun because it was an effort to comply with the Voting Rights Act, and by Justices Stewart and Powell because the plan was not shown to have any discriminatory purpose. Justice White, joined by Justice Stevens, emphasized that white voters had not been subjected to unconstitutional discrimination. The plan did not "fence out" the white population from political participation in the county or unfairly cancel out white voting strength; neither did it involve discriminatory intent against whites nor stigmatize whites. Justice Rehnquist held that the redistricting was valid because it resulted in a fair allocation of political power between whites and nonwhites.

Proponents of minority preferential admissions took comfort from the Court's *Williamsburgh* decision. Justice White's opinion indicated that Equal Protection did not prohibit the use of racial factors in districting and apportionment and, further, that "the permissible use of racial criteria is not confined to eliminating the effects of past discriminatory districting or apportionment." Several other justices seemed disposed to distinguish positive from negative race discrimination on the grounds that the former lacked any discriminatory intent against whites and did not invidiously stigmatize whites.

Justice Brennan gave both sides to the *Bakke* dispute food for thought in his observations about the circumstances under which race could be taken into account and how much weight could be assigned to race. Proposing a balancing test akin to what the New York high court had suggested in the *Alevy* case (see chapter 10), Brennan noted that courts should consider whether the particular race preferences adopted might in reality perpetuate the disadvantaged treatment of minorities, might stimulate "society's latent race consciousness," or might stigmatize minorities; in addition, courts should recognize that benign racial classifications were viewed as unjust by many Americans. Applying these considerations, Justice Brennan weighed the "balance" struck by the Voting Rights Act and the Brooklyn redistricting plan:

> In my view, if and when a decisionmaker embarks on a policy of benign racial sorting, he must weigh the concerns that I have discussed against the need for effective social policies promoting racial justice in a society beset by deep-rooted racial inequities. But I believe that Congress here adequately struck that balance in enacting the carefully conceived remedial scheme embodied in the Voting Rights Act. However the Court ultimately decides the constitutional legitimacy of "reverse discrimination" pure and simple, I am convinced that the application of the Voting Rights Act substantially minimizes the objections to preferential treatment, and legitimates the use of even overt, numerical racial devices in electoral redistricting.[4]

Although these *Williamsburgh* opinions were germane to the broad subject of racial classifications, their revelance for gauging Court attitudes toward racial preferences in selective admissions was difficult to assess. The *Williamsburgh* situation was both distinctive and markedly different from *Bakke*; it involved the elective franchise and an explicit congressional mandate as expressed in the Voting Rights Act of 1965. Since there was no abridgment of the "one person, one vote" standard, no exclusion factor was involved with respect to individual whites. What had occurred was the dilution of a white group's collective voting power in order to enhance the voting power of minorities. But the right to be fairly evaluated in medical school admissions was a personal, not a group membership, right. Allan Bakke was neither asking for nor interested in being "represented" by other whites who were admitted to UCDMS. No matter how many other white applicants were accepted, the fact remained that he had been "fenced out" of competing for the 16 seats reserved for the special admissions program. To urge that the model of group representation in the construction of legislative districts should be transferred to medical school admissions was to argue, in effect, for the redefinition of equal opportunity in terms of proportional group outcomes.

Several other Court decisions in the eighteen-month pre-*Bakke* period, none of which dealt with racial classifications, were also worth noting. In mid-1977, just four years after the Court established every woman's right to have an abortion, the Court ruled 6–3 that the Constitution did not require that government pay for abortions (through Medicaid or other medical expenses reimbursement procedures).[5] Central to the Court's position was Justice Powell's insistence that the decision to provide government funds was properly one for each state and the national government to make, not for the courts. Would that same deference to the political process be applied to the issue of racial preferences involving reverse discrimination?

In March 1978, a Court majority held that due process of law did not require a public university to grant a formal hearing to a student dismissed for academic reasons.[6] The backdrop to the decision was the Court's previous expansion of procedural due process rights for students with respect to disciplinary punishment for violations of rules of conduct. In indicating the Court's unwillingness to extend that development to academic dismissals, Justice Rehnquist's majority opinion stated, "Like the decision of an individual professor as to the proper grade for a student, [academic dismissal decisions are not] readily adapted to the procedural tools of judicial or administrative decisionmaking." Would this reaffirmation of the professional autonomy of educators carry over to judicial deference to educators' control over admissions criteria?

A month later, the Court in a 6–2 decision ruled that it was illegal sex discrimination for an employer to require women to make larger contributions to a company pension plan in order to receive the same retirement benefits as male employees.[7] Although Justice Stevens in his majority opinion conceded that the statistical group generalization that women lived longer than men was true, he emphasized that Title VII focused on the individual and "preclude[d] treatment of individuals as simply components of a racial, religious, sexual, or national class." Since some women do not outlive some men, Stevens concluded that "even a true generalization . . . is an insufficient reason for disqualifying an individual to whom the generalization doesn't apply." Would the Court take the same position on evaluating professional school applicants by the group standard of race rather than by individualized assessments?

In sum, the Court's holdings in other 1977–78 cases provided ambiguous clues as to how the Court was likely to decide *Bakke*. As public suspense about that imminent decision built during the closing months of the Court's term, the attitudes of *Bakke* partisans seemed to undergo a shift toward greater moderation. There was less talk of the cataclysmic potential of the decision and more discussion about the probability of a narrower rather than a broader ruling. Fears were less often raised that Affirmative Action might be undercut by the *Bakke* decision. Perhaps in anticipation of a ruling that would outlaw racial quotas, some anti-Bakke leaders denied that a banning of quotas would necessarily harm Affirmative Action. "Neither the set-aside places of the *Bakke* case nor the occasional quotas courts order," asserted EEOC's head, Eleanor Holmes Norton, "are central to affirmative action."[8]

As the deadline for *Bakke* approached, all sides to the dispute warned that the public's perception of the decision was perhaps of greater importance than the decision itself. The Court could provide no help in this regard because it allowed its written opinions to speak for themselves and undertook no explanatory, public relations, or rebuttal activities to ensure that Court decisions were not misunderstood by the public. This meant that the Court depended on the news media to translate its case decisions, on television and in the newspapers, for the lay public. Nonetheless, the more complex and divided the Court's views on a case, and the larger the number of significant separate opinions, the greater the likelihood that reporters, working under tight deadlines, might present oversimplified or distorted accounts. (One media expert urged—in vain—that the Court provide a one-week alert before decision day on *Bakke* so that newspapers and broadcasters could ready their ablest staff to handle the decision and could budget enough space and air time to ensure ample and accurate coverage of the Court's ruling.[9]) About all that could be hoped was that the media would take special pains to avoid misleading the public on what the *Bakke* decision signified.

"A Notable Lack of Unanimity"

The Court usually reports its decisions on Monday of each week; toward the close of its term, however, the large number of cases involved means the Court must announce decisions on other days of the week as well. During spring 1978, the capital's favorite guessing game was "waiting for *Bakke*," the affectionate name given to the pastime of predicting what day the Court would deliver its opinion on the case. Wrong guesses and false alarms abounded, but as April, May, and the first half of June went by, the odds on selecting the correct day improved greatly. On Wednesday, June 28, there were telltale indications in the Court chambers that something important was afoot. Well before the session was scheduled to begin, the chamber was packed with press and public. Solicitor General Wade McCree was there, as were many Court employees and several veteran civil rights leaders. The clincher was the arrival, minutes before the session began, of the wives of five of the justices. Decision day on *Bakke* had finally come.

At exactly ten o'clock, as Chief Justice Warren Burger and the eight associate justices entered the chamber to take their seats at the bench, Alfred Wong, the marshal of the Court, sang out the ritualized cry: "*Oyez! Oyez! Oyez!* The Court is now sitting," and invoked the blessing of God on the "United States and this honorable Court." The Chief Justice began by asking Justice Potter Stewart to announce the decision on a pension benefits case; immediately after that was done, Burger reported a minor decision himself. Then, responding to the chamber's atmosphere of hushed silence and expectancy, the Chief Justice requested Justice Lewis Powell to announce the decision in "Case No. 76–811. *Regents of the University of California* versus *Bakke.*"

"Perhaps no case in my memory has had so much media coverage," began Justice Powell. "We speak today with a notable lack of unanimity. I will try to explain how we divided." In a two-sentence summary, Powell stated that Allan Bakke was entitled to admission to the Davis medical school but the university had the right to take race into account in its admissions criteria. "It will be evident from several opinions," Justice Powell went on, "that the case, intrinsically difficult, has received our most thoughtful attention over many months." For the next seventy minutes, five of the six justices who wrote opinions in the case—Powell, Stevens, Brennan, Blackmun, and Marshall*—took turns reading from and commenting on them.

The Court's *Bakke* decision involved an unusual three-way split, 4–1–4, in which Justice Powell played the pivotal role in the construction of the three majority judgments on Bakke's admission, the Davis program, and the use of race as an admissions factor. Justice Stevens's opinion, joined in by Burger, Stewart, and Rehnquist, held the Davis special admissions program invalid as a violation of Title VI of the Civil Rights Act. Justice Brennan's opinion, joined in by White, Marshall, and Blackmun, upheld the Davis program under both Equal Protection and Title VI; each of the three justices who joined in the Brennan opinion also wrote separate opinions. With eight justices evenly divided, the critical "swing" vote rested with Justice Powell. Believing the Davis program to be impermissible under both Equal Protection and Title VI, Powell added his vote on this issue to the Stevens group; as a consequence, five justices voted to strike down the minority preferential admissions program and to order the admission of Allan Bakke to the Davis medical school. But Justice Powell also believed that Equal Protection and Title VI countenanced a university's use of race as one among many admissions factors. Since the Brennan group approved of more extreme race preferences than that, they voted to support Powell's endorsement of a more moderate use of race in admissions decisions. Hence a different majority of five justices produced the Court's other judgment, which condoned some consideration of race in admissions. Accordingly, the Court reversed the portion of the California Supreme Court's decision that prohibited the university from taking race into account in the admissions process.†

Court majority positions on *Bakke* could be said to exist, however, only in the numerical sense that five votes had produced each of

---

* The sixth opinion, that of Justice White, dealt entirely with the technical question of whether an individual could sue to enforce Title VI of the Civil Rights Act.

† Had the justices decided *DeFunis* as they did *Bakke*, the vote for Marco DeFunis would have been 4–4, with Douglas (whose seat was taken by Stevens) technically for remand of the case. Substantively, however, UWLS's admissions program could not meet the admissions standards (race-neutral individualized assessments of applicants) set by Douglas. Moreover, the Burger bloc was much more cohesive in 1974 than in 1978, which increased the statistical probability that Justice Blackmun might have been in support of DeFunis's claim. The odds appeared high, therefore, that if *DeFunis* had not been mooted, the Court's judgment would have been in favor of DeFunis.

three judgments. Powell, who provided the fifth vote in each instance, was the only justice who agreed with all three judgments. The 4–1–4 division characterized the rationales underlying the voting pattern; neither the Stevens nor the Brennan group endorsed Powell's reasoning on the key sections of his opinion. By not developing a controlling rationale subscribed to by at least a bare majority of its members, the Court prevented its *Bakke* decision from being a landmark case in the determination of the limits on affirmative action for minorities. Indeed, with three disparate minority opinions and no doctrine-setting majority opinion, the *Bakke* decision did not serve as effectively as it might have in meeting the more modest objective of providing clear Court guidelines and principles for future resolution of that issue.

Title VI Forbids Quotas: Stevens, Burger, Stewart, Rehnquist

Justice John Paul Stevens's opinion (joined in by Burger, Stewart, and Rehnquist) exhibited a determinedly narrow view of the case, one that parallel in many respects Reynold Colvin's litigation strategy on behalf of his client, Allan Bakke. This group of four justices viewed *Bakke* as a "controversy between two specific litigants" that could appropriately be settled by reference solely to Title VI of the Civil Rights Act, without need to consider constitutional questions. Title VI, in their interpretation, was not merely a statutory restatement of the Equal Protection Clause of the Fourteenth Amendment; it had, instead, "independent force, with language and emphasis in addition to that found in the Constitution." Measured by "the plain language" of Title VI—"race cannot be the basis of excluding anyone from participation in a federally funded program"—the Davis program was obviously unlawful because it "excluded Bakke . . . because of his race." Having disposed of the matter on statutory grounds, Stevens's opinion concluded that "one need not decide the congruence—or lack of congruence—of the controlling statute [Title VI] and the Constitution [Equal Protection]. . . ."

The Stevens opinion took an even narrower perspective on whether it was "necessary or appropriate to express any opinion about the legal status of any admissions program other than [the Davis program]." The justices argued the technical point that because the California trial court had barred the university from using race only in connection with Bakke's application and because the

California Supreme Court had ordered Bakke's admission, the Court need do no more than invalidate the Davis program as a violation of Title VI. "Whether the judgment of the state court is affirmed or reversed, in whole or in part," said Stevens, "there is no outstanding injunction forbidding any consideration of racial criteria in processing applications." It followed, in their view, that "it is perfectly clear that the question whether race can ever be used as a factor in an admissions decision is not an issue in this case, and that discussion of that issue is inappropriate." In sum, the Stevens group sought to dispose of *Bakke* by overturning the Davis program and ordering Bakke's admission, without providing any guidance on whether other uses of race were permissible.

The posture taken by Justices Stevens, Burger, Stewart, and Rehnquist was in keeping with the Court's general practice of avoiding constitutional or broad grounds when deciding cases, especially when contentious issues on which the Court had not yet developed a position were involved. As a sensible strategy, however, this was better suited for a Court majority, not a minority, to adopt. In *Bakke*, once five justices held Title VI to mean what Equal Protection meant and then proceeded to decide the case on constitutional grounds, it was ineffective for the remaining four justices to continue their refusal to engage the constitutional dimensions of the problem.

In like manner, it was unhelpful for the Stevens group to avoid dealing with those nonquota uses of race, if any, that were permissible in school admissions. Moreover, their argument on that point was much weaker than their insistence on disposing of the quota question on statutory grounds. As Justice Powell pointedly remarked in the opening footnote in his opinion, the California Supreme Court had not simply invalidated Davis's special admissions program but had required the university to operate its admissions process in accord with the standard of racial neutrality, which was how the state court had interpreted the constitutional requirements of Equal Protection. The U.S. Supreme Court was obligated, therefore, to face up to the question of whether and how race could be considered in the admissions process.

Equal Protection and Title VI Permit Quotas:
Brennan, White, Marshall, Blackmun

Justice William Brennan's opinion (joined in by White, Marshall, and Blackmun) was the opposite of the Stevens group in its expansive conception of Title VI and Equal Protection as justifying remedial race preferences. The context for their views was established at the outset of the opinion. After citing the historical and present background of racial inequality in America, Brennan asserted that

> . . . claims that law must be "colorblind" or that the datum of race is no longer relevant to public policy must be seen as aspiration rather than as a description of reality. . . . [W]e cannot let color-blindness become myopia which masks the reality that many "created equal" have been treated within our lifetimes as inferior both by the law and by their fellow citizens.

Their argument began by merging Title VI and Equal Protection: as the discrimination prohibited under the statute was also unconstitutional under the Fourteenth Amendment, so also whatever remedial use of race was constitutionally permissible under Equal Protection was allowable under Title VI. As the Brennan group saw it, both Title VI and Equal Protection permitted the broad remedial use of race-conscious measures to help minority groups overcome their past mistreatment by society. Thus the permissibility of race preferences was not confined to situations where institutions had engaged in demonstrated discrimination or where minority individuals could be identified as victims of specific discrimination. Support for this broad position was found in the Brennan group's reading of congressional intent and of the implementing regulations by HEW, especially though not exclusively with reference to encouraging voluntary efforts to eliminate racial discrimination that violated the Constitution. On the question of what Congress intended by the Civil Rights Act, Justice Brennan argued that no static definition of the Constitution, whether of color-blindness or otherwise, was meant; instead, Congress "favor[ed] . . . broad language that could be shaped by experience, administrative necessity, and evolving judicial doctrine."

Having established to their satisfaction that race-conscious remedial action was permissible under Title VI, the Brennan foursome next turned to the analysis of Equal Protection. Since racial classifications were not invalid per se, what review standard was appropriate for classifications that were assertedly "benign" or "compensatory"? Rejecting both the strict scrutiny and rational-basis standards as inappropriate for racial classifications designed to further remedial purposes, Justice Brennan opted for the intermediate review standard the Court had developed for use in sex discrimination challenges: "[the classification] must serve important governmental objectives and must be substantially related to achievement of those objectives."[10]* On the ends portion of the standard, then, justification of a remedial racial classification required that "an important and articulated purpose for its use" had to be shown and, above all, that it could not "stigmatize any group or . . . single out those least well represented in the political process to bear the brunt of a benign program."

In applying this review standard to the racial classification employed by the Davis special admissions program, Justice Brennan had no difficulty in finding the program constitutional. On the first of the two ends tests—"an important and articulated purpose"— he observed:

> Davis' articulated purpose of remedying the effects of past societal discrimination is . . . sufficiently important to justify the use of race-conscious admissions programs where there is a sound basis for concluding that minority underrepresentation is substantial and chronic, and that the handicap of past discrimination is impeding access of minorities to the medical school.

On the second ends test—whether any group or individual was stigmatized—whatever injury the Davis program caused for rejected white applicants, it plainly did not include attributing racial or personal inferiority to them.

What of the program's effects on minorities? Justice Brennan argued that preferential admissions could not "reasonably be regarded as stigmatizing the program's beneficiaries or their race as inferior." Unlike several of the *amici* briefs, and the UC brief as well, the Brennan group did not even concede the possibility that such programs ran the risk of promoting stigmatization. Instead, they simply asserted that there was no "reasonable basis" for stigmatization because minority special admittees were deemed fully

---

*This standard was used in the Oklahoma case, discussed in chapter 9, involving the setting of different minimum ages at which men and women could legally drink beer.

qualified, their admission was generally understood as compensation for educational disadvantage caused by "state-fostered discrimination," and their school performance and earned degrees had to meet the same standards as everyone else.

As applied by the Brennan group, the means part of the intermediate review standard—was the means "substantially related" to achieving the objective?—was easily met by the Davis program. First, only race-conscious measures could satisfy the objective of reducing the underrepresentation of minorities within the medical school. Second, from the standpoint of constitutionality, there was no significant difference between Davis's mode of racial preferences, involving a set-aside of a predetermined number of entering places, and other ostensibly more moderate forms of preference. (This last point was a direct response to one of Justice Powell's key positions, which will be discussed shortly.) Unlike the strict scrutiny standard, which required the use of "less onerous means," the slacker standard adopted by the Brennan group for affirmative racial preferences enabled them to give the school discretionary authority to determine what kind of preference policy to adopt. This position, it will be recalled, was one of the central arguments advanced by the University of California to justify the particulars of the Davis special admissions program.

Having upheld the Davis program on both Title VI and Equal Protection grounds, the four justices concluded their opinion by calling for the complete reversal of the California Supreme Court's decision:

> Accordingly, we would reverse the judgment of the Supreme Court of California holding the Medical School's special admissions program unconstitutional and directing respondent's admission, as well as that portion of the judgment enjoining the Medical School from according any consideration to race in the admissions process.

Justices White, Marshall, and Blackmun wrote separate opinions in addition to joining in the opinion written by Justice Brennan. Justice Byron White spoke entirely to the question whether a private individual could file suit under Title VI; White argued that only the government could enforce Title VI. This question had been put aside by the Court; the Stevens group had assumed the right of private action for purposes of the *Bakke* case because the university had not contested Bakke's right to sue at earlier stages of the litigation, and the other four justices considered *Bakke* a poor vehicle for addressing the merits of the question. The issue, though technical, had considerable practical importance. For example, if Title VI could not be enforced by private action, private universities might be freer than public institutions in using race as an admissions factor, depending on how HEW chose to enforce Title VI on reverse discrimination claims. (Because public institution were directly governed by Equal Protection requirements, applicants to public higher education units could always file a reverse discrimination suit as an Equal Protection claim.) Moreover, the resolution of the Title VI enforcement issue could affect whether women could file private lawsuits alleging sex bias under Title IX of the Education Amendments of 1972; that law was closely modeled on the provisions of Title VI of the Civil Rights Act.

Justice Thurgood Marshall, who as counsel for the NAACP had successfully argued for an end to de jure school segregation in the landmark *Brown* case of 1954, wrote a passionate opinion tinged with bitterness over the lot of the Negro minority in America. Tracing the history of the nation's discrimination against Negroes from the early days of slavery through the Court's endorsement of Jim Crow legislation through the "separate but equal doctrine," Marshall concluded:

> The position of the Negro today in America is the tragic but inevitable consequence of centuries of unequal treatment. Measured by any benchmark of comfort or achievement, meaningful equality remains a distant dream for the Negro.

"The experience of Negroes in America," Marshall observed, "has been different in kind, not just in degree, from that of other ethnic groups. . . . The dream of America as the great melting pot has not been realized for the Negro; because of his skin color he never even made it into the pot."

Against this backdrop of "several hundred years of class-based discrimination against Negroes," Marshall wrote, "it is more than a little ironic that . . . the Court is unwilling to hold that a class-based remedy for that discrimination is permissible. . . . It is because of a legacy of unequal treatment that we now must permit the institutions of this society to give consideration to race in making decisions about who will hold the positions of influence, affluence and prestige. . . . I do not believe that anyone can truly look into America's past and still find that a remedy for the effects of that past is impermissible."

Concluding his opinion on a somber note, Justice Marshall expressed great anxiety about the adverse effects of the Court's *Bakke* decision on affirmative action. "I doubt . . . that there is a computer capable of determining the number of persons and institutions that may be affected by the decision in this case. . . . I cannot even guess the number of state and local governments that have set up affirmative action programs, which may be affected by today's decision." Referring more generally to recent Court opinions that he viewed as restrictive of equal opportunity for minorities, Marshall warned, "I fear we have come full circle." Just as the Court had earlier "destroyed the movement toward complete equality" by sanctioning racial segregation, "*Now*, we have this Court again stepping in, this time to stop affirmative action programs of the type used by the University of California."

In his separate opinion, Justice Harry Blackmun discursively commented on several themes of concern to him. One theme was to affirm that educators, not judges, had the responsibility and competence to determine admissions programs: "For me, therefore, interference by the judiciary must be the rare exception and not the rule." Another theme was to note, as "somewhat ironic," how deeply disturbed" the Court members were "over a program where race is an element of consciousness," and yet all were aware of the range of preferences (e.g., athletes, children of alumni) that colleges and universities used in their admissions practices. Furthermore, race and ethnicity were "fact[s] of life," and "[t]he sooner we get down the road toward accepting and being a part of the real world, and not shutting it out and away from us, the sooner will these difficulties [the need to take race into account] vanish from the scene."

On the particulars of the Davis program, Justice Blackmun acknowledged that the kind of admissions program favored by Justice Powell—"where race or ethnic background is only one of many factors" considered—"is a program better formulated than Davis' two-track system." Nonetheless, Blackmun reiterated that the Davis program "is within constitutional bounds, though perhaps barely so," because "[i]t is surely free of stigma." Unlike Powell, Blackmun was "not convinced . . . that the difference between the

Davis program and the one [Powell used as a model] is very profound or constitutionally significant." As to the solution proposed by the California Supreme Court and by Justice Douglas in *DeFunis,* Justice Blackmun commented, "I suspect that it would be impossible to arrange an affirmative action program in a racially neutral way and have it successful. To ask that this be so is to demand the impossible."

Justice Blackmun also emphasized that while he hoped the period of racial preference policy would not be too long, such a period was required if the issue of race was ever to be laid to rest:

> I yield to no one in my earnest hope that the time will come when an "affirmative action" program is unnecessary and is . . . only a relic of the past. . . . Then persons will be regarded as persons, and discrimination of the type we address today will be an ugly feature of history that is instructive but that is behind us. . . . In order to get beyond racism, we must first take account of race. . . . And in order to treat some persons equally, we must treat them differently. We cannot—we dare not—let the Equal Protection Clause perpetrate racial supremacy.

If there was anything of a "landmark" quality about the *Bakke* decision, it lay in the joint opinion of Justices Brennan, White, Marshall, and Blackmun. For the first time, four justices of the Supreme Court—just one short of a majority—developed and subscribed to a constitutional justification of pro-minority racial preferences and reverse discrimination that would transform the meaning of Equal Protection and equal opportunity. Since the thesis they presented was not labeled in those terms, it must first be reconstructed; it can then be appraised to determine whether the characterization of it made here is warranted.

In reviewing the Court's treatment of Title VII (employment discrimination) cases, the Brennan opinion argued that the Court's decisions demonstrated that the permissibility of race-conscious actions did *not* turn on *any* of the following conditions:

1. Recipients of preferential advancement did not have to be confined to those who had been individually discriminated against; "it is enough that each recipient is within a general class of persons likely to have been the victims of discrimination."

2.   The fact that minority preferences would "upset the settled expectations of nonminorities" constituted no effective objection to the preferences.
3.   "Judicial findings of discrimination" were not required to justify preferences. Indeed, voluntary compliance was always preferable; "[j]udicial intervention is a last resort to achieve cessation of illegal conduct or the remedying of its effects rather than a prerequisite to action."
4.   "The entity using explicit racial classifications" did not itself have to be in violation of Equal Protection or an antidiscrimination regulation.

Summing up their reading of Title VII case law, the Brennan group concluded:

> Properly construed . . . our prior cases unequivocally show that a state government may adopt race-conscious programs if the purpose of such programs is to remove the disparate racial impact its actions might otherwise have and if there is reason to believe that the disparate impact is itself the product of past discrimination, whether its own or that of society at large.

The foregoing position, "properly construed," was nothing other than a redefinition of equal opportunity in terms of group proportional equality (as discussed in chapters 2 and 13). The added condition specified above—"if there is reason to believe that the disparate impact is itself the product of past discrimination"—had no independent standing. It was, rather, a tautology meriting dismissal because the prevailing explanation for disparate racial impact was that it was the product of previous discrimination, broadly defined. In effect, then, the Brennan thesis posited that disparate racial impact in and of itself provided sufficient constitutional jurisdiction for race-conscious activities intended to modify or eliminate that impact.

Consider, to illustrate the point, the previously quoted excerpt from the Brennan opinion that dealt with the first part of the intermediate review standard:

> Davis' articulated purpose of remedying the effects of past societal discrimination is . . . sufficiently important to justify the use of race-conscious admissions programs where there is a sound basis for

concluding that minority underrepresentation is substantial and chronic, and that the handicap of past discrimination is impeding access of minorities to the medical school.

But what reason other than "the handicap of past discrimination" would be considered an acceptable explanation for the inability of minorities to compete effectively with nonminorities on the basis of traditional admissions criteria? Hence the actual position advanced in the foregoing excerpt was as follows: where an institution had persistent and severe minority underrepresentation, it could adopt racial preferences to reduce or end that underrepresentation.

Consistent with their implicit endorsement of group proportional equality, the Brennan opinion carried the idea to its astonishing but logical conclusion: whites displaced by racial preferences were really not "innocent victims" because they would not have won out in the competition had minorities not been handicapped by previous discrimination. Such a view resolved the problem of reconciling racial preferences and no reverse discrimination by defining reverse discrimination out of existence.

The argument proceeded by analogy to the adverse effects on white employees of remedial race preferences required of a company that had violated the antidiscrimination provisions of Title VII (e.g., seniority adjustments and promotions favoring minorities). Even though the employer was to blame and the employees were technically innocent, the expectations of nonminority workers (as to seniority, promotions, and so on) that were upset by the racial preferences were "themselves products of discrimination and hence 'tainted.'" In that sense, the claims of the burdened white employees were entitled to less deference; the white worker whose promotion opportunity was delayed or lost was not really harmed because if the minority employees had not been discriminated against, they would have been ahead of him anyway. "The same argument," asserted Justice Brennan, "can be made with respect to respondent [Allan Bakke]."

If it was reasonable to conclude—as we hold that it was—that the failure of minorities to qualify for admission at Davis under regular procedures was due principally to the effects of past discrimination, then there is a reasonable likelihood that, but for pervasive racial discrimination, [Bakke] would have failed to qualify for admission even in the absence of Davis' special admissions program.

In other words, because Bakke was a "tainted" beneficiary of societal discrimination against minorities, his exclusion from consideration for one of the 16 set-aside seats at the Davis medical school did not really deprive him of anything he otherwise would have had.

"The breadth of this hypothesis," observed Justice Powell, "is unprecedented in our constitutional system." From a legal point of view, Brennan's thesis flew in the face of the *Griggs* doctrine (discussed in chapter 9), which provided the governing principle for Title VII cases.[11] In *Griggs*, a unanimous Court (Justice Brennan not participating) carefully rejected racial preference in employment:

> [Title VII] does not command that any person be hired simply because he was formerly the subject of discrimination, or because he is a member of a minority group. Discriminatory preference for any group, minority or majority, is precisely and only what Congress has proscribed. . . .

Under *Griggs*, findings of disparate racial impact triggered the requirement of validating job qualifications and the measurement of those qualifications. Once validated, however, the job qualifications and measures were entirely proper to use regardless of their disparate impact on racial groups. In short, the *Griggs* doctrine repudiated the notion that minority underrepresentation per se justified the adoption of racial preferences.

More broadly, the Brennan thesis would enshrine as a constitutional standard the speculative premise that, had there been no discrimination, the distribution of racial and ethnic-group members would be about the same in academic credentials, occupations, and the like. By treating equality in terms of statistical parity among groups, Brennan's position inescapably implied a definition of Equal Protection as providing rights for persons in their capacity as members of a racial or ethnic group, and not as individuals. Yet, evidently unaware of the full implications of the rationale he endorsed, Justice Blackmun saw no inconsistency in commenting matter-of-factly, in his separate opinion, "I, of course, accept the proposition that . . . Fourteenth Amendment rights are personal."

How could preferences be kept restricted to certain groups and denied to others? Although the Brennan foursome professed to see no difficulty in this regard, their position was incomplete and misleading. According to Brennan's opinion, if a white ethnic group also demanded preferential admissions treatment on constitutional grounds, all that a court had to do was to determine whether the school had a rational basis for concluding "that the groups it preferred had a greater claim to compensation than the groups it excluded." Consequently, Brennan stated, "claims of rival groups, although they may create thorny political problems, create relatively simple problems for the courts."

The fallacy of this position became evident once the dynamics of rival group claims were more fully considered. For reasons discussed in the previous chapter, the political process was likely to support expanding the number of groups that merited preferred treatment. Should this prove true, the problem for the courts would be the opposite of what Brennan had supposed. Whereas the problem posed by Brennan was whether the courts could easily support a school's denial of preferential treatment to other groups, the real problem was more likely to be whether the courts could do anything to contain or strike down the preferences to other groups that the school had extended in accord with political decisions taken on the issue. Under Brennan's formula, the courts would not be able to halt the proliferation of preferences as long as each newly preferred group was able to demonstrate (to both the legislature and the courts) that it was significantly underrepresented as a group— which was the essential justification for racial preferences set by the Brennan thesis. In sum, if Brennan's position on the constitutionalization of racial preferences were adopted, and political considerations then led to a multiplication of group preferences, his criterion for justifying group preferences would not provide an effective principled basis for either courts or legislatures to block that development.

What share of the available places could be allotted to qualified minorities on a preferential basis? Since Bakke had made no claim that the reservation of 16 seats for minorities was unconstitutionally excessive, there was no need to settle the question of the permissible scale of preferences. Although the Brennan group's opinion avoided fixing criteria for determining the allowable scale of preferences, the subject was discussed in ways consistent with their overall thesis. "The constitutionality of the special admissions program is buttressed," their opinion said, "by its restriction to only 16% of the positions in the Medical School, a percentage less than that of the

minority population in California. . . . This is consistent with the
goal of putting minority applicants in the position they would have
been in if not for the evil of racial discrimination." Where a program
preferentially admitted "racial minorities in numbers significantly
in excess of their proportional representation in the revelant population . . . [it] might well be inadequately justified by the legitimate remedial objectives." To allow themselves full elbow room on
the whole subject, the Brennan group commented, "our allusion to
the proportional percentage of minorities in the population of the
State administering the program is not intended to establish either
that figure or that population universe as a constitutional benchmark." Nevertheless, the logic of the statistical parity thesis advanced by the Brennan group obviously led to "constitutional benchmarks" of this type.*

Would the new review standard suggested for positive race-
conscious actions serve as a capable check on race preferences? Just
the opposite seemed to be the case. The ostensibly exacting intermediate standard offered by the Brennan group, when judged by
their application of it to the Davis program, promised to provide few
real limitations on racial preferences. The ends part of the review
standard turned on the question of stigma, which was a genuine
and severe problem generically associated with the use of race preferences in competitive situations (e.g., selective admissions to postcollege professional schools). In the Brennan opinion, however, the
stigma test was so formalistically and superficially applied as to
deprive it of any effectiveness as a constraint or a criterion. The
means part of the new review standard fared no better. The means
had to be "substantially related" to the achievement of the objective,
but since that test was held to countenance the extreme exclusionary
quota system used by Davis, it could hardly be relied upon to moderate what racial preferences might permsisibly be adopted.

The foregoing review and commentary should make clear why
the doctrine endorsed by Justices Brennan, White, Marshall, and

------

* All the opinions in *Bakke* talked about an undifferentiated category
termed "minorities"; none addressed the question of the appropriate
scale of preferences for each particular minority group (e.g., blacks,
Chicanos, Puerto Ricans, Asian-Americans, American Indians). Since
black underrepresentation, for example, could hardly be remedied by
promoting Chicano admissions, the logic of the Brennan approach called
for establishing a scale of preference separately for each minority group.

Blackmun must be considered a remarkable major effort, not simply to legitimate racial preferences intended to reduce minority under-representation as presumptively constitutional, but to redefine equality of opportunity and Equal Protection in group parity terms. Whatever one's views on the merits and demerits of the position they advocated (discussed in chapters 2 and 13), it was highly question-able for the Court to attempt to settle the matter by judicial fiat, under the guise that both the Court and the Congress, when their actions were "properly construed," had already approved or adopted the interpretation of the Constitution the Brennan foursome fully articulated for the first time in *Bakke*. If, to make use of the title of the *New York Times'* special editorial on the Bakke problem,[12] the issue (or the solution) was "Reparation, American Style," that de-cision was one properly to be made by politically accountable bodies, not by the judiciary or the faculty of professional schools.

Quotas Prohibited but the Use of Race Allowed:
The Powell Opinion

Justice Lewis Powell's opinion, which created the majority judg-ments of the Court, also addressed the constitutional dimensions of *Bakke*. Powell began with two points that set the stage for his views. First, he agreed with the Brennan opinion that Title VI had no inde-pendent force: "Title VI must be held to proscribe only those racial classifications that would violate the Equal Protection Clause or the Fifth Amendment [Due Process Clause]." Second, dismissing the "semantic distinction" between goal and quota as "beside the point," Powell characterized the Davis program as a racial classification: "it is a line drawn on the basis of race and ethnic status." What had to be analyzed, then, was the meaning of Equal Protection with respect to racial classifications.

Equal Protection was an individual, personal right whose mean-ing was clear to Justice Powell:

> The guarantee of equal protection cannot mean one thing when applied to one individual and something else when applied to a person of another color. If both are not accorded the same protec-tion, then it is not equal.

It followed that racial classifications of any sort, whether pur-portedly "benign" or otherwise, were inherently suspect and were subject to the same standard of constitutional review, namely, the strict scrutiny standard. "When [public policies] touch upon an individual's race or ethnic background, he is entitled to a judicial determination that the burden he is asked to bear on that basis is precisely tailored to serve a compelling governmental interest."

In concluding that all racial classifications warranted strict scrutiny, Justice Powell rejected the Brennan opinion's use of "stigma" as an effective way to distinguish benign from malevolent classifications: "[Stigma] has no clearly defined constitutional meaning" and "[i]t reflects a subjective judgment that is standardless." Moreover, Powell argued, race preferences for some groups stimulated other groups to make equivalent demands for preference. No less important, "there are serious problems of justice connected with the idea of preference itself." Consequently, if positive racial discrimination was granted a slacker constitutional standard then negative racial discrimination, judicial scrutiny would "vary with the ebb and flow of political forces." The result would be to "exacerbate racial and ethnic antagonisms" and, by promoting "the mutability of a constitutional principle," to undermine "the chances for consistent application of the Constitution from one generation to the next. . . ."

Did the objectives of the Davis program satisfy the "compelling interest" test, which was the first part of the strict scrutiny standard? Justice Powell discussed four objectives, three of which he turned down. He brusquely dismissed the purpose of securing "some specified precentages of a particular group merely because of its race" as "facially invalid" and as "discrimination for its own sake." Another objective, that of improving the delivery of health care services to underserved communities, was said to meet the test. Nevertheless, Powell agreed with the California Supreme Court that the university had not shown that the Davis special admissions program was likely to have any significant effect on achieving that objective, let alone that the program was a necessary means for doing so.

The third objective Powell cited was the amelioration or elimination of "the disabling effects of identified discrimination," in which the state did have a compelling interest. In Justice Powell's view, this meant a focused and bounded "racial remedy for specific racial wrongs" approach (see chapter 9), not the "societal discrimination" approach taken by the Brennan opinion. Powell's elaboration of this point constituted, in effect, his rejection of the core thesis of the Brennan group.

> We have never approved a classification that aids persons perceived as members of relatively victimized groups at the expense of other innocent individuals in the absence of . . . findings of constitutional or statutory violations. . . . Without such findings . . . it cannot be said that the government has any greater interest in helping one individual than in refraining from harming another. . . . [R]emedying . . . the effects of "societal discrimination" [is] an amorphous concept of injury that may be ageless in its reach into the past.

Applying these arguments to the particulars of the *Bakke* situation, Justice Powell concluded:

> [T]he purpose of helping certain groups whom the faculty of the Davis Medical School perceived as victims of "societal discrimination" does not justify a classification that imposes disadvantages upon persons like respondent [Allan Bakke], who bear no responsibility for whatever harm the beneficiaries of the special admissions program are thought to have suffered. To hold otherwise would be to convert a remedy heretofore reserved for violations of legal rights into a privilege that all institutions throughout the Nation could grant at their pleasure to whatever groups are perceived as victims of societal discrimination. That is a step we have never approved.

It was the remaining objective of the Davis program—"the attainment of a diverse student body"—that Powell seized on as fully meeting the "compelling interest" test. He credited this purpose as being a countervailing constitutional interest: "Academic freedom, though not a specifically enumerated constitutional right, long has been viewed as a special concern of the First Amendment." The relationship of student diversity to fulfillment of a university's mission was obvious, as was the relationship of admissions criteria to achieving diversity. With the "compelling interest" segment of strict scrutiny satisfied, the final step of the analysis was to apply the "less onerous means" test to the Davis program.

In Powell's judgment, the Davis special admissions program failed the means test. Its chief defect was its disregard of the Equal Protection Rights of the individual, especially its denial to Bakke of the right "to individualized consideration without regard to his race."

[T]he . . . program involves the use of an explicit racial classification never before countenanced by this Court. It tells applicants
who are not Negro, Asian, or "Chicano" that they are totally excluded from a specific percentage of the seats in an entering class.
No matter how strong their qualifications, quantitative and extracurricular, including their own potential for contribution to educational
diversity, they are never afforded the chance to compete with applicants from the preferred groups for the special admission seats. At
the same time, the preferred applicants have the opportunity to compete for every seat in the class.

Powell's condemnation of the Davis program reflected his recognition that some universities took race into consideration as an admissions factor without assigning a fixed number of places to minorities. Powell was much taken, in particular, by the Harvard College
program, a description of which had been filed with the Court in the
joint *amicus* brief of Columbia University and other private universities. (This description is reproduced in the appendix at the end of
this chapter.) The Harvard College admissions system emphasized
the importance of student diversity, which included students from
"disadvantaged economic, racial and ethnic groups." Race was a
factor "in some admissions decisions" in selecting from among the
large middle group of admissible applicants. No "target-quotas" were
fixed for the number of minorities to be admitted, and candidates
were compared competitively. At the same time, some attention was
paid to numbers (though minimum numbers were not set) in order
to promote diversity and prevent a "sense of isolation" among
minority enrollees.

Using the Harvard College process as his model, Justice Powell
laid out how race could be used as one among many admissions
factors in a constitutionally acceptable way in order to permit a
university to achieve the compelling objective of student diversity.
Explained Powell:

In such an admissions program, race or ethnic background may be
deemed a "plus" in a particular applicant's file, yet it does not insulate the individual from comparison with all other candidates for
the available seats. The file of a particular black applicant may be
examined for his potential contribution to diversity without the factor
of race being decisive when compared, for example, with that of an
applicant identified as an Italian-American if the latter is thought to
exhibit qualities more likely to promote beneficial educational pluralism. Such qualities could include exceptional personal talent, unique

work or service experience, leadership potential, maturity, demonstrated compassion, a history of overcoming disadvantage, ability to communicate with the poor, or other qualifications deemed important. In short, an admissions program operated in this way is flexible enough to consider all pertinent elements of diversity in light of the particular qualifications of each applicant, and to place them on the same footing for consideration, although not necessarily according them the same weight. Indeed, the weight attributed to a particular quality may vary from year to year depending upon the "mix" both of the student body and the applicants for the incoming class.

This kind of program treats each applicant as an individual in the admissions process. The applicant who loses out on the last available seat to another candidate receiving a "plus" on the basis of ethnic background will not have been foreclosed from all consideration for that seat simply because he was not the right color or had the wrong surname. It would mean only that his combined qualifications, which may have included similar nonobjective factors, did not outweigh those of the other applicant. His qualifications would have been weighed fairly and competitively, and he would have no basis to complain of unequal treatment under the Fourteenth Amendment.

Concluding his opinion, Justice Powell cast the deciding vote on each of the three judgments of the Court. On the issue of the legality of minority preferential admissions at the Davis medical school, he joined with the Stevens group to overturn the program; his grounds were Equal Protection whereas that of the Stevens foursome was Title VI. On the issue of the race-neutral standard set by the California Supreme Court, he was joined by the Brennan group in reversing "so much of the . . . court's judgment as enjoins [the university] from any consideration of the race of any applicant." On the issue of Allan Bakke's admission to the Davis medical school, Powell had the theoretical option of remanding the case to permit Davis to reconstruct what might have happened to Bakke if it had been operating a valid program; the Department of Justice, you will recall, had urged that option in its *amicus* brief. Observing, however, that a remand would result "in fictitious recasting of past conduct," Justice Powell joined the Stevens group and confirmed the California court's injunction directing Davis to admit Allan Bakke.

It was suggested in the preceding chapter that in-between positions that sought to allow some kinds of race preference but not others were likely to be better defended on political than on legal grounds. Justice Powell's idiosyncratic use of a student-diversity rationale nicely illustrated the point: it was more effective as a political solution than as a constitutional argument.

On the constitutional dimension, one key test of the adequacy of Powell's position was whether it established a general principle or merely asserted a special exception to secure a desired result. Justice Powell's thesis ostensibly granted higher education units a general though narrow exemption from Equal Protection prohibitions in recognition of their First Amendment academic-freedom rights, specifically their right to set admissions criteria to secure the kind of student body they thought most suitable for their educational goals. In *Bakke*, a university happened to be exercising its rights in the direction of promoting student diversity, including racial diversity. In response, Justice Powell was willing to approve the university's limited use of race as one among other admissions factors so that the university could achieve its compelling objectives that were protected by the First Amendment.

Suppose, however, that a university chose to exercise its rights in the direction of promoting a more homogeneous student body? In pursuit of that objective it might assign a "plus" to middle-class white applicants and then operate its admissions process in exact conformity with the Harvard College model. This admissions program would undoubtedly be struck down by the courts. But if Powell's thesis was truly a general principle, the program would have to be upheld as a permissible exercise of a university's rights. In sum, Powell's approval of a university's objective of racial diversity in its student body was not based on a general exemption of universities, because they had academic-freedom rights, from Equal Protection requirements. Rather, his approval was best understood as a special exception justified not on a principled basis but on ad hoc grounds of whose ox was gored.[13]

The Brennan group, it should be emphasized, did not endorse Powell's stand on student diversity. The four justices joined Powell in his approval of Harvard-type programs only as a practical necessity, in order to ensure that universities would be allowed to consider race in their admissions decisions. In their view, the objective of student diversity did not by itself justify race preferences: "[The Harvard admissions process] is constitutional under our approach, at least so long as the use of race to achieve an integrated student body is necessitated by the lingering effects of past discrimination."

Another basic question about the adequacy of Powell's constitutional argument was whether a constitutional difference really existed between Davis's use of a racial quota, which Powell found unacceptable, and the use of race as an admissions factor, which he endorsed as permissible. Powell acknowledged there was only a narrow boundary line between the two, but he insisted the boundary line was there. That still left open the question whether it was a *constitutional* boundary line. The issue could be argued either way because as forms of race preference the two programs showed common characteristics, but they were also distinguishable in terms of their relative severity and rigidity.

Justice Powell emphasized, for example, that the Davis program displayed "a facial intent to discriminate," in contrast to the "facially nondiscriminatory" admissions process he favored. Broadly, Powell considered the key attributes of the Harvard College-type program— competitive evaluations of each applicant against all others, individualized assessments, no set numerical "target-quotas," and race as one factor among many—as the critical elements of a constitutional line that separated legitimate from illegitimate use of the race factor in admissions. Justice Powell recognized that a university could operate a "Harvard-type" program "as a cover for the functional equivalent of a quota system," but he stated that "good faith would be presumed in the absence of a showing to the contrary."

The Brennan group was not persuaded that the differences in the admissions programs cited by Powell added up to a constitutional dividing line. Race was a substantive qualification under both programs. "The 'Harvard' program," the Brennan opinion observed, "openly and successfully employs a racial criterion [to] ensur[e] that some of the scarce places . . . are allocated to disadvantaged minority students." At Davis, race was the exclusive dispositive factor for 16 seats; under a Harvard-type system, race would be the ultimate dispositive factor for X number of seats. From the viewpoint of the effect of the race preference on the constitutional rights of white applicants, Powell's program could not be said to involve any "less burdensome means" than the Davis program: "any given preference that results in the exclusion of a white candidate is no more or less constitutionally acceptable than [the Davis program]."

In like manner, the Brennan group rejected the view that constitutional significance attached to whether the number of minority admittees was set in advance precisely or only approximately, or to whether the admission of minorities was accomplished by giving minorities extra points on their application or by reserving a number of seats for them. Such differences might have significant practical implications for program operation, but they did not rise to the status of constitutional distinctions. Universities were free, therefore, to adopt any of these forms of race preference they wished. As to the Harvard College plan, the Brennan opinion wryly noted that because "it proceeds in a manner that is not immediately apparent to the public . . . it may be . . . more acceptable to the public than is the Davis 'quota,' " but that provided no basis for holding the one constitutional and the other not.

On the political dimension, Powell's diversity theme had obvious attractiveness as a compromise view containing "bottom line" results that had something for everyone. Quotas were banned and Bakke was admitted, but schools could still secure significant levels of minority enrollment under the banner of student diversity. By supplying a racially neutral rubric for schools to consider race, Powell's formula took some of the sting out of the issue because it provided a less controversial justification than a defense of racial preferences per se. The diversity thesis would enable some to argue —as Powell did—that being an inner-city black represented a "plus" in no way different from the "plus" that might be assigned the farm boy from Kansas or the trombonist from anywhere. At the least, an emphasis on student diversity, together with use of the form of a Harvard-type admissions program, would tend to mask rather than isolate and spotlight the special treatment of race.

Nonetheless, the diversity "solution" had its own large complement of liabilities and dangers. For one thing, it combined an affirmation of enormous discretion and authority for universities with the constitutionalization of an objective—student diversity— that was inherently undefinable and unmeasurable. Justice Powell argued, you will recall, that the Brennan group's attempt to distinguish good from bad racial classifications on the basis of the stigma factor was unsatisfactory because "stigma" was a "pliable notion" that lacked "clearly defined constitutional meaning" and that reflected "a subjective judgment that is standardless." Could not the same evaluations be fairly applied to Powell's concept of "student diversity?" (To test the point, the reader is encouraged to review the description of the Harvard College program reproduced in the Appendix.) It was instructive, in this regard, to note that Powell was able to provide only very limited grounds for a litigant to challenge a university's use of race on behalf of the goal of student diversity.

> So long as the university proceeds on an individualized, case-by-case basis, there is no warrant for judicial interference in the academic process. If an applicant can establish that the institution does not adhere to a policy of individual comparisons, or can show that a systematic exclusion of certain groups results,* the presumption of legality might be overcome, creating the necessity of proving legitimate educational purpose.

Since no university would find it difficult to satisfy these two conditions (the first was easily met in form and the second was not likely ever to occur), the ability of rejected applicants to seek court protection against a university's misuse of race would seem to be severely constricted.

In view of the ambiguity and formlessness of the notion of diversity, and of the difficulty of monitoring or checking its implementation in the admissions process, schools would find it simple to employ covertly the kinds of race preferences Justice Powell held impermissible. By inviting duplicity and subterfuge, Justice Powell's prescription was vulnerable to the charge of disingenuousness that had been leveled against the California Supreme Court's holding on racially neutral admissions.

The basic difficulty was that universities genuinely committed to greater minority enrollment were motivated mostly by purposes that Powell said were improper justifications for extending racial preferences. To be sure, student diversity was an important concern for many, but the more compelling reasons related to beliefs about the moral claims of compensatory justice, the social necessity and rightness of minority advance, the reduction of minority underrepresentation in the professions, and the like. A telling example of the root tension caused by the mismatch between Powell's focus on educational diversity and the schools' focus on societal concerns was

---

* A brief explanation of the reference to "a systematic exclusion of certain groups" may be helpful. All sides to the *Bakke* dispute were agreed that if preferential treatment of minorities was accomplished by, or was associated with, the deliberate exclusion of specific white groups (e.g., Italo-Americans) rather than an undifferentiated grouping of white applicants, the minority preferences would be invalid.

unintentionally provided by a senior admissions officer from Harvard (whose program was Powell's model), who submitted the following letter to the *New York Times* the day after the Court's *Bakke* decision:

> To the Editor:
>
> It is strange that on the day of the famous Bakke decision ABC televised a frightening documentary, "Youth Terror: A View From Behind the Gun," about the millions of bitter and hopelessly lost members of minorities in the urban center of this country.
>
> If that documentary accurately reflects the existence of these young people (I have no reason to think it does not), then debating the correctness of the Supreme Court's Bakke decision is like arguing over sun-deck chairs on the *Titanic*.[14]

Although leaving the concept of diversity vague would create one set of problems, translating it into a specific formula would create another set. The greater the emphasis on racial and ethnic diversity as a central ingredient of genuine student diversity, the greater the likelihood that considerations of group advancement and statistical group parity might come to dominate the meaning attributed to equality of opportunity. Notions of group "overrepresentation" and "underrepresentation," at present a seductively plausible or fashionable way to view the world, would gain added currency. In such circumstances, the acceptable formulas for student diversity would involve the idea of group proportionality, measured by the population mix of the area from which a university normally drew its applicants.

Many universities in the 1920–40 period, it is worth remembering, justified keeping down the number of admittees from white groups they disfavored by citing the need for diversity. At that time, "geographic diversity" was in part a code word for hidden quotas against particular groups. If diversity came to be defined in terms of group parity, it would again serve as the basis for restricting the intake of persons from certain groups, especially those who members would be "overrepresented" because they had disproportionately high academic credentials. This development would not be a matter of history coming full circle; it would be something much worse. Whereas the group-restricting effects of the "old diversity" were widely understood to constitute a denial of equal opportunity, the comparable effects of the "new diversity" would be justified as promoting equal opportunity.

The Post-Bakke World
The news media covered the *Bakke* decision effectively, for the most part taking special care not to mislead the public through distorted early accounts or headlines that told only part of the story. Equal emphasis was given to key results: Bakke won, quotas lost, and affirmative action by universities was upheld. As would be expected, the media emphasized a political approach in commenting on the Court's decision and necessarily had to spend considerable time or space to explain the three-way split of the nine justices and the unusual pattern of majority judgments brought about by Justice Powell. Much less attention was paid to the quality of reasoning in the opinions, the major rationales presented, or the constitutional as distinct from the political implication of the decision.

"No one lost," said the *New York Times* of the Court's action on *Bakke*,[15] and at least the *public* statements of major participants seemed to bear out that judgment. UC's president said it was "a great victory for the university." Allan Bakke authorized his attorney, Reynold Colvin, to express his (Bakke's) pleasure at the outcome, but reiterated that he intended to keep his privacy and say nothing more. Attorney General Bell, HEW Secretary Califano, and other Carter administration officials praised the decision as reaffirming the validity of affirmative action programs. Spokesmen for higher education welcomed the decision, stating that few schools had a Davis-like system of set-aside seats and that most schools were already operating admissions programs consistent with the Court's ruling. The American Jewish Committee expressed satisfaction that racial or ethnic quotas in admissions had been declared illegal.

The congressional Black Caucus stressed that a Court majority had upheld the use of race in admissions and strongly urged the necessity of publicizing that Court ruling to ensure that the public was not misled and that support for affirmative action would not be undermined. Within a month of the decision, the NAACP held a special symposium on its implications and announced that it would lobby to inform congressmen and top federal administrators of the importance of continuing affirmative action programs. Another strand of black opinion, though supportive of efforts to resist any weakening of affirmative action, was more negative about the impact of *Bakke.* "Bakke—We Lose!" asserted the banner headline of Harlem's *Amsterdam News.* And some black leaders, such as Jesse Jackson, publicly followed the gloomy assessment of the *Bakke* ruling set by Justice Marshall in his separate opinion.

Some law professors and political columnists reached high in their praise of Justice Powell's opinion: "an act of judicial statesmanship," "a Solomonic judgment," "a brilliant compromise." Other commentators were markedly less impressed: a "straddling and confused" opinion, "expedient, not principled," "good politics does not necessarily make good constitutional law." What seemed indisputably clear was that *Bakke* had turned out not to be a landmark case. Not only was the Court badly split, but no governing opinion existed; two blocs, each composed of four justices, advanced opposed positions—and the ninth justice, who created the numerical majorities, agreed with neither bloc and spoke only for himself. Moreover, the controlling judgment accomplished no major transformation of legal doctrine or national policy in the manner, say, of the landmark education desegregation case of 1954, with which *Bakke* had been frequently compared while the nation awaited the Court's resolution of the case. (Had the Brennan group's opinion been the majority decision for example, *Bakke* would have qualified as a watershed case.)

For those in higher education, the practical consequences of the *Bakke* decision were summed up in the majority judgment endorsed by Justice Powell and the Brennan group: ". . . the State has a substantial interest that may legitimately be served by a properly devised admissions program involving the competitive consideration of race and ethnic origin." Clearly forbidden were quota reservations of places for minorities and separate, insulated evaluations of minority applicants without comparison with other applicants. The Harvard plan provided the model for what a university should emphasize for an acceptable program, including the development of a comparable statement of admissions objectives, with special reference to diversity and how it would be assessed in the admissions process.

Although these broad guidelines were helpful, the design and operation of admissions programs consistent with them was hardly the uncomplicated task that Justice Powell's opinion implied. (Several associations of professional schools and other higher education organizations set up task forces or conferences to evaluate the effects of *Bakke* on admissions programs.) There was no certainty, for example, that the Harvard college model could usefully be transferred to less selective colleges or professional schools. Even with the best "good faith" effort to implement (rather than circumvent) what Powell and the Harvard plan called for, it was not self-evidently clear how race could be used competitively as but one factor in a genuine comparative assessment of all candidates when the admissions objective included enrolling a sizable number of minorities at well above a token level. Thus, despite the ready assurance of higher education spokesmen that the admissions standards set by *Bakke* were consistent with those already in force at most places, considerable reassessment and revamping of existing practices were likely to occur, together with a persistent effort to puzzle out just what an acceptable program involved.

The higher education community could take comfort from the Court's affirmation that, apart from matters of race and ethnicity, admissions policies were the responsibility of educators. Maximum flexibility was given to universities both to select admissions criteria and to apply them; the Court's opinions did not instruct educational institutions how much to weigh academic credentials or how to determine the better qualified from the lesser qualified within the ranks of those deemed admissible. In addition, the Court decision affirmed that a university that had not itself discriminated was not obliged to undertake remedial race-conscious activities to increase minority enrollment. The effect of the *Bakke* ruling on minority admissions to professional schools, as to other higher education units, thus would depend largely on their own decisions and actions.

In speculating about the implications of the *Bakke* decision for affirmative action in employment, several cautionary observations must be made. For one thing, the *Bakke* decision did not reveal the views of four justices (the Stevens group) on the issue of the constitutionality of racial classifications and racial preferences. Although it was plausible to assume that the Stevens group would take a restrictive position on the issue, there could be no certainty on the matter short of an actual case opinion on the subject from each of the four justices. For another, Title VII (covering employment discrimination) had its own language, legislative history, administrative implementation, and case law. How a justice interpreted Title VI, therefore, was not necessarily controlling for how he would interpret Title VII. Finally, however effective Powell's diversity formula might be in settling *Bakke*-type problems in selective admissions, it obviously could not be extended to noneducation fields where it had neither relevance nor any connection to the First Amendment.

On the assumption that the key to the Court's majority position on affirmative action in employment lay with Justice Powell (rather than with any member of the Stevens group), a concentration on his opinion in *Bakke* seems warranted. Powell's decision was usually described as endorsing affirmative action by colleges and universities, but that description perhaps obscured more than it revealed. In its practical effects on higher education's ability to admit minority students, Powell's decision was obviously supportive of an objective shared by affirmative action. In terms of doctrine, however, Powell's thesis on student diversity could be considered a substitute for affirmative action rather than a variant of it. Consider, on this point, Powell's evaluation of the Davis program's purposes by the "compelling interest" test of strict scrutiny. The two affirmative action objectives—reducing minority underrepresentation in the school and the profession and remedying the effects of societal discrimination—were emphatically rejected by Justice Powell as not meeting the test. The nontransferability of the diversity thesis to fields outside education also suggested that the thesis was as much an escape from affirmative action as a confirmation of it.

These comments on Powell's avoidance of resolving *Bakke* up or down on a straightforward affirmative action approach should not be misunderstood as implying his opposition to affirmative action. The Powell opinion indicated, explicitly and implicitly, considerable support for affirmative action programs, though on the basis of a significantly less expansive view than that argued by the Brennan group. Two dimensions of Powell's views on this subject are discussed below.

In reviewing the objectives asserted for the Davis special admissions program, Justice Powell concluded that "in some situations a State's interest in facilitating the health care of its citizens is sufficiently compelling to support the use of a suspect classification [such as race]." (Powell then held that the university had not shown that minority preferential admissions was an effective, much less a necessary, means for promoting health care delivery to deprived citizens.) Powell's acceptance of this objective as justification for a racial classification suggested that comparably important and urgent objectives might persuade him to allow race classifications in employment (e.g., the social costs and problems associated with inner-city poverty).

In their *Bakke* opinion, the Brennan group undertook to meld Powell's views with their own in order to state "the central meaning of today's opinions," as they saw it:

> Government may take race into account when it acts not to demean or insult any racial group, but to remedy disadvantages cast on minorities by past racial prejudice, at least when appropriate findings have been made by judicial, legislative, or administrative bodies with competence to act in this area.

This action provoked a tart response from the Stevens group: "Four members of the Court have undertaken to announce the legal and constitutional effect of this Court's judgment. It is hardly necessary to state that only a majority can speak for the Court or determine what is the 'central meaning' of any judgment of the Court." Still, putting the feuding to the side, the Brennan group's statement was accurate. What is portended for affirmative action hinged on how the critical ambiguities in the statement would be resolved, namely, what did "appropriate findings" mean and by what means could government act to "remedy disadvantages?"

Since findings of past discrimination justified the remedy of preferential treatment, the question of "appropriate findings" boiled down to determining what would be accepted as proof of past discrimination. (The Brennan group argued that disparate racial impact, attributed to societal discrimination, was sufficient proof; but Powell thoroughly rejected that view in his opinion.) The question was particularly critical for the fate of Affirmative Action programs based on contract compliance, which were built on statistical measures of "underutilization" and required corporations to adopt goals and timetables to remedy underutilization of minority and women workers. To date, a finding of underutilization has not meant a finding of proven past discrimination. Did it follow that Affirmative Action was in jeopardy? Were goals and timetables invalid by analogy to the *Bakke* ban on Davis's quota system, or were they, as antibias officials insisted, sharply distinguishable from quotas? On the other hand, would findings of underutilization become an acceptable way of proving discrimination for purposes of upholding remedial racial preferences? Should that development occur, it would provide the functional equivalent of the "societal discrimination" rationale advanced by the Brennan group.

The importance of the question of what provided "enough" proof of discrimination to vindicate racial remedies was likely to put considerable pressure on the Court to reconcile its constitutional and statutory standards on employment discrimination. As discussed earlier, the Court interpreted Title VII in terms of disparate racial effects but defined Equal Protection in terms of discriminatory intent. Finally, and of no small importance, the *Bakke* court provided no settlement of the question of how far a remedy could go once discrimination has been proven.

Not surprisingly, *Bakke* left far more unresolved than it settled. Whether great social conflicts lend themselves well to judicial resolution is doubtful. Certainly it was unrealistic to anticipate or to hope that the Court in one great decision would definitively dispose of the most pressing racial and civil rights problem of our age. The appearance, instead, of a deeply divided Court was fully understandable; it reflected the nation's conflict and uncertainty about how to reconcile the racial claims of historic justice with the social imperative of racial neutrality.

APPENDIX

Harvard College Admissions Program

For the past 30 years Harvard College has received each year applications for admission that greatly exceed the number of places in the freshman class. The number of applicants who are deemed to be not "qualified" is comparatively small. The vast majority of applicants demonstrate through test scores, high school records and teachers' recommendations that they have the academic ability to do adequate work at Harvard, and perhaps to do it with distinction. Faced with the dilemma of choosing among a large number of "qualified" candidates, the Committee on Admissions could use the single criterion of scholarly excellence and attempt to determine who among the candidates were likely to perform best academically. But for the past 30 years the Committee on Admisssions has never adopted this approach. The belief has been that if scholarly excellence were the sole or even predominant criterion, Harvard College would lose a great deal of its vitality and intellectual excellence and that the quality of the educational experience offered to all students would suffer. Final Report of W. J. Bender, Chairman of the Admission and Scholarship Committee and Dean of Admisssions and Financial Aid, pp. 20 *et seq.* (Cambridge, 1960). Consequently, after selecting those students whose intellectual potential will seem extraordinary to the faculty—perhaps 150 or so out of an entering class of over 1,100—the Committee seeks—

variety in making its choices. This has seemed important . . . in part because it adds a critical ingredient to the effectiveness of the educational experience [in Harvard College]. . . . *The effectiveness of*

*our students' educational experience has seemed to the Committee
to be affected as importantly by a wide variety of interests, talents,
backgrounds and career goals as it is by a fine faculty and our
libraries, laboratories and housing arrangements.* (Dean of Admissions Fred L. Glimp, Final Report to the Faculty of Arts and Sciences,
65 Official Register of Harvard University No. 25, 93, 104–105 (1968)
(Emphasis supplied)

The belief that diversity adds an essential ingredient to the educational process has long been a tenet of Harvard College admissions. Fifteen or twenty years ago, however, diversity meant students from California, New York, and Massachusetts; city dwellers
and farm boys; violinists, painters and football players; biologists,
historians and classicists; potential stockbrokers, academics and
politicians. The result was that very few ethnic or racial minorities
attended Harvard College. In recent years Harvard College has expanded the concept of diversity to include students from disadvantaged economic, racial and ethnic groups. Harvard College now recruits not only Californians or Louisianans but also blacks and
Chicanos and other minority students. Contemporary conditions in
the United States mean that if Harvard College is to continue to
offer a first-rate education to its students, minority representation
in the undergraduate body cannot be ignored by the Committee on
Admissions.

In practice, this new definition of diversity has meant that race
has been a factor in some admission decisions. When the Committee on Admissions reviews the large middle group of applicants who
are "admissible" and deemed capable of doing good work in their
courses, the race of an applicant may tip the balance in his favor
just as geographic origin or a life spent on a farm may tip the
balance in other candidates' cases. A farm boy from Idaho can bring
something to Harvard College that a Bostonian cannot offer.
Similarly, a black student can usually bring something that a white
person cannot offer. The quality of the educational experience of all
the students in Harvard College depends in part on these differences in the background and outlook that students bring with them.

In Harvard College admissions the Committee has not set target-
quotas for the number of blacks, or of musicians, football players,
physicists or Californians to be admitted in a given year. At the same
time the Committee is aware that if Harvard College is to provide a
truly heterogenous environment that reflects the rich diversity of

the United States, it cannot be provided without some attention to numbers. It would not make sense, for example, to have 10 or 20 students out of 1,100 whose homes are west of the Mississippi. Comparably, 10 or 20 black students could not begin to bring to their classmates and to each other the variety of points of view, backgrounds and experiences of blacks in the United States. Their small numbers might also create a sense of isolation among the black students themselves and thus make it more difficult for them to develop and achieve their potential. Consequently, when making its decisions, the Committee on Admissions is aware that there is some relationship between numbers and achieving the benefits to be derived from a diverse student body, and between numbers and providing a reasonable environment for those students admitted. But that awareness does not mean that the Committee sets a minimum number of blacks or of people from west of the Mississippi who are to be admitted. It means only that in choosing among thousands of applicants who are not only "admissible" academically but have other strong qualities, the Committee, with a number of criteria in mind, pays some attention to distribution among many types and categories of students.

The further refinements sometimes required help to illustrate the kind of significance attached to race. The Admissions Committee, with only a few places left to fill, might find itself forced to choose between A, the child of a successful black physician in an academic community with promise of superior academic performance, and B, a black who grew up in an inner-city ghetto of semi-literate parents whose academic achievement was lower but who had demonstrated energy and leadership as well as an apparently-abiding interest in black power. If a good number of black students much like A but few like B had already been admitted, the Committee might prefer B; and vice versa. If C, a white student with extraordinary artistic talent, were also seeking one of the remaining places, his unique quality might give him an edge over both A and B. Thus, the critical criteria are often individual qualities or experience not dependent upon race but sometimes associated with it.

Chapter 1. A Ripe and Pressing Controversy

1. Ronald Dworkin, "Why Bakke Has No Case," *New York Review*, 10 November 1977, p. 11.

2. *Amicus* brief, U.S. Supreme Court, *Bakke*, University of Washington, p. 20. This was the higher education institution centrally involved in the *DeFunis* litigation.

3. *Amicus* brief, U.S. Supreme Court, *Bakke*, Jewish Community Council of Queens, New York City, and the Jewish Rights Council, p. 4.

4. *Amicus* brief, U.S. Supreme Court, *Bakke*, Howard University, p. 48.

5. *Amicus* brief, U.S. Supreme Court, *Bakke*, Anti-Defamation League of B'nai B'rith, p. 13.

6. *Amicus* brief, U.S. Supreme Court, *Bakke*, Committee on Academic Nondiscrimination and Integrity, p. 63.

7. *Change*, October 1977, editorial, p. 18.

8. *San Francisco Chronicle*, 19 March 1977, and *Chronicle of Higher Education*, 11 October 1977.

9. Oral argument, U.S. Supreme Court, *Bakke*, 12 October 1977, pp. 65–66.

10. Oral argument, California Supreme Court, *Bakke*, 18 March 1976, p. 12.

11. Harold Fleming, quoted in Robert Reinhold, "Civil Rights Road Has Become More Complicated," *New York Times*, 5 February 1978, sec. 4.

Chapter 2. Divergent Notions of Equal Opportunity

1. The survey data in table 1 are reported in Seymour Martin Lipset and William Schneider, "The Bakke Case: How Would It Be Decided

at the Bar of Public Opinion?," *Public Opinion*, March/April 1978, p. 42. This article (pp. 38–44) is an excellent review of public attitudes on alternative means to advance minority equality and is the primary source for my comments on that theme.

2. *New York Times*, 18 March 1977.

3. *Chronicle of Higher Education*, 28 March 1977.

4. Ibid.

5. *San Francisco Chronicle*, 1 April 1977.

6. The statement is that of Dean Paul Minton of Virginia Commonwealth University. *New York Times*, 24 November 1977.

7. *Amicus* brief, U.S. Supreme Court, *Bakke*, Chamber of Commerce of U.S., p. 3.

8. Ibid.

9. *Change*, May 1977, editorial, pp. 11, 49.

10. Brief, University of California, U.S. Supreme Court, *Bakke*, p. 2.

11. *Amicus* brief, Petition for Writ of Certiorari, U.S. Supreme Court, *Bakke*, Committee on Academic Nondiscrimination and Integrity, p. 5.

12. *Amicus* brief, California Supreme Court, *Bakke*, Anti-Defamation League of B'nai B'rith, p. 2.

13. The quotations are from the "classic" dissent of Justice Harlan in *Plessy* v. *Ferguson* (1896), 163 U.S. 537, at 559, the case in which the U.S. Supreme Court upheld the "separate but equal" doctrine justifying state-imposed racial segregation.

14. *Associated General Contractors of Massachusetts, Inc.* v. *Altshuler*, 490 F.2d 9, at 16 (1st Cir. 1973). The U.S. Supreme Court refused to hear the case in 1974, by denial of certiorari, and thus let stand this unanimous federal appellate court decision.

15. *Amicus* brief, U.S. Supreme Court, *DeFunis*, Anti-Defamation League of B'nai B'rith, pp. 16–17; see also Alexander Bickel, *The Morality of Consent* (New Haven: Yale University Press, 1975), p. 133. The late Professor Bickel (Yale Law School) and Professor Philip B. Kurland (University of Chicago Law School) prepared this *amicus* brief.

16. *Stanford Observer*, March 1977, p. 2. The extracts are from a lengthier response by President Lyman to an audience question at a Los Angeles gathering, 27 February 1977.

Chapter 3. Law School Admissions and Marco DeFunis, Jr.

1. Justice Douglas's observation was made in his opinion in *DeFunis;* the quotation is from Wigmore, "Juristic Psychopoyemetrology—or

How to Find Out Whether a Boy Has the Makings of a Lawyer," *Illinois Law Review* 24 (1929): 454, at 463.

2. The 1960 data on Boalt are drawn from *amicus* brief, Petition for Writ of Certiorari, U.S. Supreme Court, *Bakke*, University of California Law School Deans, p. 8.

3. Franklin R. Evans, "Applications and Admissions to ABA Accredited Law Schools: An Analysis of National Data for the Class Entering in the Fall 1976," a publication of Educational Testing Service, May 1977, pp. 2–3. The difference between the two specified percentages would be slightly reduced if corrected for the number of persons taking the LSAT more than once, since they comprise a rising proportion of LSAT-takers in recent years. The essential point remains unchanged, however, namely, that applicant demand outstripped the supply of places.

4. Ibid., pp. 1–2.

5. Ibid., p. 4.

6. *Amicus* brief, Petition for Writ of Certiorari, U.S. Supreme Court, *Bakke*, University of California Law School Deans, p. 9.

7. Evans, "Applications and Admissions to ABA Accredited Law Schools," p. 6.

8. Ibid., p. 2.

9. Much of the data in this paragraph are drawn from *Selective Admissions in Higher Education, A Report of the Carnegie Council on Policy Studies in Higher Education* (San Francisco: Jossey-Bass, 1977), table 6, p. 100. Hereinafter referred to as *Selective Admissions in Higher Education*.

10. Evans, "Applications and Admissions to ABA Accredited Law Schools," pp. xv, 26.

11. The fact record is not as complete on admissions details as one would wish. The accuracy of the numbers stated in the text may, therefore, be off a bit; but the major inferences presented would remain unchanged in any event. Data inadequacies do raise problems on how to categorize admissions of the seven Asian-Americans. I have decided to treat them as having taken places "assigned" to them by UWLS, even though each had a PFYA above the cutoff and was formally admitted through the regular admissions process. It is reasonable to infer from the way UWLS treated the other three minority groups that it also considered Asian-Americans as a distinctive group with a special "claim" on admissions.

Chapter 4. Medical School Admissions

1. *Selective Admissions in Higher Education*, Appendix D-1 and p. 109.

2. *Amicus* brief, U.S. Supreme Court, *Bakke,* Association of American Medical Colleges, p. 7.

3. Antonin Scalia, "Guadalajara! A Case Study in Regulation by Munificence," *Regulation,* March/April 1978, pp. 23, 28.

4. Peter Van Houten, director of the Office of Student Advising and Assistance, UC Berkeley, quoted in "California Pre-meds Face Tough Odds," *Daily Californian* (UC Berkeley student newspaper), 14 March 1977. This article is the source of some of the data presented here.

5. Charles E. Odegaard, *Minorities in Medicine* (New York: The Josiah Macy, Jr. Foundation, 1977), table 2, p. 31. Odegaard, who conducted this study for the Josiah Macy, Jr. Foundation, was formerly the president of the University of Washington and, as such, was the formal defendant in DeFunis's suit.

6. Ibid.

7. Odegaard, *Minorities in Medicine,* table 1, p. 30.

8. The difference in the percentages cited for the minorities' share of added seats was actually less than the figures suggested because the law school's figure included Asian-Americans and the medical school's did not.

9. *Selective Admissions in Higher Education,* table 12, p. 109 and Appendix D-2.

10. "Fact File: The Progress of Women in 4 Professional Fields," *Chronicle of Higher Education,* 16 January 1978.

11. Trial record, Deposition of George H. Lowrey, M.D., 23 July 1974, p. 29.

12. The trial record did not reveal how many nondisadvantaged minority members were reviewed under the regular admissions program and hence the 11 percent figure is my estimate. Of the total of 10,-680 applicants, 968 (9 percent) were minority candidates who were referred to the special admissions program. To this must be added the 49 minority enrollees (one-half of 1 percent) accepted through regular admissions. Finally, I have arbitrarily but generously estimated another 1.5 percent (160 persons) for other minority applicants considered but rejected under regular admissions. In any event, the difference between the 11 percent and 27 percent figures is much too great to be accounted for by whatever the correct number of minority applicants who came under the regular admissions program might be.

13. Trial record, p. 67.

14. Ibid., p. 153.

15. Ibid., p. 154.

16. Oral argument, California Supreme Court, *Bakke,* 18 March 1976, pp. 19–20.

17. Trial record, pp. 166–67.

18. Ibid., p. 171.

19. Oral argument, U.S. Supreme Court, *Bakke,* 12 October 1977, p. 54.

20. Ibid., p. 56.

21. Oral argument, California Supreme Court, *Bakke,* p. 25.

22. Ibid., p. 54; the phrase is that of U.S. Justice John Paul Stevens.

Chapter 5. Allan Bakke Gets Turned Down

1. Trial record, p. 276.

2. The comments are by Peter Storandt, who himself figures prominently in events reported later in this chapter; quoted by Robert Lindsey in "White/Caucasian—and Rejected," *New York Times Magazine,* 3 April 1977, p. 45.

3. Trial record, p. 237.

4. Ibid., p. 245.

5. Ibid., p. 233.

6. Ibid., p. 260.

7. Ibid., p. 244.

8. Ibid., pp. 48–49, 51–52. This information was supplied in written form by Bakke, as plaintiff, as his answers to a "set of interrogatories" put to him by the defendant, the regents of the University of California.

9. Ibid., pp. 224–25.

10. Ibid., p. 69.

11. Ibid., pp. 260–61; Bakke's letter was dated 30 May 1973.

12. Ibid., p. 259.

13. Peter C. Storandt, letter to the editor, 20 June 1977; *New York Times,* 3 July 1977.

14. "UC Official Suggested Bakke Suit," *San Francisco Sunday Examiner and Chronicle,* 13 February 1977.

15. Lindsey, "White/Caucasian—and Rejected," p. 45.

16. "UC Official Suggested Bakke Suit."

17. Ibid.

18. Trial record, p. 263–65.

19. Ibid., pp. 268–69.

20. Ibid., p. 266.

21. Ibid., p. 270.

22. "UC Official Suggested Bakke Suit."

23. Trial record, pp. 228–29.

24. Ibid., p. 271; Bakke's letter was dated 11 September 1973.

25. Ibid., pp. 226–27.

26. Ibid., p. 230.

27. Ibid., p. 275; Bakke's letter was dated 9 December 1973.

28. Ibid., p. 274; Storandt's letter was dated 4 January 1974.

29. Ibid., pp. 256, 273.

30. Ibid., pp. 108–09.

31. Oral argument, California Supreme Court, *Bakke*, pp. 21–22, 23.

32. Trial record, p. 281. Petitioner (UC) entered Bakke's 9 November 1973 letter in the record; the copy sent UC by HEW deleted the name of the other school (Stanford) and the details of Bakke's complaint about its 1973 admissions process.

33. Ibid., pp. 278–80; the HEW-OCR letter was dated 8 April 1974.

34. Ibid., p. 279.

35. Ibid., p. 254.

36. Ibid., p. 277.

37. Ibid., p. 275; Bakke's letter was dated 9 December 1973.

38. *Anderson* v. *San Francisco Unified School District*, 357 F. Supp. 248, at 249 (N.D. Cal. 1972).

39. *San Francisco Chronicle*, 22 November 1976.

40. Trial record, p. 268.

41. *San Francisco Chronicle*, 18 February 1976 and 28 February 1975. The suit was filed by Glen De Ronde, a white male rejected by the Davis law school.

42. *Amicus* brief, U.S. Supreme Court, *Bakke*, United States (Department of Justice), p. 73.

43. *New York Times*, 25 September 1977.

Chapter 6. Racial Quota?

1. Bickel, *The Morality of Consent*, p. 133.

2. Edited transcript, trial court, *DeFunis*, in Ann Fagan Ginger, ed., *DeFunis versus Odegaard and the University of Washington* (Dobbs Ferry, N.Y.: Oceana Publications, 1974), 1:109.

3. Ibid., p. 110.

4. Ibid., p. 97.

5. Odegaard, *Minorities in Medicine*, p. 108, citing John S. Wellington and Pilar Gyorffy, "Report of Survey and Evaluation of Equal Educational Opportunity in Health Profession Schools" (draft), 1975, table 2. Eighty-nine of 112 white medical schools responded to the questionnaire sent them. All those responding had recruitment programs for minorities, half of them begun by 1969.

6. The comment is that of Eleanor Holmes Norton; *National Journal*, 17 September 1977, p. 1439.

7. Brief, University of California, U.S. Supreme Court, *Bakke*, p. 45.

8. Ibid.

9. *New York Times*, 25 April 1977.

10. *Amicus* brief, Petition for Writ of Certiorari, U.S. Supreme Court, *Bakke*, National Urban League et al., p. 23, n. 12.

11. In the university's Reply to Brief of Amici Curiae in Opposition to Certiorari, there was a passing comment that the 1974 episode "evidences . . . that the [special admissions] program had a goal, not a quota" (p. 5, n. 4). In UC's brief for the U.S. Supreme Court, the new fact was mentioned only to correct the trial record listing of 16 special admittees in 1974 (pp. 3–4, n. 5).

12. Donald Reidhaar, responding to a question from Chief Justice Wright; oral argument, California Supreme Court, *Bakke*, p. 19.

13. Oral argument, U.S. Supreme Court, *DeFunis*, in Ginger, ed., *DeFunis versus Odegaard*, 3:1338.

14. Evans, "Applications and Admissions to ABA Accredited Law Schools," p. 30.

15. For the medical school data, see *amicus* brief, U.S. Supreme Court, *Bakke*, Association of American Medical Colleges, pp. 8–9; for the law school data, Evans, "Applications and Admissions to ABA Accredited Law Schools," pp. xvi, 39.

16. John Z. Bowers, president of the Josiah Macy, Jr. Foundation, in Odegaard, *Minorities in Medicine*, p. vii.

17. William R. Havender, "The 'Gauze Curtain' at Harvard Medical School," *American Spectator*, March 1978, pp. 22–23.

18. Brief, University of California, U.S. Supreme Court, *Bakke*, p. 46.

19. Brief, Allan Bakke, U.S. Supreme Court, *Bakke*, p. 27.

20. *Amicus* brief, Petition for Writ of Certiorari, U.S. Supreme Court, *Bakke*, University of California Law School Deans, pp. 14–15.

21. *Amicus* brief, U.S. Supreme Court, *Bakke*, Lawyers' Committee for Civil Rights Under Law, p. 25.

22. *Amicus* brief, U.S. Supreme Court, *Bakke,* Committee on Academic Nondiscrimination and Integrity, p. 10, n. 4.

23. *Amicus* brief, U.S. Supreme Court, *Bakke,* United States (Department of Justice), p. 61. The executive agencies that negotiated the policy statement were the Justice and Labor departments, the Civil Service Commission, and the Equal Employment Opportunity Commission.

24. Winton H. Manning, "The Pursuit of Fairness in Admissions to Higher Education," in *Selective Admissions in Higher Education,* p. 57.

25. *Amicus* brief, U.S. Supreme Court, *Bakke,* Association of American Medical Colleges, p. 14.

26. *Amicus* brief, U.S. Supreme Court, *Bakke,* United States (Department of Justice), p. 61.

27. Ibid.

28. Ibid., p. 70.

29. Ibid., p. 69.

30. Odegaard, *Minorities in Medicine,* pp. 109–10.

31. Oral argument, U.S. Supreme Court, *Bakke,* pp. 10–11.

32. Ibid., pp. 27–28.

33. Oral argument, California Supreme Court, *Bakke,* p. 23.

34. Brief, Allan Bakke, U.S. Supreme Court, *Bakke,* p. 14.

35. Ibid., p. 39; see pp. 35–39 for Colvin's full discussion of this theme.

36. Brief, University of California, U.S. Supreme Court, *Bakke,* p. 46.

37. Ibid., p. 47.

38. *Amicus* brief, U.S. Supreme Court, *Bakke,* State of Washington and University of Washington, p. 27.

39. *Amicus* brief, U.S. Supreme Court, *Bakke,* Columbia University et al., p. 27, n. 18.

40. Ibid.

41. Gloster B. Current, quoted by Tom Wicker in "Quotas, Goals and Justice," *New York Times,* 14 June 1977.

Chapter 7. Comparative Academic Qualifications

1. *Amicus* brief, U.S. Supreme Court, *Bakke,* Association of American Law Schools, p. 29.

2. *Amicus* brief, U.S. Supreme Court, *Bakke,* Association of American Medical Colleges, pp. 8–9.

3. *Amicus* brief, U.S. Supreme Court, *Bakke*, National Employment Law Project, pp. 8, 42; these data were drawn from Grace Zeim, "Social and Educational Determinants of the Race, Sex and Social Class Origins of U.S. Physicians" (Ph.D. dissertation, Harvard School of Public Health, 1977), p. 88, table 37 (reproduced in this brief, p. 42).

4. Ibid. (brief, p. 41; Zeim, p. 89, table 38).

5. Thomas Sowell, "New Light on Black I.Q.," *New York Times Magazine*, 27 March 1977, p. 57.

6. For an informative nontechnical review of many aspects of admissions tests and the controversy over them, see Diane Ravitch, "The College Boards," *New York Times Magazine*, 4 May 1975, pp. 12 ff.

7. *Wall Street Journal*, 28 February 1978.

8. For an excellent account of the meaning and validity of the LSAT, see *amicus* brief, U.S. Supreme Court, *Bakke*, Association of American Law Schools, pp. 14–16, including note 12. The explanation presented in this study leans heavily on that source.

9. This paragraph is adapted from Robert Reinhold, "What The Test Scores Do and Don't Say About a Child," *New York Times*, 1 May 1977.

10. Bernard D. Davis, "Academic Standards in Medical Schools," *New England Journal of Medicine* (1976), p. 1118. It was the appearance of Dr. Davis's comments in this communication to the journal (the "Sounding Board" section) that triggered the dispute over Harvard Medical School's minority admissions, as noted briefly in the last chapter.

11. Davis G. Johnson, Vernon C. Smith, Jr., and Stephen L. Tarnoff, "Recruitment and Progress of Minority Medical School Entrants, 1970–1972," *Journal of Medical Education*, July 1975, pp. 713–55, especially pp. 738–54. This study was made use of by the University of California in its brief on *Bakke*, U.S. Supreme Court, p. 45, n. 54; the data from the study reported on in the text also may be found in Odegaard, *Minorities in Medicine*, table 3, p. 35. Right after the U.S. Supreme Court's *Bakke* decision, UC released data on the program completion rate of UCDMS's special admittees. The findings were comparable to the national data reported in the text; for the 1973 entering class, for example, 13 of the 16 graduated on time, 2 took a fifth year, and one dropped out. See *San Francisco Chronicle*, 29 June 1978.

12. The attrition data presented in the *amicus* brief of the Association of American Law Schools was reproduced in *Selective Admissions in Higher Education*, table 7, p. 100. In its original form, the data compared minority students and all students (which included minority students); for greater accuracy I have adapted the data to show the comparison with all nonminority students. See also Evans, "Applications and Admissions to ABA Accredited Law Schools," attachment B, table 1, p. 108.

13. Personal communication to the author.

14. Alfred B. Carlson and Charles E. Werts, "Relationships Among Law School Predictors, Law School Performance, and Bar Examination Results," *Law School Admissions Council* (1976), p. vii; cited in *amicus* brief, U.S. Supreme Court, *Bakke*, Association of American Law Schools.

15. *New York Law Journal*, 7 February 1977.

16. "Analysis of the Budget Bill, California, Fiscal Year 1976–77, Report of the Legislative Analyst to the Joint Legislative Budget Committee," *Postsecondary Education*, pp. 819–20, especially table 30, p. 820; cited and discussed in *amicus* brief, U.S. Supreme Court. *Bakke*, Association of American Law Schools.

17. *Amicus* brief, Petition for Writ of Certiorari, U.S. Supreme Court, *Bakke*, University of California Law School Deans, p. 25.

18. *Wall Street Journal*, 28 February 1978.

19. This description and commentary on the BITCH test is adapted from "Standardized Tests Under Fire," one of the weekly advertisement-columns of Albert Shanker, president of the United Federation of Teachers, appearing in the Sunday *New York Times;* the newspaper date for this column was 29 October 1974.

20. Thomas Sowell, "The Plight of Black Students in the United States," *Daedalus,* Spring 1974, pp. 179–96; see also his *Black Education: Myths and Tragedies* (New York: David McKay, 1972) for the full range of his unconventional views.

21. *Selective Admissions in Higher Education,* Appendix A-4, pp. 156–57.

22. *Amicus* brief, U.S. Supreme Court, *Bakke*, Association of American Law Schools, pp. 31–32; the data were drawn from the report of Evans, "Applications and Admissions to ABA Accredited Law Schools."

23. Doug Lavine, "The Black Experience in Law," *New York Law Journal,* 3 April 1978.

24. *Chronicle of Higher Education,* 11 November 1977.

25. Supplemental *amicus* brief, U.S. Supreme Court, *Bakke*, United States (Department of Justice), p. 8. The quoted extracts are the department's own characterization of the central argument in its principal *amicus* brief.

26. *Amicus* brief, U.S. Supreme Court, *Bakke*, United States (Department of Justice), p. 59.

27. Ibid.

28. *New York Times,* 20 September 1977.

29. Ibid.

30. *Amicus* brief, U.S. Supreme Court, *Bakke*, United States (Department of Justice), p. 59.

31. *Selective Admissions in Higher Education*, Appendix D-3, p. 198.

32. *Amicus* brief, U.S. Supreme Court, *Bakke*, United States (Department of Justice), p. 55.

33. Ibid., pp. 61–62.

34. Ibid., pp. 55–56.

35. Ibid., pp. 63–65.

Chapter 8. Another View of Qualifications

1. Evans, "Applications and Admissions to ABA Accredited Law Schools. For a summary account of the study, see "The Social Impact of *Bakke*," *Learning and the Law*, Spring 1977, pp. 1, 51–52; or *New York Times*, 24 July 1977.

2. The data on Boalt are drawn from *amicus* brief, Petition for Writ of Certiorari, U.S. Supreme Court, *Bakke*, University of California Law School Deans, pp. 20–24, especially table 4, p. 20.

3. *Amicus* brief, U.S. Supreme Court, *Bakke*, Association of American Medical Colleges, p. 18. The 1977 study commissioned by the AAMC was B. Waldman, "Economic and Racial Disadvantage as Reflected in Traditional Medical School Selection Factors: A Study of 1976 Applicants to U.S. Medical Schools."

4. *Selective Admissions in Higher Education*, table 8, p. 112.

5. Boyd C. Sleeth and Robert I. Mishell, "Black Under-Representation in United States Medical Schools," *New England Journal of Medicine*, 24 November 1977, table 3, p. 1147.

6. Brief, University of California, U. S. Supreme Court, *Bakke*, p. 31.

7. For a discussion of these two alternate models of admission, see Manning, "Pursuit of Fairness in Admissions to Higher Education," pp. 27–31.

8. *Selective Admissions in Higher Education*, p. 11.

9. See Odegaard, *Minorities in Medicine*, pp. 66–95, for an excellent account of the scientific and research values dominant in medical schools, which establish an unhospitable environment for students with relatively weak academic credentials.

10. Manning, "Pursuit of Fairness in Admissions," p. 47.

11. *University Bulletin* (UC), 14 February 1977, pp. 79–81. President Saxon's themes were fully consonant with the argument advanced in the university's brief on *Bakke*, U.S. Supreme Court, pp. 51–54. See also, for a parallel position, Manning, "Pursuit of Fairness in

Admissions," pp. 45–51. However, Manning used his two-stage model of the admissions process to justify only the consideration of race as a factor and explicitly rejected the use of "predetermined quotas" as "undesirable" (p. 58).

12. Ibid., p. 81.

13. Ibid.

14. Ibid.

15. *Harvard Magazine*, January–February 1978, p. 76.

16. *Amicus* brief, U.S. Supreme Court, *DeFunis*, Law School Admissions Council, p. 11; in Ginger, *DeFunis versus Odegaard*, 2:709.

17. *Amicus* brief, U.S. Supreme Court, *Bakke*, NAACP, p. 19.

18. *Amicus* brief, U.S. Supreme Court, *Bakke*, Columbia University et al., p. 2.

19. Nathan Glazer, "University Autonomy and the *Bakke* Case," *New York Times*, 30 July 1977.

20. *Amicus* brief, U.S. Supreme Court, *Bakke*, National Association of Minority Contractors, pp. 21–23.

21. *Selective Admissions in Higher Education*, p. 147.

22. Sleeth and Mishell, "Black Under-Representation in United States Medical Schools," tables 1–3, p. 1147. This article fully documents its central conclusion that the number of qualified black applicants must be increased if the present level of black enrollment in medical schools is to be exceeded.

23. Ibid.

24. *Newsweek*, 26 September 1977, p. 57.

25. Steven V. Roberts, "Educators Fear a Ruling for Bakke Would Undo Minorities' Vast Gains," *New York Times*, 25 October 1977, p. 21.

26. *Amicus* brief, U.S. Supreme Court, *Bakke*, Law School Admissions Council, p. 29.

27. *Selective Admissions in Higher Education*, table 9, p. 104.

Chapter 9. Equal Protection of the Laws and Racial Classifications

1. This theme was prominent in the *amicus* brief, *Bakke*, submitted to the U.S. Supreme Court by the NAACP Legal Defense and Educational Fund.

2. Martin H. Redish, "Preferential Law School Admissions and the Equal Protection Clause," *UCLA Law Review* 22 (1974):357; for use of this quotation and reiteration of this theme, see the University of California brief on *Bakke*, U.S. Supreme Court, p. 72.

3. *San Antonio Independent School District* v. *Rodriguez,* 411 U.S. 1 (1973). This case dealt with the disparities in local district school financing caused by a heavy reliance on the property tax in combination with large differences in the value of the taxable property base among school districts.

4. *United States* v. *Carolene Products Company,* 304 U.S. 144 (1938), p. 152, note 4.

5. *San Antonio* v. *Rodriguez,* p. 28. Justice Powell delivered the majority opinion, which denied applying the "suspect classification" rule to certain distinctions based on district taxable wealth.

6. *Johnson* v. *Robison,* 415 U.S. 361 (1974). Justice Brennan spoke for the whole Court, except Justice Douglas.

7. *Dunn* v. *Blumstein,* 405 U.S. 330 (1972), pp. 342–43.

8. *Korematsu* v. *United States,* 323 U.S. 214 (1944). A year earlier, the Court upheld the imposition of curfews on Japanese-Americans, in *Hirabayashi* v. *United States,* 320 U.S. 81 (1943).

9. The seminal article was that of Gerald Gunther, "The Supreme Court, 1971 Term-Foreword: In Search of Evolving Doctrine on a Changing Court: A Model for a Newer Equal Protection," *Harvard Law Review* 86, no. 1 (1972). For an attempt to develop a middle-ground position directly on positive race discrimination, see Kent Greenawalt, "Judicial Scrutiny of 'Benign' Racial Preferences in Law School Admissions," *Columbia Law Review* 75 (1975):559.

10. *Craig* v. *Boren,* 429 U.S. 190 (1976).

11. *Califano* v. *Goldfarb,* 97 U.S. 1021 (1977).

12. *North Carolina State Board of Education* v. *Swann,* 402 U.S. 43 (1971), pp. 45–46.

13. Brief, University of California, U.S. Supreme Court, *Bakke,* pp. 19–21.

14. *Amicus* brief, U.S. Supreme Court, *DeFunis,* Rutgers University, pp. 9–10; in Ginger, *DeFunis versus Odegaard,* 2:785–86.

15. *Albemarle Paper Co.,* v. *Moody,* 422 U.S. 405 (1975), p. 418.

16. *Lau* v. *Nichols,* 414 U.S. 563 (1974).

17. *Swann* v. *Charlotte-Mecklenburg Board of Education,* 402 U.S. 1 (1971), p. 16.

18. Robert M. O'Neil, *Discriminating Against Discrimination* (Bloomington: Indiana University Press, 1975), p. 161.

19. Brief, University of California, U.S. Supreme Court, *Bakke,* p. 66.

20. *Griggs* v. *Duke Power Co.,* 401 U.S. 424 (1971).

21. David E. Robertson, a professor of management, as quoted in *New York Times,* 23 September 1977.

22. *Washington* v. *Davis*, 426 U.S. 229 (1976).

23. *International Brotherhood of Teamsters* v. *United States;* decided on 31 May 1977; see *New York Times*, 1 June 1977, or *Time*, 13 June 1977, p. 60, for a summary review of the majority and minority opinions.

24. *National Education Association* v. *South Carolina;* decided 16 January 1978. For a background account of the litigation, see *New York Times*, 24 June 1977.

25. *Amicus* brief, U.S. Supreme Court, *Bakke*, Fair Employment Practices Commission of the State of California.

26. *Amicus* brief, U.S. Supreme Court, *DeFunis*, Lawyers' Committee for Civil Rights Under Law, p. 21; in Ginger, *DeFunis versus Odegaard*, 3:987.

27. See, for example, the *amicus* brief on *Bakke* of the American Medical Student Association (California Supreme Court) and that on *Bakke* of the National Employment Law Project (U.S. Supreme Court).

Chapter 10. *DeFunis* in the Courts

1. *Plessy* v. *Ferguson*, 163 U.S. 537 (1896), p. 559.

2. *Amicus* brief, U.S. Supreme Court, *Bakke*, Anti-Defamation League of B'nai B'rith, pp. 13–14.

3. See O'Neil, *Discriminating Against Discrimination*, pp. 83–85, for a good account of why a standard more rigorous than the rational basis test was required for positive racial classifications.

4. Reply brief, University of California, U.S. Supreme Court, *Bakke*, p. 18.

5. Brief, University of California, U.S. Supreme Court, *Bakke*, p. 73.

6. Ibid., p. 85.

7. Oral decision, Judge Lloyd Shorett, *DeFunis* v. *Odegaard*, No. 741727, Superior Court, King County, Washington, 22 September 1971; in Ginger, *DeFunis versus Odegaard*, I:115–17.

8. 82 Wn. 2d 11 (1973).

9. *Anderson* v. *San Francisco Unified School District*, 357 F. Supp. 248 (N.D. Cal. 1972).

10. Oral argument, U.S. Supreme Court, *DeFunis*, 26 February 1974, p. 7.

11. Ibid., p. 42.

12. 416 U.S. 312 (1974). Although the Court opinion was *per curiam* (unsigned), both the number and composition of the majority were ascertainable because four justices signed the dissenting opinion.

13. Oral argument, U.S. Supreme Court, *DeFunis*, pp. 14–21, 24–27.

14. *Alevy* v. *Downstate Medical Center of the State of New York*, 384 N.Y.S. 2d 82 (1976).

15. Justice Thurgood Marshall developed a comparable intermediate review standard that called for drawing a balance based on the invidiousness of the classification, the importance to the individuals discriminated against of the benefits denied them, and the significance of the state interests held to justify the classification. For Marshall's views on this, see *Massachusetts Board of Retirement* v. *Murgia*, 96 S.Ct. 2562 (1976); and *San Antonio Independent School District* v. *Rodriguez*, 411 U.S. 1 (1973).

Chapter 11. *Bakke* in the California Courts

1. *Anderson* v. *San Francisco Unified School District*, 357 F. Supp. 248, at 249 (N.D. Cal. 1972).

2. Anthony Lewis, *Gideon's Trumpet* (New York: Random House, 1964), p. 55.

3. *New York Times*, 13 October 1977.

4. *Amicus* brief, U.S. Supreme Court, *Bakke*, United States (Department of Justice), p. 68.

5. Ibid., p. 69.

6. Ibid., p. 68.

7. Ibid.

8. Oral argument, U.S. Supreme Court, *Bakke*, 12 October 1977, pp. 18, 25.

9. *Amicus* brief, U.S. Supreme Court, *Bakke*, United States (Department of Justice), pp. 69–70.

10. Ibid., p. 70.

11. Ibid., pp. 70–71.

12. Lacey Fosburgh, "Coast Suit May Be Test Case for University Special Admissions Program," *New York Times*, 16 January 1975.

13. 18 Cal. 3d 34 (1976).

14. *San Francisco Chronicle*, 10 June 1977.

15. *Amicus* brief, Petition for Writ of Certiorari, U.S. Supreme Court, *Bakke*, Committee on Academic Nondiscrimination and Integrity, p. 7.

16. *San Francisco Chronicle*, 10 June 1977.

17. Brief, University of California, U.S. Supreme Court, *Bakke*, p. 81.

Chapter 12. *Bakke* Goes to the Supreme Court

1. Derrick Bell, "The High Price of Non-Representation," *Phi Beta Kappa Journal*, Winter 1978, p. 19.

2. *San Francisco Chronicle*, 25 May 1977; the regent was Charles Field, representing the alumni on the board.

3. *San Francisco Chronicle*, 29 June 1978.

4. *Amicus* brief, U.S. Supreme Court, *Bakke*, Timothy J. Hoy; the quotation is from his letter to the *New York Times*, 29 March 1977.

5. *Amicus* brief, U.S. Supreme Court, *Bakke*, Ralph J. Galliano, pp. 1–2.

6. For an incisive explanation of Jewish attitudes on group-defined concepts of equality and rights, see Leonard Fein, "The War Inside the Jews," *New Republic*, 15 October 1977, pp. 16–18.

7. Ken Bode, "Unions Divided," *New Republic*, 15 October 1977, pp. 20–22.

8. The account that follows relies on John Osborne, "Carter's Brief," *New Republic*, 15 October 1977, pp. 13–15; James W. Singer, "A Brief in Detail," *National Journal*, 1 October 1977, p. 1538; and the *New York Times*, especially for September 1977.

9. Osborne, "Carter's Brief," p. 14.

10. *New York Times*, 24 August 1977.

11. Osborne, "Carter's Brief," p. 13.

12. Martin Tolchin, "The Mondales: Making the Most of Being Number 2," *New York Times Magazine*, 26 February 1978, p. 2; Osborne, "Carter's Brief," pp. 14–15.

13. Osborne, "Carter's Brief," p. 14.

14. Ibid., p. 15.

15. *New York Times*, 12 September 1977, for all three quotations.

16. Osborne, "Carter's Brief," p. 15.

17. *New York Times*, 12 September 1977.

18. *Newsweek*, 19 September 1977, p. 97.

19. *New York Times*, 13 September 1977; Osborne, "Carter's Brief," p. 15.

20. *New York Times*, 13 September 1977.

21. Ibid.

22. Ibid.

23. *Chronicle of Higher Education*, 26 September 1977.

24. *New York Times*, 20 September 1977.

25. Ibid.

26. Reply brief, Allan Bakke, U.S. Supreme Court, *Bakke*, p. 12.

27. Ibid.

28. *New York Times*, 12 September 1977.

29. Supplemental brief, U.S. Supreme Court, *Bakke*, United States (Department of Justice), p. 8.

30. Personal observation of the author.

31. Oral argument, U.S. Supreme Court, *Bakke*, pp. 3–4.

32. Ibid., p. 45.

33. Ibid., p. 58.

34. Ibid., p. 65.

35. Ibid., pp. 58–64.

36. Ibid., p. 68.

37. Ibid., pp. 54–56.

38. Ibid., p. 57.

Chapter 13. Ends and Means

1. *Amicus* brief, U.S. Supreme Court, *Bakke*, Lawyers' Committee for Civil Rights Under Law, p. 12.

2. *Selective Admissions in Higher Education*, p. 17.

3. Brief, University of California, U.S. Supreme Court, *Bakke*, p. 43, n. 53.

4. *Amicus* brief, U.S. Supreme Court, *Bakke*, Law School Admissions Council, p. 28.

5. Ibid.

6. Brief, University of California, U.S. Supreme Court, *Bakke*, p. 43, n. 53.

7. *Amicus* brief, U.S. Supreme Court, *Bakke*, United States (Department of Justice), pp. 53–54.

8. Jeno F. Paulucci, "For Affirmative Action for Some Whites," *New York Times*, 26 November 1977.

9. Nathan Glazer, *Affirmative Discrimination* (New York: Basic Books, 1975), pp. 75–76.

10. Sowell, *Black Education: Myths and Tragedies*, p. 292.

11. Dr. Charles DeLeon, as quoted by the *New York Times*, 7 April 1974.

12. The term "liberal racism" is taken from Midge Decter, "Looting and Liberal Racism," *Commentary*, September 1977, pp. 48–54; this article, though focusing on white explanations for high crime rates among minorities, incisively discusses the subtle racism that infuses the general racial outlook of liberal white elites.

13. Alex Inkeles, "American Perceptions," *Change*, August 1977, p. 27.

14. Ibid.

15. Seymour Martin Lipset and William Schneider, "An Emerging National Consensus," *New Republic*, 15 October 1977, p. 8.

16. *Amicus* brief, U.S. Supreme Court, *Bakke*, Association of American Law Schools, p. 61.

17. Brief, University of California, U.S. Supreme Court, *Bakke*, p. 49.

18. Joseph Adelson, response to letters from readers on his article, "Living with Quotas," *Commentary*, July 1978, p. 7; Adelson's article, in the May 1978 issue of *Commentary*, is a sensitive account of the campus environment of deception surrounding minority special admissions.

19. *Report on Special Admissions at Boalt Hall After Bakke* (1976), pp. 1, 8.

20. See, for example, Evans, "Applications and Admissions to ABA Accredited Law Schools," pp. xviii, 59–62.

21. Oral argument, U.S. Supreme Court, *Bakke*, p. 73.

22. William K. Coblentz; quoted in *Daily Californian* (UC Berkeley student newspaper), 13 June 1977.

23. *New York Times*, editorial, 19 June 1977; the theme of this editorial, "Reparation, American Style," was described in chapter 12.

24. The broad argument was made by John Hart Ely, "The Constitutionality of Reverse Racial Discrimniation," *University of Chicago Law Review* 41 (1974): 723. For appropriately critical reviews of Ely's argument, see Terrance Sandalow, "Racial Preferences in Higher Education: Political Responsibility and the Judicial Role," *University of Chicago Law Review* 42 (1975): 653; and Kent Greenawalt, "Judicial Scrutiny of 'Benign' Racial Preferences in Law School Admissions," *Columbia Law Review* 75 (1975): 559.

25. Brief, University of California, U.S. Supreme Court, *Bakke*, p. 73.

26. Ibid.

27. *Amicus* brief, U.S. Supreme Court, *Bakke*, State of Washington/University of Washington, p. 23.

28. See Sandalow, "Racial Preferences in Higher Education: Political Responsibility and the Judicial Role," pp. 653–703, esp. pp. 693–703, for an alternate Court position and a general review of the theme indicated in the article's title.

29. Assembly Concurrent Resolution No. 151 (1974); reprinted in *amicus* brief, U.S. Supreme Court, *Bakke*, NAACP Legal Defense and Educational Fund, pp. 26a–27a.

30. 122 *Congressional Record*, House 4316 (daily edition, 12 May 1976); cited in supplemental *amicus* brief, U.S. Supreme Court, *Bakke*, United States (Department of Justice), p. 20.

31. Education Amendments of 1976, Public Law 94–482, 90 Stat. 2233, adding Section 440(c) to the General Education Provisions Act, 20 U.S.C. (1976 ed.) 1231i(c); cited in supplemental *amicus* brief, U.S. Supreme Court, *Bakke*, United States (Department of Justice), p. 21.

32. *New York Times*, 18 June 1977; *Chronicle of Higher Education*, 5 July 1977.

33. Lipset and Schneider, "The Bakke Case: How Would It Be Decided at the Bar of Public Opinion?," p. 40.

34. *New York Times*, editorial, 3 July 1977; the pro-UC editorial appeared on 19 June 1977.

35. *San Francisco Chronicle*, 12 October 1977; the two UC campus newspapers opposing Bakke were at Santa Cruz and the medical center at San Francisco.

Chapter 14. The Supreme Court Decides

1. Warren Weaver, Jr., "High Court Opening: Nixon Imprint Seen," *New York Times*, 3 October 1977.

2. *New York Law Journal*, 29 May 1978.

3. *United Jewish Organizations of Williamsburgh, Inc.* v. *Carey*, 430 U.S. 144 (1977).

4. Ibid., pp. 173–74.

5. "Abortion: Who Pays?," *Newsweek*, 4 July 1977, pp. 12–13; "The Supreme Court Ignites a Fiery Abortion Debate," *Time*, 4 July 1977, pp. 6–7.

6. *Board of Curators of the University of Missouri* v. *Charlotte Horowitz*. For a summary account of the case, see *New York Times*, 2 March

1978, *Wall Street Journal*, 2 March 1978, or *Chronicle of Higher Education*, 6 March 1978; the latter source also contains the text of Justice Rehnquist's majority opinion.

7. *Wall Street Journal*, 26 April 1978; *Chronicle of Higher Education*, 1 May 1978.

8. *New York Times*, 7 May 1978.

9. Fred W. Friendly, "Bakke, Unmuddy," *New York Times*, 15 June 1978.

10. *Craig* v. *Boren*, 429 U.S. 190 (1976).

11. *Griggs* v. *Duke Power Company*, 401 U.S. 424 (1971).

12. *New York Times*, 19 June 1977.

13. The same conclusion is reached by Robert H. Bork, "The Unpersuasive Bakke Decision," *Wall Street Journal*, 21 July 1978.

14. *New York Times*, 6 July 1978; David L. Evans was the writer of the letter, which was dated 29 June 1978.

15. *New York Times*, section 4, "The News in Review," 2 July 1978.